The Draft
and
Public Policy

A Publication of the Mershon Center for

Education in National Security

THE DRAFT
AND
PUBLIC POLICY

*Issues in Military
Manpower Procurement
1945-1970*

JAMES M. GERHARDT

OHIO STATE UNIVERSITY PRESS: COLUMBUS

Standard Book Number 8142-0143-1
Library of Congress Catalogue Card Number 70-105723
Printed in the United States of America
Copyright © 1971 by the Ohio State University Press

TO MY PARENTS

Contents

LIST OF TABLES

Acknowledgments

For their counsel and helpful criticism, I wish to thank Professors Arthur Smithies and Samuel P. Huntington, who directed and read the dissertation from which this book has grown.

Several persons in the Office of the Assistant Secretary of Defense (Manpower) in 1964-66 were most generous with their time and knowledge: Dr. Harold Wool, staff coordinator for the Defense Manpower Study; Colonel Erwin R. Brigham, U.S. Army, administrative coordinator for the study; Albert Kay of the draft policies group; Dr. Walter Oi, director, and Dr. Stuart Altman, consultant, of the economic analysis group; Keene Peterson, director of the military-civilian substitutability group; and Dr. C. W. Bateman of the qualitative requirements group.

For interviews granted in summer, 1967, I wish to thank Dr. Wool; Bradley Patterson, executive staff director for the National Advisory Commission on Selective Service; William E. Bonsteel, examiner in the Bureau of the Budget; Carl W. Clewlow, deputy director of the Task Force on the Structure of the Selective Service System; Colonel Bernard T. Franck, III, chief of the Office of Legislation, Liaison, and Public Relations, and Kenneth H. McGill, chief of the Research and Statistics Division, of the Selective Service System; Senator Edward M. Kennedy, and Don Gifford, a member of the senator's staff; William H. Darden, chief of staff for the Senate Committee on Armed Services; Frank M. Slatinshek, counsel to the House Committee on Armed Services; Robert W. Carr, staff assistant to Representative Donald Rumsfeld; David Newhall, III, administrative assistant to Representative Robert Schweiker; and Douglas Bailey, staff director for the Wednesday Club.

I am deeply grateful to General Lewis B. Hershey, director of the Selective Service System until last year, for a generously long interview in 1968.

None of these persons is responsible, of course, for any errors or misinterpretations that may have crept into my use of their information and views.

I am especially indebted to Dr. James A. Robinson, then director of the Mershon Center for Education in National Security and now vice-president and provost of the Ohio State University; his interest and support, and the assistance of the Mershon Center in granting a summer fellowship in 1968, were invaluable in helping me to revise this study for publication.

Mrs. Jean Kuenn, formerly of the Ohio State University Press, gave extensive and wise advice on smoothing the roughness of my earlier draft.

Finally, I thank all those friends and family who, by their tolerance and encouragement, sustained me in my work.

Introduction

In the course of World War II, the United States was propelled from its prewar position and attitudes of isolation into new and heavy international responsibilities. The accompanying national changes in domestic character and international stance have been profound, and most of these changes have not come easily. In few areas of activity has this been more true than in military affairs; and in few aspects of these activities has the struggle to create workable and acceptable policies been more difficult than in that of procuring men for the armed forces.

The extensive engagement of American resources and efforts in the pursuit of external goals since World War II, and the outside attention to American domestic actions resulting from our position as the leading world power, have combined to assure that hardly any American policy can fail to have both domestic and external consequences. Some aspects of military policy respond predominantly to the changing character of external threats and military technology. But military policy also rests on decisions as to what resources, material and human, the nation is willing to devote to its security. Thus in other aspects of military policy—and manpower procurement is one of these—domestic considerations can and do influence decisions as much as, sometimes more than, external and technological considerations.

This study traces the evolution of American military manpower procurement policy over the past twenty-five years, and examines current pressures for changes in Selective Service and related programs. The analysis is cast in terms of explicit and implicit issues debated by major participants in this area of policy-making: the presidency, the defense establishment, the Selective Service System, and other executive agencies; Congress and its armed services committees; and various organized pressure groups. Although support of national security has been the predominant goal, policy has evolved only partly in response to changing perceptions of what constitutes an effective military establishment; policy and programs have also been shaped by shifting attitudes toward four other issues: costs, compulsions, equity, and impact on nonmilitary social goals.

Given the importance and the broad range of these issues, it is not surprising that military manpower procurement policy has been the object of recurring congressional and public debate, and a matter of almost constant concern for the defense establishment throughout this period. These policy debates, the varying emphases on goals among participants, and the nature of policy and program outcomes, constitute the major content of this study. At the outset, then, it will be helpful to outline the major policy goals, the programs and administrators that implement policy, and the major participants in policy-making.

Military manpower procurement policies and programs are linked to the predominant goal of national security in a number of ways. In *The Common Defense* (New York: Columbia University Press, 1962), Samuel Huntington developed a distinction between strategic and structural military policies. Clearly, military manpower procurement belongs in the structural category, with other policies concerning how military forces will be acquired, organized, equipped, supplied, and maintained. Yet manpower procurement, like other structural policies, has important effects on strategic policy questions of how much and what kinds of military forces will be available and how they will be used in pursuit of national security. For example, our response to the 1948 Soviet challenge in Berlin, employing an airlift instead of forcing open the ground access routes, reflected a strategic decision to respond non-violently; but it also reflected the structural fact that we had neither the forces on the ground nor the ability to acquire, train, and equip such forces in time to meet the challenge. Again, the decision to cut back ground forces after the Korean War reflected decisions on deterrent strategy as well as decisions about optimum levels of spending for defense and other governmental purposes.

The linkages between military strategy and military force structure are of major importance to manpower procurement policy. This study does not examine these linkages at technical levels of military staff planning nor does it examine very closely such higher level questions as how many divisions, how many major naval vessels, how many bomber and missile groups, and what mixtures of types within these kinds of military forces should be available. But considerable attention is given a yet broader question about force structure, one that has been a recurrent source of policy dispute: how much of each kind of military force should be kept active, ready to use on little or no notice, and how much should be kept at lower levels of strength and readiness, not under direct control of military leadership. The much debated balance between forces-in-being and mobilizable reserves has important implications for military strategy, and is at the same time directly related to policies and programs of manpower procurement. Linkages of manpower procurement policy to force structure, and ultimately to military strategy, can be subsumed under one general goal for that policy, the goal of military effectiveness. But force effectiveness also depends on aspects of manpower procurement more distinctly structural in character, particularly the quantity and quality of manpower procured for the armed forces. For their sources of manpower, the armed forces tap the pool of qualified but untrained men not in service, and they seek to retain trained men who have been in service for varying periods of time. Thus force effectiveness depends not only on force structure, but also on service entry standards, recruiting and reenlistment programs, and the material and psychological attractiveness of military service.

As an element of military policy, then, manpower procurement involves both devising an appropriate force structure and supplying the quantity and quality of manpower required, all to the end of making the armed forces effective instruments for national security. But—as with other elements of military policy, so with manpower procurement—the goal of force effectiveness cannot be considered apart from that of cost efficiency. Pay and benefit scales affect the quantity and quality of men the armed forces can recruit and retain. These results, along with the character of the force structure, determine the gross military pay budget. This budget, in total and by its various parts, may be compared with the costs of alternative force structures and recruiting and retention programs to assess the military cost effectiveness of a particular manpower procurement system.

Decisions on force structure and manpower procurement systems have important implications for more than military effectiveness and defense cost efficiency. A decision to raise spending on manpower by a given amount represents in part a decision not to spend that amount on other elements of military strength and needs—weapons, supplies, training facilities, housing and the like. But it also represents a decision not to spend those funds on other governmental activities, or not to release them through lower taxes for private spending decisions in the marketplace. Moreover, manpower acquired by the armed forces is at least temporarily not available for other activities, governmental or private. At the same time, at least part of the manpower outflow from the armed forces has more skills to contribute to the economy than it had upon entry. All these considerations suggest that military manpower procurement needs to be adapted to a variety of social goals. Negatively, these may include minimizing the impact of manpower procurement on the general economy, on defense production, on education, and on family and community life. But manpower procurement may also be adapted to such positive goals as socialization of youth into the national community, promoting education in particular fields, and expanding the pool of skilled manpower available to industry. Moreover, the possibility of promoting such positive benefits suggests still another goal for manpower procurement policy, that of equitably distributing the benefits of military service.

Men may be compelled, as well as persuaded, to serve; and government's use of its power to conscript sharpens the need to consider the impact of manpower procurement on nonmilitary goals for the development and use of manpower. Moreover, compulsions in American society, especially those of military conscription, are not usually considered good in and of themselves; indeed, their application normally requires considerable justification. Thus yet another goal of policy is to reduce these compulsions to a minimum consistent with broadly acceptable demands of national security. At the same time, both to mitigate the felt impact of compulsions and as an end in itself, means are sought for distributing the burdens of involuntary service fairly and equitably.

In sum, military manpower procurement is important to military security policy because without men the machines of war are useless; and it is important to domestic policy both because of its aggregative impacts on the economy and society and their various parts, and because of its implications for individual members of society and their relations with each other. The conflict between national security demands for armed manpower and domestic reluctance to provide it has made manpower procurement a major object of political pressures and debate, especially in a time when military needs for manpower have been higher than in any other extended period of American national history, and when the social and economic rewards to nonmilitary manpower have also been higher, and rising.

Conflicts in the policy-making process arise, however, not so much among goals as among men and organizations that participate in the process and bring to it differing priorities among goals—priorities based in part on differing perceptions of past and present facts and events and of future trends, and based in part on personal and institutional preferences among inherently conflicting ends.

The armed services themselves are, of course, participants in almost all manpower procurement decisions; but they are relatively independent policy-makers only in their own recruiting programs and, to a lesser extent, in setting entry standards for volunteers; and even these aspects of policy are subjected occasionally to higher-level executive amendment and congressional scrutiny. The task of setting strength goals is a part of the military programing-budget-ing process, involving decisions by the services, the Joint Chiefs of Staff, the Defense Department, the Bureau of the Budget, and the president; except for some long-suspended statutory ceilings on individual service strengths, and generously conceived over-all ceilings on active and reserve forces, congressional attention to military manpower strengths is generally limited to the appropriations process. Proposed changes in pay scales and other material inducements are usually developed through interservice agreements, closely supervised by the Defense Department and the Bureau of the Budget, and are often subjected to intense scrutiny and amendment in the committee or floor stages of congressional action.

On the compulsory side of manpower procurement, monthly calls are set by the military services, normally only the Army, and the Department of Defense; the examination of men forwarded for induction is conducted at military service examining stations; and standards of acceptance are set by the Defense Department within limits determined by Congress. The chief participants in selecting men to be forwarded for induction, as well as in classifying and deferring others, are the 4,000 or so local boards of the Selective Service System, an agency independent of the Defense Department; these boards make their decisions under more or less close supervision by state and national headquarters of the System, depending on the nature of the decisions to be made. National headquarters issues regulations based on the statutes and its interpretation of them, governing the processes of registration with Selective Service, classification, induction, deferment, and exemption. Most of these regulations are standardized, as in any other governmental agency, but some, especially those dealing with certain deferments, are simply guidelines which leave the local boards and state organizations considerable room for discretion. Major changes in Selective Service regulations usually require the president's approval by executive order, and thus are scrutinized by the Bureau of the Budget; usually these must first be coordinated with the Defense Department, and sometimes with such other interested agencies as the Labor, Commerce, Agriculture, or Health, Education and Welfare departments, or the National Security Council. The statutes provide that local board decisions shall be final unless reversed on appeal, and establish appeals panels in each federal judicial district, under supervision of the state headquarters; final administrative recourse may be had under certain circumstances to the president, or more precisely to a National Appeals Board which exercised his powers in this respect. Congress and its Armed Services Committees have played a major role in establishing the Selective Service System, and in writing its statutory guidelines and occasionally amending them. The most consistent, year-to-year congressional interest in the System is shown by the House and Senate Subcommittees on Independent Offices Appropriations, which oversee the System's budget; but that oversight has had no discernable effect on the military manpower procurement operations of the System, and little if any on its work in managing the pool of registrants who have not been inducted.

In all of these manpower procurement policies, programs, and activities, compulsory or voluntary, there is a community of interest groups which play more or less active roles. The most steadily interested of these participants are the National Guard Association, the Reserve Officers Association, and other organized spokesmen for the military reserves. Their chief interest is in actions affecting reserve programs, although they speak out on other subjects as well. To a limited extent, representation of their interests is built into the military service and Defense Department staffs; but their chief access to the policy process is through the congressional committees and their staffs and, to a lesser extent, through local community pressures on individual members of Congress. A second set of interest groups are the veterans organizations, especially the American Legion and the Veterans of Foreign Wars. These groups, too, show interest in reserve policy, though not to the same extent as the reserve associations; they see themselves as the general public voice of national security interests, and have been staunch supporters of compulsory manpower procurement in one or another form. They have no formal representation in the administrative policy process, but do have fairly ready access to the Armed Services Committees and many individual senators and representatives; more than the reserve associations, they are able to depend on a general public audience for their views, both locally and nationally. While the reserve associations and the veterans groups take some interest in most aspects of military manpower procurement, it is the compulsory side of procurement that stirs a wide variety of other interest groups to action; these include the familiar representatives of organized labor, business, and farm interests, as well as secondary and college education groups, the whole spectrum of church and peace groups, minority political groups, and ad hoc groups organized to support or, more often, oppose particular manpower procurement proposals. On some issues, usually involving induction and deferment of special categories of registrants, the medical, dental, scientific, engineering and other professional associations have also played an active role.

Although this study follows a chronological structure, it is not a detailed policy history. (Such a history may become possible, and at the same time less interesting as an independent study, when the passage of time yields better perspectives on America's whole response to the cold war than historians have yet achieved.) The study relies almost entirely on publicly available documents and contemporary journalistic accounts for its construction of events. Moreover, it uses that construction of events for analytical and prescriptive purposes not usually pursued by the historian.

This study explains policy outputs and outcomes in terms of purposeful, goal-oriented actions by participants of varying influence and importance in the political process. It attempts no complete explanation of why participants took the positions they did. Thus the participants' perceptions of their personal, institutional, and substantive stakes in policy results are taken to be reflected in attitudes and actions regarding substantive policy goals or, in a few instances, some very obvious organizational aims.

This study does not prescribe optimal or efficient solutions to the problem of setting military manpower procurement policy; indeed, such prescription is technically impossible, given the complexity of the problem and the current state of the art and science of policy analysis and evaluation. Despite such limitations, an exploration of how this problem has been solved in the past, focusing on substantive policy goals and assessments, can contribute to evaluation of past results and to discovery of better solutions for the future. At least it can provide better understanding of the impact past decisions have had on policy goals, and in this way help clarify the real character of those goals. It can also improve understanding of the impact current policy alternatives may have on these goals in the future. Finally, it can reveal weaknesses in the policy process, and suggest ways of strengthening the translation of military manpower procurement goals into satisfactory public policy results.

The Draft
and
Public Policy

chapter one

Frustration
of Postwar Policy

During the years immediately following World War
II, military manpower procurement policy was a matter of constant,
nagging concern to the armed services and the Administration. It
was also the subject of nearly continuous, and occasionally furious,
public and congressional debate. This debate focused on two policy
proposals pursued by the Administration: universal military training (UMT), to provide a large and stable pool of trained manpower
available for recruitment into the organized reserves and for quick
mobilization in any future crisis; and extended Selective Service, to
meet immediate needs for large numbers of new men in the active
forces following the wholesale release of wartime veterans. UMT
was considered by the Administration, and especially the Army, to
be the essential foundation for a permanent postwar military establishment. Selective Service extension, on the other hand, was

proposed as a transitional measure, to support and supplement voluntary recruiting into the temporarily large forces needed for occupation and other immediate postwar tasks.

The early debate over these two proposals developed in response to three major legislative initiatives by the Administration: first, an unsuccessful attempt to secure adoption of UMT during the months immediately preceding and following V-J Day; second, a partly met request in early 1946 for a one-year extension of Selective Service, which would otherwise expire in May, 1946; and finally, a second unsuccessful campaign for UMT in 1947.

The outcome of this early debate over military manpower procurement policies was, by early 1948, stalemate and frustration for the Administration in its search for a stable postwar policy, accompanied by serious military manpower shortages, especially for the Army. The reasons for this outcome, and its consequences for later policy initiatives, are summarized in the concluding section.

I.   FIRST CAMPAIGN FOR UMT

1.   *The Administration's Case*

In his annual message to Congress on January 6, 1945, President Franklin Roosevelt included this brief declaration: "I am clear in my mind that, as an essential factor in the maintenance of peace in the future, we must have universal military training after this war and I shall send a special message to Congress on this subject."[1] So saying, Roosevelt endorsed a proposal which would be part of the Administration's formal legislative program for most of the next seven years, and a proposal which became the object of intensive debate in the months just before and after the end of World War II.

Within the Administration, the primary sponsor of UMT was the War Department. As early as 1943, adoption of some form of UMT was already one major assumption in that department's planning for its postwar establishment.[2] This assumption was, in turn, rooted in the thinking of the interwar years and the experience of mobilization for World War II.

In 1939, American military forces were woefully small, a consequence of two decades of neglect: the active Army was authorized

280,000 men by the National Defense Act of 1920, but had never received appropriations to reach this strength, and had less than 190,000 officers and enlisted men; the Navy and Marine Corps were no better off, numbering 125,000 and 19,000 active officers and enlisted men.[3] These prewar inadequacies were recognized by both the Army and the Navy, but from rather different points of view based on differing ideas about what constituted an appropriate force structure.

The prewar Navy tended toward a structure primarily based on active forces, in concept if not in fact. The Navy considered itself the nation's "first line of defense," and it was so regarded by the public and Congress. In an emergency, the Navy's first task would be to buy time with its existing forces, time in which the nation's full war strength might be mobilized in a secure home base. For this task, a two-ocean Navy was needed, and it was toward this end that a rebuilding program began in the mid-1930's. Such a naval force, it was expected, should be able to defend the coasts and keep open the sea-lanes to our Pacific bases and across the Atlantic. If strong enough, its existence at the outset of a war emergency might even preclude any need for mobilizing ground forces to fight outside the country. Naval reserves did exist, but their immediate role was to be that of filling out existing peacetime crews rather than providing the base for large-scale wartime expansion.

The prewar Army force structure was, in concept, a small professional force backed by large, mobilizeable reserves. Thus the Army could hope to play a decisive role in war only after extensive mobilization. The active forces would have two tasks at the outset of a war emergency: to provide small holding or delaying forces, mostly stationed overseas in the Philippines, Hawaii and the Canal Zone; and to provide training and leadership cadres for the creation of a large wartime force. Like the Naval and Marine reserves, the Army's Officer Reserve Corps was to provide immediate fillers. The National Guard, on the other hand, was intended to provide additional combat units, available at the onset of war, to supplement the active Army in its initial defensive and mobilization tasks. The real key to any wartime mobilization, however, would be the as yet untrained millions of American youth.

Both the Army and Navy structures were supported by voluntary recruiting alone. This system was adequate to the Navy's needs, as they conceived them; that service experienced no serious difficulties in meeting prewar appropriated strength goals, even during the mild expansion after 1937. The Army, however, had difficulties. Once past the depths of the depression, and especially after the decision to enlarge the active Army somewhat after 1939, that service was hard-pressed to meet its strength goals through voluntary enlistment; and the National Guard was even worse off.

From the Navy's prewar point of view, the important weaknesses were those of its active forces. These were given formal recognition, and limited remedy, in the naval expansion program. Given the Army's force structure concept, concern over its weaknesses included doubts about the adequacy and readiness of its organized reserves as well as worries about the adequacy of the active Army in face of its emergency defense and mobilization tasks. Events would soon prove that while neither service was ready when war arrived, the Army's broader fears were a better anticipation of wartime needs than was the Navy's intent to rely on its fleet-in-being.

The nation's mobilization for war began in earnest in 1940, with a declaration of national emergency in May, accompanied by a call-up of the National Guard and much of the reserves, and with enactment and activation of Selective Service in the late summer and early fall.[4] The size and pace of this mobilization are recorded in Table 1. The Army reached its greatest rate of expansion in the first year of mobilization; the multiplication of strength was more than five-fold in fiscal year 1941. Thereafter expansion continued at a slower rate, but by mid-1945 the Army had reached a strength more than thirty times its 1940 size. The Navy's expansion was only a little less explosive, bringing it to a 1945 peak strength more than twenty times its 1940 size. It differed from the Army's mobilization, being much slower in the first year, and thereafter outstripping the Army increases both in rate and, beginning in 1943, in numbers.

The prime engine of this expansion was the Selective Service System. At first only the Army accepted inductees; but with active entry into the war, the Navy, and later the Marine Corps, also began placing induction calls. Voluntary enlistment also continued, and the relative attractiveness of the Navy soon made for serious distortion in the procurement system: the Navy was able to select fairly

TABLE 1

ACTIVE DUTY MILITARY PERSONNEL,
JUNE 30, 1938-JUNE 30, 1945
(In Thousands)

	1938	1939	1940	1941	1942	1943	1944	1945
Army (incl. Air Force)	185	190	269	1,462	3,076	6,994	7,995	8,268
Navy	119	125	161	284	641	1,742	2,981	3,381
Marine Corps	18	19	28	54	143	309	476	475
Total	323	334	458	1,801	3,859	9,045	11,452	12,123

SOURCE: U.S. Department of Defense, Directorate for Statistical Services, *Selected Manpower Statistics* (Washington: Department of Defense, April 11, 1966), pp. 7, 9. (N.B. Details do not add to totals due to rounding.)

carefully, and to keep its standards relatively high, while the Army was left with what men it could get. In December, 1942, a presidential order banned further volunteering, except through the Selective Service System, on the part of men in the draft-liable age groups. This only partly remedied the distortions, however, as the Navy continued to enlist youths under age eighteen.

This experience, first with the gap between prewar force concepts and realities, and then with the need for an enormous wartime expansion, suggested to the Army and the War Department a fairly simple line of reasoning about postwar plans: the United States, in order to discharge its peace-keeping responsibilities, must not return to the old feast-and-famine cycle of military preparedness—small forces in peacetime, starved for men and equipment, followed by a frantic effort to mobilize in the midst of a war crisis. The needed peacetime military strength might be achieved by maintaining large standing forces, but the American people would provide neither the financial support nor the manpower to support such forces. Hopefully they would support much smaller professional forces and the necessarily large, well-trained organized reserves to back up the active forces; but such a force structure would also require a large pool of trained men. The most effective and acceptable method of providing this pool would be to require all, or nearly all, young men to undergo a period of military training sometime between age eighteen and twenty. Finally, by exposing all young men to the nature and opportunities of military service, UMT would also promote voluntary recruiting into the organized reserve units and even into the active services. This reasoning, and the conclusion that UMT was essential, formed the baseline of Army and War Department planning for a postwar establishment.

Army and War Department planning in turn became the foundation of the Administration's initial case for UMT, a case which, except for some shifts in programmatic details, varied little through all the years of the early debate over military manpower procurement policies. This case was first presented in full, to Congress and the public, in hearings before the House Select Committee on Postwar Military Policy held in June 1945.[5]

Opening the Administration's presentation, Acting Secretary of State Joseph Grew testified to the need for American military power in the postwar world. He argued that German and Japanese assessments of and contempt for our prewar military weakness had played an important part in their miscalculations leading to war. In the years ahead, he urged, even granting reasonable success in concluding peace treaties at the end of World War II and in creating collective security machinery under the new United Nations Organization, the United States' responsibilities toward our own security and world stability would require military forces considerably larger and better trained than those of the prewar years. This argument was either seconded or assumed by all the military and other Administration witnesses. The remainder of the case then, was a matter of showing that UMT would be the most effective and acceptable means of assuring greater postwar military strength.

The key witnesses in making this showing were two Army officers, General of the Army George C. Marshall and Brigadier General John McAuley Palmer. As chief of staff, General Marshall had insisted that UMT be made an integral part of the Army's planning for demobilization and a postwar establishment; to him, UMT was to be the central feature in postwar military policy. For General Palmer, UMT was more than a mere policy proposal; it was an article of faith. Palmer had been a key Army staff assistant in the ill-starred campaign for UMT after World War I; following his retirement, he became a writer with a major interest in the history of American military policy; in 1940, he advised the civilian group promoting the Selective Service Act; and, in November, 1941, Marshall recalled him to active duty as a special staff advisor. In the planning for UMT, Marshall and Palmer seemed almost alter egos; it is difficult to decide just where Palmer's role as old friend, historian, and staff advisor ended and Marshall's position as prestigious wartime chief of staff became the major weight.

Palmer's argument began with " . . . a fundamental principle of military organization which is as valid in 1945 as it was in 1790."

> No nation is fully prepared for war unless it is organized to deploy all or any necessary part of its manpower to meet any possible military emergency. From this flows the corollary that no nation can be fully prepared for sudden military emergency unless all of its able-bodied young men are trained in peace time to do their several parts in the military defense of their country and its interests.

In the American context, the most acceptable realization of this principle would be the maintenance of a small regular force, " . . . no larger than necessary to perform its normal peacetime duties and to meet sudden minor emergencies, to be reinforced when necessary by reserve forces organized from the trained young men of the Nation." The alternative, Palmer stated, would be a standing regular force " . . . large enough to meet any contingency in the foreseeable future. But such . . . a standing force without trained reserves would have no power of rapid expansion and would therefore have to be very large indeed." Moreover, recalling the Army's experience with recruiting prior to the war, Palmer argued that, barring "prohibitively expensive" pay raises, such a large standing force could be maintained only by means of compulsory service. This would mean that " . . . no able-bodied American would be free from the threat of peacetime conscription in his early manhood."[6]

To escape this choice among military weakness, national bankruptcy, and perpetual conscription, Palmer proposed UMT, yet another form of compulsory procurement. What was the difference between conscription and universal training? As Palmer and other witnesses argued it, the crucial difference lay in the distinction between military *service* and military *training*. Conscription, said Palmer, involves compulsory service; just as in wartime, peacetime conscripts would be full-fledged members of the armed forces, subject to their discipline, and required to perform any tasks in any place where military force was required. UMT, on the other hand, would impose no such obligations. Young men would, to be sure, be required to undergo one year of military or naval training. But they would be called for training only, in special training units, and they would not be subject to military service. After training, any obligation for actual military service could only be acquired by volunteering for the regular or organized reserve forces, or as a consequence of a declaration of national emergency by Congress. The latter would, of course, lead to conscription for actual service; but the precedents for such emergency and wartime conscription already existed. In the United States, Palmer concluded,

> . . . men have been, are and will be liable to compulsory military service in wartime whether they are trained or not.
> The primary purpose of universal military training is to see to it that, hereafter, America's young men are to be trained before they become subject to compulsory military service.[7]

General Marshall supported Palmer's arguments by adopting them as his own, and he gave special emphasis to the matter of economy. He doubted that even World War II had taught a strong enough lesson to induce national support for a large active force in peacetime, given Congress's reaction to military budgets in election years. The cost of such a force would certainly in this sense be prohibitive. Moreover, " . . . the necessary men to fill its ranks could not be hired in time of peace; and it would be repugnant to the American people." "So," argued Marshall, "the problem boils down to some system that is within our financial possibilities and still is an acceptable procedure. Other than a large standing army, I know of no other system except one based on universal military training. . . . If you do not have that, you cannot expect to maintain before the world a respectable military posture. . . ."[8]

Secretary of War Henry Stimson testified in a similar vein, but he went beyond the arguments of Marshall and Palmer to cite a number of "incidental advantages" to trainees under UMT: they would gain "lasting benefit" from its contribution to their physical well-being; by mixing with youth from all sections and social classes they would "rub smooth the sharp edges of prejudice"; they would discover and be encouraged to develop new vocational skills; and they would learn, through "patriotic training and discipline," the lessons of decent and mutually considerate human behavior. Nevertheless, the primary aim of UMT would be " . . . to fit men to protect the national security."[9] Stimson was one of the few official witnesses to lay any great stress on these "incidental" benefits of UMT. Moreover, the attention given by others to nonmilitary aspects of the program was largely defensive. Their emphasis clearly was on the military arguments for UMT, and on what they saw as the political and economic realities affecting the survival of any American military system.

In addition to making a political-military case for UMT, witnesses for the Army and Navy also presented general outlines and some details of the anticipated training programs. For both services, the plan was to induct young men, through a civilian agency similar to the Selective Service System, for one year of continuous training, normally at age eighteen, or at age seventeen with parents' consent, or as late as age twenty to permit completion of high school. Exceptions would be minimal, with emphasis on equality of obligation. To this end, there would be no provisions for occupational or dependency exemptions. Nevertheless, since the purpose was to train men for possible service in time of war, some men would not be taken by reason of physical or mental deficiency. The Navy suggested, in fact, that the current wartime standards for induction were the minimums which should be allowed for UMT. The 800,000 to 900,000 men inducted annually for training would be given some choice of branch of service, limited by overall quotas on the ratio of $8 : 2\text{-}1/2 : 1/2$ for the Army (including Army Air Forces), Navy, and Marine Corps. The actual training programs would, of course, differ according to service needs. In the Army, all trainees would undergo nine weeks of common basic training. The next thirty-five weeks would provide individual and unit training fitted to the special tasks of the Army Ground, Service and Air Forces. The final eight weeks would be devoted to combined field maneuvers involving trainee units from all three branches. Navy trainees would spend their first nine months in three stages—recruit training, specialized schools, and operational training. The remaining three months would be devoted to practical experience on board ship or with aircraft squadrons. (The Marine Corps program was not discussed). To gain maximum economy of training facilities and staff, trainees would be called in four classes each year rather than one. Following their one year of training, graduates of the program would be discharged into reserve pools for a period of five years; they would have no further obligation for training or service during this period except at the call of Congress. They would, however, have the opportunity to volunteer for the regular forces or the organized reserves; or they could volunteer for further specialized training to fit them for more advanced tasks in the reserves; or, if otherwise qualified, they could apply for officer training in the college ROTC programs, or for appointment to the Military or Naval Academy.

Besides Grew, Stimson, Marshall, Palmer and the two staff officers already mentioned, other chief Administration witnesses included top civilian and military leaders of the Navy, Marine Corps, and Army Air Forces. While each of these men developed and emphasized particular points about UMT, the general thrust of their testimony supported the case developed by Army witnesses. Nonetheless, some differences of emphasis in the testimony, and later evidence, suggest there were difficulties in maintaining a unified Administration position on UMT.

One of these difficulties was internal to the War Department and the Army, and was apparent in the contrast between two plans produced by the Special Planning Division of the General Staff. Both plans aimed at the final goal of demobilization, the achievement of a permanent peacetime establishment. The first, dated May, 1944, proposed an Army of 870,000 active officers and enlisted men, 630,000 UMT trainees annually, and 3,000,000 in organized reserve units, including both World War II veterans and graduates of UMT. General Marshall refused to approve these estimates, terming them "improbable of accomplishment," and suggesting that even rumor of them could hurt the chances for a realistic postwar establishment. He ordered a resurvey of postwar active force requirements, in light of assumed destruction of Axis military power, our own resources of surplus war material, and "the vastly increased power" to be derived from UMT. The Special Planning Division later produced new figures of 275,000 for active Army strength, plus a UMT training overhead of 110,000 composed of one-half regulars and one-half reservists on active duty. Marshall approved the new estimates in February, 1945. This approval ignored, however, strong dissent from the Army Air Forces (AAF). Despite later attempts to persuade this increasingly independent Army command of the political-military realism of these estimates, the AAF never formally retreated from its dissent.[10] Heir presumptive to the Navy's prewar position as the nation's "first line of defense," the AAF felt the postwar active forces would have to be much larger than Marshall thought possible. The February, 1945, estimates were never mentioned in the June hearings, and it seems probable that this omission was the price paid for public support of UMT in the hearings by AAF witnesses.

There were interservice, as well as intraservice, differences underlying the apparent Administration unity on UMT. As an independent service and department, the Navy had its own plans for a postwar establishment. The postwar active Navy would have some 500,000 enlisted men, but the experience of a twenty-fold expansion in World War II had taught the Navy that a much larger force would be needed to fight a war. Some 1.8 million men would be "required to man the vessels it is planned to retain at the end of this war in active, training and reserve status and to man the naval air force and shore stations to support the fleet." Thus about 1.3 million additional enlisted men would be needed to mobilize the Navy in wartime. These the Navy hoped to obtain from UMT, either as volunteers in the organized Naval Reserve or in unorganized reserve pools. Although these figures suggest that the Navy, as a result of wartime experience, had moved closer to the Army's concept of a proper peacetime force structure, the contrast between the Navy's and the Army's estimates also suggests significant differences between the two service's expectations.

One of these differences arose from the services' contrasting experiences with voluntary recruiting before and during the war. Asked whether the estimate of 500,000 enlisted men in the postwar active Navy was based on a realistic estimate of recruiting prospects, Admiral King responded cautiously that "there may be a problem . . . and that is something we will have to consider when we are confronted with the condition." Against this cautious optimism stood Marshall's pessimistic response when pressed for his "idea as to the correct size" of the postwar active Army: "by a great recruiting campaign and by rates of pay which I think would be prohibitive we might reach a strength of 250,000."[11] Even more striking was the contrast between the service's planned ratios of active strength to reserves; the Army's February plan estimated one active to eleven organized reserves, while the Navy's figure was one active to less than three reserves. Finally, the Navy was willing to take much the lesser share of UMT trainees in each annual class; the ratio was to be eight for the Army to three for the Navy and Marine Corps, based roughly on current relative wartime strengths.

In planning for postwar military establishments, then, UMT was vital to the Army because it would provide the trained reserves without which that prospectively small professional service could not fight any war. It was important to the Navy as well, but less so; for that service had not wholly abandoned its "fleet-in-being" concept in favor of the Marshall-Palmer vision of strength through UMT. But the Navy did not make a point of this difference, and indeed gave UMT its enthusiastic public support. Potentially the strongest dissenter, the Army Air Forces did not disagree publicly with the Administration position and the Marshall-Palmer vision for nearly three more years, well after becoming independent from the War Department.

Still a third potential threat to a unified Administration position on UMT was obscured in the hearings by the fact that all the official witnesses were from the State, War and Navy Departments. This was the possibility that some in the Administration might wish to promote UMT as not so much a defense measure as a general welfare program. Two years earlier, President Roosevelt had publicly expressed interest in a postwar youth training program which would be only partly military; and more recently he had suggested that a public study be made of a postwar program much like the old Civilian Conservation Corps, but broader in scope and including all male youths.[12] Roosevelt's endorsement of UMT in the 1945 State of the Union message may have marked the end of his indecision on this question; and the character of the opposition which developed against any form of UMT suggests Administration witnesses were wise to emphasize the program's purely military virtues.

Aside from these differences, actual or potential, there were no visible cracks in the Administration position that UMT was the most effective, the most acceptable, and perhaps the only way to meet the nation's postwar needs for trained military manpower; nor did any open dissent develop during the early years of debate, through the first and second campaigns for UMT.

2. *Debate Before V-J Day*

Internal unity, or the appearance of it, was essential if the Administration were to make its case persuasive, for it faced an uncertain Congress and a divided public. Most of the nation's large, permanent interest groups had taken sides on UMT. From their ranks, the Administration had gained the early, active, and wholehearted support of the veterans groups, with the American Legion playing the leading role. The opposition of these groups could have killed UMT quickly, but their support was not enough, and support from other groups was either disappointingly mild or nonexistent. The military reserve associations favored UMT in principle, but were more concerned to stress their own special interests than to fight the Administration's battles. Support came also from the U.S. Chamber of Commerce, a few prominent educators, and a small number of religious groups and leaders. Against these was a formidable array of opponents, including organized labor, most of organized education, a majority of religious groups, the major farm groups, the NAACP and other Negro groups, a variety of left-leaning political groups, and an extensive structure of ad hoc citizens committees. The opposition to UMT displayed great diversity in both specific and general purposes, yet it maintained remarkable stability, and efficacy, throughout the early years of debate.

The House Select Committee on Postwar Military Policy was not empowered to propose legislation to the House; so its hearings in June, 1945, served no formal purpose other than as a public forum. That purpose was well served, though. The hearings provided a focus for all the energy, emotion, reason, and logic that the Administration, its allies, and its opponents could bring to bear on the complex issues surrounding UMT. The resulting debate dealt, expressly or implicitly, with all the major goals of military manpower procurement policy: force effectiveness, cost efficiency, minimal compulsions, equity, and adaptation to social goals.

Military Force Effectiveness

The Administration's case for UMT argued that large, trained reserves would be an essential part of the postwar military and naval establishments, and that UMT would be an effective way of getting them—perhaps the only way. Opposition to these claims took several main lines: one questioned whether the United States would really need as much military force in the postwar period as the Administration and the military services seemed to think; a second questioned whether UMT would produce the sort of military force structure required in the postwar world; and a third argued that UMT was not the only way, and certainly not the best way, of providing forces to fit the structure desired by the military services.

The core of the first line of argument, questioning whether we would really need very large military forces in peacetime, was not the open and outspoken isolationism of the 1930's and of the 1940 debate over Selective Service, though there were echoes of this. Lewis Hines, representing the AFL, was not alone in asking: "Preparedness for what? If we are on the brink of another war, should we not have the right to demand to know with whom, when, and where?"[13] Yet the context of such questions had changed. The experience of World War II had not completely suppressed the attitude that we could be secure by minding our own business. But a different attitude, one also firmly held by some in the interwar period, had now come to the fore as the prime argument against maintaining sizeable postwar military forces. This was the notion, or hope, that national security must in the future rest on a foundation of international collective security. It was this hope and faith which had led the great majority of Americans to support creation of a postwar United Nations Organization. And it was faith in the idea of a United Nations based on international understanding and good will, but supported too by internationally controlled armed forces, which led many to question America's need for large forces of our own. It was in this context that Hines raised his question. In a similar vein, Byrl Whitney, speaking for the Brotherhood of Railroad Trainmen, closed his formal statement with this observation: "There is something pitifully ironical about a nation vigorously preparing for the next war and delaying the problems of peace while fighting a war to destroy militarism and to establish enduring world peace."[14] Although willing to admit he had been "delinquent" in opposing Selective Service in 1940, Whitney, like many others, felt the lessons of 1940 simply were not applicable to the coming period of international peace. Moreover, spokesmen for labor and for church groups expressed concern that American action to sustain a strong military posture in the postwar era might very well jeopardize the chances for creating stable and peaceful international arrangements.

To these arguments, Administration witnesses answered that military force would not only be a necessity in the postwar world, it would also be a positive good. Obviously they could not cite our wartime ally in answer to Hines's rhetorical question. But they could and did treat these arguments as simply a new version of the old isolationist misunderstanding of the role of power and force in relations among nations. Undersecretary Grew set the tone, arguing that without adequate military force "our diplomacy becomes weak and ineffective." General Marshall was a little more blunt in observing that to preserve the postwar peace "we must either depend completely on a new and, I might well say, unheard-of idealism among European nations or we must be prepared to back up what we put into the terms of the peace." Secretary Forrestal was just as blunt and a bit more colorful, though no more explicit:

> Proponents of military training frequently are asked whom we are preparing to fight. Quite simply, we are going to fight any international ruffian who attempts to impose his will on the world by force. We should make that determination clear—by deeds as well as words—to any frustrated paperhanger who may be dreaming of world domination.[15]

The pro-UMT argument was not without its appeal to the internationalist spirit, as evidenced by Secretary Stimson's appeal to a sense of duty toward preserving the peace, and in other witnesses' observations that what our allies feared most was not our military power but that we might once again withdraw from the world. But it did insist that strong American military forces in the postwar era would be necessary and positively helpful, as the absence of such force in the 1930's had been harmful, to both American security and world stability.

A second line of argument against UMT as a means to military effectiveness granted that postwar American military strength should be greater than in 1939, but questioned whether the intended force structure would be appropriate to postwar needs. Opponents of UMT taking this line emphasized the need for forces-in-being rather than the mobilizeable reserves which UMT was to provide; and the forces-in-being they had in mind were more often than not air and naval fleets, not ground divisions.

An outspoken proponent of this view was Josephus Daniels, secretary of the navy in Wilson's wartime cabinet. Forrestal had recorded Daniels' view, some months before the June hearings, that it was dangerous to promote public reliance on the UMT concept rather than on maintaining a large, effective Navy.[16] Daniels presented a similar argument at the Postwar Military Policy Committee hearings, this time placing "the main emphasis on a navy that flies, with adequate military strength on land and sea. Aviation has passed its infancy, but has not yet reached its stride. I would take leave to be strong in the air. If our country dominates the sky, no enemy can land on any part of our terrain."[17] Strong standing forces were also urged by two education group witnesses, but they gave a little more credit to the need for ground forces. The most articulate spokesman for reliance on forces-in-being did not appear at the hearings; this was Hanson W. Baldwin, military editor of the *New York Times*, whose views on peacetime conscription[18] were so widely quoted by some witnesses, and paraphrased by so many others, that he was in effect a participant. His argument amounted, in essence, to downgrading the need for reserves, and indeed the need for armed manpower, in modern war. World War II mobilization had produced American military forces several times larger than ever before in our history, and had drawn even larger numbers into the armed forces of other nations. Nevertheless, Baldwin was not alone in approving the view that, while past wars had been decided by manpower, World War II and future wars would be won primarily by machines; and he and others assumed this change in the character of war would enable the United States to buy more military security with less manpower.[19] To this common premise, Baldwin added some of his own. Geography, he argued, reinforced by a strong Navy and Air Force and complemented by a well-protected system of overseas bases, would preclude the need for a great land army in defense of the continental United States, at least in the first year of a war. He did recognize that a large ground force might be required in a later stage, but argued that the necesssary equipment for such an army could not be produced in less than a year to eighteen months. This, he implied, would be sufficient time for raising the army, too. Thus, while granting the need for a sizable corps of reserve officers, Baldwin saw no real need for large numbers of trained reserves, and thus no military requirement for peacetime UMT.

By admitting the possibility of some future wartime mobilization, Baldwin made the argument against UMT a better reflection of experience in World War II than were arguments for simple reliance on strong naval and air forces. But in so doing, he also yielded much of the grounds of the pro-UMT case. It remained for the Administration, in response, to emphasize the problem of time. Here, again, World War II experience supported those who argued that quick wartime mobilization would require peacetime preparation and training. The United States had not been able to launch a large-scale operation involving ground forces until the invasion of North Africa, more than two years after the beginnings of serious mobilization in 1940. To Marshall, the alternatives were clear: "Either universal military training or the hope—that is all you can possibly have—the hope that you will have better than a year for preparation."[20]

To the argument that geography, bases, and a strong Navy and Air Force would provide that time, General Ira Eaker of the Army Air Force responded by emphasizing the enormous advantage air power would give an attacking force. Were such an attack to be launched against the United States, surely an early target in any future war, "there will certainly be no time to mobilize our Army, Navy or Air Force from men untrained in the modern complicated weapons of war." But how much mobilization of manpower would be needed? Would not the increasingly complex technology of war preclude mass employment of men? Admiral Aubrey Fitch, representing the Naval air arm, took note of this "dangerous fallacy . . . that since war is becoming more and more a matter of machines rather than masses of men, future wars may be fought by small corps of technicians controlling vast destructive machines. Our ex-

perience is quite the contrary." The very complexity of war machines, he argued, had increased the demands for manpower to
maintain and supply the machines and train men to use them.
"There is nothing in the trend of military development," he added,
"which indicates that, if the United States ever engages in another
great war, the manpower needs of the military forces will not be
greater still."[21]

In short, the advantage of having a large pool of trained reserves
was that, without maintaining unacceptably large standing forces,
the nation could produce very quickly the kind of forces required to
fight a large-scale war. The Army hoped to avoid the total unpreparedness of 1940 and "the breathless haste and improvization involved in the subsequent years of preparation . . . which were
necessarily wasteful and exorbitantly expensive."[22] The Navy expected that, with UMT and the concomitant reserves, it could expand immediately to 1.8 million men, a process that had taken 18
months after Pearl Harbor. And the Army Air Forces intended,
with the aid of UMT, to create reserves "capable of being formed
into units, not merely for service as fillers or replacement, but actually operating units. . . ."[23]

These claims led, in turn, to a third line of argument against UMT
as a military requirement, that the training contemplated simply
could not provide the kind of reserves alleged to be required.
Baldwin conceded that UMT could produce mobilizable reserves,
but argued that these reserves could not be immediately employed as
operating forces. Given the one year of continuous training called
for in the Administration plans, given even some periodic refresher
training, which the plan did not make obligatory, nevertheless after
five to eight years the military effectiveness of a UMT graduate
would have declined drastically, possibly 40 percent to 60 percent.
Time, a year or more, would be required to mobilize an effective
force.[24]

The answer of UMT proponents to this argument lay in their
basic case and the nature of their plan. The whole purpose of UMT
was to speed mobilization; obviously this process would be quicker
if those called to active duty at the onset of an emergency had had
some military training. By placing UMT graduates in reserve pools
for only five years, the plan recognized the need to call first those

whose training was recent enough to be adequate for active service. Nor were reserve pools to be the only source for mobilization. From UMT graduates would be recruited members of the organized reserves, whose training activities would not just maintain, but actually increase, their skills. From this source would come not only ready units, but also the necessary augmentation of military and naval technicians. Finally, in direct answer to the argument that changes in the technology of warfare would rapidly make the training in any one year obsolete, UMT supporters relied on Dr. Karl T. Compton's expert testimony:

> The same type of argument would say that we should not train an electrical engineer at M.I.T. today because some of the techniques of electrical engineering may be different 5 or 10 years hence. Actually, details will change and new elements will be introduced into the picture, but the fundamentals do not change so much, and anyone with the fundamental training can pick up the developments of the next five years with relative ease and in a short time.[25]

On the last point, opponents of UMT could and did cite the section of the Selective Training and Service Act of 1940 which required inductees to remain on reserve rolls for ten years after discharge. To this the UMT proponents made no direct response. Theirs was a program for the future, for the long-run future security of the nation. Their plans for the postwar armed forces, especially for the Army, depended not on the short-run usefulness of veteran reservists, but on early enactment of a system to augment and eventually replace those veterans.

Cost Efficiency

A major point in the Marshall-Palmer case for UMT was that, whether it would provide the most effective peacetime force structure or not, UMT did offer the only hope of providing any effective force at all within the postwar appropriations Congress and the public were likely to allow. The argument assumed these appropriations would be larger than those of the interwar period, but hardly large enough to support active ground, naval and air forces large enough to make up for a lack of well-trained reserves. None of the UMT opponents argued directly to this point; but the indictments of UMT by Baldwin and others rested implicitly on one or both of two unstated assumptions: Either postwar military appropriations would be significantly larger than those expected by UMT proponents, or the funds to be spent on UMT would produce less additional military effectiveness than the same funds spent on additional active forces. Neither the fiscal and political judgment of the first assumption nor the cost effectiveness analysis implied by the second was explored openly at this stage of the debate. Some UMT opponents did suggest a broader cost efficiency issue, questioning whether the three billion dollars they had heard UMT would cost annually might not be better spent on public education, national health and scientific development; but Administration witnesses ignored this argument, and were not pressed for a UMT cost estimate.

Limiting Compulsions

The main power and passion of those urging adoption of UMT was spent in relating the proposed program to the security needs of the nation. The equivalent energy and emotion of those opposed was focused on the remaining issues. Of these, the proponents of UMT were particularly sensitive to the issue of compulsion. This is directly apparent in the pains taken by almost all the Administration witnesses, and many of their interest group allies, to follow carefully the distinction elaborated by General Palmer between obligatory training (UMT) and obligatory military service (conscription).

By whatever name, compulsory performance of military duties in peacetime was a most unattractive prospect for large numbers of Americans. The single argument most often voiced against UMT in the hearings was that peacetime conscription would run counter to all of American tradition and experience with military forces, and that to adopt it would be to emulate our wartime enemies, or at best to follow the hapless example of our defeated French ally. Peacetime conscription, whether for training or for service, would militarize America, smother democracy, regiment the minds of American youth, destroy the spirit of free labor, contradict the principle of free conscience, and insult the memory of the millions who had fled conscript tyranny in Europe to find freedom and peace in a New World. Indeed, if the UMT proposal was not a conscious plot to subvert American liberties, it was to some opponents clearly a means to perpetuate the wartime military hierarchy which had been established by the war.

To argue that compulsory military training in peacetime was against all American tradition was to overlook a good bit of American history. In the early periods of colonization, every one of the thirteen colonies had imposed by legislation a universal obligation on its able-bodied male citizens to service in the militia. Moreover, these statutes required continuous training in time of peace, as well as service in a military emergency, and these requirements were enforced.[26] But, as colonial military needs declined, these statutes were altered considerably. By the time of the Revolution, colonial legislatures had introduced provisions for avoiding wartime duty by paying a fine or hiring a substitute; and they had introduced contractual systems of military service, with bounties paid for volunteering, which tended to displace the traditional obligation to serve.[27]

Experience with manpower procurement in the Revolutionary War taught conflicting lessons. One of these was that dependence on volunteering and lack of peacetime training afforded a very poor basis for military security. The lesson was reflected in the proposals of Secretary of War Knox and President Washington to the First Congress for plans incorporating local militia units in a national army system and requiring all young American men to undertake three summer military training periods, and it was this lesson and this response that General Palmer emphasized in the June, 1945, hearings.[28] The Washington-Knox plan finally emerged in a much watered-down version as the Militia Act of 1792, which rejected the principle of compulsory training. To Palmer, peacetime UMT would not so much contradict American tradition as it would restore the wisdom of Washington and, before him, of the early colonial legislatures. Against this lesson, however, most Americans accepted the legend of the Minutemen, yeoman farmers ready and willing to spring to the nation's defense whenever needed, but desiring to be left alone in peacetime.

American experience following the Revolution did support the anti-UMT view that compulsion was not the accepted basis for American military service in peacetime. Through the nineteenth century, the concept of peacetime militia obligations withered continuously, to the point that after the Civil War even the requirement of militia enrollment was abandoned. It was only after more than a hundred years that the Congress finally reaffirmed, in the Militia Act of 1903, the membership of all able-bodied American men in the militia. Even then there was no recognized obligation to train or serve except as the citizen might voluntarily accept it.[29]

At the same time, the post-Revolutionary concept of military obligation as a matter of a voluntary contract had come to dominate even wartime service. An attempt to enact a federal draft law in the War of 1812 was rejected as unconstitutional; and the unhappy experiences of both the Union and the Confederacy with drafts in the Civil War seemed only to affirm the incompatibility of the voluntary-contract and forced-draft concepts. It was not until 1917 that the United States achieved its first successful implementation of the principle that citizens owe the nation their services in war.[30] By 1945, the idea of wartime military conscription had gained general acceptance, even something of the aura of tradition. But, with their familiar tendency to make sharp distinctions between war and peace, many Americans saw no obligation to train for war in time of peace.

The attacks by opponents of UMT on the Administration's estimate of postwar military requirements, and on the value of peacetime training of reserves in meeting those requirements, were also assertions that compulsion in peacetime was unnecessary—and if unnecessary, therefore undesirable. The Administration answered this in its basic case for UMT, specifically linking peacetime training to effective wartime service. If compulsory service was justified in wartime as essential to national security—this being the generally accepted defense of it—then compulsory training in peacetime was equally justified on the same grounds.

The main attack on peacetime compulsion focused not on these questions of need, but on allegations that it would destroy or drastically alter the basic fabric of American life and liberty. One answer of UMT supporters to these allegations was to emphasize the lack of militaristic spirit displayed by veterans returning from World

War I and by GI's during World War II. Moreover, the real danger of militarism, so General Palmer argued, would stem from a large, permanent active force, not from annual classes of trainees. Far from being an unmitigated evil, some supporters added, UMT would be of positive, if only incidental, benefit in promoting civic virtues among American youth. Two witnesses laid special stress on such benefits, General Luther D. Miller, acting Army chief of chaplains, and Dr. Daniel A. Poling. Their testimony was intended to counter the charge of various church groups and the Women's Christian Temperance Union that UMT would expose impressionable young men to temptations which only their homes and local communities could protect them from. In answer they pointed to the work of the military and naval chaplains and argued that UMT would provide an unparalleled opportunity to bring the influence of the church to American youth.

Such arguments left opponents of UMT unconvinced; theirs was a conclusion not so much from logic as from fear, not so much from the mind as from the gut, or from the bible belt. If they did not quite equate the military realism of Marshall and King with the militaristic outlook of the Prussian generals or the Samurai, still they did see dangers of militaristic indoctrination and regimentation. To expose one or another generation of Americans to military service was one thing, especially when that service also entailed direct experience with the consequences of war; but to fasten upon the American people a permanent system of military education for all able-bodied young men might, and eventually probably would, have quite different and disastrous results. The argument that UMT would produce side benefits in civic education was hardly reassuring. Not even such arguments as that offered by Secretary Forrestal —that UMT need be only as permanent as the Congress and the people saw fit to make it—could quiet all the fears expressed by church groups, labor leaders, educationists, and staunchly anti-military private citizens.

By and large, proponents of UMT chose to ignore these fears rather than answer them. The Administration preferred to rest its case on grounds of military necessity, not social advantage, and to emphasize the limited nature of the training obligation proposed.

A number of witnesses at the June hearings, more or less favorable to the principle of UMT, offered alternatives to the Administration's plan that tended to mitigate the impact of compulsion by reducing or otherwise altering the training obligation. Typical of these was a plan presented by the Catholic War Veterans Association. The central feature of their proposal was that military drill and tactics be required courses at all high schools, colleges and universities in the country; ROTC would be available as an optional course at all schools; and all military courses would be conducted by Army or Navy officers. In addition, all young men reaching age eighteen would be required to participate in two consecutive summer camps of thirteen weeks each at military or naval training bases. In offering this plan, the association stressed its wish to avoid a prolonged separation of youth from home and community life. The plan of the Veterans of Foreign Wars (VFW) had a similar aim. It called for compulsory enlistment in a reserve component for a three-year period. During this time, trainees would attend weekly drill periods at a local armory and annual two-week summer camps.

The Administration's reaction to such plans was indirect, but clearly unenthusiastic. Nearly every government witness stressed and restressed the need for one continuous year of training if UMT were to produce effectively trained reserves. Indeed, Admiral King implied that the Navy perhaps should have a longer period, though he was satisfied to support the one-year plan.

The Question of Equity

When attacked on the question of compulsion, the Administration's response was to stress military necessity. When attention turned to the question of equity, military necessity was pictured as a social virtue. There was, in fact, hardly any argument raised against UMT on grounds of equity; that field was left largely to UMT's supporters.

Of interest, then, was not the argument on this question, but the ambiguity in the proposed plan. On the one hand, the Administration emphasized universality of obligation. It would make the discharge of this obligation a prerequisite to specialist or officer training; the only alternative to training would be direct enlistment in the regular Army, Navy or Marine Corps; and there would be no privileged avenues of avoidance. On the other hand, the Navy proposed limiting trainee induction to those who could meet current Selective Service standards. The Army's witnesses did not discuss the matter of screening out those with physical or mental deficiencies, but presumably the Navy's logic would apply to the Army as well: the purpose of UMT was to train men for possible war service, and current induction standards represented minimums for such service. Yet rejection rates under Selective Service were at that time a little over 35 percent, which posed a rather serious potential compromise of the equal obligation concept. Opponents of UMT did have comments to make on this limitation, but not in relation to equity.

Adapting to Social Goals

UMT's possible impact on other goals for the development of the nation's youth was also questioned at this early stage of debate. Some of these questions had to do with the extra-military benefits claimed for UMT, not so much by the Administration as by its more enthusiastic allies. Even among Administration witnesses, however, there was a general sense of optimism over what UMT could accomplish beyond its strictly military goals. General Vandegrift, for example, asserted that "Total abolition of illiteracy in the male population, sound physical condition of participants, few men in occupations for which they are not fitted, resulting from service classification. . . . These are not just possibilities, they are practical certainties."[31] Such claims were at best questionable, given that proposed standards for trainee induction would screen out many of those most in need of such benefits, as several labor and education group witnesses pointed out. UMT's appropriateness to such goals was also attacked. Typical was the comment of the AFL representative, that any national program promoting health and physical well-being ought to be aimed at youths well under the age for military service. Even more to the point was Hanson Baldwin's argument that a UMT program must either educate young men for civil life or train them for military duties; it could not do both.[32] In response, the Administration argument was that UMT would in fact be a military training program, but that its other benefits, if only incidental, would nonetheless be real.

The fears noted earlier concerning the impact of UMT on youthful character and morals were not simply arguments against compulsion; they suggested strong conflicts over goals and means for the development of American youth. Homes, churches and schools were said to be the proper place to shape the attitudes and govern the actions of youths, not military training camps. The answering emphasis on military chaplains and on molding character through discipline was not very convincing.

The most difficult charge for the Administration to answer was that UMT would interfere seriously with education. Daniel Marsh, president of Boston University, spoke for the American Association of Colleges, and for most other education witnesses, in arguing that the interruption of education "would simply be disastrous to an overwhelming number of the young fellows. They get out of the habit of study, are broken away from their fellows, and want to get into some kind of employment; or their ideals have been changed." A representative of the National Association of Secondary School Principals, NEA, stressed the dangers in UMT for professional and scientific education, pointing out that there were already severe shortages developing in these fields as a result of wartime interruptions, and that such education would take five to eight years. Having stressed the military nature of the training it proposed, the Administration could not very easily argue that UMT would promote technical and professional education; and its claims that the program might uncover and develop latent vocational skills were halfheartedly made and indifferently received. It remained, then, for Dr. Karl Compton of M.I.T. to offer the most complete response to this problem. Compton began by rejecting any thought of exempting scientific and engineering students from UMT. "The difficulty with this . . . as I see it, is that once it is acceded to for any one group, the pressure cannot be resisted to grant exemption to many other groups, and the whole military training program hence breaks down." Beyond considerations of equity and efficacy in the program, Compton saw some positive benefits in holding potential scientists and engineers to a UMT obligation. For one, he noted the need of the armed forces for officers with technical education. Second, he argued that the individual student would benefit from the practical experience of working with technical equipment and learning to work in an organization. Finally, he suggested that interruptions of education to earn money for further schooling were neither uncommon nor harmful, but often beneficial. UMT should have a similar effect, he reasoned: "They would come out of it with greater maturity, more realistic social adjustment, and greater determination to make the best use of their future educational opportunities."[33]

Results of the June Hearings

The June, 1945, hearings provided a broad-scale test of strength between supporters and opponents of UMT, but the results were hardly decisive. To be sure, the committee did recommend "that the Congress adopt, as a matter of broad policy, a system of universal military training for the critical years ahead." In so recommending, the committee accepted not only the argument of the War, Navy and State Departments for the necessity of military strength in the postwar world, but also the Army and Navy pleas that early congressional action setting out the major features of their postwar establishment was essential to provide "the predicate for an orderly transition from the wartime to the peacetime military organizations."[34] But the committee was not empowered to produce a bill of its own; its report, though highly favorable to the Administration, could only urge still more committee hearings. Thus UMT's opponents also got the delay they wanted, and they revealed to the Administration, Congress, the public, and themselves, their very considerable strength.

3. Impact of Demobilization

Within days after the atomic explosions at Hiroshima and Nagasaki, the chairmen of the House and Senate Military Affairs Committees both began pressing for changes in manpower procurement activity; and even before V-J Day, both committees invited military spokesmen to public hearings on their demobilization plans.[35] Members of these committees, while expressing no firm consensus on any specific demobilization program, nonetheless seemed to have a fairly clear goal in mind: the most rapid possible conversion of the huge Army and Navy war machines into much smaller, permanent, peacetime establishments supported by voluntary enlistments.

Such a goal was implicit in the interest expressed by committee members in three kinds of manpower action: acceleration of demobilization, promotion of voluntary recruiting, and early cessation of Selective Service inductions. Moreover, the goal, and the interest, were a reasonable representation of public desires.

The Administration and the armed forces were well aware of these congressional and public desires; and the Navy's plans, at least, seemed to be in keeping with them. The Navy intended to complete its demobilization in twelve months—by September 1, 1946; strength goals for that date were 558,000 officers and enlisted men in the Navy, and 116,000 in the Marine Corps. Moreover, these services intended to launch a recruiting drive which they hoped would get them to an all-volunteer status in that one year's time. Navy witnesses did not go into detailed plans for the permanent postwar establishment; that was considered a subject more appropriate to the Naval Affairs Committees.

By contrast, the Army presented a plan for only the first ten months after V-J Day, and emphasized that this was merely part of its demobilization plan. Its strength goal for July 1, 1946, was 2.5 million. This was, to be sure, a major reduction from V-J Day strength of a little over 8 million; but the contrast between that goal and the Navy's was sharp and unpleasant. There were other contrasts, also displeasing. Of the 2.5 million men, 1.7 million would remain involuntarily from the V-J Day force. Despite plans for its own recruiting drive, moreover, the Army expected to enlist only 300,000 by July 1. The remaining 500,000 would have to be inducted through Selective Service, in monthly quotas of 50,000.

To take the edge off the Army-Navy contrasts, Army witnesses stressed two points about their plans. First, the 2.5 million figure was not a firm one, but simply the best estimate then available of Army needs for occupation troops and other overseas and home base tasks. Second, the figure was not a final goal for the Army's permanent postwar establishment, but rather an interim goal for a particular point in the period of transition between war and genuine peace. The length of that transition could not be predicted, and the final goal had yet to be determined by Congress. In addition, Army witnesses carefully avoided suggesting that Selective Service inductions were anything other than a temporary expedient to meet transitional strength requirements.

One obvious reason for the contrasts in Army and Navy demobilization plans was the much larger size of the Army on V-J Day: 8.03 million compared to 3.9 million for the Navy and Marine Corps. Equally obvious was the expectation that the chief burden of occupation in Europe and the Far East would fall to the Army. These help explain the gross difference in projected Army and Navy strength for the summer of 1946; and the second point also partly explains the Army's vagueness about the timing and character of its final demobilization goals. Another reason for the Army's reluctance to be specific was not even mentioned in the initial demobilization hearings: UMT, the central feature of the Army's postwar plans, was still only a hope, not a reality. That the Navy was not similarly reluctant, that it intended to reach its peacetime strength in twelve months without apparent concern over adoption of UMT in the interim, suggests again the lesser importance of UMT to the Navy's plans.

These Army-Navy differences were probably of less immediate interest to the congressional committees than was the major V-J Day prospect of rapid and massive discharges of World War II veterans over the coming year. The performance of the two services in this respect, during the first four months after V-J Day, was even greater than their initial predictions.

In mid-October, the Navy presented to the Senate committee a revised schedule of discharges indicating that, by year's end, it would have released almost 1.2 million men, a 44 percent increase over the V-J Day predictions for that period. As there was no change in the final goal for September 1, 1946, however, it would be necessary, after January 1, to reduce the discharge rate well below that originally scheduled for the following months. This fact was not stressed or questioned; it was simply lost in a table of figures which emphasized the current step-up of demobilization. The Army was less fortunate in its public and congressional relations. On January 4, the War Department formally announced that it would have to slow the pace of its demobilization, and that the discharge of men with two years' service would have to be postponed from March 20 to June 30, 1946.[36] Reaction to the announcement was stormy; and eleven days later General Eisenhower, the new Army chief of staff, offered a detailed defense of the decision to a joint meeting of senators and representatives in the Library of Congress. The major reason for the change in policy, he argued, was the "spectacular success" of demobilization in the first four months; nearly 4.2 million had been discharged, a 65 percent increase over the original prediction of 2.5 million.[37]

To call demobilization a "spectacular success" was to stress only one aspect of it, albeit the aspect most appealing to the public and Congress. More pessimistic judgments were being shaped within the Administration, and for good reasons. The rate of discharge in the first four months was precipitous, and the impact of these reductions on combat potential was exponential rather than linear. Both services discharged men individually rather by unit, giving discharge priority to those with the longest service and the most operational experience. This system stripped units and ships' complements of their key men, particularly non-commissioned officers and skilled technicians. The concurrent elimination and consolidation of organizations alleviated quantitative manpower shortages in the remaining units, but left these filled with inexperienced personnel. The constant turmoil of personnel turnover in those remaining units also reduced their effectiveness. By mid-November, 1945, the estimated combat efficiency of existing Army ground units was about 50 percent of wartime norms. Of the major warships available to the Navy on V-J Day (carriers, battleships, cruisers and submarines), by mid-October only one-third to one-half were considered "ready to fight."[38]

Within the Administration, Secretaries Stimson and Forrestal cautioned early against a too rapid dismantling of American military and naval power. The State Department also sensed the danger. Representatives from the State, War, and Navy Departments, meeting on October 16, readily agreed "that it was most inadvisable for this country to continue accelerating the demobilization of the Armed Forces. . . ." Nevertheless, Secretary of State Byrnes "demurred somewhat" when Forrestal went on to propose that the president be urged to acquaint the public with the facts of Russian intransigence in current negotiations.[39] Nor did President Truman take any such action. He did, however, note the warning from Forrestal and Patterson, in an October 26 cabinet meeting, that the acceleration of demobilization "threatened to jeopardize our strategic position in the midst of the postwar tensions that were building up around the world." He concluded that "so far as I was concerned, the program we were following was no longer demobilization—it was disintegration of our armed forces."[40]

Given these attitudes on the part of President Truman and his senior cabinet advisors, the question arises why nothing was done before January to slow the pace of demobilization and to relieve its impact on military and naval potential. One answer is that the Administration, as Sparrow says of the Army, "resigned itself to a rapid demobilization and ascribed this fate . . . to the 'spontaneous expression of the will of the American people.' "[41] But resigning himself to fate was not one of Truman's major personality traits. Granted that public pressure was enormous, there is no evidence that the president, even in this early stage of his term, was inclined to avoid pressing unpopular actions or to yield to public outcries without a struggle. The fact is that the Administration did respond. And, although its proposal apparently had little to do with the immediate consequences of demobilization, it proved very unpopular indeed. In his memoirs, Truman writes: "Our frenzied demobilization, in fact, grew out of our antagonism toward maintaining a large standing Army. There was only one alternative, in my opinion, and that was a prepared soldier-citizenry. I have held this view for thirty years—ever since World War I."[42] The response at this point, thus, was an address to a Joint Session of Congress on October 22, 1945, urging early enactment of a universal military training program.[43]

4. The First Campaign Ends

President Truman's October 22 address was not a quixotic response to the impact of demobilization, but rather a natural next step in the campaign for UMT. To give it its best face, the renewed request for UMT was a call upon Congress for a declaration of intent: if the United States could not be expected to maintain its wartime strength-in-being after V-J Day, at least we could declare our willingness to keep our huge military potential in a respectable state of readiness. Such a declaration would encourage our cooperative friends and, at least by implication, give pause to our intransigent ones.

The UMT campaign resumed in a very changed atmosphere. The focal scene was once again a committee hearing room, this time that of the House Military Affairs Committee.[44] This committee was considering a specific bill, which had been drawn up late in 1944 with the cooperation of the American Legion and introduced by Chairman Andrew May in January, 1945. The president's message and committee consideration of specific legislation both gave the Administration's UMT proposals a greater sense of formality. At the same time, the ongoing demobilization, with its disintegrative impact on military strength, plus growing concern over Soviet intransigence in the peace negotiations, suggested a greater sense of urgency than could have been conveyed in June. A final difference lay in the introduction of atomic weapons some three months earlier. This ultimate product of World War II technology had somehow fundamentally changed the nature of war, but no one yet knew just how. Despite these changes, though, this second round of debate over UMT sounded very much like the June, 1945, hearings.

There were, to be sure, some changes in the Administration's argument for UMT, at least in emphasis. Secretary of War Patterson and other Army witnesses now stressed even more the need for well-trained reserves to effect a rapid mobilization in event of war. In any future war, Patterson argued, the United States would be the first target of attack. Such an attack might come with "lightning speed," employing "weapons of great power" carried by guided missiles. Survival in such a war would depend in part on our ability to retaliate in kind. Equally, it would depend on our ability to launch "an immediate counteroffensive" aimed at gaining "control of the enemy's launching sites and production facilities." Time, said Patterson, would be of the essence. "There will be no time in which to prepare . . . if we wait until we are in danger." Hence the need for immediately available reserves, which UMT was to produce. Furthermore, UMT would assure " . . . as no other method would that trained men would be near at hand to alleviate the effects of the initial attack, wherever it might be felt—men to organize disaster services, restore public utilities and lines of communications, and, if necessary, repel air-borne invaders."[45]

It was difficult, at best, to convey any public sense of urgency and military danger in the victory euphoria of late 1945, despite the worries of some over demobilization and Soviet attitudes. Talk of attacks on the United States with atomic bombs and rockets was not very convincing; after all we had the secret of the bomb, and the most sophisticated rockets yet produced could just make the trip across the English Channel. And why should we want to seize launching sites and destroy production facilities with trained manpower? Would not our own aircraft and A-bombs suffice? UMT just did not seem an urgent question to the public or Congress. Nor was it all that urgent for the Administration and the military services. Since UMT was a training program only, it could not provide men for active service. The War Department was urging immediate enactment of UMT; but it planned to defer implementing the program ". . . until we are in a position to meet the need for occupying hostile territory in Europe and the Far East without further resort to inductions. . . ."[46]

Opponents of UMT were thus strengthened in their argument that there was still time for further study; and by the fall of 1945, this argument had resolved itself into two separate but not conflicting proposals. One of these emphasized that UMT, even if desirable, was only one part of a total postwar defense program which still had to be determined. A statement signed by Harvard University President James Conant, and thirty-three other college and university presidents, urged appointment of a "national defense commission" to study not only the manpower needs of the military services but such other defense problems as manpower for essential industry, stock-piling of strategic materials, resource conservation, and scientific research. "If, after thorough study, such a commission finds universal military training an indispensable part of our long range national defense program, we would support it."[47]

A second proposal for delay focused on the Martin Resolution, which was a call on our government to seek an international agreement eliminating compulsory service of all kinds from all nations' military systems.[48] If the proposal of Conant and his colleagues represented the hard-headed, realistic school of UMT doubters, this one surely sprang from a kind of dreamy optimism. But there was no conflict. While most of the signers of the first proposal might not have lent their names to the second, most promoters of international abolition of conscription were willing to have the UMT decision delayed for some sort of futher study.

The proponents of delay included most of the same organizations which had appeared at the June hearings. If any change had occurred among them, it was toward even more determined opposition to UMT by organized religion, education, and labor, and their lesser allies among farm, Negro and ad hoc citizens groups. Their arguments against UMT hardly changed at all, except that a number of them cited the atomic bomb as further evidence of the futility of UMT in modern war.

Partly in response to earlier arguments and questions, the Administration revised some details of its UMT plan and added others. The major change offered the nearest estimate yet of the alternative costs of postwar establishments with and without UMT, but still this analysis was not cast in dollar terms. By now the War Department was proposing, and proposing publicly, a postwar Regular Army of 500,000—almost twice that approved by Marshall nine months earlier. With UMT, this would assure an M-Day (mobilization day) Army of 1,500,000 with an additional 400,000 available ninety days later. By contrast, providing the same effective M-Day force without UMT would require a standing army of 1,750,000, the additional 250,000 being needed at M-Day to train National Guard and Organized Reserve units rendered ineffective for lack of trained UMT graduates.

Additions to the plan included a group of War Department amendments to the May bill which would emphasize and reinforce the separateness of the UMT program from service in the armed forces. These included provisions for: a civilian selection system modeled after the current Selective Service System, to perform all registration, screening and other pre-induction duties; a separate universal military training corps, with a special code of discipline (in lieu of the Articles of War) and a special oath or affirmation; a civilian advisory board to determine policies for the religious, moral, physical training, and educational aspects of the program; and a special reserve component of the armed forces for graduate trainees. In addition, War Department witnesses suggested one exception to the requirement for a full year of training, for those few trainees having outstanding qualifications for highly specialized education. These men, after completing the basic phases of their military training, could be sent to college with government financial aid, on the condition that they join an ROTC program and agree to a period of active duty after graduation. Selection for such scholarship aid would presumably be one function of the proposed civilian advisory board.

These alterations in Administration proposals were not so much a yielding to opposition arguments as they were an attempt to clarify the plan in light of some of the objections to it. Much more significant to the course of the debate, and the outcome, were shifts in the position of some important groups which had been Administration allies in the June hearings.

Most important among these was the American Legion, the leading non-governmental voice supporting UMT. This organization did not abandon its support, but it did propose major alterations to the Administration plan which it hoped would be sufficient concessions to change the minds of many UMT opponents and some of its questioning friends.[49] The main feature of the American Legion plan was a one-year training program broken into two phases. The first phase would be basic training, conducted as in Administration's proposal, except that it would last only four months. Thereafter each trainee would have open to him a number of options under which he could complete his training obligation: (1) training in specialist or technical subjects with the regular armed forces; (2) training in basic sciences, professions or technical subjects in the armed services schools, civilian colleges and universities, or industry; (3) completion of a four-year college and ROTC program, including at least one summer of field training; (4) enlistment and training in the National Guard or other organized Army, Navy or Marine reserve component for three years; (5) enlistment in the regular armed forces; or (6) completion of the year of training under the Administration's UMT program.

This plan was not greatly different from the alternative offered in June by the VFW, and presumably had that group's general support. More important, the new American Legion plan received direct and vigorous support from the National Guard and Reserve Officers Association. These groups emphasized, as had the VFW earlier, the need for some provision to fill up the organized reserve components, and they saw the fourth option as doing just this.

Administration witnesses rejected the Legion plan on two

grounds. First, it was not equitable; the options offered simply were not equal in their burdens. Second, and more important, four months of basic training would not be sufficient to " . . . produce the trained soldier who would make our National Guard and Organized Reserve immediately available for combat."[50]

The American Legion plan looked, on its face, like a reasonable compromise among the various interests supporting some form of UMT. Yet its effect was to divide the Administration and the military services even more sharply than before from their potential allies among the veterans groups and military associations. The plan was also intended to attract additional support from groups previously opposed to UMT; but UMT's opponents were not moved.

The House Military Affairs Committee hearings opened early in November, 1945. At the second meeting, a move to postpone further hearings indefinitely was defeated in a straight party vote. Thereafter, the hearings dragged on until the Christmas recess, reopened again for three days in February, 1946, and then closed, with many private citizens and small groups still clamoring to be heard. They were followed by two days of hearings on the Martin Resolution,[51] which provided a further opportunity for vocal opposition to UMT. In the end, both the May UMT bill and the Martin Resolution died in committee. No steps were taken, either, to meet the demands of those wanting a special UMT study commission.

The first campaign for UMT ended, not in defeat, but in inanimate suspension. Its opponents might feel they had talked the plan to death. The Administration hoped not; but by early 1946 it had another, more urgent military manpower debate on its hands.

II.   FATE OF SELECTIVE SERVICE

1.   *Demobilization and Manpower Crisis*

At the initial hearings on demobilization in August, 1945, a major goal of military witnesses was to avert any congressional action which might shut off Selective Service inductions. This was chiefly an Army concern. For the Navy, Selective Service quickly became only a secondary factor in manpower procurement and planning. They continued to accept a token number of inductees and they expected that continued Army inductions would aid Navy recruiting, but they clearly intended to rely on new enlistments and reenlistments as their major procurement source. The Army, on the other hand, argued from the beginning that continued inductions were essential to achieve the hoped-for pace of discharging wartime veterans while maintaining the necessary interim strengths. Over the months after V-J Day both the planned interim strengths and the pace of discharging changed; but the Army's insistence on its need for 50,000 inductees each month remained firm.

The Army's concern for continuing inductions stemmed partly from the peculiar termination provisions of the Selective Service Act. The original act was set to expire on May 15, 1945; and from March to May of that year the Administration and Congress had jousted over a bill to extend it. Debate had focused on issues other than extension of the authority to induct; but growing congressional hostility toward the War Department was partly reflected in a new provision: that inductions would end on May 15, 1946, or earlier upon proclamation of the war's end by the president or by concurrent resolution of Congress, or on any earlier date specified in a concurrent resolution.[52]

This provision for termination by concurrent resolution explains the Army's worried reaction to rumblings from the two Military Affairs Committees' chairmen and other congressmen that Selective Service ought to be discontinued immediately. This danger passed fairly quickly; by V-J Day, Chairman May had come around to support continued inductions; and by the end of September the Senate committee had bottled up Chairman Thomas's proposals for drastic limits on induction powers.[53] More serious was the automatic expiration of Selective Service, set less than nine months away. Any further extension would require a positive initiative from the Administration and active acceptance by Congress. Neither the initiative nor the acceptance came easily.

When General Eisenhower spoke out in mid-January, 1946, to explain and defend the slowdown of Army demobilization announced earlier that month, he urged that the Army be allowed to pursue a new plan approved by the War Department in late December. That plan called for an Army of 1.5 million on July 1, 1946, including 150,000 officers, 650,000 enlisted volunteers for the new Regular Army, 500,000 involuntary service men remaining from the V-E Day force, and 200,000 involuntary service men remaining from the total inductions since V-E Day.[54] To reach this goal, the Army planned phased reductions in all overseas theaters and at home. Included in the plan was a firm commitment to establish the maximum term of involuntary service at two years by July 1, 1946. Eisenhower's audience was clearly pleased with the reduction in total Army requirements for July 1, 1946—one million fewer men than predicted at V-J Day.

There was even greater interest in the revised estimates of recruiting. Wartime restrictions on voluntary enlistment had been lifted before V-J Day.[55] By early October the president had signed new legislation which substantially increased the pay and furlough benefits for men enlisting and reenlisting and provided enlistment terms in the Army of three years, two years, eighteen months, or one year.[56] By January 1, 1946, the Army was employing a recruiting service of 10,000 men; and it had surpassed the ten months' recruiting estimate announced at V-J Day, with 393,000 enlisted men already in the new Regular Army. Nevertheless, there were major qualifications to the Army's optimism about future recruiting prospects. It expected to gain only about 260,000 during the first six months of the year, and predicted even greater difficulties thereafter.[57] Only about 55 percent of those already enlisted had chosen three-year terms, and the majority of these were former Regular Army men who chose to continue their careers. This source was rapidly drying up, and the proportion of three-year enlistments had dropped steadily since the beginning of the recruiting campaign. Of the remaining enlistments, over half were for one year, an option available only to men who had already been in service at least six months; and the inducement for this option would disappear after July 1. Another 16 percent of total enlistments were for eighteen months; presumably some of these were true volunteers, but this option was also open to new inductees who wished to fix the shortest possible term of service. The Army contended that most of the one-year and eighteen-month enlistments were an indirect product of continued Selective Service inductions and that, should the act expire as scheduled on May 15, this source of volunteers would also dry up rapidly.

While Eisenhower stressed the dependence of the new Army plan —especially the two-year involuntary service limit—upon getting 50,000 replacements monthly through Selective Service, he did not suggest that the Selective Service Act be extended beyond the May 15 deadline. The Administration had reached no decision on extension; and Eisenhower and other Army witnesses were warned sharply against any such recommendation by Senator Edwin Johnson, subcommittee chairman and second ranking Democrat on the Military Affairs Committee:

> . . . I am very certain—and I am only predicting now; this is speculation on my part—I don't believe that Congress is going to continue Selective Service after May 15, and if you are going to get your replacements . . . my suggestion is that you begin getting them for the whole period until July 1, between now and May 15.[58]

Despite the Army's dependence, however, actual deliveries of acceptable men had fallen well below the needed 50,000 per month; and General Lewis Hershey, director of Selective Service, was asked by the Senate committee to explain this record and to offer his assessment of future inductions. Hershey admitted that the estimate of 50,000 inductees had been based on his V-J Day expectations, not the Army's desires. But this expectation had reckoned without any of the major changes in induction rules since V-J Day, other than a planned reduction in the age bracket to eighteen to twenty-five years. Most important of these changes was the lifting of wartime restrictions on enlistments; both Army and Navy recruiters were draining the pool of eligible youths. In addition, the Army would no longer accept the number of illiterates (4,000 to 6,000 per month) that it had been taking earlier from the group who failed to meet minimum educational standards. Of minor importance was the Selective Service System's liberalization of deferments for students, teachers, and research workers in various scientific fields. Of greater impact was its decision to defer all high school students rather than only those in their last semester. Finally, the services themselves had tightened their physical standards. A further major reason that actual inductions had fallen short of the goal, Hershey suggested, was that local board members were increasingly reluctant to induct men, in view of the possibility of an early end to Selective Service.

This reluctance, he predicted, would increase sharply as the May 15 deadline drew near.

As to the future, General Hershey thought that, given current conditions, he might produce about 150,000 or 160,000 men, or 35,000 per month, who would be acceptable to the Army, between January 1 and May 15; but he noted that about 70,000 high school seniors, currently deferred by law, would not be available until June. His other recommendations were more palatable to the senators. Arguing that men could not be held for two years of inducted service when Congress had already permitted reducing service to eighteen months by enlistment, he recommended amending the Selective Service Act to provide a definite maximum service term of eighteen months. Third, he urged that the services apply physical standards to inductees low enough to pass the numbers of men needed. Finally, all else failing, he recommended the reinduction of men with less than six months' service.

In his State of the Union Message on January 21, President Truman gave limited support to Hershey's first recommendation, saying extension of Selective Service would be necessary if voluntary recruiting fell short of military needs. Nevertheless, the Administration hesitated in making a formal request. Officially its position was that it still wanted UMT, and President Truman also repeated that request in his January message. Three weeks later, Secretary Patterson was willing to state only that a War Department recommendation for Selective Service extension was "probable."[59]

In the meantime, the Army continued to place calls of 50,000 a month, despite Hershey's estimate that he could provide only 35,000. To meet Hershey's criticism of the rejection rate, the Army announced in February that it was lowering its physical standards for induction. It hoped that an additional 75,000 men could be found acceptable by rescreening men under age twenty-six who had been rejected; these were to be inducted in April, over and above the normal quota of 50,000, at which time the lower standards would be made operative for newer registrants as well.[60] At the same time, the Army continued to press its recruiting efforts. Moreover, to speed the conversion of new recruits and inductees into replacements for long-service and combat veterans, the Army had already cut its basic training period from the wartime low of seventeen weeks to only thirteen weeks, and then again reduced it to eight weeks.

Despite these actions, and despite hesitancy about making a firm declaration on the subject, through the month of February it became increasingly clear that the Administration was going to ask for extension of Selective Service beyond the May 15 deadline. On February 21 the House Military Affairs Committee closed its hearings on UMT, and the very low probability of further action on this subject no doubt spurred the Administration to seek a more immediate solution to its manpower problems. Yet congressional resistance was expected to be strong, and at the end of the month Secretary Patterson was speaking of a "compromise" extension plan. Finally, in mid-March, Patterson, General Eisenhower, and General Spaatz (Army Air Forces commander) appeared before a closed session of the House Military Affairs Committee to make a formal request to extend Selective Service.[61]

2.   Debate over Extension

Extension of Selective Service remained in doubt for three more months, a period marked by fitful activity in various quarters, alternating with frustrating delays. Both the Senate and House Committees on Military Affairs held hearings in late March and early April, and before mid-April each committee reported a version of extension which would have satisfied the Administration.[62] The House acted quickly and devastatingly, accepting one amendment by its Military Affairs Committee chairman to exclude the only sizable pool of young men available, those under age twenty, and another by its Naval Affairs Committee chairman to suspend inductions until October 15. Floor consideration of the Senate bill was delayed so long that a last-minute resolution, briefly extending Selective Service to July 1, 1946, was required to gain time for a later debate; and a balky House forced Senate acceptance of an amendment excluding eighteen- and nineteen-year-olds from induction during this temporary extension. The Senate acted again in early June, approving a pro-Administration version of extension not much changed from that recommended by its committee. Late in June, after a two-weeks House-Senate conference, Congress finally agreed to an extension act which, with some important exceptions, met much of what the Administration had asked for.

The Selective Service extension debate ranged over a large number of general and specific issues, mostly related to the manpower procurement goals of military effectiveness, cost efficiency and limited compulsions; but some of the argument touched on questions of equity and nonmilitary social goals as well.

Military Effectiveness

The Administration's major contention in the extension debate was that if Selective Service came to an end on May 15, the military services, especially the Army, would fall seriously short of their manpower needs in the succeeding months. Its recommended solution was an extension of Selective Service, with minor changes, for one year, until May 15, 1947.

The Navy Department's role in this debate was secondary, and its argument was simple. The department's military manpower requirements were 558,000 for the Navy and 108,000 for the Marine Corps, strengths they intended to reach by September 1 and maintain thereafter. These goals were not much different from those set at V-J Day, and the two naval services still expected to be on a completely volunteer basis by that date. But Secretary Forrestal warned that Navy recruiting would suffer from a termination of Selective Service, and that the goal of an all-volunteer Navy could not be guaranteed in the absence of a continued induction threat.

The burden of the Administration's case was once again carried by the War Department. Army manpower requirements were now set at 1,550,000 for July 1, 1946, and 1,070,000 for July 1, 1947 and thereafter, barring changes in occupation needs. By this time the Army was no longer much concerned about meeting its mid-1946 goal, largely because of continued though somewhat declining success with recruiting. Nonetheless, they were certain that termination of Selective Service on May 15 would result in a serious shortage of active manpower by mid-1947, and even worse shortages thereafter. Not only would a May 15 termination shut off actual inductions, but it would also remove a major incentive to enlistments.

In justification of the stated requirements, War Secretary Patterson listed the Army's many tasks: providing occupation forces, garrisoning overseas bases, maintaining supply and communications lines and installations, training new men, maintaining programs in intelligence and research and development, providing forces which could be made available to the United Nations Organization, and "the overriding requirement to present a strong military front in these unsettled times." He also stated the assumptions about future developments which had guided Army planning: Despite decreases in occupation forces, the people in the occupied areas would remain "tractable"; occupation duties in Germany would continue to be shared by the four powers; assistance could be expected from the British, Chinese, and Filipinos in the occupation of Japan; early peace treaties would relieve us of occupation duties in Italy and Austria; foreign civilians would be hired in greater numbers to reduce overseas requirements; disposal of surplus property would be expeditious; and, finally, the United Nations would become "increasingly effective in the maintenance of world security." Given these tasks and these optimistic assumptions, Patterson argued, the Army's stated requirements were minimal.[63]

Some committee members and opposing witnesses questioned the need for so many men in the Army, but this proved a difficult and frustrating line of attack. When a senator asked what Army tasks would be dropped if the shortages predicted for mid-1947 actually occurred, Patterson side-stepped the question, saying he would abandon any function that Congress might tell him to abandon. In the end, Congress accepted the stated military strength goals at face value.

Accepting manpower strength goals was not the same as accepting extension of Selective Service, and the Administration had much more difficulty presenting a convincing case for its contention that terminating Selective Service would produce severe Army manpower shortages.

Part of the trouble with the argument that voluntary recruiting would not suffice was that it sounded just a little like a cry of "Wolf." At V-J Day, the Army had said it could expect only 300,000 regular recruits by July 1, 1946. In January, 1946, with 393,000 already recruited, the estimate for July 1 had been revised to 650,000, plus 150,000 mostly volunteer officers. Now, in March, the esti-

mate was for a volunteer Army of 950,000, including 150,000 officers, on July 1; an increase to over a million by October; and then
a tapering off to 930,000 on July 1, 1947, and 905,000 on January
1, 1948. All this assumed the termination of Selective Service on
May 15. Given the past experience of recruiting estimates exceeded
by the actual successes of the Army Recruiting Service, it was difficult to avoid the impression that the predicted manpower shortages were merely the hypothetical result of overly conservative staff
work.

Adding to doubts about the shortages was the Administration's
inability to make the size of this hypothetical wolf precisely clear.
General Hershey testified that much of the Army's recruiting, and
the Navy's for that matter, was at the expense of Selective Service
inductions; take away the induction threat, he warned, and the recruiting effort would collapse, leaving the Army 400,000 short of
its goal by January 1, 1948. The War Department offered not one,
but two estimates of the expected shortage on that date should inductions cease. One, apparently a compromise between personnel
and recruiting staff estimates, predicted a shortage of 165,000. The
other, the result of a special Army staff study ordered by Secretary
Patterson, estimated the shortage at 336,000.

The confusion among these estimates of shortages led opponents
of extension to question the probability of any of them. Most effective was a review of the more pessimistic War Department estimate by a young Methodist minister, who concluded that the internal figures proved manpower needs could easily be met by voluntary recruiting alone. On close examination, it is clear that the minister saw only what he wanted to see in the staff analysis; but he was
not alone in thinking the Army's recruiting estimates too gloomy.

In the Senate hearings, Senator Revercomb (R., W.Va.) questioned the Army's good faith in its promises to push recruiting as
hard as possible. Had not the Army, as recently as February, actually
raised its mental standards for enlistment? An Army staff witness
admitted this was so, but noted the new minimum standard was a
mental test score roughly equivalent to a fifth-grade education,
rather than the earlier fourth-grade standard. He justified this on
the grounds that the Army was already getting too many recruits in

the lower mental categories, and that a smaller Army was relatively less able to absorb less effective men. The new standard would soon be applied to inductees as well. General Eisenhower supported this argument, but stressed that at the same time physical standards had been lowered. "We went so far," he said, "that the doctors told me that if I insisted on going lower we would be filling the hospitals and getting other men to take care of them."[64]

Congress responded to all these doubts over predicted shortages and recruiting estimates by accepting the services' own strength goals at face value, but writing them into the extension legislation as strength ceilings, and requiring that future induction calls take into account both these ceilings and performance in recruiting. The extension provided was shorter than the Administration wanted. Splitting the difference between House and Senate versions, the conference committee settled for an expiration date of March 31, 1947.[65]

These two provisions in the extension act were not the only important reflections of congressional reluctance to accept the Administration's case for a direct relation between continued inductions and future military effectiveness. The high point of this resistance came when the House accepted an amendment by Carl Vinson (D., Ga.), chairman of the Naval Affairs Committee, suspending inductions for five months, from May 15 to October 15. This would, Vinson argued, properly test whether voluntary recruiting might not meet the Army's needs; thereafter inductions could be resumed if the president found this necessary. The Senate, on the other hand, decisively rejected a proposal by three Republican senators that inductions be discontinued until and unless Congress declared in a separate action that resumption was necessary to national security.[66] In the end, President Truman was saved the possible embarrassment of having to decide about resuming inductions just weeks before the first postwar congressional elections, when the conference committee dropped the Vinson amendment without comment.

The potential contribution of Selective Service extension to military force effectiveness was modified, though not seriously compromised, and in one respect complemented, by the outcome of debate over a number of other issues.

Cost Efficiency

The issue of cost efficiency entered the debate, albeit implicitly rather than directly, as proponents and opponents of Selective Service extension both sought to increase recruiting prospects through a military pay raise. The pay raise was actually a separate proposal of the Administration, which sponsored a 20 percent across-the-board increase for all ranks. In the extension hearings, General Eisenhower and Secretary Patterson were several times drawn to admit this would improve recruiting prospects; but here, as in House hearings on the pay bill itself, their theme was guarded pessimism.

Pay raises somewhat more generous than the Administration's proposal were supported by some as a means to preclude any further need for inductions or an induction threat. Senator Edwin Johnson (D., Colo.) was a prominent proponent of this view:

> . . . In all other categories of service, civil service and everything else, our country is able to get all the employees it needs by paying wages commensurable with the services required. . . . The only reason why we have any difficulty getting international police, or soldiers in the Army is because this great and powerful and rich Nation of ours refuses to pay the price of such services, and has to resort to drafting, merely to save a few paltry dollars. . . . [67]

Others were not so sure, however, that even a generous pay raise would produce enough volunteers; and certainly the Administration was not prepared to concede the point. The outcome was a compromise pay raise, providing a 50 percent increase for the lowest enlisted grades and relatively smaller increases up through the enlisted and officer ranks.[68]

Limiting Compulsions

As in the earlier debate over UMT, the chief concern of the Administration in proposing Selective Service extension was military force effectiveness. The chief concern of those opposing Selective Service extension was once again the question of compulsion, of peacetime conscription.

The opponents' argument was familiar: conscription means militarism, a reversal of American traditions and eventual loss of freedoms. Indeed, not a few witnesses charged or implied that the effort to extend Selective Service was simply another way of imposing the same sort of military system as that allegedly contemplated under UMT: "Militarism, refused the front door, is seeking a second-story entry of conscription into the heretofore military-free domicile of peacetime American democracy."[69] A representative of the American Federation of Labor suggested an even closer relation between the two proposals: "I think that if it, Selective Service, extends for 6 more months, they will be in here asking for another extension in the hope they can whip up enough sentiment for universal military training."[70]

This issue was raised early in the hearings, and Secretary Patterson later took the opportunity to emphasize that the goals of two programs were entirely separate. Stressing the long-range nature of UMT, he argued that, even if adopted immediately, it could not meet the problem at hand, the potential shortage of men in active service to meet current occupation and defense tasks. General Eisenhower also carefully noted that there was "no possible connection" between Selective Service extension and UMT. "What we are talking about now is the providing of the interim army for a very specific job, a large part of which is an aftermath of the shooting war that has been completed."[71] Further emphasizing the point, Eisenhower assured his audience that not one man in the Army's manpower estimates was earmarked to a training cadre for UMT.

Still another point indicates the separation of the two programs in the thinking of the War Department. As they had said in the UMT debates, implementation of that program would have to await the end of Selective Service inductions. Plans for the peacetime establishment envisioned UMT in support of an all-volunteer active force, and the War Department simply did not think in terms of mixing UMT with an inducted active army. Said Secretary Patterson: "We do not recommend conscription as a long-range military policy. We do not recommend it."[72]

Patterson and Eisenhower also stressed their hope that, given continued induction pressure to spur recruiting, even the forces needed to meet the war-produced demands might be raised mostly by voluntary enlistment; and they promised there would be no inductions beyond those needed to make up whatever deficit did develop between actual strength and stated goals. To further ease the impact of compulsion, they agreed that if Selective Service were extended the term of involuntary service could be reduced to eighteen months shortly after July 1. They also agreed that there would be no harm in formalizing the earlier Selective Service System decision to defer, and effectively exempt, fathers. The House and Senate committees nailed down this War Department promise by setting ceilings on service strength; and they readily accepted the concessions on term of service and exemption of fathers, adding a requirement that fathers already in service involuntarily be discharged after August 1. A different and much more important proposal was the chief aim of those seeking to limit compulsions. At the outset, Chairman May of the House Military Affairs Committee formally proposed reducing the bracket of age liability to the ages from twenty-one to thirty, inclusive, giving major emphasis to raising the minimum age. This proposal was hardly discussed in the House hearings, but General Hershey told the Senate committee just what such a change would mean: Given the deferment of fathers, agricultural workers and merchant seamen, he could produce practically no men in age groups over twenty-five; age groups nineteen to twenty-five would yield about 5,000 per month, perhaps through August; after that, almost the sole source of inductees would be eighteen-year-olds. In addition, most of the short-term enlistments in the Army were also coming from this group of younger men. In writing a new extension bill, a closely divided House Committee defeated May's proposal, set the upper limit at age thirty, but left the lower limit at age eighteen. On the floor, May announced he would vote for the Committee's bill, but he intended to propose a major amendment exempting eighteen- and nineteen-year-olds. He won his floor fight easily. Later, when the House considered the joint resolution extending Selective Service temporarily to July 1, it insisted on attaching this same limitation; and, time being short, the Senate had little choice but to accept it.[73]

President Truman signed the resolution, but expressed deep dissatisfaction, especially on this point. Two days later, he authorized raising the effective age of induction to twenty-nine years. This gesture had only dramatic value, if even that. General Hershey had already stated that the higher age groups were devoid of draft-eligible men, and late in May, Selective Service Headquarters announced there were only 36,000 men left in the pool of eligibles to meet the Army's call for 50,000 in June. Possibly more effective was the War Department's announcement that it would retain its two-year involuntary service requirement; if given a full year's extension, however, it would consider reducing the requirement to eighteen months and discharging fathers early.[74] This Administration pressure may have helped persuade the Senate to restore the original age bracket when it produced its own extension bill.[75] The age limit then became the major issue delaying a House-Senate conference report, and the final result was a compromise excluding only eighteen-year-olds.

Groups other than youths under age nineteen were also the objects of proposals to limit the reach of Selective Service; but these proposals were considered more in relation to the question of equity than to that of limiting compulsions.

Equity in Selective Service

To the Administration, the question of Selective Service extension itself had important implications for the question of equity, as did the attempt to exclude the younger men from induction liability. As an Army staff witness put it, if War Department estimates of recruiting proved correct, and Selective Service were not extended, the only other way to meet manpower needs would be to keep those already inducted in service for longer periods. Given the contemporary congressional and public mood, it is doubtful that these men could have been kept in service indefinitely; nor did the War Department wish to do so. The real implication of the argument, then, was not a threat; it was a suggestion that the war veterans had done their service, that it was now up to Congress, by extending Selective Service and not crippling it, to provide replacements from among these youths who, in different circumstances, might themselves have gone to war.

Congress was not willing, as it turned out, to admit that demands of equity precluded protecting eighteen-year-olds from induction. Much less was Congress, nor the War and Navy Departments for that matter, ready to accept General Hershey's implication that

Selective Service, not voluntary recruiting, should be the main reliance in providing postwar occupation troops. Accused in the Senate hearings of believing in an "impressed Army," Hershey responded that he could match any man present in his resentment of regimentation. "I have written more nonconcurrences, I could probably qualify as a revolutionist, but on the other hand I don't like to see the poor and the willing have to carry the responsibility of everybody."[76]

No one in the extension debate raised the equity implications in early discharge and exemption for fathers, measures readily accepted on all sides. But a parallel proposal for early discharge of married men failed in a close House vote. On the other hand, an amendment exempting short-term veterans, mostly men discharged early when wartime in-service college and other training programs were discontinued, gained easy acceptance in the Senate and survived the conference report.[77] It was the category of occupational deferments, however, that gave Congress the greatest trouble in drawing the line between protection for special groups and protecting the impartiality of Selective Service.

Under the wartime act, the only occupational groups given specific statutory protection were clergymen and divinity students, who were exempted, and agricultural workers, for whom a special deferment provision had been added during the war. One attempt to expand these protections in 1946 was a proposal to credit Merchant Marine service against the military obligation; this was readily defeated in the House. Another attempt was an amendment offered to exempt all persons studying for a degree in science, enrolled in a medical, dental, osteopathic or theological school, pursuing graduate work in science, or engaged in scientific work. This, and a substitute amendment limiting the exemption to scientists and science students (subject to presidential regulation), were also rejected in the House. A version of the substitute was accepted in the Senate,[78] but this provision was dropped in conference. The conference version of the extension act stated instead that no occupational deferments for industry could be allowed except those essential to the national health, safety or interest, thus leaving the problem to presidential regulation and local board discretion.

Adapting to Other Social Goals

One import of this final decision on occupational deferments was that Congress was reasonably satisfied with the wartime and post-V-J Day operation of the Selective Service System and its local boards in seeing to civilian as well as military needs for manpower. By the time of the extension debate, there certainly was no shortage of civilian manpower; the precipitous demobilization resolved whatever difficulties had led to the "work-or-fight" proposals more than a year before. What special protections were added to the act, then, were added more in the spirit of limiting compulsions than of consciously promoting social goals, although the latter motive might be read into the provisions exempting fathers and eighteen-year-olds. Where further special protections were denied, moreover, the decisions reflected more a desire to protect the integrity of Selective Service than any careful judgment on nonmilitary manpower needs. Judgments of the latter kind would not have an important impact on Selective Service until some years later, when this manpower procurement device acquired a permanence no participant in the debate foresaw in the spring of 1946.

Congress, Crisis, and Selective Service

Even before the hearings on Selective Service extension ended, the committee members and many of their House and Senate colleagues realized they faced difficulties of more than ordinary political proportions. They had heard one witness refer to "those jingo coteries of our Government departments who are whipping up the Russian war-scare campaign either to secure vast peacetime armies for their own interests or, in Hitleresque fashion to use as a threat to force other nations to do our bidding. . . ."[79] Those sectors of group opinion most heavily represented in the hearings—church and peace groups, organized labor, organized education, and the ad hoc citizens groups—all emphasized their belief that conscription is a necessary evil in wartime, perhaps, but indefensible in time of peace. Nearly seven months had passed since V-J Day, and it was high time to get our armed forces on a peacetime footing. The way to do this would be to force the Army, as well as the Navy and Marine Corps, to rely on volunteers. Against these views were the urgent pleadings of the Secretaries of War and the Navy, of leading military officials, and of Secretary of State Byrnes; and the crisis over Soviet troops in Azerbaijan was fresh in congressional minds. In the end, then, the issue was not whether to meet the services' manpower requests, but how.

After long delay, Congress discharged itself of a distasteful task with a fairly positive response to Administration requests. Senator Chan Gurney (R., S. Dak.), a leading champion of the Administration request, probably expressed the dominant congressional reaction when he argued for extension because "we do not know and can only guess at the number of volunteers the armed forces may expect to get . . . with or without the Selective Service Act on the books and with or without a pay raise." "We play it safe," said Gurney, "if we extend the act as proposed. We gamble with disaster if we do not."[80] Responding to this mood, Congress resisted moves to restrict extension to a very short period and thus aim it almost solely at the high school graduating class of 1946. It resisted pressure to exempt the very age groups comprising the major pool of availables, and thus to emasculate Selective Service as a direct supplier of inductees and a spur to enlistments. And it rejected moves to suspend inductions, attempts that is to have Selective Service without peacetime conscription.

Apart from the needed help given a Democratic Administration by Republican congressional leaders, perhaps the most surprising aspect of this response was that the major case for extension did not rest on current shortages of military manpower; the shortages were expected to begin several months hence, if at all, and to become serious only after a year or more. Time was short from the viewpoint of Administration and military planners; but Congress has seldom been accused of being too far-sighted. Yet Congress did take the longer view.

Given this extension of Selective Service, and a military pay raise to help attract and retain recruits, the Administration once again faced on its own the tasks of meeting military manpower requirements.

3. End of Wartime Selective Service

If Congress had, in a sense, taken the long view, still the Selective Service Act had been given only another nine months' life. More important, the authority to induct had been tied closely to current rates of enlistment. The remaining history of wartime Selective Service was largely the consequence of these two decisions.

Even as the House was considering the conference report, one consequence of the extension bill was taking effect. In a letter to Representative Thomason (D., Tex.), Secretary Patterson stressed once more his and the War Department's desire for an all-volunteer Army. Citing new hopes in this direction stirred by the pay bill, and noting the limitation of inductions to only that number needed to meet specific shortages, he announced the War Department would place no calls on Selective Service for July and August. He could not, however, go as far as the Vinson amendment had proposed. Discharges of eighteen-month men would begin in October, and eight weeks were required to train replacements. Thus the possibility of a September call was left uncertain.[81]

The length of the induction holiday depended directly on the Army's success in sustaining its recruiting drive, and the prospects for this were mixed. The goal of 800,000 enlistments by July 1, announced in the March hearings, had almost been reached by the end of May;[82] and the Army Recruiting Service was pushing hard on the theme "make it a Million," emphasizing heavily the postwar advantages in ". . . good pay, travel, education, and adventure."[83] But the rate of enlistment had fallen sharply. The peak had been reached in November, 1945, with nearly 184,000 enlisting in that month alone. In December, the figure fell to 132,000. That this was not solely a consequence of the holiday season became clear when January brought a further drop to 114,000. Thereafter, the monthly intake fell steadily until, in May, 1946, the total was only 48,000.

In June, spurred by the prospects of continuing Selective Service inductions, high school graduations, and the June 30 deadline for enlistment with full dependency benefits, enlistments rose to over

62,000. But enlistments fell during July; and in early August Secretary Patterson said an induction call for 25,000 in September and succeeding months seemed likely.[84] August enlistments, down to 40,000, confirmed the decision to resume inductions.

By the end of September, with current enlistments indicating little improvement over the August rate, the Army announced an increase in its draft call for October to 35,000. But September enlistments improved sharply in the second half-month, under the double incentive of renewed draft calls and an approaching October 5 deadline for enlistment with full veterans' benefits. In mid-October, a new decision was reached: the War Department cancelled the unfilled portion of its October call, cancelled its November call, and announced it would place no call for December. As the Navy Department had placed no calls since May, this meant that, within six weeks of the resumption of inductions, the draft holiday had returned.[85]

At this point, probably even earlier, other pressures came to bear on the military services' strength goals—most notably those of the budget. The act extending Selective Service had set maximum strength goals for the Army, Navy, and Marine Corps at 1,070,000, 558,000, and 108,000 respectively, on July 1, 1947. By the end of September, the Navy was down to 572,000; it was enlisting about 1,500 per month, and actually had a backlog of volunteers. In January, however, President Truman announced that the average Navy strength, including the Marine Corps, for FY 1948 would be 571,000—a 95,000 reduction under the total Congress had authorized for these two services. The Army, on September 30, stood at 1,745,000 including 200,000 "ineffectives" not chargeable against the congressional authorization. The Army strength goal announced in January was 1,070,000, exactly that of the congressional authorization; but the presidential ceiling included ineffectives, and the Army anticipated this would cut its effective strength by about 80,000.[86]

In December and January, therefore, the War Department was faced with conflicting pressures on its manpower planning. October enlistments had dropped to 49,000. With the resumption of the draft holiday, and the end of veterans' benefits inducements, enlistments fell to only 18,000 in November, and the same number in

December. Moreover, only about 51 percent of the total enlistments since V-J Day had been for three-year terms. Almost all the rest had enlisted for eighteen months (30 percent) or one year (17 percent). To sustain such a short-term Army over the long run would require, the War Department estimated, monthly enlistments of about 37,000, or more than double the November-December rates. Understandably, there was some desire in the War Department to use the induction authority while it still existed, and perhaps to ask for a further extension. At the same time there was now the problem of assuring that Army strength stayed within the president's ceiling, just six months away.[87]

When the War Department had asked for extension of Selective Service in March, 1946, its case had rested ultimately on a projection of future shortages. The same would be true of any new request for extension. At the same time, in the earlier fight for extension the Army had been enlisting and inducting every man it could get, and holding on to its men as long as possible. Now, in early 1947, the War Department was contemplating early release of some men— an act which would not affect long-term Army strength, but which might be necessary in response to the short-run cut in strength targets.[88] And it faced, in the Eightieth Congress, a body presumed to be even more hostile to Selective Service than Congress had been in 1946. The chances that this Congress would take the long view of manpower procurement must have seemed dim indeed.

In his 1947 State of the Union message, President Truman stressed the current inability of the Army to meet its basic manpower needs by voluntary enlistments; but in mid-January the War Department decided to place no further calls on Selective Service prior to the March 31 expiration date. This decision, and the rise of January enlistments to 37,000, pointed clearly to a quiet end of Selective Service.

The death warrant was not formally sealed until March 3, just four weeks before the act was to expire. In a message to Congress, President Truman offered this reasoning to support his decison:

> The Army and Navy are still reducing their forces and the Army is not using inductees for the full term the law allows; consequently, an extension of Selective Service at this time would be solely on the basis of predicted shortages during the next year. With a recent brightening of

recruiting prospects, this appears to be the logical time to shoulder the risks involved.

Therefore, I recommend that no extension of Selective Service at this time be made. . . .

On the same day the War Department announced that 100,000 inductees, all that remained of its involuntary service men, would be released by June 30. All that remained was for the president to recommend, and Congress to provide, a transfer of certain continuing Selective Service functions to other offices, and the creation of a new Selective Service Record Office to preserve the important records and produce studies of wartime Selective Service for the sake of some future emergency.[89]

III. SECOND CAMPAIGN FOR UMT

Unwillingness to fight for another extension of Selective Service in 1947 can hardly be laid to any fundamental lack of combativeness on the part of the Truman Administration, though certainly the War Department and the Army must have felt the bruises of the earlier extension struggle. Rather, it seemed to be a matter of priorities—a decision to concentrate on one major manpower measure at a time. Thus the end of wartime Selective Service was partly the consequence of recruiting success and budgetary pressures, and partly a result of unwillingness to do battle with the new Eightieth Congress to preserve yet another unpopular wartime control. But it was also partly a result of the second major Administration drive for a postwar program of UMT.

1. *New Moves by the War Department*

In this second campaign, as in the first, the starting point of the Administration's case for UMT was the Army's, and the War Department's, vision of its permanent postwar establishment; but if that vision were ever to become reality, the Army and the Administration first had to do some homework. The American Legion plan of late 1945, proposing a reduced basic training period of four months, had not gained UMT any identifiable new support; but its associated proposal for completing a year's training in one of several optional programs had attracted the strong support of the National Guard and Reserve Officers Associations, who saw in it a means of assuring the promised build-up of Guard and Organized Reserve units. In their support, they exposed what they felt was a practical weakness in the Administration's plan: once a man had finished his twelve months' training under that earlier plan, there was no way other than patriotic suasion, supported by the small benefits of reserve drill pay, to get men into the Guard and Organized Reserve units which the Army hoped to have ready on M-Day. The Legion plan, by including enlistment in these units among the various options for discharging the remaining training obligation, would go a long way toward patching over this weakness. What good would it be, the civilian components argued, to have a training program if the units supposed to benefit most could be bypassed as easily as the Administration plan allowed? The Administration's response was a counter-question: what good would the reserve units be, even if filled up, if the men going into them were not properly trained? This response pointed logically, not to a defense of the Administration's original proposal, but to a need for compromise.

The Administration's need to compromise was political as well as practical. Without the whole-hearted support of the veterans groups and the reserves associations, there was no hope of persuading a reluctant Congress to accept UMT; and the major weight of these organizations by the end of 1945 was behind the Legion's plan, not the Administration's. It was not until mid-September, 1946, however, that Secretary Patterson announced, in an address to the annual NGA meeting, that the War Department would soon propose a modified version of UMT. Two weeks later the new plan was released to the public, with appeals for support from the public at large and the American Legion in particular.[90]

The new War Department plan was very much like that proposed earlier by the American Legion. It called for six, rather than four, months of common training, and offered nine options for completing the training obligation. As in the Legion plan, these included completion of training within the initial UMT framework, enlistment in the regular services or enlistment in the National Guard or Organized Reserves. The War Department plan, unlike the Legion's, included a service academy option. Like the Legion plan, the War Department proposed options for ROTC or for other professional or technical training in colleges or schools; but the latter tied these options to acceptance of reserve commissions, to prior enlistment in an unorganized reserve pool that could serve as a control over individuals failing to complete such courses, or to some other guarantee of attachment to a reserve or active component. Thus, while yielding on the length of continuous training, the War Department plan also sought to assure that those options providing individuals with desirable advanced training and higher education would carry with them burdens roughly equivalent to the less desirable enlistment options.

Announcement of this plan was only one of a number of moves over the next few months designed to attract new support for UMT. The next was the announcement, late in November, that the Army would begin an experiment at Fort Knox, Kentucky, where new Regular Army recruits would undertake, in lieu of standard basic training, a six months' training program shaped as closely as possible to that proposed for UMT.[91] The experiment was intended, among other purposes, to prove to skeptics inside and out of the services that a program incorporating the promised UMT features of added special off-duty educational opportunities, added chaplains' services, and sports, cultural and other recreational activities, could at the same time be an effective military program.[92] Like most "experiments" in the military services, this one was expected to work. It was also intended to produce results far beyond the confines of the training center and the Army. Use of the Fort Knox experiment as a public showcase for UMT was so extensive that it spurred investigation by an unfriendly subcommittee, which condemned this public relations campaign as well as some more specific and individual examples of the War Department's zealous efforts to promote UMT.[93]

2. *Promotion by Advisory Commission*

The most important Administration initiative in the second UMT campaign came not from the War Department but from the White House. Opponents of UMT had many times called for creation of a commission to study the concept and its relation to the broader issues of national defense and preparedness; and in December, 1946,

President Truman did so. This President's Advisory Commission on Universal Training was truly a blue-ribbon panel, and one which was not, as UMT opponents charged, "stacked" in favor of UMT. To be sure, its chairman, Karl Compton, and one other member, Daniel Poling, were on public record as favoring the concept; but another member, Harold Dodds, had publicly expressed his skepticism and general opposition; and other members had taken no public positions at all. Indeed, the commission probably surprised its creator by both the timing and the nature of its report. As to timing, President Truman expressed the hope that the group could produce a report soon after the new Congress convened in January. The commission, however, decided to make a much more thorough study than this would have allowed. It heard or consulted with some two hundred individuals—representing all the groups and interests which had taken some public stand on the subject of UMT. Despite White House anxieties over the delay, the commission did not submit its formal report until late in May, leaving little time for congressional consideration of it at the end of the session.[94]

As for content, if the main thrust of the commission's report was a surprise at all, it must have been a pleasant one for the major supporters of UMT. President Roosevelt, it will be recalled, had been rather ambiguous on the question of how much emphasis the program should give to strictly military training. This issue seemed to be resolved within the Administration, by the time of the June, 1945, hearings, in favor of a military program; but the question cropped up once again in late 1946. The letters of invitation and the initial announcement indicated that the commission was to consider UMT as part of the total defense program. Nevertheless, President Truman shifted the emphasis somewhat by deleting the word "military" from the commission's original title. This incident, and indeed the discussion of UMT in his memoirs, suggest a degree of ambiguity in Truman's intentions for the training program. Recalling his plea for UMT in October, 1945, he wrote:

> This was not a military training program in the conventional sense. The military phase was incidental to what I had in mind. While the training was to offer every qualified young man a chance to perfect himself for the service of his country in some military capacity, I envisioned a program that would at the same time provide ample opportunity for

self-improvement. Part of that training was calculated to raise the physical standards of the nation's manpower, to lower the illiteracy rate, to develop citizenship responsibilities, and to foster the moral and spiritual welfare of our young people.

Addressing the new commission, Truman stressed this theme of extra-military goals for the program. But Truman also wrote of his 1945 proposal that "the basic reason . . . was still to guarantee the safety and freedom of the United States against any potential aggressor." He was "morally certain" that, had UMT been enacted in 1945, "we would have had a pool of basically trained men which would have made the Soviets hesitate in their program of expansion. . . ."[95]

The advisory commission's own work reflected the president's ambiguity, but only to a point. The commission's staff produced or procured a number of studies relating to health, education, and welfare programs at all levels of government, and to the mutual impact of a training program and the civilian labor market on each other. The commission's report also emphasized the importance of the nation's health—physical, moral, economic, political—to the security of the nation; and it expressed concern for deficiencies in these areas revealed by the work of its staff and other public and private agencies. Nevertheless, the commission concluded that, in the absence of other needs for UMT, benefits in these areas "could be secured more surely and more appropriately through a strengthening of existing public and private agencies in these fields rather than by a separate system of universal training." In its mind, the sole justification for UMT would be "a demonstration that it is needed to insure our safety in a world in which peace is not yet secure." Thus, in recommending approval of UMT by Congress and the public, the commission urged it as "a matter of urgent military necessity. . . ."[96]

The Compton Report, once published, became both the Administration's case for UMT and the focus of subsequent debate over the proposal. It restated, and in some respects refashioned, the whole range of arguments for UMT, and attempted to answer most of the objections to it. It also presented the most comprehensive plan thus far offered for implementing UMT; and this, in part, stood as further answer to many earlier objections.

As in earlier Administration arguments, the crucial issue developed in the commission's report was the relation of UMT to national security, and of that to world peace. On the latter point, the commission rejected arguments that any build-up of American military force would contradict our intent to seek and preserve peace through the United Nations. "One of the deterrents to the effectiveness of the United Nations," their report declared, "is the belief of other nations that we are stripping ourselves of the strength necessary to support our moral leadership and are thus encouraging powers that may not share our peaceful aims to plan campaigns of aggression." The commission expressed alarm over the impact of demobilization on American military strength: "At a time when war can strike without warning and with devastating force, our Ground Forces have only 2-1/3 full combat divisions available for duty. Our air and sea strength is somewhat more formidable, but it is dwindling so rapidly that it cannot long be considered a shield against attack." Moreover, it rejected arguments that we could, for more than a short time, rely on either our atomic weapons monopoly or the trained manpower resources of World War II veterans. The commission urged that those weaknesses must be corrected by an extensive national defense program, including UMT:

> . . . The only way in which we can lend authority to our voice in international affairs and inspire confidence in the ability of the United Nations to enforce peace is to maintain our armed forces at a level of efficiency and comprehensiveness that will defy challenge by any would-be aggressor. If the people of this country will declare in convincing fashion their determination to support such a program in all its elements for as long as may be necessary to guarantee the attainment of a stable world order through the United Nations, they will make the greatest contribution to perpetual peace within their power.[97]

In relating UMT to a total program for national defense, the commission yielded somewhat to arguments of the realist school of UMT critics. They admitted that "universal training is not our first line of defense. . . ." UMT, they argued, should be one part of an "integrated national security program" which would include a strong, healthy, educated and united people; coordinated intelligence services; scientific research and development; industrial mobilization capabilities and stockpiling; strong regular military forces, emphasizing both a striking air force and highly competent, well-equipped ground, sea and air formations; a unified military command—all these as well as universal training.

> We do not give it [UMT] priority over any of the other elements we have set forth. . . . Neither do we put it behind the others. It has neither purpose nor effect, except as part of a balanced structure. All of them are necessary if we are to feel secure in this world.[98]

The commission's vision of a future war, and the essential role of military training in preparing for it, was not much different from that offered by Secretary Patterson in late 1945. It argued that "the era of push-button warfare, in which inter continental rockets with atomic warheads wipe out tens of millions overnight, has not yet arrived." Moreover, it "is not a development of the foreseeable future" although "it was freely predicted by the scientists that such warfare might become a reality within 25 years." In the meantime, our atomic monopoly would probably not last beyond 1951, although we need not expect any enemy to be able to launch an atomic attack in quantity before 1955. One of the prime needs in any foreseeable future war, would be large numbers of trained men.

> . . . The United States simply cannot take the chance of facing future warfare without large reserves of men trained and disciplined in the use of weapons and in the techniques of warfare. Apart from the need of them during the after-effects of the first attacks upon us – a desperate need which cannot be fulfilled in any other way than UMT – they will be needed to secure bases from which to launch air and sea and land attacks upon our enemy, to carry our bombs over the targets, to transport and supply our forces all over the world, to invade the land of the enemy, to repel attacks upon us of large forces of men on land, sea, and in the air, and to occupy conquered bases and countries.[99]

In addition to arguing the general need for trained manpower reserves, the commission also concluded that such training must be compulsory. Given the large numbers required at the outset of a war, the nation could not afford to provide them all in the form of professional forces; nor could enough volunteers be found to fill up such forces, or even smaller forces backed up by volunteer reserves. Compulsory training was thus the only practical and economical way to supply the trained reserve of men needed for both organized military reserve units and for civil defense.

The commission sought to meet arguments against compulsion in a number of ways. UMT, they observed, would be no more un-American or undemocratic than compulsory education or the levying of taxes. "One of our basic tenets is that every citizen owes service to his country as needed. That need of lack of need is determined by the democratic vote of the representatives of the people, subject to certain safeguards provided in the Constitution."[100] Not satisfied with Constitutional safeguards, however, the commission recommended still others in its plan. Most importantly, the entire program was to be placed under the general control and direction of a three-man commission reporting directly to the president. This group would set policies and standards for the program and would have power to direct other agencies, especially the military departments, in matters relating to UMT. Specifically, they would have the final say on annual UMT estimates submitted to the Bureau of the Budget, and the authority to allocate funds appropriated for UMT. They would be assisted in their work by a professional staff, working under a presidentially appointed executive director, by a corps of full-time civilian inspectors, and by an advisory board of civilian and military experts in the fields of recreation, religion, education, and health. Thus, while actual operation of the program would be in the hands of agencies giving the training, the civilian commission and its subsidiary structure would assure responsible civil control. In addition to these agencies, the report recommended creation of a civilian selection system, patterned after Selective Service, which would be responsible for inducting trainees and could assist in supervising completion of their training obligations after release from training camps.

The advisory commission saw little danger that UMT would lead to any militarization of American youth. It did provide in its plan, as had other plans before it, that trainees in the program would have only limited military status and obligations, and would be subject to a specially devised disciplinary code rather than the Articles of War. The commission made special mention, in this regard, of the Fort Knox experience with trainee courts to try minor offenses.

Partly in mitigation of the compulsory aspects of the program, the commission recommended limiting the initial training period to six months, to be followed by completion of the training obligation under one of a number of options. In this respect, the Compton Report generally followed the 1946 War Department plan. One option was added—a catch-all for those unwilling, unqualified, or unable by reason of occupation or locale to opt for further education, enlistment in an organized reserve unit, or completion of training under UMT auspices; this would allow men to enlist in an unorganized reserve pool for six years, subject to call for one month of training each summer.

The optional features of the Legion, War Department and Compton Report plans all had three purposes in common: mitigation of compulsion, channeling of some partially trained men into special nonmilitary training in the national interest, and filling up the Guard and other organized reserve units. The War Department's and advisory commission's plans had a fourth purpose—the equalization, as nearly as possible, of the burdens imposed by the training obligation. Thus both plans attached to the desirable educational options an additional obligation of reserve or active service, and increased these obligations where the education was to be supported by government financial aid.

The commission was more explicit and detailed than any other UMT proponents had been before on the issue of equity. Recognizing that equal obligation does not necessarily mean identical obligation, the commission nevertheless insisted, as a first principle, that a successful program "must be universal in its application to all persons of a given age or status, and the obligation which it imposes on each must be substantially equal." The commission urged

> that the training, in one form or another, apply to all those who are physically and mentally able to prepare for any form of useful service to their country in time of crisis . . . whether or not such service is of a direct military character. We recommend that the Congress exclude only those unfortunately handicapped persons who could make no material contribution of any kind, and those whose absence in camp would create extreme hardship.[101]

The commission's plan recognized that a significant minority of men brought into the program under such standards would not be qualified for full military training. Nevertheless they recommended that these men be given training, following the pattern of six months of basic training and various options for completion of the obligation, which would take into account their limitations but still prepare them for useful service in some future emergency. Such training would be exclusively under civilian control, probably with the Federal Security Agency as operating agent. Programs for conscientious objectors would be conducted as they had been in World War II. Presumably similar arrangements might eventually be made for including women in the universal training program, for the commission recommended their initial exclusion only on practical grounds.

By emphasizing the military nature of the training to be given the majority of young men, and the defense-related nature of training for others, the advisory commission closed what had been a gap between presidential and military goals for the program. At the same time, it came closer than any earlier proponents of UMT to grappling with the challenge that emphasis on military purposes raised against the goal of equity.

In playing down the possible benefits from UMT to nonmilitary national goals for manpower, the commission did not yield the whole ground in this area. It suggested, as had Stimson, Truman and others before them, that UMT could strengthen the commitment of American youth to the nation and its ideals, both through specific instruction and as a result of commonly shared obligations and experiences. The commission did admit the potential danger to general morals of separating young men from home and community and placing them in large military camps. Pointing to the experience at Fort Knox, the commission argued that such measures as careful selection and training of the cadres, expansion of chaplains' functions, and extensive on-post recreational and educational activities could alleviate these problems. The commission also called for wide-spread duplication of the Fort Knox innovation of a local advisory council drawn from nearby civilian communities, strict enforcement of existing laws relating to liquor and prostitution, and strengthening of these laws where necessary.

The commission was very concerned with reducing as much as possible the disruptive impact of UMT on civilian education. As in other plans, young men would, within generous limits, be allowed to complete high school prior to their training. Moreover, apparently agreeing that a year's interruption between high school and college might be damaging, the commission carefully studied ways of precluding this. The Legion plan would have reduced the time in training camps to four months, with those going on to college presumably having priority for the period June-September. The commission rejected such a solution, on grounds that any period less than six months would be too short to accomplish the basic training objective of the program. On the other hand, while admitting that a one-year training period might be best for many military purposes, they still felt that six months would be adequate, and that the program of options would have additional advantages not available under a straight one-year program. Moreover, limiting the initial training to six months still offered some chance of reducing the impact of UMT on the transition from high school to college. By giving college-bound youths priority for the period May-October, the commission felt that secondary and college institutions could adapt themselves fairly easily to the loss of one month each at the end or beginning of a four-year academic cycle.

3.   *The Second Campaign Peaks and Stalls*

The Compton Report, formally submitted in late May, 1947, and made public a few days later, offered the most complete case for UMT yet formulated. Together with its relatively detailed plan of implementation, it afforded an impressive if not eloquent argument for its adoption. Even so, even while the report offered newly formulated, or at least freshly recast, arguments for and defenses of UMT, its publication did little to stir new and creative debate.

Despite the lateness of the report, the new House Armed Services Committee decided to open hearings on UMT. These continued, off and on, for a month; and the task of further hearings was then turned over to a subcommittee.[102] The major witnesses appearing in support of UMT were: four members of the Advisory Commission, who defended their report and asserted their group had indeed approached the problem with open minds; representatives of the American Legion and the Veterans of Foreign Wars, who supported the commission in general and were willing to leave the details to Congress; former Justice Owen Roberts, who headed a newly formed citizens committee; and representatives of the military services, who expressed willingness to accept any program worked out in line with the Advisory Commission's report. None of these witnesses had anything new to add to the arguments of that report. In opposition to UMT came representatives of the familiar church, education, labor, farm, Negro, left-wing, and ad hoc citizens groups, who mostly repeated the arguments they had been offering for the past two years and more. In a report submitted in late July, the House Armed Services Committee answered charges that it had terminated hearings without giving all opponents a fair chance to be heard: "The record of hearings on the subject including those held in 1945 and 1946 reveals a singular uniformity of argument employed by opponents of UMT . . . and, equally, by its advocates. The committee believes, accordingly, that no new light would have been shed on the subject had hearings been extended. . . ."[103] Indeed, by that standard, the hearings might well have ended once the Advisory Commission members had reviewed their report.

The only argument approaching a fresh debate on UMT came prior to publication of the Compton Report, in an indirect exchange between Hanson Baldwin, military expert for the *New York Times*, and Secretary of War Patterson. Long an articulate opponent of UMT (in conflict with his own newspaper's editorial policy), Baldwin once again chose as his major ground of attack, not the often expressed fears that UMT was an un-American attempt to militarize youth and corrupt their morals, but the Administration's own claims that UMT was essential to military security. If war came, Baldwin argued, it would come initially as an air and sea attack on the United States. Given short-term military technology, over the coming ten years, American victory in such a war would depend in part on ground force action, but only after we had retaliated with our own air-sea forces; for this period, our reserves of World War II veterans would suffice to reinforce the ground armies. The real current need was to create an air-sea force capable of instant retaliation. Over the longer term, should push-button war become a reality, it would neither require nor permit any ground action in its initial and probably decisive stages. Should such a future conflict deteriorate into a long war of attrition, there would then be time to train the needed forces. The major prewar training effort should therefore be put into regular forces, existing reserves, and civil defense; the National Guard could take care of civil defense training on a local basis as well as or better than UMT. No amount of UMT could possibly make the National Guard and other organized reserve units instantly ready for active combat. Indeed, far from solving military problems, UMT would simply add to the Army's already difficult manpower problems by imposing additional burdens on it for training cadres. Finally, far from enhancing military security, adoption of UMT might well lead to starving other defense needs, both by reason of practical budget limits and as a consequence of UMT's producing a false sense of security.[104]

There is little doubt that the advisory commission, or most of its members, took note of Baldwin's assault on the military value of UMT, as is suggested by the nature of their own arguments. Moreover, they paid him the compliment of incorporating his last arguments into a warning that UMT, if accepted at the expense of other elements of defense rather than being integrated with them, might do more harm than good.

It was left to Secretary Patterson to provide a more explicit answer to Baldwin. By invitation, he wrote a letter to Senator Lodge (R., Mass.), ticking off Baldwin's points one by one, and generally anticipating the commission's report. Modern war, Patterson wrote, cannot be prosecuted successfully either by mass armies or by air-sea forces operating alone. Even the ground component of the necessary forces must be a balanced organization capable of operating highly complicated machines and weapons, not a mass army. Such forces require training, and UMT is the way to provide it. The reserve of World War II veterans, he argued, could not be relied on for more than another five years. A push-button war, reaching its conclusion in hours or days, was not, Patterson insisted, a foreseeable reality. The best way to assure that some future war would not deteriorate into a long defensive battle on our part would be to train our manpower, at least partially, prior to an emergency. Far from making the Army's current manpower problems more difficult, UMT would, by supplying trained reserves, reduce the need for men in the standing forces. To be sure, UMT might not make the organized reserves instantly ready; but it would greatly reduce that task at the time of emergency. In addition, UMT would be the surest way of providing men in all parts of the country with civil defense training. In sum, Patterson argued:

> Mr. Baldwin's whole article is based on a basic misapprehension. . . . He treats UMT as essentially a negation of modern developments in air, sea and land power. Whereas, actually, it is the very speed and complexity of modern warfare which makes UMT, for the first time, an absolute essential to our military security. Further, UMT is the only substitute for the strong allies who in our last two wars bore the brunt of the attack while we were building up our fighting forces.

Secretary Patterson also acknowledged the danger of relying on any one element of national security, even UMT, to the exclusion of others. In the wary language of budget compromise he asserted: "All elements of preparedness must be balanced within the funds that can reasonably be made available."[105]

This clash between Baldwin and Patterson, and the issues of military strategy and manpower policy it raised, had little visible impact on congressional treatment of UMT at the time. In the Senate there was little inclination to act at all. In the House the Armed Services Committee met on July 25 and voted unanimously to report favorably a bill sponsored by subcommittee chairman Towe (R., N.Y.), but the vote was deceptive. Of the committee's Republican majority, the four ranking members (after the chairman) and seven others managed to be absent. The twenty favorable votes were a clear majority of the committee, but twelve of those were Democrats. Indeed, it is probable that Chairman Andrews and Towe were able to get a report at all only on the promise not to seek further action during the current session.[106]

Still, the Towe bill had been reported, and the tone of the report was more favorable than the committee's vote. Agreeing with the Compton Report, the committee argued that modern warfare still required, and would for the foreseeable future, large numbers of trained men, and that the only practical way to assure their availability in an emergency would be adoption of UMT.

In their reluctance to act on UMT, it is doubtful that many senators and representatives accepted the dictum of Senator E. C. Johnson: "Such an un-American innovation would substitute sex training and guzzling for spiritual training and moral stagnation for the development of a healthy, wholesome, self-reliant and energetic morale." A significant number, however, may have accepted the lead of Senator Taft. Warning of the dangers of militarism inherent in UMT, he asserted: "We are indeed bankrupt of ideas if we cannot provide a method by which necessary military forces and reserves are provided by an American voluntary system."[107]

Public opinion, at least in its raw and unorganized form, strongly favored some such innovation as UMT;[108] but there was no accompanying surge of congressional support for the measure. Surveying the 1946 election results, the Army's legislative experts had not expected to get even a committee report favoring UMT.[109] In February, 1947, Representative Clarence Brown (R., Ohio), a prominent member of the House Rules Committee, told Secretary Forrestal that there was no chance of getting UMT through Congress.[110] The House committee's report represented the high-water mark thus far in efforts to legislate UMT; as it turned out, the report was to retain that distinction for nearly five more years.

Through the rest of 1947 there were no major developments in the UMT campaign—and certainly there was no rallying of the people and Congress behind the Compton Report and the Towe bill. The American Legion met in late August, and once more voted its support. Through the summer and fall, and into the winter, other groups expressed their by now nearly traditional opposition. Presidential hopefuls began to express themselves: President Truman's support was known, and he was joined in this by Governor Dewey; Senator Taft continued his opposition, questioning the need for ten million "half-trained" men, and promising his support for an antisegregation rider to any UMT bill; ex-Secretary Wallace also made his opposition known in announcing his third party candidacy, making repudiation of UMT one condition for his return to the Democratic party; and Harold Stassen entered the debate with a plea for compromise; any compromise, apparently, would do.[111]

President Truman repeated once again his formal request for UMT in his State of the Union Message of 1948; and the Defense budget for FY 1949 included $400 million in anticipation of starting the program later that year. Early in February, 1948, the advisory commission informally reported to the president on rising congressional sentiment for the measure, and Representative Wadsworth confidently predicted success.[112]

Such optimism was not very well founded. As the new session of Congress opened, House Armed Services Committee Chairman Andrews began an effort to move the Towe bill through the Rules Committee and onto the floor. Rules Committee Chairman Leo Allen (R., Ill.) responded to Andrews's requests for a hearing in a condescending letter, stating that the session promised to be a busy one, that he must consider all important measures, and that this one would get attention in due time. The tone of the letter strongly suggested that the bill had been indefinitely shelved by the House leadership. Speaker Martin denied this, but his claims that the delay was due to lack of information on costs were not wholly convincing. At the end of February, the Rules Committee still showed no signs of acting on the bill, and Chairman Allen paraded his confident opposition by taunting UMT proponents with failure to activate a pending discharge petition. Thus the second campaign for UMT ended, as had the first, with this central feature of the Administration's hopes for a postwar military establishment resting quietly on the congressional shelf.[113]

IV. SUMMARY OF THE POSTWAR DEBATES

1. *Major Issues and Outcomes*

By early 1948, three years of debate had produced much heat and some light, but very little in the way of satisfactory solutions to the complex issues of military manpower procurement policy. Instead, these early debates over UMT and Selective Service extension revealed wide differences between proponents and opponents of those policies which, in turn, affected policy outcomes at the time.

Central to the Administration's position on both proposals was the Marshall-Palmer vision of a postwar Army establishment (with Navy, Marine Corps and Army Air Force variations on the theme) consisting of small professional forces backed by large, well-trained reserves. Procurement for the active forces of this peacetime establishment would be by voluntary recruiting; but compulsory UMT would train young men and, hopefully, would spur them into joining organized reserve units. During the transition from wartime forces to a peacetime establishment, it soon became clear that postwar international tensions were generating unusually high, though presumably temporary, requirements for active forces. Under these circumstances, extension of Selective Service was proposed as a temporary measure; once the peacetime establishments were in operation, the direct supply function of Selective Service would be unnecessary, and its function as a spur to recruiting would be taken over by UMT.

The Administration and its supporters argued, of course, that both UMT and temporary Selective Service were necessary and sufficient means to achieve adequate postwar military effectiveness. Opponents disagreed, on a variety of grounds. Some questioned the need for very much at all in the way of postwar military forces; but the impact of this argument on policy outcomes, peripheral at the outset, steadily waned as the nation slowly shook the euphoria of V-J Day and demobilization. More important were the doubts raised about the need for Selective Service as a temporary supplement and spur to voluntary recruiting in support of the transitional forces; these doubts helped modify, though they did not prevent, extension of Selective Service; and they were later cited by the Administration itself when it decided to let Selective Service lapse. On the matter of the peacetime establishment, some opponents argued that postwar needs could best be met with strong, well-equipped, highly-trained professional forces-in-being; that the concept of mobilizable reserves was obsolete; and that the appropriate procurement system would be voluntary recruiting only, supported by higher pay and benefits and other improvements in military life. A modified version of this position accepted the need for some reserves, but stressed that UMT could not produce the quickly mobilizeable reserves needed; here again, the proper procurement system was said to be voluntary recruiting. These arguments were partly, but only partly, responsible for deferring adoption of UMT throughout the early postwar years. They were also responsible for modifications to the original UMT proposal, tying UMT more directly to the task of supplying trained men and officers for the National Guard and other organized reserve components.

Questions of cost effectiveness were more implicit than conscious in the debates over UMT and Selective Service extension. The Army case for UMT argued that the postwar establishment this was to support would be the most effective one possible within the limited appropriations it expected to get; but opponents avoided the cost issue simply by questioning whether such a force would be effective, or necessary, at all. In the debate over Selective Service, opponents did suggest that a pay raise might enable the services to meet their needs through voluntary recruiting; but both sides in this argument were hampered by lack of any estimates, reliable or not, of how large a pay raise would be needed.

Next in importance to military effectiveness as an issue in these debates was the question of compulsion. These issues were closely related; for if military needs, properly defined, could be met by voluntary recruiting, then it was generally agreed that compulsory procurement would not be desirable. But opponents of UMT and Selective Service went further, arguing that peacetime conscription was inherently so undesirable, so dangerous to American traditions, ideals and social structure, that it should be avoided even if this weakened military security. It is difficult to separate these pragmatic and ideological facets of opposition to compulsion from each other, and that whole issue from the debate over military effectiveness and its cost implications. Some opponents so abhorred military conscription that they were willing to define military requirements and costs so as to deny the need for it; others viewed compulsion as simply the unnecessary and undesirable by-product of a poor definition of military needs. Nonetheless, it is fair to conclude that resistance to peacetime conscription played a major role in deferring adoption of UMT, and a lesser role in modifying the UMT proposal by shortening the requested basic training period in that program. It also played a major part in modifying postwar Selective Service, eventually inducing the Administration to drop the draft entirely.

A fourth potential issue, that of equity, proved much less controversial. UMT was promoted, in part, as the most equitable way of distributing the burdens and obligations of military preparedness across the whole society. There was no debate over this claim; but maintaining it required adjustments in the original proposals for UMT, seen most clearly in the emphasis the Compton Report gave to making the basic training program as nearly universal as possible and to equalizing the burdens of various options for completing the required training. Questions of equity also played a minor role in the debate over Selective Service. No one disagreed that fairness to war veterans required replacing them with other men in the occupation forces; and Congress generally followed the rule that fairness to inductees required limiting special deferments to a minimum.

Finally, a series of issues was raised which reflected concern over the impact of military manpower procurement policies on nonmilitary goals for the development of the nation's youth. One focus for these issues was the claims made for the extra-military values of UMT to its graduates—improved health and physical conditioning, a greater sense of obligation to one's community and nation, a heightened appreciation for the virtues of teamwork, a greater toleration for differing sub-cultures in the nation, and acquisition of skills useful in civilian life. Against these claims lay the arguments of education, church and labor groups that a military environment could not produce these benefits, and that there were more appropriate means for pursuing such goals. The Administration and its allies played down the claims of extra-military benefits, thus making arguments against them largely beside the point. This tactic was not pursued consistently, however; it is probable that most supporters of UMT deeply believed these claims could be made good. Opponents, on the other hand, went beyond arguments of infeasibility and inappropriateness, charging that UMT would in fact be counterproductive in the area of non-military benefits. Here their arguments were really an aspect of more general fears about the long-term effects of peacetime conscription on American traditions of liberty and civilian control of the military. The major impact of these fears on the UMT proposal and Selective Service extension has already been noted. There were more specific charges of counter-productiveness, however, the major one being that peacetime conscription would interfere with education. This argument played only a small part in persuading Congress to shorten the term of service for inductees to eighteen months. Its impact in modifying UMT proposals was much more direct and clear—best illustrated in the Compton Report's concern with adjusting the length and scheduling of basic training to the constraints of academic schedules, and in the educational character of many of the UMT options proposed by the advisory commission and others.

In sum, major differences in the perception of policy goals and policy means led to modifications in the original UMT proposal, but modifications still insufficient to gain wide acceptance of that program. Similar differences over goals and means led to the dismantling of wartime Selective Service before the military services, particularly the Army, could achieve their peacetime establishment goals.

2. *Assumptions Underlying Policy Frustration*

Beneath these differences over policy goals and means lay two assumptions about postwar military policy, assumptions held by proponents and opponents alike in the debates over UMT and Selective Service extension. These shared assumptions, within which almost the whole policy debate was framed, were fundamentally responsible both for the frustration of the Administration's postwar military manpower procurement policy and for the increasing political discomfort of many opponents of that policy.

One assumption was that a general transition on the international scene from war to peace would allow the reduction of American wartime military forces to much smaller, permanent, peacetime levels. No one questioned the desirability of these reductions, although there were major arguments over how fast the transition could be achieved, whether Selective Service was necessary during the transition, and how small the peacetime establishments should be. Accompanying this assumption in the early stages of debate was the Administration's unwillingness to challenge those urging the shortest possible war-to-peace transition by openly voicing its growing fears over the prospects for peace in the postwar world. President Truman's message to Congress in October, 1945, urging adoption of UMT, was hardly calculated to resist the rising pressure for demobilization. Rather, this move reflected the Administration's position that confirming the peacetime establishment by statute was the most important goal for military policy at the time, as well as its reluctance to provoke the Russians. Indeed, the Administration probably chose this response partly in order to capitalize on the strong public and congressional sentiment for a rapid war-to-peace transition. Only after it was clear that UMT could not be achieved quickly did the Administration act directly to slow the demobilization tide with a drive for Selective Service extension. And even this move was conceived, argued, and accepted as only a temporary, transitional measure.

A second assumption was also underscored by the debates over Selective Service, the assumption that the active forces in a peacetime establishment could and should be supported by voluntary recruiting. For a variety of reasons, including but not limited to its own strong attachment to this assumption, the Administration eventually accepted constraints on involuntary procurement during the transitional period as well, abandoning Selective Service even before Congress had confirmed the legislative outlines of a peacetime establishment.

During the early years of debate, then, the Administration's case was built mostly on the claim that its programs were the best, perhaps the only feasible ways to meet military requirements, both for a peacetime establishment and for the period of transition to peacetime conditions. The most effective opposition to the Administration, resting on the same assumptions, grew out of the claim that peacetime, and possibly even transitional, military requirements could not justify imposing conscription on American youths. The practical outcome of the debate, up to 1948, was a twofold frustration of Administration policy: its goals for a permanent postwar establishment were not yet accepted; and its plans for transitional forces were compromised by the ending of induction powers.

3.   *Minor Themes and Shifting Grounds of Debate*

Related to the opposition's general rejection of peacetime conscription was a minor theme of recurrent suspicion about the Administration's good faith in assuming the twin goals of transition-to-peace and voluntarism in the active forces, especially the latter. Was not the extension of Selective Service a denial of that second assumption? Most emphatically not, the Administration asserted; Selective Service was only a temporary measure designed to meet the unusual demands of a transitional period. In response, opponents restricted the period of Selective Service extension, and helped induce its abandonment in March, 1947. But suspicions and charges of bad faith continued, as evidenced in this bristly exchange among Representatives Bishop (R., Ill.) and Short (R., Mo.), both opponents of UMT, and General Collins, the chief military witness in the 1947 UMT hearings;

> Mr. Bishop. I understand that when this UMT program is inaugurated, you are going to come back and ask for selective service.
>
> General Collins. This is not the case. In our judgement, if we can't make this program operate without selective service, we would never get it. In other words, we don't believe the country will have both selective service and universal military training.
>
> Mr. Short. And you stopped selective service in order to get this?
>
> General Collins. This is—no, sir. We stopped selective service—
>
> Mr. Short. Oh, yes, you did.
>
> General Collins. No sir. We stopped selective service in order to see whether or not we could maintain the Regular Army on a fully voluntary basis, which is what we want to do.[114]

This exchange questioned the Administration's good faith not merely on the issue of conscription for the active forces, but ultimately on its intentions for the whole general course of postwar procurement policy. Did the Administration intend no transition to peacetime forces at all? Given its devotion to UMT, it would seem the Administration was still thinking in war-to-peace terms; but the "transition" had been going on for nearly two years, and there was no end in sight. Despite his very proper response to Representative Short, General Collins gave cause for alarm later in the hearings by predicting that Selective Service might have to be reactivated in 1948. It helped very little that the context of his prediction was the continuing "transitional" demand for an extraordinarily large active Army, or that he was making obvious reference to the conditional nature of President Truman's March, 1947, recommendation on Selective Service expiration. Still another exchange in these hearings went to the heart of the basic assumptions shaping the policy debate, and lent strength to suspicions that the Administration might be abandoning them. Representative Bates (R., Mass.), who clearly preferred Selective Service to UMT, got this response from Father Walsh, a member of the advisory commission. "I don't think the menace [to American security] is dramatic enough yet to get another draft act. It has to be dramatized to the people, and although I know, and I think you would agree it is there, I don't think they are convinced of it yet, sir."[115]

In terms of political factions, the core of congressional opposition to Administration manpower procurement proposals had generally been conservative Midwestern Republicans and the congressional heirs of old-time Populism. These men were as attached to the assumptions of voluntarism and transition-to-peace as General Marshall and the Administration had ever been, although they rejected most of the rest of Marshall's reasoning about postwar military policy. Allied with this group, in both respects, was a congeries of liberal-pacifist and left-wing groups which, in the months after the 1947 UMT hearings, gathered around Henry Wallace and eventually produced his Progressive party campaign for the presidency. This faction also raised charges of bad faith in Administration military policy; but they linked these to further charges of bad faith in American relations with and intentions toward the Soviet Union. Their mostly Republican allies, on the other hand, avoided and even denounced the charges of "red-baiting" so popular among the Wallaceites; but they continued to nurse their suspicions about the Administration's military policy intentions. At the same time, perhaps out of deep conviction, but more likely out of need to distinguish their criticism from that of the new Progressives, the congressional and national political groups then rallying around Senator Robert Taft began to shift their critique to a new emphasis on what had been a second minor theme of opposition to the Administration's proposals.

Throughout the early debate over manpower procurement, opponents of the Administration had posed conscription, and its implications for American social and political traditions, as the crucial issue, subordinating all others to it. From this viewpoint, utopian objections to any sizeable postwar military establishment at all were just as serviceable as attacks based on technical criticism of the proposed force structure; and these two lines of attack were almost invariably intermingled and confused in the debate.

While the emotional heat of opposition to conscription tended to obscure the more technical critique of military requirements, the latter did have a life of its own, and an increasingly vigorous one as the debate progressed. The major target of this critique was Marshall's concept of small professional forces, dependent in an emergency on mobilizable reserves. The argument was a newer version of the prewar differences between Army and Navy manpower policies—mobilization base versus force-in-being. But in this postwar era, the prime candidate for the force-in-being was the Air Force rather than the Navy; and differences over force structure became, as they had not realy been before World War II, the subject of public political debate.

This critique began with the argument that the technical requirements of modern war made any UMT-produced reserves, alleged to be the base for "mass armies," outmoded. This view was not so much pertinent as it was persistent. Great "masses" of servicemen had been employed in World War II, in large part to perform the expanded tasks of supply, maintenance and communication that the new war technology required; and most of the technological developments envisioned by early critics of UMT were not likely to reduce these tasks. One line of development, however, did suggest an enticing alternative to the sort of ground armies which UMT implied. Air power, particularly long-range bombing, made even more plausible in the closing months of the war by the introduction of long-range rocketry, came to seem for many not just a first line of defense, but the major, perhaps only, force required for war. The potential strength of this case was obscured early in the debate by the apparently willing support that Army Air Forces representatives gave to UMT in the June, 1945, hearings. Largely concealed by this public position was the AAF's earlier dissent from the postwar Army plan approved by Marshall, in which they objected that the small active force proposed could not provide the air power necessary for a proper defense.

Air power as an alternative to ground forces in general, and to UMT in particular, gained new support in the wake of the atomic explosion at the end of the war; one prominent UMT critic suggested almost immediately that our whole defense would have to be built around these weapons;[116] In time such arguments against UMT were capsulized in the popular notion of "push-button" warfare.

The case for air power lay at the roots of an increasingly vigorous competition between the AAF and the rest of the Army for men, missions, and, above all, money; and the growing strength of the AAF in this struggle was reflected in congressional action on military appropriations during 1947. Despite the strong economizing trend in the new Eightieth Congress, the House took the unusual step of restoring a cut in aircraft procurement which its own Appropriations Committee had recommmended; and the Senate actually increased this amount, preserving most of the increase in conference.[117]

The early postwar debates over military manpower procurement touched on a broad range of issues, but the major aspect of these debates was the clash between the Administration's emphasis on military requirements and the opposition's stress on the undesirability of conscription. Despite general acceptance by both sides of the twin assumptions concerning transition-to-peace and voluntary active forces in peacetime, the debate led only to stalemate and frustration. At the same time, two minor themes of opposition appeared. The first, responding to proposals to extend Selective Service, was suspicion of the Administration's sincerity in accepting the generally agreed assumptions. The second was a more technical line of attack on the proposed peacetime force structure, stressing the need for active air power and the possibilities of relying on this as the major feature of a proper postwar establishment. Over the next two years, these minor themes would take on new importance, as the Administration sought new solutions to its military manpower problems, and critics sought new and less emotional grounds for opposition.

chapter two

The Return of
Selective Service

I. CRISIS AND RESPONSE

In January, 1948, stalemate seemed the order of the day in military manpower procurement policy. But events of the next six months shattered that stalemate, produced a partial resolution on policy and programs, and reshaped the policy debate. The climax to this sudden shift in postwar military policy came on March 17, as President Truman, in a hurriedly arranged address to a joint session of Congress, urged speedy passage of the European Recovery Program, enactment of universal military training, and temporary reenactment of Selective Service.[1] The first two requests were hardly new in and of themselves; but they took on a fresh and dramatic character when presented with the third as responses to a series of alarming international events which preceded them. In this sense, the address bore much the same relation to the revolution in military policy that the Truman Doctrine and the Marshall Plan proposals had to the more general revolution in America's postwar foreign policy.

More than eighteen months earlier, Hanson Baldwin had called into question one of the fundamental assumptions of postwar military planning. International events, he observed, are blurring the distinction between "interim" and "permanent" military policy.[2] If any single event were chosen from the postwar years to illustrate this thesis, it would have to be the coup d'état in Czechoslovakia on February 24, 1948. Perhaps nothing less menacing could have at once persuaded the public and the Administration of the need for fresh initiatives in military policy, and at the same time suggested that these new initiatives might properly involve abandoning the cherished concept of a transition-to-peace. Other events of the time also brought pressure on the Administration to break the stalemate in military policy; but no other served so well to make, in Father Walsh's candid phrase, "the menace . . . dramatic enough."

The Czech coup underscored what had been apparent to the Administration for some months. The winter of 1947-48 was marked by deep concern in the government over the gap between military strength and potential force commitments. The arithmetic of the problem was laid out for the president in a Defense briefing on February 18 (see Table 2): Air Force manpower was not considered

TABLE 2

ACTIVE MILITARY SERVICE STRENGTHS, FEBRUARY 1, 1948
(In Thousands)

	Actual Strength	Budget Authorization	Congressional Authorization
Army	552	560	669
Navy	476	526	664
(Marine Corps)	(79)	(87)	(108)
Air Force	346	362	382
Total	1,374	1,448	1,715

SOURCE: Walter Millis, ed., *The Forrestal Diaries* (New York: The Viking Press, 1951), p. 375. Reproduced by permission of W.C.C. Publishing Company, New York, New York, and Princeton University, Princeton, New Jersey.

a serious problem, and the current shortages in the Navy were expected to decline by July 1; the really serious concern was over the

Army and Marine Corps, that is, ground strength. The Army was short of meeting requirements in every major overseas area and at home, and its strength was dropping. Moreover, the general reserve of active ground forces available for deployment from the United States, including Army and Marine Corps units, amounted to only 46,600 men—roughly equivalent to two and one-third divisions.[3] Both the retiring Army chief of staff, General Eisenhower, and Secretary of State George Marshall warned that this growing military weakness could have disastrous consequences for our European and Far Eastern policies.[4]

This sense of alarm had not been conveyed to Congress and the public before the president's March address. Indeed, the Budget Message in January had observed that fiscal year 1949 estimates for military pay would provide a total active strength equal to existing levels, and went on to state that "existing recruitment inducements appear to be adequate to maintain these forces."[5] This was in sharp contrast to a statement three days later, by Army Secretary Kenneth C. Royall, that the Army's enlistment drive had been a failure.[6] The facts, as revealed in a later House report, were on Royall's side. Between July 1, 1947, and March 1, 1948, monthly gains from enlistment and reenlistment averaged under 14,000, while gross losses were over 29,000 a month, and total Army enlisted strength dropped from 594,100 to 469,500. At the same time, enlisted strength in the Navy dropped from 434,500 to 351,200, and in the Marine Corps from 84,800 to 74,000. Only the Air Force enjoyed steady net gains, rising over this eight month period from 263,100 to 317,100.[7] These trends through the last half of 1947 suggest the Budget Message really meant that the Administration had already gone as high as it cared to in individual pay and allowances as a means of attracting recruits; although the Administration was aware of the dangerous state of military manpower strengths, it was not clear on a course of action.

In early March, 1948, the formal position of the Administration on new manpower policies was support for UMT legislation introduced the year before (the Towe bill) and currently bottled up in the House Rules Committee. One reaction, thus, was to seek a fresh impetus for UMT by working through the Senate Armed Services Committee. In view of the crisis in active military strength, this reaction seems almost atavistic, recalling a similar response in October, 1945. But it was not simply a reiteration of a long-standing vision of postwar military policy and problems. The reaction also reflected a long-term view of America's role in the growing postwar international crisis. Just as the older vision of military policy had been personified in Army Chief of Staff George Marshall, so now were the vision and the long-term view of foreign policy personified in the same man as secretary of state. Marshall had never faltered in his support of UMT. Now Marshall reasoned that, just as with his current chief interest, the European Recovery Program, a major American investment in UMT would be a convincing gesture to the rest of the world of our determination and ability to back our policy with deeds.[8] At best, of course, adoption of UMT would not simply be a gesture; one hoped-for result of the program had always been that it would stimulate recruiting for the active forces. Nor was the direct goal of UMT, building up the ready reserves, entirely beside the point in the crisis of March, 1948. The briefing for President Truman on February 18 had stressed that partial mobilization would be required to support the deployment of any force larger than a division in any of the world's potential trouble spots; but the effectiveness of such a mobilization in producing ready men and units was still in doubt. There had been some improvement in the condition of the organized reserves since the 1947 House Armed Services Committee report on UMT had pronounced them to be "in an advanced state of confusion," but by early 1948 they were still grievously short on manpower.[9]

Whether as a measure to meet clearly perceived military needs, or as a gesture of determination, a renewed campaign for UMT was the Administration's first military policy response to the Czech coup. On March 2, Secretary Marshall conferred with members of the Senate committee and urged action. Within a week, following a closed committee meeting with Secretary Forrestal and the military department secretaries, the Senate Armed Services Committee announced it would begin public hearings on UMT.[10] After a brief delay to avoid conflict with the president's address, these hearings opened on the afternoon of March 17.

By this time it was clear that a drive for UMT would not be the only Administration response to the crisis in military manpower;

for the president, in his morning address, had also called for a restoration of Selective Service. The decision to ask for Selective Service had not come until almost two weeks after the renewed UMT campaign was launched, despite its obviously more direct relation to current shortages in the active forces.

Asserting the failure of the enlistment drive in mid-January, Army Secretary Royall also suggested that renewed draft calls might be necessary if the European Recovery Program were not approved.[11] The subject came up again, obliquely, in a National Security Council meeting on February 12; here Secretary Forrestal mentioned recourse to Selective Service as a possible consequence of our U.N. obligations and the situation in Palestine. Nevertheless, in succeeding weeks the defense secretary still approached the subject with caution. On March 3, he agreed with Representative Walter Andrews that the president would have to think seriously not only about UMT but about reviving Selective Service; but in a press conference as late as March 10, Forrestal only went so far as to suggest a need for Selective Service should UMT fail of enactment.[12]

The apparent reason for Forrestal's caution up to this point was the lack of an agreed position on Selective Service among the joint chiefs of staff. This was not remedied until March 14, when the joint chiefs accepted a staff paper on the subject. Their study recognized the failure of voluntary enlistments to meet authorized strengths and the slowness of any UMT program in providing new manpower; and they called for an immediate reenactment of a recourse to Selective Service. Forrestal reported this conclusion to President Truman late in the afternoon of March 15. By that time the president, who had heard of this recommendation from other sources, had already decided to include Selective Service in his March 17 address.[13]

The president's request for a dual answer to military manpower shortages came as a surprise to Congress and the public, as well it might. For three years, a major strategem in the Administration's case for its manpower procurement proposals had been to maintain the distinction between Selective Service and UMT, and between the different goals to which these two measures were appropriate. One means of keeping the distinction clear had been the often repeated advice to Congress that UMT could be made operative only after Selective Service had passed from the scene. Now, suddenly, Congress was being asked to enact both procurement measures, and the apparent intent was to operate them together. The Administration did still emphasize the differing, if complementary, purposes of the two measures. The president urged UMT as a long-range preparedness measure, "the only feasible means by which the civilian components of our armed forces can be built up to the strength required if we are to be prepared for emergencies." Echoing Secretary Marshall's argument, Truman asserted that "adoption of universal training by the United States at this time would be unmistakable evidence to all the world of our determination to back the will to peace with the strength for peace." At the same time, echoing the conclusion of the joint chiefs of staff that voluntary enlistments had failed to keep pace with minimum needs, the president urged the need for Selective Service to maintain active forces at their authorized strengths. Anticipating the charge that the two programs would be redundant rather than complementary, the president emphasized that Selective Service would support the regular forces, UMT the reserves. Finally, bringing the case for these twin proposals as close as possible to the logic of earlier arguments, President Truman stated that Selective Service would be only a temporary measure, "necessary until the solid foundation of universal training can be established. Selective service can then be terminated and the regular forces may then be maintained on a voluntary basis."[14]

The new sense of urgency conveyed by President Truman's March 17 address did serve, so it seems in retrospect, to break the 1945-47 stalemate in military manpower procurement policy. But it took three more months of renewed and restructured debate to produce formal policy decisions in response to the Soviet challenge.

II.   THE SELECTIVE SERVICE ACT OF 1948

1.   *New Shape of the Debate*

The policy debate that followed President Truman's dual request for enactment of UMT and renewal of Selective Service differed from earlier legislative struggles over these two proposals, in political setting and in content, as well as in results.

In 1948 the Administration faced a Republican-dominated Congress anxious to make a record for the impending presidential campaign, which most observers felt sure that party would win. But in 1948 the Administration enjoyed, as it had not in the 1946 Selective Service debate, the fairly willing cooperation of the legislative committee chairmen most concerned, even though it could hardly hope for wide support from their party colleagues.

In 1946 the Administration had asked for, at most, a one-year extension of a wartime procurement system to meet "war-generated" demands for military manpower, and had carefully distinguished this request from its longer-range plans for a peacetime military establishment and procurement system. Opponents of the proposal had argued that compulsion was simply unnecessary, either because volunteers would be forthcoming to meet military demands for manpower, or because those demands were unrealistically high for the postwar period. Almost inextricably mixed with their arguments had come the charge that conscription in peacetime could only be destructive of traditional American social and political relations, and would inevitably lead to the militarization of American youth and society. The outcome, limited extension of a modified Selective Service program, had reflected an uneasy acceptance of, or inability to disprove, Administration estimates of the necessary military strengths and the probable lack of sufficient volunteers. The debate and its outcome had also affirmed the strength of public and congressional desires for a rapid return to the traditionally American peacetime system of voluntary forces; and they had uncovered suspicions that the Administration and military leaders intended to prolong conscription as a means to extending their wartime powers indefinitely into the postwar period.

Desires for peacetime normalcy and suspicions of Administration and military motives had affected policy in 1946 partly because of the inherent strength of these attitudes among highly vocal factions in Congress and the body politic. By contrast, the Administration's position had lacked dramatic appeal. Unwilling to discuss the relation between its postwar aims and the threats posed by Soviet intransigence and our own precipitate demobilization, the Administration could only assert that its manpower calculations were correct, that they demonstrated a continued need for Selective Service, and that extension of that program would provide for an orderly transition, at a time unspecified, to a permanent postwar establishment. To support this future peacetime establishment, the Administration wanted UMT; but public support for this proposal was mostly passive, too weak to overcome a highly organized and vocal opposition.

By contrast, in 1948 the Administration made clear that its proposals were responses to a dangerously unsettled international situation in which one nation, the Soviet Union, posed a threat to the peace and security of ourselves and our friends in Europe. In this new openness, the Administration was, in effect, answering the misleading question of whether our responses to the cold war should be military or diplomatic by urging that both responses were necessary; the president called for expansion of American military capabilities as an essential underpinning for our political and economic initiatives.

The cold war logic of this position, which both affected and reflected the public and congressional temper of the time, had the important effect of exposing and underscoring growing divisions in the opposition to the Administration's military policy proposals. Most of those opposing the Administration on details of these proposals nonetheless accepted the need for greater military strength. Arrayed against this conclusion were only the Wallace Progressives and their close allies. In the words of their nominal leader, the Truman address was "a shameful call for world remobilization, a complete admission of the failure of the Truman Doctrine and a call for an American police state. . . ."[15] Such harsh expressions of long-standing antimilitary and anticonscription prejudices provided much of the fireworks in the renewed debate over military manpower procurement; but their real effect was probably opposite to that intended. The 1945-47 alliance of left and right in opposition to "militaristic conscription" came apart in 1948, as most conservatives found it more important to be anti-Soviet than antimilitary.

While the Administration's ambiguity on the source of threats to our security was erased, its position on military manpower policies to meet that threat seemed more ambiguous than ever. In a sense, the Administration's position resembled that of 1945; UMT was intended to provide the trained reserves needed for a permanent peacetime establishment, while Selective Service was labeled a "temporary" expedient. But to ask for both programs at once left unanswered the question of how the two procurement systems could be operated in tandem with fairness and efficiency. There were even more important unanswered questions: How temporary was a temporary reenactment of Selective Service to be? Was Administration policy still built on the Marshall-Palmer vision of a postwar military establishment? The president had gone far to make it appear so in his address. But how much longer could the transition to peace be stretched out without calling this vision and its fundamental assumptions into question? Was Selective Service to operate only until UMT could produce sufficient trained reserves to make transition to a small peacetime establishment feasible? Or was the need for large active forces now relatively independent of the status of reserves? If so, then Selective Service might operate for the duration of the international crisis. Were this to last long enough, the concept of transition to peace could no longer be said to govern policy. The second fundamental assumption about postwar policy would, in turn, become irrelevant: if voluntary recruiting could be relied on to support the active forces only in some unforeseeable future peacetime situation, then to suggest that peacetime conscription for the active forces had become the real goal of the Administration was realism, not suspicion.

These ambiguities suggest only part of the Administration's mid-March difficulties in setting a clear course for manpower procurement policy. Much more immediate and obvious than questions about the long-term relation between UMT and Selective Service was a growing challenge to both of these proposals on grounds that there was a more effective, less expensive, and more necessary means to national security—air power.

All other things being equal, just the 1947 creation of a separate Air Force, with its own cabinet-level secretary, would have made an air power challenge to the Administration's ideas about force structure more likely to be heard in 1948 than in 1945. The powers of the secretary of defense and the joint chiefs of staff to maintain a unified front on defense policies were far from clear, but they certainly did not match the earlier impact of General Marshall's prestige on the wartime Army Ground and Air Forces.

Moreover, other things were not equal; for by 1948, air power had acquired powerful friends in Congress. In urging new economic and political directions in foreign policy on the Republican-dominated Eightieth Congress, the Administration enjoyed the effective cooperation of Senator Arthur Vandenberg. But Vandenberg's persuasiveness with his party colleagues did not extend to military policy, especially those aspects having a direct effect on manpower strengths and procurement. The Administration did have a willing Republican friend, at least on UMT, in Senator Chan Gurney, chairman of the Armed Services Committee. On UMT, however, and eventually on a wider range of defense policy issues, Gurney had a powerful rival in Senator Robert Taft. Long an outspoken opponent of both UMT and Selective Service, Taft had phrased his opposition largely in terms of the general anticonscription argument. By early 1948, he had shifted his attack to new ground, promoting air power as the principal means of defense and an alternative to UMT.[16] The partisanship of this challenge was soon diluted, however, and the challenge itself gained new strength as leading congressional Democrats also took up the fight for air power.

Both administration and congressional champions of air power found fresh support for their views in the early months of 1948, with the publication of the Finletter report on January 1, and the parallel Brewster-Hinshaw report in March. Both reports dealt with the question of air power, and both accepted Air Force arguments for a seventy-group force, a substantial increase over the fifty-five groups proposed in the current budget.[17] Despite their obvious value to the Air Force's claims on the defense budget, though, these reports reflected a review only of air power problems, and those largely in the context of an "all-out" war contingency.[18] The Administration tended to discount their recommendations on those grounds, and continued its formal support for a system of mobilizable reserves based on UMT. But the reports did lend new prestige to the position of the Air Force and its congressional allies.

Out of all this came a major Air Force challenge to Secretary Forrestal's position as spokesman for a supposedly unified defense establishment, a challenge which forced the debate over air power versus balanced military forces into two stages: first, the struggle to achieve a united front within the Administration—specifically among the joint chiefs of staff and the military services; and second, the attempt to win a majority for the resulting compromise from a reluctant and skeptical Congress. These two stages, much to Forrestal's embarrassment, erupted simultaneously during congressional committee consideration of the Administration's proposals. Thus what had been a latent critique of the Administration's plans in 1946 became a dominant line of attack on its 1948 program, and it had a major impact on the outcome of the 1948 debate.

In sum, the events and new attitudes of early 1948, especially the open assertion of cold war logic and the growing enthusiasm for air power, reshaped but did not wholly revolutionize the debate over military manpower procurement. In both the development of Administration proposals and consideration of these by the Congress, most of the really pertinent and effective argument was addressed to questions of how, not whether, to achieve greater military effectiveness. For the first time the debate dealt explicitly, if not too cogently, with questions of cost efficiency. In committee, and during the later floor debates and decision in the House and Senate and conference, opposition to the compulsions of conscription was still lively; it had important, but no longer dominant, impact on the content and outcome of the debate. Problems of equity and of adapting military programs to other social goals, which had been obscurely present in the earlier debates over UMT and Selective Service extension, had even less impact on the 1948 discussion and results.

2. *The Administration's Initial Proposals*

By coupling a plea for reenactment of Selective Service with his expected request for UMT, the president evidently surprised not only many congressmen and much of the press and public, but parts of his own Administration as well. That afternoon the Senate Armed Services Committee opened its scheduled hearings on UMT, with Secretary of State Marshall as the lead-off witness. Predictably, Marshall vigorously supported enactment of UMT. Only at the very end of his prepared statement did he refer to the second part of the president's manpower requests, and then only in a brief observation: "Due to the rapid dwindling in the strength of the armed forces, the temporary application of selective service is necessary."[19]

Nor was Marshall the only one caught unprepared by the sudden request for Selective Service. A meeting of representatives from the Defense Department, Selective Service, the Budget Bureau and other agencies in the evening of March 17 marked only the start of internal negotiations to produce an Administration bill for Selective Service, a process which took several more weeks even to reach the stage of review by the Bureau of the Budget.[20]

The draft of legislative proposals was not the only Administration homework still uncompleted at this point. Secretary Forrestal appeared before the Senate Committee on March 18, along with the other service secretaries, and reviewed the need for both UMT and Selective Service in only the most general terms. Then, citing a recommendation by the joint chiefs of staff for increases in the strengths of the armed forces, Forrestal said he needed time to study the proposal before approving or modifying it. He did indicate that his recommendation would include expansion not just up to but beyond the strengths currently allowed by Congress; but he was not prepared to specify what this would mean either in numbers of men or in added costs.[21] He was not prepared because the Administration, while generally agreed on the need to expand military capabilities, was not yet agreed on the content or scope of that expansion.

A week later, on March 25, Forrestal presented his program to the Senate committee, in company with the service secretaries and the joint chiefs of staff. The general goal, said Forrestal, was to achieve a balance among manpower needs of the Air Force, the Army, and the Navy. For the short-term, this meant increasing the strength of the active forces by about 25 percent, with most of this going to the Army (see Table 3). These increases would be supported by a supplemental budget request for $3 billion for FY 1949, including $775 million for aircraft procurement, research and development for the Air Force and naval aviation, and about $760 million for military personnel costs. Forrestal asserted but did not elaborate on the need for Selective Service to support this short-term program. Although the Administration's draft legislation was still in preparation, Forrestal did suggest that it would apply to young men aged nineteen through twenty-five, and that not all those eligible would be needed: excluding veterans, the unfit, and others entitled to exemption or deferment, about 1,350,000 men would

TABLE 3

FORRESTAL'S ACTIVE FORCES MANPOWER PROPOSALS,
MARCH 25, 1948

	Current Strength	Proposed Increase	Proposed Total
Army _____	542,000	240,000	782,000
Navy _____	478,000	74,000	552,000
(Marine Corps) _____	(81,000)	(11,000)	(92,000)
Air Force _____	364,500	35,500	400,000
Total _____	1,384,500	349,500	1,734,000

SOURCE: U.S. Congress, Senate, Committee on Armed Services, *Universal Military Training,* Hearings, 80th Cong., 2d sess., 1948, p. 331.

be available in those age groups; but of these the services would take only a little over half—some 500,000 by voluntary enlistment and about 220,000 through Selective Service.[22]

For the long-term, Forrestal turned to the task of providing adequate reserve forces through UMT. In three years, he stated, that program could be in full operation, producing about 850,000 basically trained men annually. Forrestal noted that the FY 1949 budget had already asked for expenditure of $400 million to begin the UMT program, later confirmed a recommendation to the Senate committee calling for expenditures of $880 million in the program's first fiscal year, and said he hoped the annual cost of the program in full operation could be held under $4 billion. (These amounts were for the UMT training programs alone; they did not include the costs of providing, maintaining, and operating facilities for the expanded organized reserves that were to be an important end product of the program. Presumably these demands would not be felt until after FY 1949.) But, Forrestal insisted, this $4 billion would not all be additional cost. UMT would be necessary to avoid the "inordinate costs" of maintaining large enough active forces to make up for the current lack of reliable reserves. With UMT, he argued, it may be possible "substantially to reduce" spending for the active forces.[23]

Other witnesses gave more specific information. The Army was to get most of the increase in active forces manpower, and would use a major part of this to expand its "mobile striking force" based in the United States. Most of the Navy's smaller increase was earmarked for the operating fleet, naval aviation, and fleet support activities. Marine Corps increases would expand the Fleet Marine Force, supporting establishments, and training. The Air Force intended to use most of its increase to bring its fifteen skeletonized groups (out of a total of fifty-five active) up to peacetime strength, and to bring six of its thirteen heavy bomber groups up to wartime strength. The UMT program would bring in 850,000 out of an expected 1.2 million youths reaching age eighteen each year (allowing for those enlisting ahead of a call into UMT and for those not physically or mentally fit for military training). Again the Army would be the chief beneficiary. The annual flow of trainees would be divided into half for the Army, three-tenths for the Navy, and one-fifth for the Air Force. UMT was expected to increase the Army National Guard to 650,000, and its Organized Reserves to 505,000; and the Army's general reserve pool, currently numbering about 2 million, would increase to 3 million by 1957, instead of declining over that same period to a half million in the absence of UMT.[24]

Despite this filling in of details, much of the ambiguity in the president's proposals remained. Neither the witnesses nor the committee faced at this point the question of how the dual operation of Selective Service and UMT would affect an individual's military obligation—whether, specifically, a UMT graduate would still be eligible for induction. Presumably this could be worked out in the details of the new Selective Service Act. More fundamental was the question of the relation between these two manpower procurement programs and the current emergency to which they were responses. It was not at all clear from Forrestal's testimony that UMT, in full operation, would allow cuts in the active forces and an end to Selective Service. What he did say was more cautious: "When these immediate needs [for active forces] have been met, and the long-term program is adequately functioning, we should be able *in a more peaceful world* to curtail or eliminate the short-term program."[25] In other words, Selective Service and the enlarged active forces it was to provide, might be necessary only until UMT could produce the trained reserves needed to complete the Administration's long-standing vision of a proper peacetime establishment. But if these programs, even in combination with our political and economic policies, failed to produce "a more peaceful world," then Selective Service might be needed for quite a long time. At least this is what

Forrestal's careful statement seemed to mean. Neither he nor other witnesses nor the committee members tried to clarify the point.

The problem of dual operation of the two procurement programs was resolved, not to the Administration's liking, at a later stage in the debate. Questions about the duration of the current emergency, which were crucial to the issue of compulsions, did not emerge until even later, and even then were not answered clearly. The first month of the debate was dominated, instead, by yet another issue: what kind of active forces were really needed? The answers to this question, and the process of reaching them, had major effects on the rest of the 1948 manpower procurement debate.

3. Balanced Forces versus Air Power

Debate over the character of active forces erupted as air power enthusiasts challenged Forrestal's emphasis on a "balanced" defense establishment. The honor, or onus, for raising this challenge fell to Air Force Secretary W. Stuart Symington.

Symington was in an awkward position as he began his initial presentation on March 25. His testimony followed Forrestal's; it also followed presentations by the civilian and military heads of the Army and Navy, each supporting his service's part of Forrestal's total program, and by General Collins, who represented all services on UMT. In his formal statement, Symington also supported the short- and long-term parts of Forrestal's program. Although the Air Force could get the additional men proposed for its active forces through voluntary recruiting, Symington supported Selective Service as the means to assuring that the Army could continue its extensive logistical support of the Air Force and could, if necessary, "defend those bases we must use." So far, so good; even General Bradley had cast the Army's requirements largely in terms of its potential contribution to a general air war: defending and seizing bases for our own Air Force, and denying bases to the enemy. But Symington's support of UMT was briefer and less enthusiastic. The Air Force, he said, "considers essential to the national security those requirements found necessary to the other services." This was no deep bow to inter-service unity; in the context of what followed, it was merely a hint that the Army and the Navy should return the compliment by supporting what the Air Force found necessary. At this point, Symington shifted his emphasis, implying that Forrestal's program was good, but not good enough. The proposed FY 1949 budget, he said, would allow continuation of the current fifty-five active air groups, and would authorize "a rate of procurement for aircraft that will eventually provide us with 34 combat groups that have modern airplanes." He then recalled recommendations by Generals Eisenhower and Spaatz, made two years before the current emergency, for over twice that number of modern air groups. Finally he stressed the even more critical time ahead, when the Russians would have their own atomic bombs. At that date, he warned, "we will not have an adequate modern Air Force . . . unless we start building the Air Force now."[26]

Despite Chairman Gurney's objections, other members of the committee pressed Symington and his chief of staff, General Spaatz, for specific recommendations. Symington emphasized that he was only being consistent with testimony he had given earlier to the Finletter Commission on air policy; that commission, he noted, had accepted the goal of a seventy-group Air Force, and had recommended almost twice as much in procurement funds as was proposed by Forrestal, even with the FY 1949 budget supplement. The latter proposal was for only fifty-five groups. Why the drop from seventy to fifty-five? "My answer," said Symington, "is we have not got the men because we have not got the money and we have not got the airplaines because we have not got the money." Was a seventy-group Air Force essential to national security? "Well, under a direct question like that, I would say, yes, sir, it is, and it has been for two years." Spaatz was even less reticent, agreeing quickly that the seventy-group program was the minimum necessary to national security.[27]

Symington and Spaatz did not, at this point, offer their case as a direct challenge to Forrestal's manpower proposals. They simply stressed the contrast between a seventy-group force and the Administration's plans for an Air Force smaller than that minimum. Nor did Forrestal accept their challenge in terms of the manpower program. Instead, he chose to argue in budget terms. Invited to reappear at the end of the March 25 hearing, he concentrated on the concept of balanced forces. Balance was the goal of his proposed $3 billion supplemental budget and the inauguration of Selective Service and

UMT. Balanced forces at this budget level (a total for FY 1949 of $14 billion) meant a fifty-five-group Air Force. To buy a seventy-group Air Force, and at the same time balance the whole defense establishment at that higher level, might cost another $15 billion.[28]

Shortly after the March 25 hearing, Forrestal attempted to set his Defense Department house in order. In a memorandum to the joint chiefs of staff, he reminded them that at the time of the Finletter Commission's hearings they had recommended a seventy-group Air Force, but also had advised that this would require parallel expansion of the other services. He now asked the joint chiefs to be specific. Did they still support the larger Air Force? Would this still require increases in the Army and Navy, or would they support the Air Force program without such increases? If the former, how large should the increases be? And, "In case sufficient funds cannot be obtained for the entire foregoing balanced force, what elements do the Joint Chiefs of Staff recommend for activation and support and in what priorities?"[29]

Before Forrestal got his answers, he had to defend his program in public again, at hearings by the House Armed Services Committee. Already, at an executive session on April 7, that committee had unanimously approved a resolution favoring the seventy-group program.[30] Thus, the Air Force's cause had progressed well beyond the point of being simply a convenient platform for Republican opposition to the Administration's defense policies. Indeed, in the open hearings of the House committee on April 12, the leading proponent of the seventy-group program seemed to be the ranking minority member, Representative Carl Vinson (D., Ga.), who served notice that he would support an amendment to the aircraft procurement appropriation adding some $900 million in aircraft contract authorizations.[31] Pressed hard, and receiving open support from only one committee member, Forrestal responded with a determined defense of the "balanced force" concept. Repeatedly he emphasized that he was not opposed to a seventy-group Air Force or any other specific program, but that this program alone did not represent a rounded judgment on military needs. That judgment would not be available until the joint chiefs of staff answered his earlier memorandum. Until then, he could not support any particular air program.[32]

The following day, Secretary Symington appeared before the

House committee, and revealed a shift in his tactics. Once again he stated his support of Selective Service, given the Army's need for it. Then Representative Lyndon Johnson (D., Tex.), raised the question Symington was waiting for, posing a choice between UMT and a seventy-group Air Force as national security measures. "Well," Symington answered, "if my two boys have to go back into the Army and the marines, I would rather see them have a minimum Air Force than I would a group of younger boys trained for six months or a year. . . . The Compton report said that if UMT had to be at the expense of the military services they would not only not be for it, they would be against it. That is our position."[33]

This position was neither new nor unique to the Air Force. It underlay the older Army Air Force dissent from the Army's plan for a postwar establishment in February, 1945, and had been an important part of the technical critique of UMT ever since. Senator Taft had espoused this view some months earlier, and now the cause had been taken up by important Democrats in the House committee. What was new, and what Symington had obviously come to this hearing to accomplish, was that the Air Force was now clearly on public record favoring its seventy-group program ahead of UMT.

Up to a point, Symington was only anticipating the joint chiefs' response to Forrestal's questions, which he received one day later, on April 14. The joint chiefs again unanimously recommended "a military establishment commensurate with the seventy group air program."[34] Such an establishment would require active manpower levels of 502,000 for the Air Force, 837,000 for the Army, and 668,000 for the Navy and Marine Corps; and quick achievement of this enlarged active establishment would require additions to the original FY 1949 defense budget of $9 billion, in contrast to Forrestal's $3 billion supplemental. But this was not the whole story. The joint chiefs admitted their recommendation was solely a military judgment, and they granted the need to phase such a program with regard for the national economy and the productive capacities of aircraft and other defense industries. These would be, by inference, matters for judgment by civil authorities. It was these judgments, of course, that Symington hoped to influence.

On the day of the joint chiefs' report to Forrestal, General Bradley met the issue head on, telling the House committee he was "not unmindful" of the growing pressure for a seventy-group Air Force as an alternative to Army expansion. He set forth the Army's needs, emphasizing that these were concomitants, not alternatives, to a strong Air Force. And he offered a blunt defense of UMT against air power enthusiasts. It was wrong, he argued, to consider any specific number of air groups as an alternative to UMT. "The alternative to UMT if we are to have the barest type of security is a standing army big enough to carry the Army portion of a war burden . . . until mobilization can be effected."[35] This, he said, would mean twenty-five active divisions, or about 1.5 million men. Assuming UMT would be approved, however, Bradley asked for only twelve active divisions plus supporting elements, a standing force of 822,000 men (or 837,000 if Air Force increases required added Army logistical support).

This request was as much a departure from Forrestal's March 25 program as was Symington's call for a seventy-group Air Force. Nevertheless, all three programs reflected one common assumption about strategy, widely held in the late 1940's. The war that both Bradley and Symington wanted to prepare for was what today goes by the term "central war," a direct, all-out confrontation between the United States and the Soviet Union. The assumption that this kind of war was *the* military threat to the United States pervaded the entire public debate over strategy, as reflected both in the 1947 Compton Report and in the 1948 debate over Selective Service and UMT. Bradley's own attitude is clear from his assertion that: "The whole trouble is over toward Europe. Period."[36] And Forrestal's public case for active force expansion focused solely on the plight of West Europe and the threat to it and to the United States posed by the Soviet Union. (He did have other worries, especially the possibility of an explosion in Palestine;[37] but he kept these out of the public debate.) If anyone had in mind that expanded American military forces might be used as a deterrent or counter-force in more limited situations, no one was saying so or acting as if he thought so.

Forrestal's immediate problem was to keep the Army's and the Air Force's demands for central war forces from getting out of hand. In this context, Bradley's testimony probably helped more than it hindered. By keeping his case within that for "balanced forces," and by demonstrating the consequences of pursuing each service's "minimum" needs independently of a unified defense program, Bradley made it easier for Forrestal to impose his own program, at least within the defense establishment.

A week before Forrestal announced his revised program, the House rendered its own judgment on priorities, by amending the aircraft procurement bill to add $822 million toward building a seventy-group Air Force.[38] But, as Forrestal concluded, this judgment was not final. A meeting with the joint chiefs on April 19 climaxed the long process of reaching agreement on an Administration program.[39] Here Forrestal stressed that the Air Force's real concern should be, not the House appropriation, but the funds available under the current presidential budget ceiling plus whatever added amount they might hope to get. Forrestal extracted from the joint chiefs their "unanimous" agreement to a final force expansion proposal, which he then presented to the Senate Armed Services Committee on April 21. This proposal included a budget supplemental of $3.481 billion, and manpower levels reflecting only a partial shift from the original proposal toward what the joint chiefs had asked (see Table 4).

TABLE 4

ADMINISTRATION PROGRAMS FOR EXPANSION
OF ACTIVE FORCES, MARCH-APRIL 1948.

	March 25 Proposal*	JCS Proposal†	Final Proposal†
Army	782,000	837,000	790,000
Navy (incl. Marine Corps)	552,000	668,000	552,000
Air Force	400,000	502,000	453,000
Total	1,734,000	2,007,000	1,795,000
Budget Supplement	$3 billion	$9 billion	$3.481 billion

* SOURCE: U.S. Congress, Senate, Committee on Armed Services, *Universal Military Training*, Hearings, 80th Cong., 2d sess., 1948, p. 331.

† SOURCE: Secretary Forrestal's statement on April 21 concerning his testimony at an executive session of the Senate Committee on Armed Services; see *New York Times*, April 22, 1948, p. 13.

Millis summarizes this outcome as, at least on the surface, an Air Force victory. In this April 21 proposal, that service would get enough men for eleven new air groups, four short of its seventy-group goal; and the Air Force was not overly concerned about the troop carrier and light bomber groups being deferred. The proposal would give the Air Force money to re-equip and maintain its existing fifty-five groups; and there was added hope, in the

House's vote for $822 million in additional procurement funds, for early progress in equipping the new groups.[40] In manpower, the Air Force would get all it had ever requested for the next fiscal year, while the small additional increase for the Army merely rec-ognized its obligation to provide supply and other services to an enlarged Air Force.

In a larger sense, Forrestal's initial concept of a short-range program for expanding the active forces remained intact. The Army was still to get the major share of the manpower increase over current strengths (248,000 out of 410,500); and the need for Selective Service to achieve this expansion had never been questioned within the defense establishment (although the Air Force, and to a lesser degree the Navy, thought they themselves could get by without it). Thus the imbalance introduced by the Air Force's challenge to Forrestal was, in manpower terms, manageable. In budgeting terms, the threat was more formidable; but even here Forrestal still had strong cards to play. In its demand for a seventy-group Air Force, that service had not openly challenged either part of the short-range program—a balanced expansion of active forces, and Selective Service to support it. Indeed, by agreeing to Forrestal's $3.481 billion budget supplemental, the Air Force had renewed its public commitment to the short-range program. Moreover, the House's $822 million was for two years of contract authorizations; and Forrestal felt sure of strong presidential backing for controlling these funds even more tightly, and thus maintaining a degree of active force balance.[41]

The impact of later congressional action on balance in the short-range expansion of active forces was only superficial. The Senate Armed Services Committee eventually recommended manpower levels very much like those in Forrestal's April 21 proposal. The House committee recommended higher levels, very close to those in the joint chiefs' proposal; and this recommendation survived to the final version of the bill.[42] But these were only authorizations, and did not obligate the Administration to achieve the higher manpower levels. In the context of the whole debate over manpower policy, these authorizations did not affect Forrestal's insistence on a "balanced force" concept for the short-range expansion of active forces.

The debate over the character of active forces had a much greater impact on the Administration's long-range program. By the end of April, Symington's public statement of the Air Force's preference for a seventy-group force over UMT, combined with the symbolic House vote of $822 million for new aircraft, posed a grave threat to hopes for building up the reserves through UMT. Here, Forrestal had very few cards left to play. He could hardly argue that the joint chiefs were unanimously committed to UMT. The strongest argument suggested thus far was that only UMT could give the armed services the strong, well-trained reserves that might permit eventual reductions in the active forces and abandonment of Selective Service. But this argument had its weaknesses. In addition to the ambiguities in it, there was the cold fact that as yet no Selective Service program existed with which to bargain; and adoption of Selective Service, although by the end of April a likelier prospect than UMT, was by no means a foregone conclusion.

4.   Compulsions: Conscription for Peacetime or for Emergency?

If Congress had little effect on the Administration's decision for balance in the short-range expansion of active forces, its deliberations and actions did have major impacts on the scope and character of compulsions to be employed in manpower procurement. The outcomes of debate over this issue can be stated quite simply: the reenactment of Selective Service, and the rejection of UMT. But the reasons for these outcomes were as important to the future of manpower policy as the results themselves; and those reasons were not at all simple or clear.

Easiest to explain is the rejection of UMT. In part, this program was the victim of its own long history as a public issue. Not one important pressure group or congressional faction earlier opposed to UMT switched to support it in 1948. Moreover, resentment rankled over the War Department's 1946-47 public relations campaign, and over the active establishment's uncomplimentary views of the current reserve program. "The Army has acted," said the five signers of a House committee minority report, "as if it is the policy-making body. . . . it has said that Congress must accept a conscription program before the Army will organize, train, and equip the Reserves. Congress cannot permit itself to become the rubber stamp of the willful group of officers who want to Prussianize this Nation. . . ."[43]

At the same time, the Administration was unable to offer fresh arguments for UMT, except the dubious one that its operation might, someday, obviate the need for Selective Service. Nor could it ignore the growing public and congressional preference, symbol-ized in the House vote for additional aircraft procurement funds, for air power rather than trained reserves as the answer to long-range security needs.

By the end of April, Forrestal became convinced that UMT would never get past the Senate committee, and that the House committee no longer supported its own 1947 UMT bill with any enthusiasm.[44] Responding to initiatives from two Senate committee members, he decided to cooperate in adding several provisions to the Selective Service proposal intended to give fresh strength to recruiting for the organized reserves.[45] What came out of the Senate committee was eventually altered, on both floors and in conference, to yield four new targets for organized reserve unit recruiting. First, anyone inducted or enlisted under the new act would acquire a reserve obligation following active service—five years in a reserve pool, reducible to three by service in an organized reserve unit. Second, although most active service veterans were exempt under the new act, a small number of short-term veterans remained liable for induction; but they could gain deferment by joining an organized reserve unit. Third, youths under age eighteen and one-half could gain deferment from induction by enlisting in a National Guard (but not other organized reserve) unit. Finally, in what was misleadingly tagged a "draft-UMT marriage" provision, limited numbers of eighteen-year-olds were allowed to enlist for one year of active training and service, to be followed by four years of compulsory service in an organized reserve unit (or six years in a reserve pool); annual ceilings for this program were: Army, 110,000; Navy and Marine Corps, 36,000; and Air Force, 15,000. In addition, members of organized reserve units when the act became effective would remain exempt from induction so long as they continued their membership.

This compromise was a long way from assuring trained manpower to the reserves. Of course, it did preclude any need to mesh the mechanics of Selective Service and UMT in a tandem operation. Indeed, Forrestal's reluctant cooperation in this compromise made self-confirming his predictions that UMT was doomed. The 1947 UMT bill never got out of the House Rules Committee to the floor; and an attempt to incorporate its provisions into the Senate's Selective Service bill failed in that house on a voice vote.[46]

The outcome for Selective Service itself was more favorable, though still short of what the Administration wanted. Recommendations on this program by the House and Senate committees mostly reflected close legislative drafting cooperation with Administration officials. But several factors led to major differences between the versions passed in each house, and the final conference version included some compromises with those factions resisting Selective Service on one or another ground.

Support for and opposition to Selective Service conscription were marked by continuing confusion over the specific character of the military threat being faced, and its significance for manpower procurement policies. The core of the Administration's case for Selective Service lay in the falling levels of active force strength, especially in the ground forces. The straightforward approach, given this case, would have been a simple request for reenactment of Selective Service, citing President Truman's warning a year earlier when he had allowed that program to lapse. But the President's March 17 address injected a strong note of international crisis into the debate. While this drama may well have been necessary to get any action at all, it also tended to shift the case for Selective Service to one of support for a specific emergency measure.

Forrestal was very cautious throughout on this matter. At the House committee hearings in mid-April he repeated his earlier argument, that when immediate active force needs had been met and UMT was functioning adequately, "we should be able in a more peaceful world to curtail or eliminate the short term program." Then he added: "But not in our lifetime or that of the next generation do I foresee a time when a strong military potential will not be needed to back up our diplomacy." When Representative Vinson asked whether there was a crisis or not, Forrestal answered: "No, I should not like to use the word 'crisis.' I think we are in a state of tension, which I think may continue for a long time to come." Representative Havenner (D., Calif.) pursued the point, asking "whether we are not, in fact, embarking upon a permanent program rather than a temporary program." Forrestal answered: "I think it is permanent so long as the need for it exists. . . . We are not reacting to any temporary condition."[47]

Whether the current situation was understood as one of emergency or merely of heightened tension, as temporary or permanent, there were important signs of shifting public attitudes toward military needs and the propriety of conscription to meet them. At committee hearings, although there were no changes in the earlier line-up of UMT opponents, there were several cracks in the opposition to Selective Service. Spokesmen for the American Farm Bureau Federation and the National Grange reasserted their distaste for peacetime conscription, and doubted that the current crisis could justify even a temporary resort to Selective Service; but both suggested that information on the military threat not available to them might provide such a justification. CIO spokesman Nathan Cowan took a similar position; and AFL president William Green went even further, giving reluctant endorsement to a temporary Selective Service program to meet current needs. Spokesmen for the Association of American Colleges, the American Association of University Professors, and the American Council on Education, while maintaining their oppositon to UMT, nonetheless saw some possible justification for temporary Selective Service. They did not relate this to any current international emergency; rather they suggested inductions might become necessary should voluntary enlistments fail; but they all suggested that, with a little more effort and will, the necessary volunteers could be found.

Despite these shifts, there remained a strong current of support for the House committee's minority view, that neither the international situation nor evidence of declining enlistments was sufficient to justify a program of peacetime conscription. The threat to international peace, their report suggested, was partly of our own making; "our own country is promoting distrust and unrest in the world when we announce our intention to spend over 20 billion dollars in 1949 for military preparedness." Rejecting the Administration's call for a build-up of all three services, they proposed that the Air

Force and Navy be kept strong through voluntary recruiting. Rejecting the evidence that the Army could not even maintain its current strength, much less increase it, they urged that that service be forced to step up its recruiting program and, if necessary, to lower its standards. Finally, they offered a classic statement of the oldest and most faimilar argument against peacetime conscription—that it was simply un-American:

> America is populated by many peoples, most of whom came to the New World to escape . . . the very Prussianism which it is now proposed to fasten upon these United States for all time. Millions of Americans have fought and died to avoid just such slavery as it is now proposed that we legislate into existence. The compulsory peacetime draft will wreck the institutions upon which America is founded.[48]

Debate over Selective Service at this very general level continued on the House floor. Representative Short (R., Mo.), a minority report signer, again argued that the international crisis did not justify peacetime conscription, alleging that only the militarists wanted it: "Oh, emergency! How many crimes are committed in thy name?" Representative Cooley (D., N.C.) responded in kind, alluding to Short's votes against Selective Service before World War II: "I might even say, 'Isolation, isolation, oh what crimes have been committed in thy name. . . . If this were only a peacetime military conscription bill . . . I would certainly not vote for it . . . but, gentlemen, we are not living in normal times." Representative Cole (R., N.Y.) echoed Forrestal's earlier caution over labeling the situation an "emergency." In 1940 Selective Service had been a measure to prepare for war, he said; but in 1948 its purpose was "to prevent the situation from getting out of hand," to assure that American military strength would be an effective "deterrent to aggression." But not many members were interested in fine distinctions between forces to meet an emergency and the more modest aim of forces to provide a deterrent. Many, in the end perhaps most, were more impressed with the blunt position of Representative Leroy Johnson (R., Calif.), a converted foe of 1940 Selective Service: "There is only one question, and that is, Are you for national defense or are you against it?"[49]

The minority report signers soon realized that most of their colleagues would not accept an open hard-line stand against Selective

Service and a military build-up. No one directly challenged the proposed manpower authorizations. Given Forrestal's earlier extraction of "unanimous" agreement from the joint chiefs, those who would have preferred to concentrate on increases in the Air Force had no choice but to go along with that service's agreement to parallel increases in the Army. And those who wanted no military increases at all had to find lines of attack more promising of unified opposition than an outright rejection of any need for expanded defenses.

Such lines of attack were found in both the House and Senate debates, but most successfully in the House. One of them, a major threat to the effectiveness of the bill, consisted of a series of attempts to delay the start of inductions. As reported by committee, the House bill called for a ninety-day delay after enactment—not unreasonable in view of the time it would take to reactivate the Selective Service System and prepare training centers. Beyond this, however, there was considerable support for moves to place the burden of initiating draft calls even more directly on the president than it would be under the original provisions, requiring that he precede such calls by a formal declaration that sufficient men could not be obtained by other means. The motives behind this move were fairly clear: it would force the president to make an onerous decision in a very public manner in the midst of the election campaign; and, should he not prove equal to the challenge, it might serve to postpone inductions for quite a long time.

In the Senate an amendment incorporating this requirement (and the House bill's ninety-day provision) was defeated handily. In the House, however, Chairman Andrews apparently considered a similar amendment part of the price for getting his bill through the Rules Committee. Introduced by Andrews himself, the amendment passed easily.[50] This action only whetted the appetite of the opposition. A further amendment, proposed by Representative Shafer (R., Mich.) and supported by all shades of opposition to Selective Service, which would prohibit inductions prior to January 31, 1949, was adopted by a strong majority.[51] These votes for delay in the House were almost a high-water mark for the opposition. One implication was that the House had rejected the Administration claims that, emergency or not, quick action was required to meet the nation's security needs.

In the Senate, the nature and duration of the need for expanded active forces was questioned from a different angle. Senator Morse (R., Ore.), who had insisted in hearings that Forrestal demonstrate a need approaching emergency proportions, was apparently satisfied of the immediate need for expansion. But he questioned how long this need would last, and proposed an amendment limiting the life of the Selective Service Act to two years (as endorsed by the House bill, and in contrast to the five-year life endorsed by the Senate committee). Morse made clear his intent that Selective Service should come up for reconsideration not only soon, but preferably in an election year. Senator Gurney opposed the amendment. He was unwilling to argue directly that inductions might be required over the whole five-year period; but he insisted that the build-up of reserves, an important purpose of the Senate bill, would take more than two or three years. He also stressed the opportunities for annual review of the whole matter of active strengths and inductions inherent in the provision for strength authorizations. Nonetheless, Morse's amendment passed fairly easily.[52]

These various moves to delay or shorten the operation of Selective Service implied more than questions about the current extent or long-term nature of the threat to American security. Another of the opposition's major contentions was that voluntary enlistments could produce the necessary manpower, and that conscription was therefore unnecessary. The argument was not contested by supporters of Selective Service so far as it concerned current Air Force and Navy strengths; but, the Administration contended, the Navy probably could not expand to the desired level without at least the threat of inductions to support its recruiting efforts; and the Army could not even maintain its current strength, much less achieve the proposed major expansion, by voluntary means alone. Thus, to opponents and supporters alike, the Selective Service bill was very much an Army bill; and it was that service which bore the brunt of attacks on the Senate and House floors.

A prime target of these attacks, as in 1946, was the Army's mental standard for entry into service. From a wartime minimum Army General Classification Test (AGCT) score of 59, the requirement had risen to 80. Representative Short characterized this as such a high standard that "only a classical scholar in Greek or Latin or a Philadelphia lawyer could pass."[53] A more cautious estimate, offered by an Army witness in the House committee's hearings, was that the two standards were roughly equivalent to a fourth and fifth-grade education. The Army's defense of the higher standard was, as it had been in 1946, that a smaller force could not absorb the large number of less effective men who would have to be accepted were standards kept at the wartime level. On the other hand, as Senator Gurney pointed out in his defense of the higher standard, only 13 percent of those applying for enlistment in the Army were rejected on these grounds. Senator Gurney's arguments helped to convince his Senate colleagues, and they rejected an amendment requiring a return to the wartime standard. Similar arguments in the House did not fare so well, however; for the House adopted without vote an amendment requiring the Army to accept applicants for enlistment who could score 70 or better on the AGCT.

One other proposal was, at least in part, an attempt to open Army enlistments to a wider pool of eligibles. This was Senator Lodge's (R., Mass.) amendment which would permit the enlistment of up to 25,000 aliens, which was adopted after brief debate.[54]

In addition to attempts to widen the source of volunteers, a number of proposals aimed at making military service more attractive to those already eligible. One, which never reached the stage of a motion to amend the bill, was nevertheless the subject of considerable discussion in both houses. This was the suggestion that volunteers could be found if the financial inducements were made high enough. The only specific proposal made in this vein came from Rules Committee Chairman Leo Allen, who suggested an enlistment bonus plan ($1,000 for a two-year enlistment, $1,500 for three years) as a substitute for Selective Service, and asked that the House Armed Services Committee hold hearings. President Truman reacted to the idea by calling it "asinine," and the House committee did not take it up.[55] On the House floor, Representative Barden (D., N.C.) put the question of military pay in more general terms. How, he asked, will the men be found to build the planes called for in the earlier appropriations, and to build the barracks to house the inductees? "You will pay good salaries. . . . That is how you will get them. Yet to the private in the Army you pay $75 a month." To this, and specifically to Allen's bonus plan, Representative Durham (D., N.D.) responded:

> I would be deeply embarrassed if any Member of Congress would propose that the obligation for service in the armed forces, in this emergency, should or must be accompanied by the payment of some bonus. This would mean that men from the wealthier classes could easily avoid their responsibility by foregoing some trifling amount of money, thereby placing the burden of national security on our poorer and less fortunate classes. In addition to maligning the character of the American citizen such a suggestion presents clear evidence to the people of the world that we are in favor of world peace and security only if it does not interfere with our lives. We will give anything but ourselves.

Repeating the theme that patriotism should not be purchased, Representative Cooley also raised the inevitable question of cost: "Can the Nation ever in war or peace afford to pay the members of their own forces according to their talents? Cooley's question was rhetorical, but an answer had been given on the Senate floor. Observing that American military pay scales were already the highest in the world, Senator Gurney concluded it would be impossible to raise the necessary quantity and quality of volunteers without raising military pay "so high as to be out of all proportion or reason. It is therefore necessary," he urged, "to invoke the obligations of citizenship through selective service."[56]

Low pay was not the only condition alleged to make military service insufficiently attractive. Anticipating repetition of a number of familiar charges, especially against the Army, Senator Gurney offered an extensive survey of the Army's recruiting disadvantages in relation to the Air Force and the Navy. Given the large proportion of the Army stationed overseas, and the inherent differences in service tasks, Gurney concluded "in peace, as in war, that the daily life of the Ground Force soldier contains very little of either the glamour or the comparative luxury of the other services. And," Gurney added, reminding his colleagues of an often overlooked fact, ". . . the Army today is actually maintaining, by voluntary enlistment, a force far larger in size than in either the Navy or the Air Force."[57]

Many senators remained convinced nonetheless that some special remedial steps were needed to improve conditions of service in the

Army. The chosen vehicle was a major revision of the Articles of War (the statutory foundation for discipline in the Army), aimed primarily at providing better legal protection for soldiers brought to trial by courts-martial. These provisions were incorporated in a bill which had been passed by the House (H.R. 2575), and the contents of that bill were offered as an amendment in the Senate. The fact that this action would leave untouched deficiencies in the military justice systems of the Navy and Air Force similar to those in the Army was generally ignored, and the amendment passed.[58]

Opponents of Selective Service did not confine their attacks to questioning the need for a military build-up, delaying the start of inductions, or promoting voluntary recruiting as an alternative to conscription. Several proposals were also offered to mitigate compulsion in manpower procurement; and one of these was the equal of the Shafer delaying amendment, both in attracting support and in threatening evisceration of Selective Service.

The most serious attack on the compulsory principle, and indeed on the effectiveness of Selective Service, was launched in the House by Representative Coudert (R., N.Y.). In the opening debate on the bill, he noted that not one West European country using conscription required a service term of more than twelve months. "Yet . . . in a period when no great war is being waged . . . we are asked to impose upon the American people the harshest and most ruthless draft law in the Western World. Some days earlier, the Senate had rejected a motion by Senator Morse reducing the service period under Selective Service from twenty-four to eighteen months. A similar provision had been included in the 1946 extension of Selective Service; in response to Coudert, Representative Kilday (D., Tex.) recalled that he had been indirectly responsible for it, having successfully introduced the eighteen-month enlistment provision immediately after V-J Day. "I am now convinced," he admitted, "that perhaps the Army knew more about this than I did. They did not get very much out of the [short-term man]. . . . We spent most of the time getting him in and getting him out and darned little time using him." Despite strong objections from Kilday and other House committee members, and the Senate's earlier strong rejection of a shorter term, Coudert offered an amendment reducing the term of inducted service to twelve months. This was adopted, in the strongest mustering of Selective Service opponents in the whole debate.[59]

In contrast to this strong attack on compulsion, it is worth noting an earlier attempt to revive the 1946 debate over minimum age. An amendment proposed in the House to raise the minimum age for induction from nineteen to twenty-one years was defeated easily.[60]

Of all the foregoing changes voted during the Senate and House floor debates, only two really threatened to make Selective Service ineffective as a compulsory manpower procurement program. These were the Shafer amendment, delaying the start of inductions until February, 1949, and the Coudert amendment, shortening the term of involuntary service to twelve months. In conference, both these House threats were blunted. The induction delay was reduced to ninety days, as originally suggested by the House committee; and the requirement for a special presidential finding of strength deficiencies was omitted. The term of inducted service was set at twenty-one months, a considerable compromise toward the Senate and Administration version.

In other decisions, the conference report confirmed a two-year life for the new act; it accepted the House version on lower mental standards for induction and Army enlistment; it omitted Senator Lodge's plan for enlisting aliens; it accepted revisions to the Army's Articles of War; it accepted a House provision for twenty-one-month enlistments in the Army (matching the induction term); and it directed the service secretaries to invigorate their recruiting campaigns.

In sum, only two important compromises over the issue of compulsory procurement were forced upon the Administration. One was the shortened induction term under Selective Service. The second was the replacement of UMT with a set of weak provisions to induce recruiting into the organized reserves.

5.   Equity and Other Social Goals

As in earlier debates, so also in 1948, questions about equity in compulsory procurement and about the impact military policy might have on other social goals for manpower were overshadowed by considerations of military effectiveness, budget costs, and the use of conscription. Only two matters of equity and social goals emerged explicitly in the 1948 debate, although these issues were inherent in a number of noncontroversial decisions as well.

Organization of the new Selective Service System was never in question. Both House and Senate versions accepted Administration recommendations for re-creating the agency almost exactly as it had been formed under the old act. The only important change was a reduction in the number of local boards.

It was not organization, but rather the standards and procedures for classification and induction that were the potentially controversial aspects of Selective Service. Nonetheless, most categories for deferment or exemption were carried over from the old Selective Service provisions without objection. These included: deferment for certain federal and state officials; exemption of ministers and divinity students; and authority for presidential regulation of deferments on grounds of dependency and of physical, mental, or moral deficiencies. The 1946 regulations regarding students were incorporated and extended in the new act: induction of high school students was postponed until graduation or age twenty, whichever was earlier; and college students were entitled to postponement until the end of the academic year in which they were called. A House provision exempting "sole surviving sons" was added in the final version. Again without objection, some changes were made in the provisions for induction into noncombatant service, or for deferment, of conscientious objectors: no alternative work program was prescribed for those deferred; and grounds for claiming status as a conscientious objector were spelled out in more detail, requiring "belief in relation to a Supreme Being," and excluding "essentially political, sociological, or philosophical views or a merely personal moral code."

The problem of balancing equity and military needs against nonmilitary manpower demands did produce mild controversy over one set of classifications. There was some discussion in committee hearings of the need to avoid interference by military manpower requirements with the existing or future pool of scientists, engineers and technicians who would be the source of improved or entirely new weapons of war. In a letter to the House committee, Dr. Vannevar Bush argued that the regulations under which some scientific personnel had been deferred during World War II had not been wholly satisfactory. Even more serious, he said, was the lack of any deferment for students preparing to enter scientific and technical fields; the consequence was a current shortage in scientific manpower estimated at 40,000 to 150,000 at the B.S. level and 7,000 to 17,000 at the Ph.D. level. In response to this problem, the committees' bills included a policy declaration "that adequate provision for national security requires maximum effort in the fields of scientific research and development, and the fullest possible utilization of the Nation's technological, scientific, and other critical manpower resources." Neither committee, however, wished to specify detailed conditions for deferments to promote these goals.

The House committee's bill followed closely the 1940 act's language, authorizing presidential regulation of deferments for "any or all categories of persons whose employment in industry, agriculture, or other occupations or employment . . . or whose continued activity in other endeavors is found to be necessary for the maintenance of the national health, safety, or interest." In House debate, an amendment was proposed to defer all college students until graduation or age twenty-two. Chairman Andrews spoke strongly in opposition. The committee, he said, had considered this question at some length. He cited the bill's provisions for postponing college students' inductions to the end of the academic year, and deferring ROTC students. "The committee thought," he concluded, "that if we went so far as to exempt all college students, it would be committing a highly preferential action which would benefit only the sons of wealthy men." The amendment was rejected by voice vote.[61] Another proposed amendment would have required that all Selective Service regulations, including presidential regulations on deferments, be submitted to the Armed Services Committees, or to subcommittees designated for that purpose; either committee or subcommittee would then have fifteen days in which to exercise a veto over the regulation. Representative Kilday objected, declaring that "Congress has all that it can possibly do in passing laws, and cannot possibly administer those laws." His colleagues agreed, strongly rejecting this proposed legislative veto.[62]

The Senate committee's bill was only a little more explicit on occupational and student deferments, changing the House bill's language on "continued activity in other endeavors" to read "activity in study, research, or medical, scientific, or other endeavors." The final bill, approved in conference, accepted this Senate language.

By explicitly including "study" among the categories of deferrable activities, Congress clearly indicated its support for some form of student deferment program. But it left to the president the task of deciding how this and other deferments would, in practice, balance the private schooling and career plans of registrants, special needs for civilian manpower, and the imposition of compulsory military service, in some equitable fashion.

One other problem of equity and social goals became an important rallying point for some opponents of Selective Service. This was the problem posed by racial segregation in the armed forces. At the Senate committee's hearings, an NAACP spokesman argued that no system of conscription could be considered fair or acceptable so long as that practice continued. This was not a new argument; but it took on a new tone when A. Philip Randolph, speaking for a newly formed Committee against Jim Crow in Military Service, threatened massive civil disobedience against conscription if the argument were not heeded. He proposed a group of amendments which would ban all segregation and discrimination among races in the armed forces, and would also protect servicemen from a wide range of civil discriminatory practices. Should these provisions not be included in the new legislation, Randolph warned, "I personally pledge my self to openly counsel, aid, and abet youth, both white and Negro, to quarantine any Jim Crow conscription system. . . ."[63]

This spectacular threat had little effect on the Senate and House committees. Both their bills did include a provision from the 1940 act, forbidding "discrimination against any person on account of race or color" in selecting persons for induction and in interpreting and executing other provisions of the act. Nonetheless, as some witnesses argued, this provision had not in the past prevented the Selective Service System from issuing wartime induction calls specifying separate white and Negro quotas. Nor had it prevented the armed services from practicing highly discriminatory segregation, by unit and even by type of job. Not too surprisingly, such arguments failed to persuade either committee to add any of Randolph's proposals.

This failure left the committees' bills open to attacks in floor debates, however. These attacks, while not altering the final bill, did considerably prolong the debates; and they very nearly kept the two bills from ever reaching a conference. Only a technical error by Senator Taylor (D., Idaho) enabled the Senate to end a two-man, last-minute filibuster,[64] opening the way for acceptance of the conference report by both houses on the day Congress adjourned for the national party conventions.

The civil rights issue had no further impact on military manpower legislation until the mid-1950's; but problems inherent in occupational, and especially student, deferments would arise to plague Selective Service and the legislative process during the first year of the Korean War. For the time being, however, issues of equity and other social goals for manpower remained dormant.

6. Results of the Debate

In an immediate and limited sense, the major questions of the 1948 debate were answered: the administration had proposed, and Congress had accepted, a build-up of military forces, a build-up balanced among the three services rather than one emphasizing air power, and a build-up depending at least in part on Selective Service to procure the needed manpower. But the 1948 debate left unanswered about as many questions as it resolved, and the meaning of its answers for the future of military manpower procurement policy was far from clear.

One issue was clearly resolved—that of compulsion. From the viewpoint of die-hard opponents of conscription in any form, the proposal and passage of Selective Service marked the end of Administration hypocrisy over this question. For them, compulsion was *the* issue. Long mistrusting the Administration's good faith in its long-range military policy goals of small voluntary forces and UMT-supplied-reserves, they had chosen to see, or to depict, the Administration as bent simply on imposing one form or another of military conscription. From this point of view the debate was lost, at least temporarily. Nonetheless, the compulsions adopted could be applied only on a very limited scale, and for a limited period of time.

Fears for national security, and the apparent need for more military manpower to provide it, proved more compelling than had traditional fears of conscription and militarism. Yet the acceptance of compulsions, in the particular form of Selective Service, raised other issues which were hardly touched at all. For one, the new Selective Service Act imposed an obligation for training and service on all young men in the nineteen to twenty-five age group; but payment on this obligation would be exacted only from a little over half of them, and only for these inductees and volunteers would there be the further obligation to involuntary service in the reserves. Neither the Administration nor its supporters in Congress showed any very fine concern for the question of equity thus raised. Nor was much attention given to the impact of Selective Service on other, nonmilitary goals for the development of American youth. Here the question of higher education was of greatest concern in the debate; but the only decision on student deferments was that some, though by no means all, college students might be eligible; the details were left to administrative determination. These and other issues of equity and impact on other social goals were implicit in a peacetime operation of Selective Service; but the heated struggle to put down the general qualms over compulsion largely overshadowed concern for such questions.

The acceptance of Selective Service did not reflect any clear and unambiguous long-range decisions as to the nature of the military force expansion desired. Neither the Administration and its supporters, nor their opponents, completely abandoned the twin assumptions of the earlier debates—that there would be a transition to a permanent postwar military establishment, and that the active elements in that establishment could and should be supported voluntarily. Thus the Administration remained at least formally committed to a long-range military program stressing strong reserves and universal military training, and Congress paid lip service to these goals by adding to Selective Service some special provisions aimed at strengthening the reserves. Selective Service was promoted by the Administration as a temporary measure, and Congress's action in limiting the life of the act to two years indicates it was accepted in that same spirit. But the nagging question remained: how temporary? And more directly than ever before, this question implied still another: how deep was the administration's commitment, by mid-1948, to a long-range military program relying on UMT and mobilizable reserves?

In the early postwar years, the most effective challenge to such a program had come from those who opposed conscription in any form; their opposition to UMT precluded an assured supply of trained reserves and thus left the possibility of achieving such a force structure in doubt. At the same time there were those who doubted the value of a force structure relying on mobilizable reserves; and by early 1948 it seemed certain that the major challenge to Administration hopes for UMT would come in the form of support for a fundamentally different force structure—one stressing forces-in-being, with the Air Force as the chief component. This was in fact the course taken in the 1948 debate over UMT.

Most of the old arguments against UMT were repeated once again, especially in the hearings. But the clinching argument came with passage in the House, and then the Senate, of the special $822 million appropriation for aircraft procurement. In this limited sense Congress, at least, opted for active air forces in preference to UMT-supported reserves.

Unfortunately for the clarity of the outcome, this was much more a victory for air power over UMT than for forces-in-being over mobilizable reserves; and even that victory was open to later challenge. Left to its own devices, Congress would very likely have been content with a fairly consistent pursuit of security through air power. The Administration, however, yielded in its drive for UMT not to promote air power, but to protect the integrity of the balanced expansion of active forces. The latter, they argued, required immediate reenactment of Selective Service; and if further delay of UMT was to be the cost, then so be it. Yet this choice, like the $822 million appropriation for aircraft, was no clear victory for forces-in-being over mobilizable reserves. The commitment to UMT remained, and events were to prove it was something more than a formality.

Had the debate been conducted and resolved in terms of long-range military policy, it might have been clearer to its participants that the air-power enthusiasts and the supporters of balanced forces were arguing, not over the issue of forces-in-being versus mobilizable reserves, but over the content of forces-in-being. The rudiments of the first issue were, to be sure, present in the debate over air power versus UMT and this debate, in both its specific and its general forms, would be repeated in years to come. But American political debates, especially those with concrete legislative and administrative programs at stake, rarely if ever focus on the long-range issues if shorter-range issues are at hand; and this debate was no exception. The immediate question was: what must we have now in the way of military forces? The Administration wanted a balance among the services (or at least this proved the lowest common denominator for agreement among the services). The Congress would probably have preferred a more single-minded expansion of air power, but it ended by providing for both and letting the Administration choose. Moreover, both Congress, by allowing the choice, and the Administration, by opting for balanced forces, left open the question of long-range military policy. In so doing, they likewise postponed answering the question of how temporary Selective Service would be.

Answers to these questions depended on the answer to yet another: what was the nature of the threat which a military establishment was to meet? As it had not in 1946, the Administration did in 1948 explicitly and openly recognize a Soviet threat to national security; and the 1948 act was not billed solely or even primarily as a stop-gap measure designed to smooth the transition to a permanent peacetime establishment. The response from Congress was different, too. In 1946, it had imposed a ceiling of about 1.5 million men on the active forces, good for one year, on the understanding that even this would be further reduced as quickly as possible. In 1948, Congress authorized active forces totalling over 2 million men, more than the Administration had asked for and good for at least the two-year life of the act; and it exacted no promises of later reductions. Moreover, it was apparent on all sides that the forces being provided might have to fight a war, not simply man a postwar occupation. In all these ways, then, it was accepted that the 1948 act was a response to a situation clearly different from that posed, or perceived, in 1946.

Only in retrospect is it equally clear that the threat posed in 1948, and the response to it, also differed from the threat and response in 1940—that, in short, the 1948 act was peacetime conscription as the 1940 act had not been. However much the point may have been argued in the summer of 1940, there was general agreement by the spring of 1948 that the earlier act had been a response to an existing and growing international emergency. Moreover, the very drama of President Truman's address to Congress, and of the international events surrounding it, suggested that his 1948 proposals might be responses to a similar emergency. Secretary Forrestal, on the other hand, took some pains to distinguish the proposals for force expansion as short-run, but not emergency, measures. There was in all this, and in the congressional debates, very little open recognition that the immediate and long-range needs for military forces might be essentially the same—that the long-run required not a "peacetime" military establishment, but an active military deterrent force. The spring of 1948 brought only the beginnings of realization that the times were already "normal"—as normal as they were likely to be for some time to come.

In sum, the Selective Service Act of 1948 left unanswered some important questions about the equity and impact of its operation, about the kind of military force structure it was eventually to provide, and indeed about the very nature and duration of the security threat it was to meet. In Hanson Baldwin's judgment at the time, "fundamentally it represents—though without too much cogent reasoning about the means—America's desire for security."[65]

In practical and immediate terms, however, the act did grant Forrestal's minimum requests. Congress authorized a balanced expansion of the active forces, and it provided the manpower procurement machinery required to produce it. How that authorization and procurement machinery were used, and the implications of this use for subsequent manpower procurement policies, are examined in the next section.

III. SLOW BEGINNINGS OF PEACETIME CONSCRIPTION

1. *Budgetary Constraints on Active Forces*

The Selective Service Act of 1948 became law on June 24. The story of Selective Service in the two years following was strongly shaped, indeed very nearly determined, some six weeks earlier, in the opening round of intra-Administration bargaining over the defense budget for FY 1950.

The process of infighting, bargaining, and unsatisfying compromise which produced the FY 1950 defense budget proposals has been recounted elsewhere in detail.[66] The key to the outcome lay in the early expressed intentions of President Truman and his budget director, James Webb, to level off defense spending at about $15 billion a year. The immediate issue in May, 1948, was the size of the FY 1949 supplemental appropriation. After a month-long struggle, Forrestal had finally compromised with the joint chiefs on a figure of $3.481 billion. Webb argued that the programs and spending levels which this implied would lead to a defense budget of $18-20 billion by FY 1952, far above the desired ceiling. In the end, President Truman and Webb won their budget battle. The impact on active force manpower levels was a sharp reduction from those contemplated in the fight for Selective Service.

Over the next two years, none of the services reached the goals set by Forrestal in his April, 1948, compromise, much less the higher levels authorized in the new Selective Service Act (see Table 5).

TABLE 5

ACTIVE FORCES MANPOWER GOALS AND STRENGTHS, 1948-1950
(In Thousands)

	Total	Army	Navy (including Marine Corps)	Air Force
Actual, March 31, 1948*	1,399	540	490	368
Authorized by Selective Service Act of 1948†	2,006	837	667	502
Actual, June 30, 1948*	1,446	554	504	388
Actual, June 30, 1949*	1,615	660	536	419
Budgeted for FY 1950‡	1,616	677	527	412
Actual, June 30, 1950*	1,460	593	456	411
Budgeted for FY 1951‡	1,507	630	461	416

* SOURCE: U.S. Department of Defense, Directorate for Statistical Services, *Selected Manpower Statistics* (Washington: Department of Defense, April 11, 1966), p. 19.

† Figures authorized for the one-year training program are not included in these totals but are as follows: Army, 110,000; Navy (including Marine Corps), 36,000; Air Force, 15,000. The total manpower authorized under this program was 161,000.

‡ SOURCE: U.S., *The Budget of the United States Government, Fiscal Year 1950* (Washington: U.S. Government Printing Office, 1949), p. M-22; *Fiscal Year 1951*, p. M.29. Figures are for average annual strengths.

Strengths of all services did expand during FY 1949, but all contracted during FY 1950. Indeed, in the Navy and Marine Corps the expansion was so slight and the contraction so great that both those services finished FY 1950 at lower strength levels than they had achieved before Selective Service was reenacted.

Had Congress and the public become aware of President Truman's budget and service strength intentions at the same time Forrestal and the joint chiefs heard of them, it is doubtful that the Selective Service Act would have survived to passage. (When the president gave his budget guidelines to Forrestal, the service secretaries, and the joint chiefs on May 13, the Senate Armed Services Committee had just reported its Selective Service bill, and the House bill had yet to come up on the Rules Committee's agenda.) But press and congressional attentions were focused on the immediate legislative struggle and on ominous events in Berlin, rather than on the beginnings of a budget which would not be announced formally for nearly seven months and would not be implemented until more than a year later. Moreover, only one party to the ensuing battle over the FY 1950 defense budget stood to gain anything by publicizing the newly intended cutbacks and at the same time not lose by endangering Selective Service; and President Truman took special pains to assure that this party, the Air Force, thoroughly understood his desire to keep the new budget quarrel inside the Administration for the time being.[67] Thus the legislative battle over Selective Service went forward untouched by the Administration's concurrent, and very pertinent, change of direction regarding service strengths.

2. *Selective Service in Operation.*

The Selective Service System, once reestablished, also went forward with little initial regard for the new budgetary portents of reduced manpower demands. Indeed, there is no evidence in the System's reports that the agency was even told of the May decisions on the defense budget and their probable consequences for force goals. "From the start, the System had not expected any sizeable operation. It had looked forward to filling regular monthly calls of modest size. . . ." But by this the System apparently meant calls on the order of 30,000 a month.[68]

Before any calls could be met, the System had to be reconstituted in operating form. In the fifteen months since March, 1947, the wartime organization had been sharply reduced but not completely liquidated. General Hershey had stayed on as director of the interim Office of Selective Service Records; that office had preserved an organization at national and state levels; and it had carried on limited training programs in anticipation of some future restoration of Selective Service.[69] All this made the transition to active operations easier than it had been in 1940. To no one's surprise, Hershey was again named director. The transition was effected during July and August, and registrations began on August 30.[70]

During this time, there were weak attempts to make A. Philip Randolph's threat of civil disobedience against Selective Service a reality. Asked about this, Hershey told reporters that draft law enforcement "was a matter for the Justice Department." President Truman followed up his civil rights stand at the Democratic convention in July, by issuing an executive order calling for the orderly end to segregation in the armed forces. And the Selective Service System dropped its earlier practice of setting separate quotas for Negroes in its induction calls. The NAACP announced it could not support a program of civil disobedience, and the resistance movement soon collapsed.[71]

The initial draft call, announced on August 30 for delivery in November, was very modest indeed. Advance word was that it would be for 15,000; but the official call was for only 10,000, with the reduction accounted for by rising enlistments. Later, calls were announced for 15,000 in December and 20,000 in January, 1949, with the implication that further calls would continue at the January level.[72]

Not until early November, 1948, were the reduced active force goals reflected clearly in demands placed on Selective Service. At that time the January call was cut in half, to 10,000, and the February call was set at only 5,000. These reduced calls were publicly attributed by the National Munitions Board to the $15 billion ceiling on the FY 1950 military budget. Finally, in mid-January, with the armed forces already somewhat over the new strength goals set for June 30, 1949, and with Army enlistments up to about 35,000 per month, the February draft call was cancelled and inductions came to a halt.[73]

The downward trend in strength goals and actual service

strengths continued through 1949 and early 1950. Despite a pre-diction by General Hershey in the fall of 1949 that the armed forces might have to resort to inductions again soon, there was never any realistic basis during this period for expecting that the draft holiday would not continue indefinitely. Indeed, reduced strength ceilings also led to cutbacks in recruiting; and in January, 1950, all services temporarily halted voluntary enlistments.[74]

The cessation of inductions no doubt had some adverse impact on morale in the Selective Service System, but this was minor compared to the blow dealt the System by Congress. Its appropriation for FY 1950 was only a little over half the amount requested by the Ad-minstration for Selective Service operations. In addition to drastic cuts in national and state personnel and operations, this reduced appropriation forced the System to place almost all local boards on a part-time basis (some were open less than one day a week) and to group boards and their records into a smaller number of office lo-cations. Registration duties were, in some instances, turned over to other government officials or even private citizens. The Administra-tion submitted a much smaller budget request for FY 1951, and thus seemed prepared to accept these cutbacks and their impact on the System's potential for rapid re-expansion in response to any future manpower demands.[75]

3.   UMT versus the Seventy-Group Air Force, 1949.

In January, 1949, President Truman announced his FY 1950 de-fense budget. It included, among other items, a planned reduction in Air Force strength to forty-eight groups. It also followed up a renewed request for UMT legislation by including $800 million for the first year's operation of that program.[76] It remained for Carl Vinson, now chairman of the House Armed Services Committee, to juxtapose these two parts of the budget, and thus to touch off a brief renewal of debate over UMT versus air power.

Late that month, Vinson's committee opened hearings on a bill to make permanent the organizational and strength authorizations for the Army and the Air Force. The bill, approved by the president, included authorization for a seventy-group Air Force; and Secretary Symington readily agreed with Vinson's observation that the reason this goal was not part of the current budget program was "because of dollars and cents." Vinson then revealed his new tactic: "I hardly think," he said, "that the Congress is going to pass any universal military training bill this go-around. So . . . why wouldn't it be a good idea to use that $800,000,000 to try to carry out the objective which you all agree on, which is a 70-air-group [force]. It would help that much, would it not?" Symington responded: "You are asking me, sir?" For the moment, Vinson ignored this request for a cue, but he picked it up later and gave Symington the weekend to produce details on how much additional air strength could be bought for $800 million. Three days later, Symington reported that the addition would be nine air groups, a fifty-seven group force in FY 1950 instead of the budgeted forty-eight. A week later, the House committee formally endorsed Vinson's plan to ask the Appropriations Committee for a shift in funds.[77]

That was the beginning, and very nearly the end, of this last confrontation between the seventy-group Air Force program and UMT. Given the atmosphere created by the indefinite halt of inductions, it seems doubtful that UMT could have stirred much public or congressional support, even if considered on its merits alone. It was, in fact, hardly considered at all; and, as Millis concludes, the continued pressure for a larger Air Force certainly contributed to this result.[78] Nor did the Air Force program become accepted policy. The challenge it offered to the concept of balanced active forces was drained off into a bitter controversy over the relative merits of the B-36 bomber and sea-borne striking forces; and the result of this was yet another assertion of presidential control, vis-à-vis the Air Force and Congress, over the expenditure of appropriated funds.[79]

The implications of this brief confrontation between UMT and air power for the larger issue of forces-in-being versus mobilizable reserves were hardly considered at all. That issue did come to the fore in a rather different context, however, as the Administration sought legislative extension of the Selective Service Act.

4. Selective Service Extension, 1950.

Late in 1948, in a speech that defended Selective Service as one means of keeping the peace, General Omar Bradley voiced a need for a long-range military policy that would not shift "every time a paper is rustled east of the Elbe River." By the end of 1949, enough hints had been dropped, by Army Secretary Gordon Gray, General Hershey, and Defense Secretary Louis Johnson, to make it clear that the Administration would ask for retention of Selective Service as one means to stabilizing the legislative base for military planning. A few weeks later President Truman made the request formal: "While the world remains unsettled . . . , and as long as our own security and the security of the free world require, we will maintain a strong and well-balanced defense organization. The Selective Service System is an essential part of our defense plans, and it must be continued."[80]

There was no serious doubt that legislation preserving Selective Service in some form would pass; nevertheless, the precise form, and indeed the future of Selective Service as a working engine of manpower procurement, did remain in doubt right up to, and past, the deadline for extension on June 24, 1950. Hearings on a bill sponsored by the Defense Department, to extend the Selective Service Act of 1948 for three years without further amendment, opened in the House Armed Services Committee in late January. In early February, after seven sittings, Chairman Vinson called a halt and the committee took no action. Three months later the committee again took up the measure; it voted unanimously to report a heavily rewritten version, which the House accepted in late May.[81] Two weeks later, after only two days of hearings, the Senate Armed Services Committee reported its own version, one very close to the Defense Department's original bill. The Senate amended this, bringing its provisions a little closer to those in the House bill, agreed to this amended bill, and asked for a conference on June 22.[82] By that time, the deadline for expiration of the Selective Service Act was less than thirty-six hours away. But on the same day, the Senate and House passed a joint resolution extending the act for fifteen days, to July 9.[83] Given one very important difference between the Senate and House versions, it seems likely that the conference committee might have needed all that time, and perhaps more, to reach agreement on an extension act. As it happened, however, the major issue dividing the two houses was resolved not in conference, but in Korea. On June 27, less than three days after the North Korean Army's invasion across the thirty-eighth parallel, the conference committee agreed to a report recommending extension of the Selective Service Act for one year (to July 9, 1951) without changes, and authorizing the president to call up the National Guard and other reserves. The House and Senate quickly accepted the report, and the president signed the extension act on June 30.[84]

Of the numerous differences between the House and Senate versions prior to the conference, only one offered serious obstacles to agreement. Neither version was quite what the Administration had asked; but here, too, there was only one serious issue—the same one dividing the two houses. The Administration had asked, originally, that the Selective Service Act of 1948 be extended without alteration for three years. (This would round out the five years originally proposed in 1948. The House committee preferred a two-year provision, arguing that further extensions should be considered in election years. The Senate committee showed no particular interest in the question, but retained the three-year provision, probably for bargaining purposes.) Throughout the debate, there was no major challenge to the proposition that the Selective Service System should be retained, and little dissent from the proposition that it should continue to register and classify young men. The central issue, the one dividing the House from the Senate, and both from the Administration, was that of inductions. There had been no draft calls under the act for over a year; and, General Hershey to the contrary, there was no public suggestion before mid-June of 1950 that any new calls were being planned. It was natural, then, that Congress should question the Administration's request for a three-year extension of its authority to issue induction calls; and question it did.

Differences among Administration, House, and Senate positions on extension of Selective Service arose from two interrelated aspects of this issue of induction authority. The first was the obvious question: who should have the legal power to decide for or against any resumption of inductions? The Selective Service Act of 1948 had given that power to the president; and, by proposing a simple extension, the Administration in effect said this was where that power should remain. The House committee took a different view. Its report recommended that presidential authority to order inductions be suspended, pending a concurrent resolution by Congress that such action was necessary; and the House-passed bill included this feature. The Senate committee sided with the Administration; but on the Senate floor, an amendment was added providing that there be no further inductions under the act unless such action were declared necessary either (1) by a concurrent resolution of the Congress, or (2) should Congress not be in session, by a presidential declaration. These various answers to the first question suggested a simple disagreement over what powers the Congress might properly delegate to the president.

The second question regarding the induction authority was: what circumstances would justify a resumption of inductions? Answers to this question reflected more than disagreement over the distribution of powers. Indeed, they revealed a profound disagreement, and some considerable confusion, over the very purpose of Selective Service. On one side was the view that Selective Service should be preserved, but used only as a means of rapid mobilization in a major emergency. On the other side was the argument that Selective Service should be used whenever necessary to maintain or increase active force strengths, whether that need might arise from a specific military emergency, or from an upward assessment of active force needs, or simply from a decline in voluntary enlistments.

The key figure in the attempt to resolve these two questions was House committee chairman Carl Vinson. At the very first day of hearings, he took the position that Congress should decide on any resumption of inductions, and that this decision should be in response to emergency mobilization demands: "Why should we leave to the military the authority to induct . . . , especially in view of the fact that if an emergency arises, we have some 350,000 Guardsmen . . . [and] thousands of Reservists who can be called in, and Congress can promptly pass a concurrent resolution authorizing induction to begin."[85] Vinson stuck with this position right into the conference stage.

The Administration's position was not that clear. Its original proposal was to leave the induction authority in the president's hands. It did show willingness to compromise; under pressure from Vinson, Secretary Johnson was able to report acceptance by the joint chiefs and the president of a proviso reserving authority to resume inductions either to a concurrent resolution by the Congress, or "until such time as the President, after consulting with the National Security Council, shall make a finding that international conditions warrant the resumption of inductions."[86] But this sort of compromise would leave open the question of what circumstances might justify resumption of inductions. On this, and therefore on the question of the real purpose of Selective Service, the Administration seemed throughout to be lacking in candor, or at best confused.

From time to time in the hearings, Administration witnesses cited both purposes, saying Selective Service was equally important as a means, directly or indirectly (through pressure to enlist), of maintaining service strengths, and as a means of rapid expansion in an emergency. The former was more in keeping with the uses of Selective Service since its reenactment in 1948. But in the 1950 debate, only General Collins, the Army chief of staff, gave any clear indication that inductions might have to be resumed if enlistments failed to meet normal service needs. General Bradley, chairman of the joint chiefs, stated on the contrary: "There is no intention, so far as I know, of exercising the provisions of the Selective Service Act in the near future, or for that matter in peacetime in general." Most Administration witnesses probably recalled that the idea of emergency expansion had been uppermost in the minds of many congressmen and much of the public in the 1948 debate; and most of them, like Secretary Gray, preferred to stress the second purpose: "The basic reason for advocating the continuance of the selective service law is mobilization and its vital time element."[87]

Stressing emergency mobilization as the purpose of resuming inductions of course led back to the question of why that authority should remain in the president's hands. General Bradley gave this explanation: "It seemed to us that there ought to be some proviso that in case of an emergency so dire that you [Congress] could not assemble properly, the President ought to have that authority."[88] Of course, declining enlistments would scarcely constitute such a dire emergency. On the other hand, under the Administration's compromise proviso the president might sometime conclude that international conditions did, indeed, require resumption of inductions to supplement and spur voluntary enlistments. It is likely that the House committee recognized this possibility, and that they wondered just how firmly the Administration was committed to a mobilization concept of Selective Service.

One element almost wholly absent from the public record would easily account both for Vinson's position and for the Administration's discomfort. There was no strong mustering of support behind a move to let Selective Service expire in June, but Vinson's maneuvers can be read as an attempt to prevent just that. After squeezing a compromise out of the Administration in January, Vinson dropped the whole matter for two months. When hearings resumed in May, they followed Vinson's sudden announcement that "worsening world conditions" had forced him to pursue the subject further.[89] The second round of hearings was devoted mostly to General Bradley's "drab but realistic" litany of troubles in China, Indochina, the Philippines, Bulgaria, Hungary, and Trieste. The House committee's report argued that current world conditions differed little from those of 1948. In House debate, Vinson pointed out that his committee's version of extension was supported by many members who had voted against Selective Service two years earlier. Key opponents of the 1948 act, including former Rules Committee chairman Leo Allen (R., Ill.), testified to a change of heart. And one signer of the 1948 minority report, Representative Havenner (D., Calif.), praised the committee's return to the principles of 1940, predicting "that the Military Establishment will never again, except in national emergencies, be given compulsory authority over the lives and liberties of American men."[90] This evidence does not prove, but it strongly suggests, that Vinson's weak version of extension was the price he paid to avoid a split in his committee and a lengthy floor debate. And the lack of candor among Administration witnesses strongly suggests they realized Vinson's difficulties were their own as well, and were willing to pay a good part of Vinson's price to avoid them.

Whatever the reasons, the House committee clearly recorded its view of Selective Service as a piece of emergency mobilization machinery; it concluded that the decision to resume inductions should be left to Congress in order to protect the nation "from administrative whimsy in the implementation of Selective Service authority." Underlining this view, the committee further argued that any resolution to resume inductions should also authorize a call of reserves, and that this call "should precede, not follow, the resorting to inductions."[91]

Reporting after the House had acted favorably on its committee's bill, the Senate committee took a different view of Selective Service, though there is no record that the Administration urged this on them. It concluded that the 1948 act had been intended to meet existing manpower shortages, not some future threat of national disaster: "In summary, the 1948 act would prevent emergencies. The House version makes it necessary for Congress actually to declare an emergency in order to attempt to prevent one."[92] Rejecting fears of "administrative whimsy," the Senate committee recommended elimination of the House provisions for congressional control of inductions and a prerequisite call-up of reserves. On the Senate floor, this position was modified somewhat by adding a compromise proviso: no inductions would be permitted unless (1) Congress declared they were necessary to supplement enlistments, or (2) the president, Congress not in session, declared the existence of a "national necessity" (the word "emergency" was explicitly avoided) requiring an increase in the armed forces up to appropriated strengths.[93]

There is no way of knowing how the conference committee might have resolved this issue of induction authority had not the North Korean Army intervened. It seems highly probable that any compromise between the House and Senate versions would have impaired severely the usefulness of Selective Service as a working engine of manpower procurement, especially its usefulness as a spur to voluntary enlistments. As it turned out, Selective Service survived, eventually to become entrenched as the very core of this country's military manpower procurement policies.

IV. MANPOWER POLICY ISSUES ON THE EVE OF THE KOREAN WAR

Before this could happen, the major issues in the policy debate had to undergo further resolution than had been achieved to date. A part of one of these issues did seem to have been settled, though, and remained so until the mid-1960's. Between the Korean and Vietnamese wars there were only two important national challenges to the conclusion that compulsory military service was an acceptable feature of American military policy, one by Adlai Stevenson in 1956, the other by Barry Goldwater in 1964. Neither was at all successful. Moreover, neither of these challenges rested primarily on what had been the most effective argument against compulsion in the early postwar years—that it would destroy traditional social and political balances and end in militarizing American youth and the nation. Indeed, this ideological argument against compulsion in manpower procurement followed second only to fear of entangling alliances as an early casualty in the nation's reaction to the cold war.

Challenges to compulsion were, in the fifties and early sixties, almost invariably couched in terms of declining need for it; and for the time being, this question seemed also to have been settled. Nevertheless, given the circumstances under which the 1950 extension of Selective Service was approved, it is unlikely that many in Congress meant this approval to be a permanent decision that conscription would henceforth have to be employed or threatened to supply needed defense forces. Rather, it is more reasonable to read the conference report and the votes accepting it (315-4 in the House, 76-0 in the Senate) as an immediate response to a clear international emergency—not unlike a declaration of war.[94] Certainly, there had never been any expression of strong congressional support for Selective Service as a permanently operating manpower procurement device, and few votes for the one-year extension could be read as such.

Attitudes in the Administration and among the military leadership toward the issue of compulsion can be appraised only partly in terms of that issue alone. At no point in the postwar debate over manpower procurement policies had these groups evidenced any real moral qualms over the possible impact of conscription on the fabric of American political and social traditions. This is not to suggest that, for example, General Marshall and those who followed his lead were insincere in their professed belief that peacetime conscription for active service would be unacceptable as a long-range policy. Rather it is to emphasize that their preference for UMT (conscription for training only) involved nearly as strong a rejection of the traditionalist argument against conscription as would have an alternative preference for a permanent Selective Service operation. Nor did the enthusiasts for air power, at least those in the Administration and the military establishment, take any more than tactical comfort from the traditionalist position and its apparent strength in Congress and among the public at large. There were, on the other hand, very important differences on the Executive side over the need for compulsion. These differences emerged as a debate not over the need for compulsion alone, however, but over military requirements and cost efficiency as well.

In 1948, the Administration's official policy for a long-term, permanent military establishment had still been expressed in terms of UMT to supply large, trained reserves backing small, highly professional active forces. Open opposition to this policy, within the Administration and among some elements of Congress and the public, had been cast in terms of active air power as the most needed, and perhaps the only necessary, form of defense. Seeking a middle course, and having in mind some pressing needs for active ground forces, Forrestal had approved and fought for a balanced active establishment rather larger than the one in existence; but he had been forced to rest his case publicly on an agreement among the joint chiefs, which accepted the argument favoring an active air force and then pressed for larger ground and naval forces to make the air element viable. In the crush of interservice rivalries, and the press to get something from Congress, UMT had been postponed once again; but Selective Service had been accepted as a means to producing the manpower for a balanced establishment.

The aim of rebuilding the active military establishment, contemplated by the Selective Service Act of 1948, had been sharply revised even before the act was passed, in the form of the Truman-Webb restrictions on current and future defense budgets. One consequence of this had been to drive the joint chiefs and the Defense Department into even greater reliance on active air power, and its capability for atomic retaliation, as the central feature of American military strength.[95] During the same period the Administration, or at least the Army, had abandoned neither its hopes for UMT nor its deep-seated belief in the mobilizable-reserves force structure which that program implied.[96] Nevertheless, neither of these force structure concepts, nor the national security strategies they implied, had been pursued with any consistent vigor either before or after the 1948 enactment of Selective Service. Moreover, none of the public debate, and very little of the intra-Administration struggle among the services and between Defense and the Budget Bureau, had served yet to relate the issues of military requirements realistically to what was coming to be the accepted Administration foreign policy.

Since 1947, American foreign policy had been increasingly rooted in the concept of containment—a concept given its first public airing in George Kennan's now famous article in *Foreign Affairs*, and later elaborated in an early document of the National Security Council, NSC-20.[97] But neither the Kennan article nor NSC-20 had offered very much guidance on requirements for military forces to support, or if need be implement, a general strategy of containment. At the same time, the continuing debate over military requirements and force structure had dealt only peripherally with the military problems of containment. Instead, the primary concern at first had been with separately conceived goals of the military services—UMT and mobilizable reserves for the Army, the Navy's fleet-in-being, and the seventy-group Air Force. Eventually attention had shifted to preserving some role for ground and naval forces, as budgetary constraints pointed more and more to deterrence through atomic air power. As Samuel Huntington put it, "The two great constraints on effective military planning, the doctrinal heritage from the past and the pressure of military needs, combined to produce a serious gap between military policy and foreign policy."[98]

By January, 1950, a great deal of pressure had built up within the Administration for a thorough review of foreign and military policy and, specifically, for some attempt to establish a realistic relation between these fundamental elements of national security strategy. Perhaps the most important of these pressures came from the policy gap itself. Since 1948, the renewed pursuit of defense economy, the parallel intensification of service rivalries, the growing budgetary demands of foreign aid and the newly approved Mutual Defense Assistance Program, and the new threats to national security and international stability posed by the fall of China and the Soviet detonation of an atomic device—all these made the policy gap seem larger and more dangerous than ever before. By January, 1950, partly in response to these problems, partly growing out of intra-Administration negotiations over development of the H-bomb, and partly inspired by organizational self-conceptions, there were several moves underway which pointed toward a thoroughgoing review of military and foreign policy. Specific authorization for such a study came from the president on January 20, and by mid-March an ad hoc study group composed of representatives from the Departments of State and Defense had prepared an initial draft. After extensive circulation and considerable maneuvering, this paper was endorsed by Secretaries Acheson and Johnson and given to the president. On April 12, President Truman gave the study preliminary approval by referring it to the National Security Council. The document, henceforth known as NSC-68, lacked specific recommendations on military programs and budgets; and the president called for an NSC subcommittee, representing the Bureau of the Budget, the Council of Economic Advisors, and the Economic Cooperation Administration, as well as the State, Treasury, and Defense Departments, to do the hard work of programing and costing.[99]

NSC-68 was more than a review of American foreign and military policies; it was a call for action. "Here, for the first time, was an overall definition of goals and a general statement of methods oriented primarily to the needs of the cold war. Unlike the programs and goals of the services dating back to World War II, this was a response to existing and future conditions." Specifically, the paper "urged the expansion of American capabilities for both limited war and all-out war and the strengthening of the allies of the United States. All this would require a vast expansion of the security effort."[100] But, as noted above, the paper incorporated not even the most general cost estimates. These had been estimated variously, in terms of an annual defense budget, at about $35 billion by State Department representatives on the study group, and a much more modest $17-$18 billion by Defense Department members.[101] Moreover, the paper included neither an extensive examination of military strategy, nor any program for rearmament beyond the proposed target date of 1954 (the year by which, it was assumed, the Soviet Union would have a strategic nuclear capability). The omission of any details on military strategy was a bow to interservice conflicts which the study group wished to avoid; and the lack of programs was a consequence of both the other omissions. "What the group did do," says Hammond, "was to make the case that strategic air power was not enough—perhaps the most important single point needed in military strategy then and in the decade since then. . . ."[102]

NCS-68, both as a fresh case for balanced active forces which was much more realistic than the case Forrestal had to work with in 1948, and as a call for a rearmament of major proportions, certainly should have had some bearing on the concurrent attempt to extend Selective Service. A "vast expansion of the security effort" of the sort contemplated by NSC-68 would require sharp increases in active service strengths; and past experience suggested a central role for Selective Service in attaining and maintaining such increases. Yet the testimony of Administration witnesses supporting extension of Selective Service, especially that of Secretary Johnson, lent itself easily to Vinson's plan for converting Selective Service into a mere piece of stand-by machinery for an emergency mobilization. Even if this was not what they had in mind, Johnson and his civilian and military subordinates did little to dispel Vinson's interpretation of their intent.

To be sure, the initial testimony on Selective Service extension was given in the House committee before the study leading to NSC-68 had even begun. One can, perhaps, read into the renewed activity on the issue, in late April and early May, a Defense Department reaction to the preliminary results of the study. Nevertheless, none of the open testimony at the May hearings in the House committee or at the Senate committee's hearings in June suggested anything like a major revolution in Defense and Administration attitudes toward national security strategy, force structure, or the immediate need for compulsion in manpower procurement. Of course, NSC-68 had not proposed any specific programs. Such filling-in of the general policy position had hardly begun as the Selective Service issue approached its legislative deadline in late June.[103] Even so, it is difficult indeed to reconcile any presumed Administration intent to push strongly for the rearmament proposed in NSC-68 with its publicly recorded willingness to see Selective Service, the most likely engine of manpower procurement to support such a rearmament, converted into something useful only to an emergency-mobilization concept of strategy and force structure.

The evidence from the Selective Service debate tends to confirm both Hammond's and Huntington's findings concerning NSC-68 and the general Administration position on defense on the eve of the Korean War. First, the member of the Administration most directly affected by NSC-68's implications, Defense Secretary Johnson, was also the one least sympathetic to them; and this lack of sympathy colored the public, and even the private, advice given by General Bradley and other JCS members perhaps as much as did any intellectual hangover from older service doctrines or any immersion in the "climate of opinion" which supported drastic economies in defense budgets. As a consequence, Johnson and the Defense Department were slow to accept the full thrust of NSC-68, and it seems likely that Johnson himself never fully incorporated it into his own thinking.[104] Second, up to the outbreak of hostilities in Korea, the president and the Administration as a whole had adopted no clear course toward a major rearmament to provide military forces capable both of deterring an all-out war and of deterring or otherwise dealing with limited conflicts.[105]

On the manpower procurement issue of the need for compulsion, then, the salvaging of Selective Service in mid-1950 represented something more of a long-range commitment on the part of the Administration than it did for an emergency-minded Congress. Even so, this commitment to the need for compulsion was simply the unstated consequence of pending shifts in the Administration's position on military force needs and the related costs. It would be some time before the details of these shifts could be made clear, in terms of firm decisions on force structure, manpower requirements, and the relations of Selective Service to these. Before discussing the problems involved in these decisions (see Chapter 3), it will be useful to review the progress, or lack thereof, on other issues in the general debate over manpower procurement policy.

One of these was the effectiveness of procurement programs in providing the needed manpower. Here two sets of questions were raised, one concerning recruiting programs prior to the Korean War, the other dealing with the effectiveness of the Selective Service Act of 1948 as a large-scale manpower procurement system.

Given the halt of inductions in January, 1949, and the absence of any clear intent to resume them (until late June, 1950), it is obvious that voluntary enlistments were meeting current manpower requirements. Its is not clear, however, that the voluntary system could have continued to be successful after June, 1950, even if service strength goals had stayed low, had Congress removed the threat of inductions. Administration supporters laid great stress on the value of the induction threat to recruiting success, and upwards of 200,000 "volunteers" were credited largely to this factor alone.[106] Critics of the Administration suggested that other factors were at work, specifically the rise in unemployment during 1949, and the military pay increases enacted during that year. The point was moot; for not since June, 1948, had recruiting been conducted without support from at least a minimal threat of inductions. (The critics overlooked the facts that the new pay act did not become effective until October, 1949, and that it offered no increase in pay for the lowest enlisted grade.)[107]

Questions about the appropriateness of the existing Selective Service program to large-scale inductions were, understandably, couched in hypothetical terms during the extension debate; but the problems proved serious once inductions were resumed to meet Korean War needs. The immediate evidence for this lies in a series of actions, many involving legislation, taken during the opening weeks of the conflict. The extension act, signed on June 30, left intact the president's power to order inductions, and he authorized use of this source for manpower on July 7; the initial Defense call upon the Selective Service System was for only 20,000 in September; but by the end of July the Army raised the call to 50,000 in September and an equal number in October.[108] Late in July the president signed into law an act permitting him to extend the term of enlistment of those already in service.[109] A week later, a second law was signed, suspending the authorized strength limitations set in the 1948 act until July 31, 1954.[110] In another month Congress produced two much more complex pieces of legislation affecting manpower procurement. One restored the World War II system of dependents' allowances.[111] This had been wiped out in the 1949 pay act, and restored in effect for noncommissioned officers only; now, with a call-up of reservists and a possible revocation of automatic deferment from induction for married men, it could no longer be assumed that privates and junior corporals would be bachelors. A second act expanded the Selective Service authority to permit induction—effectively to promote volunteering—of medical, dental and allied specialists up to age fifty-one.[112] In yet another attempt to alter the manpower procurement system legislatively, the Administration sought repeal of the one-year enlistment program, which had been Congress's inventive substitute for UMT in 1948. This proposal passed the Senate in altered form, but the House committee ignored it.[113] These actions were considered to be the minimum changes required, pending a thorough review by the Administration and Congress, to make the 1948 version of Selective Service workable in a period of heavy manpower demands.

There was also some evidence that interest in the related issues of equity and the impact of military manpower demands on other sectors of the economy and society was reviving in the administration, in Congress, and among the public at large. These issues did not emerge clearly, however, until 1951.

In sum, the nation entered the Korean War period of mobilization and rearmament with a manpower procurement system not entirely suited to its needs. The major point to be made about progress in the policy debate up to this time, however, is the important difference in attitudes held by the Administration and Congress toward the central purpose of the procurement system. In the Administration there had been, through the spring of 1950, growing agreement that our foreign policy required a major expansion of active forces; and this implied a manpower procurement system able to achieve that expansion, and then maintain it. The opening of war in Korea at once served to confirm that conclusion, and created a climate in which new military force goals could be pursued. Congress, on the other hand, had expressed general satisfaction with our military forces (at least their manpower strengths) as they were in the spring of 1950, and the Administration had not begun to advise them differently. Consequently Congress had seen no reason to preserve the compulsory element in manpower procurement, except on a stand-by basis for an emergency; and the Korean War outbreak did not immediately alter this attitude toward long-term procurement policies. Thus it remained for the decisions and events of the Korean War mobilization, and of later years, to complete the process which the abortive rearmament of 1948 had begun: the entrenchment of Selective Service as the central machinery of military manpower procurement for the cold war.

chapter three

Korean Rearmament and Cold War Policy

I. DECISION FOR PARTIAL MOBILIZATION

Within hours of the North Korean invasion across the thirty-eighth parallel, American air and naval forces were committed to the defense of South Korea. Ground troops followed shortly after, and very soon practically all American ground fighting forces available in the west Pacific were locked into a desperate defensive retreat down the Korean Peninsula. In Washington, Defense officials involved in gathering, training, and transporting replacements and reinforcements for the two divisions and the air and sea elements already committed in Korea were giving these immediate needs top priority. Yet in middle- and long-range Defense planning, the war requirements for Korea were far from being the only considerations, and were not always even the most important.

Through the early postwar years, interservice debates and public discussion of military strategic policy had usually assumed that the next war, like the last, would be a general conflict calling upon all the resources of the nation to turn back a major military threat to our independent existence. The conflict in strategic debate came over just how the nation's power might best be readied for and brought to bear in such a struggle. The most important weapon in our arsenal was, clearly, the atomically armed Strategic Air Command. There were those who argued that this would indeed be the only important weapon in World War III, and that a proper strategy called only for the atomic air arm to be prepared, at a moment's notice, to strike at the heart of the enemy and destroy him before his own massive ground forces could achieve any of their objectives. Such preparation, it was argued, would have the double advantage of assuring victory should war come and, for this reason, of deterring an enemy from launching an attack in the first place. Opponents of an air-power strategy quarreled with it on both grounds. Atomic air power could not alone assure military victory, they argued; its effective application would require forward air bases, defended and supplied by ground and naval forces; and similar forces would be required, once the enemy gained a significant air capability of his own, to deny him bases from which to launch an atomic attack upon us. It was, in fact, upon just such a broader concept of the need for military forces in a general war that the joint chiefs of staff shaped their April, 1948, compromise on balanced force requirements. Already in 1948, however, and even more clearly in 1950, there was growing recognition that military forces and a strategy to shape and direct them had to meet more than the challenge of an all-out general war with the Soviet Union. Such a war continued to be the ultimate challenge, and NSC-68 recognized in 1950 the need to meet it with sharply increased air, ground, and naval forces. Recognition was also given to the possibility that all-out war might not come suddenly, but rather after a series of lesser defeats had left us and our allies with no choice but to engage in total war or accept surrender; larger forces, especially ground and naval elements, were again seen as the answer to these lesser challenges. (It was one such, in the Middle East, that played a large part in Forrestal's thinking about rearmament in 1948.) As important, perhaps more so, ground forces in place and air-naval elements to support them were considered essential in convincing our European allies that their defense was of vital concern to us; an atomic-air-power strategy could have little value for them if it meant that, as the Soviet Union was being obliterated, the Soviet armies were overrunning their homelands. Finally, larger American forces of all kinds, and for all these strategic purposes—provision of an air-power deterrent, deterring or meeting lesser challenges, and symbolizing defense of West Europe—fitted a more general strategic pattern of containment. This was, in 1950, the grand strategy: prevent, by threat or application of force, any further unilateral Soviet successes, in the hope that this might eventually persuade the Soviet Union to seek more constructive relations with the rest of the world.[1]

The outbreak of war in Korea provided an immediate military challenge to be met with the forces at hand; but the challenge appeared even greater than that, and the response to it was broader yet.

Even as the demands for units and equipment in Korea absorbed almost all of America's immediately available combat power in the summer and fall of 1950, uncertainty over Soviet intentions in Western Europe, and to a lesser extent over China's intention in the Formosa Straits, demanded plans, programs and actions toward a build-up of defense forces far beyond that intended for the active theater in Korea. This same uncertainty also required some constraints in defense mobilization. There was no obvious timetable leading to an all-out conflict with the Soviet Union. Wise and restrained use or threat of force might prevent such a conflict altogether; yet the very success of such a deterrent strategy could stretch out the need for forces to back it up over an unpredictably long period. Unlike our mobilization in World War II, aimed at bringing the maximum resources of the nation to bear toward defeating Germany and Japan, the mobilization begun in July, 1950, had strategic and programmatic aims more limited in scope but open-ended in time. Strategically it sought to deter, not to eliminate, the major threat to American security. Its programs, moreover, were aimed not at total mobilization of resources into a national war effort, but rather at achieving and then sustaining a "high plateau of preparedness" over a long period of time.[2] Indeed, despite the intensive efforts required to meet our commitments in Korea, there was not even a declaration of national emergency until the Chinese intervention forced reconsideration and acceleration of the mobilization effort in December.

The general insistence on limiting the Korean War mobilization[3] was accompanied by more open and widespread agreement on the actual programs of rearmament than on the strategic purposes of partial mobilization. The mobilization programs aimed primarily at enlarging the active forces. But it was not clear whether these enlarged active forces were to serve as a force-in-being to deter both general war and limited conflicts of the Korean type, or simply as the base from which these forces could be more readily expanded in the event of a general war. As Huntington argues, the existence of NSC-68 and its role in rearmament did not really resolve this issue; for both purposes were pursued throughout the Korean War rearmament.[4] This duality of purpose had important effects on the development of manpower procurement policies.

The immediate thrust of manpower procurement policy change during the Korean War was directed at Selective Service and allied programs. As noted in the last chapter, the Selective Service Act of 1948 was not a fully satisfactory device for rapid, large-scale manpower mobilization. Early legislative adjustments in the summer of 1950 were only a beginning, and it was clear to the Administration and interested members of Congress that a thorough review and revision of these policies would be needed. There was also a strong desire in the Administration and among some congressional leaders to achieve a more or less permanent settlement on policy; they hoped that whatever arrangements were made to meet the current needs for partial mobilization could and would, with minor adjustments, also serve in the longer period of preparedness for the cold war. The shock of the Korean War brought with it a new public willingness to support such a long-term preparedness effort—or, perhaps more accurately, a fresh recognition by Congress and the Administration of that willingness.

II.   THE UNIVERSAL MILITARY TRAINING AND SERVICE ACT, 1951

1.   Administration Proposals for a Cold War Manpower Policy

Throughout the fall of 1950, the Administration moved slowly and deliberately, laying careful plans for major revisions in manpower procurement policy. After General George

Marshall became secretary of defense in September, he personally selected Mrs. Anna Rosenberg to be an assistant secretary and his chief manpower aide. A professional consultant on labor and public relations, Mrs. Rosenberg had worked for the War Manpower Commission as regional director in New York City during the war, and had been a member of the presidential commission that produced the Compton Report on UMT in 1947. She became a key figure in the 1951 congressional hearings, delighting or disconcerting members and observers with her blunt answers and her seemingly inexhaustible willingness to turn up new facts, figures, and charts on short notice to meet criticisms and strengthen her case. Development of the Defense Department's complex legislative proposals required extensive coordination within the Defense Department and among the military services, and cooperation among a number of nonmilitary agencies. An interdepartmental committee was formed, bringing together representatives from the Defense Department, the Selective Service System, the National Security Resources Board, and the Bureau of Labor Statistics, to lay the statistical base for the Administration's case. In addition, the Defense Department worked with the Office of Education, the Department of Agriculture, and, of course, the Bureau of the Budget; and in the early planning stages it also sought advice from prominent educators and consulted with veterans, labor, and farm groups.[5] In sum, the effort at planning, coordination, and consultation was more extensive than ever in the past, or since, on this policy subject.

A major reason why the Administration had time for such deliberate preparations was that, in this same period, the Selective Service System was working hard and successfully at providing manpower for the rapidly expanding active forces. The initial induction call, for September, was quickly raised from 20,000 to 50,000; and another 50,000 were called for October. Since the suspension of inductions in early 1949, the System's machinery had contracted drastically, and this process had to be reversed.[6] Despite the suddenness of this reactivation, and despite initially high rejection rates among the men first delivered for examination, the System began with small deliveries in August and more than met the September and later calls.[7]

Nevertheless, this very success of Selective Service produced its own pressures for revisions in manpower procurement policy. As inductions and enlistments both rose after August, the pool of men on which Selective Service could draw (those classified I-A, plus those registered but not yet classified) dropped sharply—from about 3.3 million on September 30 to about 2.5 million on December 31.[8] In the same period, the Administration settled on a goal of achieving and maintaining active armed forces totalling some 3.5 million men—nearly two and one-half times the June, 1950, active strength. There was concern, especially in Selective Service Headquarters, that the pool of availables would dwindle so rapidly that it would soon be extremely difficult, if not impossible, to meet induction calls promptly.

There was also concern over too indiscriminate a widening of the available manpower pool. As the Defense Department's coordination with outside agencies suggests, there was a strong desire to avoid interfering any more than necessary with normal civilian activities, even in the current emergency.

Pressure also developed for an early solution to long-range military manpower problems. By the end of August, considerable support had developed outside the Administration for quick enactment of UMT legislation, apparently reflecting hopes of capitalizing on the very real atmosphere of emergency. Fearing that this might interfere with more pressing mobilization demands, President Truman made a strong plea that Congress delay any action on this matter until its next session.[9] The hopes of UMT enthusiasts revived, though, with the appointment of General Marshall to be secretary of defense. As Marshall said later, he did not want a repetition of past experience, "where we do something to meet the immediate emergency, and then look hopefully into the future for something that has never happened."[10] That "something" was settlement on a permanent system of manpower procurement and training supported by more than volunteering. To Marshall, this meant UMT, and he was determined to have that program authorized and ready to operate before the current emergency receded.

Out of the coordinated planning, and reflecting all these pressures, came the Defense Department's proposal for a system of universal military training and service. The chief aims and features of this proposal were:

First, expansion of the manpower pool by: lowering the minimum age for induction from nineteen to eighteen; lengthening the period of involuntary service from twenty-one to twenty-seven months; extending, for one year, enlistments scheduled to expire during the next two fiscal years; extending for two more years the president's authority to call reservists to active service; removing the induction deferment for National Guardsmen who enlisted before reaching age eighteen and one-half; and allowing the president to create a nonmilitary program of voluntary rehabilitation for men rejected as physically or mentally unfit for service.

Second, protection of the civilian economy and the nation's defense potential by assuring at least a minimal flow of men through the colleges and universities.

Third, establishment of a long-range training and service program by: imposing an eight-year training and service obligation, active and reserve, on all young men; allowing reduction or elimination of active service for the younger age groups once the current need for active forces had lessened, leaving only an obligation for active training under UMT to be followed by reserve service; repealing the 1948 active strength ceilings and extending the 1950 suspension of ceilings from 1953 to 1961; and repealing the termination date of the act.[11]

The major justifications offered for the Department's proposal, with varying emphases, were: that the Selective Service pool was falling dangerously low; that these measures were needed to improve not only the strength but the efficiency of the active services; that the actions taken should interfere as little as possible with the normal processes of civilian production and education even during the current emergency but especially over the long term, but that the system of manpower procurement should also be adaptable to an all-out mobilization; and, finally, that it was long past time for settling on a permanent military training and service policy.

Not all the Department's arguments were accepted by Congress. Of the specific measures proposed, those occasioning the most extensive examination by the committees[12] and on the House and Senate floors were the twenty-seven months' service period, the draft of eighteen-year-olds, and the student deferment program. Proposals regarding deferments for reservists and relations between the active and reserve manpower pools proved less controversial. Also at issue in the hearings and debates, on congressional initiative, were the physical and mental qualifications for service, and deferments for men with dependents. Three more matters became major issues in the floor debates: the method by which universal service would later be transformed into universal training, ceilings on active strengths, and the duration of the act. The concept of universal training and service emerged from this legislative process more or less intact, at least technically; but many of the details, and even some major provisions, underwent considerable modification.

2. *Longer Service and Younger Draftees*

Of the more controversial proposals, that for a twenty-seven-month service period occasioned the most straightforward controversy and compromise. The Defense Department gave two reasons for the change: first, it would increase combat potential in units relying on inductees, by reducing turnover and increasing the post-training contributions of inductees; and second, lower turnover would result in lower training costs. General Hershey had a third reason: lengthening the service period would significantly reduce demand for inductions. Two objections were raised against this proposal. One, championed by Senator Morse, was that the prospective budget savings from reduced turnover would be less valuable than the extra time sacrificed by inductees and the forgone long-range benefits of training larger numbers of men. The second was that the longer service period would interfere unduly with education. Mrs. Rosenberg responded that Army and Selective Service recommendations for a thirty-month period had been trimmed back just to meet that second objection. More trimming seemed to be in order, though, and the conference version finally compromised on twenty-four months.

Debate over reducing the induction age to eighteen years was more complicated. Both Armed Services Committees eventually accepted the argument that immediate demands for manpower required either lowering the draft age or some other major adjustments to expand the pool of availables, but not without very careful scrutiny and critique of the figures presented by Defense and Selective

Service witnesses. This was not an easy task, partly because of the complex interrelations among various possible ways of expanding the pool, and partly because intra-Administration coordination was not complete when hearings opened before the Senate subcommittee. Not until several days into the Senate hearings were Defense witnesses able to speak uniformly of a 3.5 million-man goal (raised from 3.2 million), and this required revision of charts and data already given the subcommittee. Also, there was confusion over just how large the pool of availables had to be to satisfy General Hershey that he could meet the calls placed on him. This "safety margin" began at 250,000, then was raised to 400,000; finally Hershey, the Defense Department, and the Senate subcommittee settled on 600,000.

Early in the Senate subcommittee hearings, given the lower safety margin, the Defense Department could not really justify the eighteen-year-old draft on grounds of a manpower shortage (at least not assuming, as they did, that Congress would grant the longer twenty-seven months' service period). Thus Mrs. Rosenberg emphasized other reasons for lowering the age limit: that induction at a younger age would cause less disruption in young men's lives, and hence in education and the economy; and that the lower age would be necessary for the UMT program. Later in the same hearings, however, General Hershey stressed the problem of his manpower pool. The Defense Department's estimates were all based on the most favorable assumptions, he argued: "they are dangerous . . . if you increase the calls, the game is over. You are completely wrecked."[13] The joint chiefs, appearing after General Hershey, warned that the alternative to drafting eighteen-year-olds would be an unfair draft of veterans or fathers. Before the House committee, however, the arguments were better coordinated. The Defense Department used General Hershey's argument for a safety margin of 600,000; and Hershey in turn adopted a broader approach, stressing reasons other than his manpower pool for lowering the draft age.

Other, non-governmental, witnesses also testified on the eighteen-year-old draft. On the Administration's side were a group of prestigious college presidents, who all asserted that induction for service or training would not hurt the eighteen-year-old and would be better for his career plans or education than induction at age nineteen. Opposed were a number of organizations and individual witnesses, the most convincing being the representative of the National Education Association. He pointed out that the only large education group which had specifically endorsed induction of eighteen-year-olds was the Association of American Universities, the smallest of the groups representing higher education. More telling were his arguments that the number of man-years of college attendance in the period 1941-51 was significantly smaller than it would have been without a war, despite the postwar surge of veterans returning to take advantage of their education benefits, and that the nineteen-year-old with a year or more of college prior to induction was much more likely to go on with his education after service than was the eighteen-year-old inducted before getting into college. The only student group to testify—Students for Democratic Action—supported the Administration on the draft of eighteen-year-olds.

The Senate committee, after sifting the conflicting testimony, finally concluded that the minimum age should be lowered to eighteen for the reasons given by Defense and Selective Service spokesmen. But it attempted to limit indirectly the numbers of eighteen-year-olds who could be inducted for service: first, physical and mental standards would be lowered, and the IV-F's in the nineteen to twenty-five age group reexamined; second, nonveteran husbands would be reclassified I-A if otherwise fit for service; third, no local board would be permitted to call eighteen-year-olds until its supply of men aged nineteen to twenty-five was exhausted; and finally when eighteen-year-olds were called the local boards would have to exhaust the older groups in this age bracket, by quarter, before calling the younger men. The committee also made it almost impossible to induct men shortly after their eighteenth birthdays, by refusing to lower the registration age below eighteen. Its version of the bill required, moreover, that men inducted before age nineteen not be sent overseas or into combat with less than four months' basic training. On the Senate floor, an attempt by Senator Morse to raise the minimum age to eighteen and one-half was rejected.[14]

The House committee started where Senator Morse left off. Recommending a minimum age of eighteen and one-half, the committee agreed that some expansion of the manpower pool was required;

but it argued that its action would provide enough men, assuming other changes required in the Senate bill were preserved. The House committee was less concerned than the Administration and the Senate over the effects of the higher minimum age on inauguration of UMT. In House action an amendment to keep the minimum age at nineteen was rejected, and the process of inducting eighteen-year-olds was simplified.[15] The conference committee eventually accepted the House version of a minimum age of eighteen and one-half years.

3.   Student Deferments

A third controversial proposal was one providing that a number of carefully selected youths might, after completing basic training, be relieved temporarily from active duty to attend college. These men, up to 75,000 annually, would be selected by civilian agencies, hopefully for leadership qualities in addition to educational achievement, to study or do research in medicine, science, engineering, the humanities, or other fields determined to be in the national interest. Eventually they would have to serve out the remainder of their active and reserve obligation, although a very few might perform important civilian service in lieu thereof. The Department also suggested consideration of national scholarships to pay for the education of men selected but unable to put themselves through college; and it stated that those who chose to work their way might be given up to six years to do so. This proposal relied most heavily on the recommendation of the Scientific Manpower Advisory Committee (Thomas Committee), appointed in December, 1950, by the chairman of the National Security Resources Board. The Defense proposal also showed signs of consultation with the Association of American Universities, in a provision that students suspended from service for study would have no military connection.[16]

In the Selective Service Act of 1948, Congress had declared that "adequate provision for national security requires maximum effort in the fields of scientific research and development, health, and education, and the fullest possible development and utilization of the Nation's technological, scientific, and other critical manpower resources." But as noted in Chapter 2, Congress had left to presidential determination, through Selective Service regulations, the question of which students, if any, should be deferred from service. Indeed, until the beginning of heavy inductions in late summer of 1950, there seemed little reason for concern over the question. In August, 1948, General Hershey had appointed a group of six committees, under the general chairmanship of Dr. M. H. Trytten, to advise him on student and occupational deferments. The committees submitted a single report in December, 1948, but no action was taken on their recommendations before the halt of inductions in early 1949.[17]

By late 1950, there was ample reason for concern. In August, 1950, the Selective Service System had issued interim regulations authorizing deferment of students who had completed at least one year and were in the upper half of their classes.[18] These regulations did not provide any further guidelines to the local boards for determining what studies were "necessary to the maintenance of the national health, safety, or interest. . . ." Nor did they provide for deferment beyond June, 1951, nor for any way of deciding which draft-eligible high school graduates should be allowed to enter college. Thus, as the Defense Department and Selective Service were readying proposals which could bring the majority of qualified college-age young men into military service, colleges and students alike were uncertain about their futures; and the nation had no definite plan for assuring an uninterrupted supply of highly educated and skilled manpower during what many felt could be a ten-year or longer period of partial mobilization.

As the Selective Service System went forward with efforts to refine student deferments, the Administration was producing a more general directive on mobilization of the nation's manpower. "The most efficient use of the Nation's manpower," the new policy statement said,

> will be of vital importance in any prolonged effort to keep the strength of the United States at a high level and will be of the utmost importance in the event of full mobilization. Consequently, it is important the manpower measures taken now be consistent with and contribute to the most advantageous use of our manpower should full mobilization become necessary.

Recognition was given to the need for "training and educational programs to expand our supply of persons with highly developed skills essential to civilian and military activities." For Selective Service policy, this meant continued deferment of men having and using critical skills and "deferment of a sufficient number of individuals in educational and training institutions to provide an adequate continuing supply of professional and highly skilled manpower."[19]

Primarily in pursuit of this last objective, the Defense Department made its proposal for annual selection of 75,000 servicemen for a special college program. Said Mrs. Rosenberg:

> We feel, Senator, that with our shortage of manpower it is essential that we make it up in skills; that the skilled manpower, the scientific manpower, the highly trained manpower is essential for the national interest. . . . It is essential that we have an educated and informed public and we want to do everything in the armed services to make sure that that process is not interrupted if we can get men without interrupting the process.
>
> At the same time, we are cognizant that if we do not support our educational institutions they will dry up and financially go bankrupt and the potential greatest good in the country will be wasted.[20]

Through this plan, the Defense Department and those groups with whom it consulted hoped to assure that the college population would not undergo the drastic decline experienced in World War II. Then, between the 1939-40 and 1943-44 school years, enrollment of male civilians in colleges and universities had fallen nearly 70 percent.[21] For the coming years of partial mobilization, the Office of Education estimated that by leaving half the 1950-51 freshman class, and all the sophomore and junior classes, in college after June, 1951, and adding the expected numbers of World War II veterans, IV-F college students, ROTC students, and the 75,000 special students proposed by the Defense Department, total male undergraduate enrollment would drop from a little more than 1 million in 1950-51 to just over 700,000 in 1953-54 (or about the 1939 level). Male college graduates would number about 275,000 in 1951, and would drop to under 180,000 by 1954. Thereafter, returning veterans would begin to affect college enrollments again.[22]

Most criticisms of the Defense proposal did not take into account those sources of college students other than the 75,000 per year input from the special program. Thus that figure came under attack by some educators and professional men as being too small to supply the nation's needs and support the educational system. The Defense Department, under pressure to keep the special program down to a minimum, argued that its consultations with educators suggested that this number would meet the need. The Senate committee agreed; it also specified a presidential commission to select youths for the program, and authorized that commission to pay tuition and other expenses for such of the 75,000 selected youths as might seem appropriate.

Related to the question of numbers was that of fields of study. The general sense of the Thomas Committee's report was that these 75,000 would be limited to study in science, engineering, and premedical fields; and some wanted the program just that strictly defined. Harold Dodds, president of Princeton, argued that "to make college a haven or refuge for even the brightest students, outside the most essential services, for the study of subjects that are not pointed immediately to the need of the defense effort, would destroy their moral capacities as future leaders of a democracy."[23] President Conant of Harvard spoke in even more restrictive terms. In 1948 and early 1949 he had associated himself with an AAU recommendation against any educational deferments. He had since then come to support deferments only for those whose special skills would be needed by the military services, and this only to avoid imposing double service on such men; and he supported the Defense proposal on this ground.

The Defense Department itself was less restrictive in its attitude toward what fields the 75,000 might be allowed to pursue; its proposal would have allowed "study or research in medicine, science, engineering, the humanities, or other fields determined to be in the national interest." Supporting this more liberal approach, Commissioner of Education McGrath noted that most students entering college do not know what their special field is going to be. Moreover, he argued, there is always uncertainty about what fields may prove critical in the future. General Hershey also supported this view: "I do have probably some little sensitivity in having the Government engage too much in telling a boy what he is going to do. I believe in the freest possible choice . . . [that] we can afford."[24] Educational and professional groups represented at the hearings also generally favored the idea of free choice. The Senate committee, in recommending its version of the Defense proposal, retained the provision for study in the humanities and other fields, but gave the selection commission reserve power to set quotas for the various fields.

A final aspect of the Defense program for students, with which the Senate committee agreed, was that it should be limited in time. In three years, it was argued, veterans should be returning in sufficient numbers to make up for the drafting of younger college candidates; and the Senate committee therefore gave the program an expiration date of June 30, 1954.

The House committee showed little interest in this Defense proposal; and later, when the committee wrote its own bill as a substitute for the Senate version, it left out the program entirely. It then heard the protests of Secretary Marshall and Mrs. Rosenberg. Chairman Vinson responded that his committee's bill made fully adequate provision for the deferment of students, in that it retained the provision of the 1948 act which permitted the president to prescribe the necessary rules and regulations. "You are complaining because we have struck it out," Vinson said. "We put it in here in a direct, positive way, giving the discretion to the President. That is what we have done." The House committee did hear other witnesses, from the world of education, on the question; but its mind was apparently made up: the student deferment program would be set by the president, preferably through the Selective Service System. Said Chairman Vinson, urging General Hershey to get on with his own plans, "we have confidence in you."[25]

Hershey had received the Trytten Report's reendorsement of its 1948 recommendations in December, 1950, and the report had been published a few days later.[26] The six advisory committees had, in reaching their conclusions, rejected several alternatives. First, to the argument that there should be no student deferment, they answered that national security would not be served by the resulting "serious hiatus in the continuing supply of critically needed specialized personnel. . . ." Nor could they countenance a blanket deferment for all college students: "Any plan adopted . . . should be capable of ready adjustment . . . in case of increasing emergency. This plan is regarded as inflexible and unrealistic and, therefore, impracticable." Finally, they rejected vigorously the suggestion that deferment go only to "those students who are preparing for 'essential' sciences and professions. . . ." As did Commissioner Mc-Grath, the Trytten Report argued that these "essential" sciences were not easily identified. "It is quite possible that fifteen years ago nuclear physicists would have been dismissed as a luxury . . . not essential to the national defense. The professor of Japanese language and literature would certainly have been viewed earlier as a luxury." Moreover, they said, entering college students rarely make a final choice of special field in the first year; nor is anyone else likely to be able to make an intelligent choice for them. In short, although the committees recognized the urgent demands for military manpower, they also insisted the national security required that no major field of learning and knowledge should be crippled for lack of men.[27]

The Trytten Report recommended two standards to be applied jointly as guidelines for the selective deferment of college students: potential ability, as established by a general aptitude test; and educational accomplishment, as measured by academic records. To be deferred, an undergraduate student would have to (1) score high enough on a general aptitude test to place him in the upper one-sixth of the general population; and (2) maintain a class rank in his school, among those qualifying under (1), above a level specified by the director of Selective Service. To enter graduate or professional school, a student would have to qualify under (1), and would have to have graduated in the upper half of his college class; to remain, he would have to continue to make satisfactory progress in a full-time program toward the degree for which he was enrolled. Certification of class rank and progress toward graduate degrees would be provided by the colleges and universities, and failure by any deferred student to meet the requirements would be reported immediately to his local board. Each year of deferment would add one year to the upper age limit of eligibility for induction. Between academic years, students otherwise qualified could maintain their deferments by evidencing intent to continue in school and to spend the interim period in related course, laboratory, or field work, or in employment to earn funds for schooling. Finally, the report urged that the director of Selective Service recommend a government scholarship program for all individuals qualifying for deferment on the general aptitude test.[28]

By the time of the House committee's report in mid-March, General Hershey was able to provide an outline of his own plan for student deferments. This was a modification of the Trytten Report recommendations in several respects. For one, it made no mention of the report's suggestions concerning scholarships, or of its suggestion for lengthening the induction liability of deferred students. Hershey's plan did fill in one detail left out of the Trytten Report; specific provisions were made for class rank qualifications for proceeding to the next year of schoooling: upper half of the freshman class, upper two-thirds of the sophomore class, upper three-quarters of the junior class (or of the next-to-last year in five-, six-, or seven-year undergraduate programs), and upper-half of the last undergraduate class for proceeding to graduate or professional school. A Selective Service College Qualification Test was also part of Hershey's plan, with a slightly higher score required of graduate school candidates than of undergraduate students.[29] In the major modification of the Trytten recommendations, General Hershey proposed to employ class standing and test scores, not in combination, but on an either-or basis. Thus a student who stood near the bottom of his class could qualify for deferment by scoring well on the test; and one failing to pass the test could still gain deferment by maintaining a high enough class standing in his school.

Dr. Trytten later offered to justify this altered application of the dual criteria:

> It became clear . . . that this double requirement (class standing and high test score) would unduly affect certain types of institutions in such a way as possibly to defeat the intent of the program. . . . The highly selective institutions, if they were to suffer the same percentage loss (by class standing) as the less selective institutions, would not be able to turn out the same number of highly qualified young men as formerly, and in many cases their graduates are of considerable significance to the nation. . . .
> But other considerations make it undesirable also that less selective institutions should lose too large a percentage of their students, as they might if the aptitude [test] criterion were made absolute. These schools serve an important social and training purpose for their clientele and their region. There are other values than strictly academic ones.[30]

Presidential approval of Hershey's plan, even before the House acted on the bill, aroused a storm of protest—most prominently from the presidents of three "highly selective institutions." President Conant, speaking for the Committee on the Present Danger, said the plan "violates the democratic principle of equality of sacrifice." President Dodds of Princeton agreed, and stated: "I . . . view the almost blanket deferment of college students as wrong for the nation and detrimental to the best interests of the colleges in the long run." Only minimal deferments to meet immediate defense needs should be allowed, he said. President Griswold of Yale was also critical, stating he would prefer a plan similar to the original Defense proposal. But he was more optimistic on the question of the colleges becoming a haven from the draft. "Deferment," he observed, "does not mean exemption."[31]

The House committee also had this last idea in mind. To prevent student deferments from becoming exemptions, the committee added a proviso to its bill that all persons deferred prior to age twenty-six would remain liable until age thirty-five. (The original bill written by the committee applied this proviso only to deferred students; as reported to the House, however, the proviso covered all deferments.)

On the House floor, friends of the Selective Service System added another very important proviso, this one also aimed ostensibly at countering opposition to a blanket deferment for college students. An amendment proposed by Representative Kilday (D., Tex.) added this limitation to the paragraph on occupational and student deferments:

> Notwithstanding any provision of this Act, no local board, appeal board, or other agency of appeal of the Selective Service System shall be required to postpone or defer any person by reason of his activity in study, research, or . . . other endeavors found to be necessary . . . solely on the basis of any test, examination, selective system, class standing, or any other means conducted, sponsored, administered, or prepared by any agency or department of the Federal Government or any private institution, corporation, association, partnership, or individual employed by an agency or department of the Federal Government.[32]

The legal effect of this amendment went beyond the stated intent. The president might establish occupational and student deferment programs, but any standards for such deferments would be guidelines only, to be followed or not at the discretion of the local boards and the appeals system. The president could, of course, choose to allow no such deferments at all; but this seemed unlikely given the Administration's earlier position on the matter and the president's recent approval of the new student deferment regulations.

In practice, this amendment produced no administrative change at all. Instead, it simply confirmed in the statutes what had been General Hershey's operating philosophy all along. During World War II, and again under the 1948 act, Hershey had sought to delegate as much discretionary authority as possible to the local boards. He had supplied the boards only informational guidelines, not hard instructions, on what activities and skills might meet the statutory test for occupational deferments, that is, the test of necessity "in the maintenance of the national health, safety, or interest." Of course, the appeals system might be used to reverse specific local board decisions. But Hershey had consistently resisted any pressure to establish national standards for decisions he thought should be based on local judgments of local conditions. The real effect of the Kilday amendment, then, was to assure that Hershey's administrative philosophy and practice could not be reversed by any presidential order to apply national standards in deciding on occupational or student deferments.[33]

Presidential approval of Hershey's plan for student deferments probably had a strong influence on subsequent congressional decisions. In the Senate, the Administration's allies had already turned back several attempts to delete the special program for 75,000 students.[34] As noted earlier, however, the House committee left this program out of its bill; and no move was made to restore it during floor debate. The conference committee accepted the House language on standards for occupational and student deferments (the Kilday amendment) and on extension of induction liability to age thirty-five for deferred persons; and it agreed to omit the special program for 75,000 students, along with the Senate's scholarship provisions for them.

4. Reservists and the Manpower Pools

In its proposed revisions of Selective Service law, the Defense Department asked for three measures involving relations between the active and reserve manpower pools: extension to mid-1953 of authority to call reservists to active duty; elimination of deferments for National Guardsmen enlisting before age eighteen and one-half; and establishment of a uniform, eight-year military obligation for all men entering active or reserve service.

The Senate accepted the Defense Department's argument for extension of the reserve call-up authority. This was still needed, the Department said, during the period of building up the active forces. The Senate also agreed to match the active service period for reservists with that for inductees.

In the House committee, these proposals met some resistance. Mrs. Rosenberg was forced to admit that the call-up of reservists since June, 1950, especially by the Army, had worked hardships and inequities upon many World War II veterans and other volunteers in the reserves. Records on reservists were simply not adequate to the task of sorting out men whose dependents or occupations might have made them ineligible for induction under Selective Service rules. The result was that nonveteran, nonreservist husbands, fathers, students, and skilled technicians were not inducted, while many veteran reservists in these same categories were called to active duty. Moreover, unlike the other services, the Army was obligated to call National Guardsmen and Organized Reservists only in whole units; what it desperately needed, though, were individual reservists with particular skills who could fill out skeletonized active units or help man the training establishment. Thus many of the reservists who had stayed out of organized training programs were called ahead of those who had joined organized units, continued their training, and received reserve drill pay. The House committee felt some changes were needed in the Defense Department's proposals, aimed at countering these incongruities.

The House accepted its committee's recommendation to extend the recall authority, but to shorten the active service period for involuntarily called, and especially veteran, reservists. The conference committee compromised the House and Senate positions: it extended the recall authority to mid-1953; it set the active service term for called reservists at twenty-four months, as for inductees; but it included provisions for early release of those reservists who were veterans.

Congress, like the Defense Department, was concerned over

charges that the National Guard and Organized Reserves had become draft havens. No one objected to the 1948 act's provisions deferring reservists who were already in organized training programs at that time, and deferring short-term veterans who joined such reserve units after the act was passed. But the Defense Department, over vigorous objections by the National Guard Association, wanted to eliminate the 1948 provision deferring those youths who joined the Guard before reaching age eighteen and one-half. Moreover, members of the House and Senate committees questioned sharply General Hershey's administrative decision to postpone indefinitely the induction of all men in National Guard and Organized Reserve units. On this matter the Defense Department was silent, neither proposing a remedy nor supporting Hershey's contention that these reserve units should not be broken up; it only noted that it had called only four of the twenty-five National Guard divisions, and planned to call only two more. But committee members, especially House committee chairman Vinson, pressed hard; he realized that, justly or not, Congress and his committee were vulnerable to criticism for having allowed the National Guard and other reserve units to become shelters from the draft.

The Senate committee proposed, and the Senate and House accepted, compromises on both these questions: the Guard might continue enlisting youths under age eighteen and one-half, who would then be deferred from induction, but only until the secretary of defense declared that a sufficient pool of reserve-obligated, post-service men was available as a source for Guard recruiting; and Hershey's practice of postponing induction for other Guardsmen and Organized Reservists was given post facto authorization, but halted for the future, by altering from June 24, 1948, to February 1, 1951, the deadline for enlistment of older men in such units in order to qualify for deferment.

The Defense Department also wanted a change in the 1948 act's provision of a five-year reserve obligation for any man entering active service who served less than three years. Instead, it proposed an eight-year service obligation, active and reserve, for any man entering active or reserve service. In addition, the department requested that details regarding apportionment of these eight years between active and reserve service, assignment of active service veterans to reserve units, and reduction of the obligation through extra active service or participation in reserve training, be left to departmental discretion or further legislation. Despite objections from the reserve associations that this left their recruiting prospects uncertain, and pressure from the House for a shorter, six-year, obligation, the Senate and the conference committee agreed to accept these Defense Department requests. (The Senate and House committees also exacted promises from the Defense Department of early proposals to revise and strengthen the reserve programs; these proposals are discussed in section III-2 of this chapter.)

5. Congressional Initiatives to Expand the Manpower Pool

Besides lengthening the involuntary service term and lowering the induction age, two other means of expanding the available manpower pool were written into the statutes on congressional initiative.

The more controversial of these, and a move strongly resisted by the Defense Department, was a provision lowering the physical and mental standards for induction. The only Department proposal regarding men classified IV-F was a recommendation that Congress authorize the president to establish a voluntary, nonmilitary rehabilitation program for them. No specific program was offered; and thanks to automatic opposition from the American Medical Association and a lack of Defense Department enthusiasm, nothing came of the idea. Yet there was concern over the high rate of rejections, especially for failure to pass the mental tests. Moreover, because of the relative popularity of the Navy and the Air Force, the Army's forced dependence on Selective Service was giving it the far greater share of the least qualified men.

Few wished to resolve the interservice recruiting imbalance by forcing all services to rely only on Selective Service for manpower, with the possible exception of General Hershey. In late 1950, a House Armed Services Committee subcommittee had recommended a different solution to the Defense Department: establish quotas for each service in various categories of fitness, and regulate recruiting quotas monthly so that no service could get more than its proper share within each category and so that men in the top categories would be available for Selective Service inductions. Mrs. Rosenberg testified that the Defense Department was implementing this recommendation. On the strength of this assurance, Congress took no action to legislate a solution.

As to the standards themselves, the Senate took no action to change them. Its committee report summarized the Defense Department's case against any lowering of standards: it could create a heavy future pension burden; it would reduce the services' flexibility in assigning men, or hamper the effectiveness of units; it could reduce the ability of the services to rotate men from the combat zones; and it would probably increase disciplinary problems, the bulk of which came from men in the lower mental categories. The House committee, however, recommended reducing both physical and mental standards to those of January, 1945, "the barrel-scraping period." The House followed suit, and in conference a compromise was reached reducing physical standards to the proposed level, but reducing mental standards only to a point between that and the minimum required in the 1948 act.

A second congressional action to increase the pool of availables proved much less controversial. The 1948 act had left the entire question of dependency deferments to presidential regulation. As one early response to the expected light inductions calls under the act, all married men were deferred; and they remained in that status through the first year of the Korean War. Although the Defense Department and the Selective Service System both favored changes in the regulations, Congress took the matter in its own hands and wrote into the statute a ban on deferment of men whose only dependents were their wives, "except in cases of extreme hardship."

Two other actions also helped expand the pool. One continued the president's authority to extend enlistments for one year, that authority to expire on July 1, 1953. The other increased an authorization for enlistments of aliens from 2,500, as enacted in 1950, to 12,500.

6. *Additional Amendments by Congress*

One vital part of the Defense Department's universal training and service proposals was the mechanism by which a transition would be made from heavy inductions for active service to a program of UMT. The attention given this matter by the committees was mild by contrast with the difficulties encountered on the Senate and, especially, House floors.

The Defense Department's proposals were simple: the president might, on recommendation of the secretary of defense, increase the period of basic training to six months and reduce or eliminate the period of active service required of inductees. These changes, to be made "when justified by the strength of the armed forces in the light of international conditions," could vary as to age groups, thus making it possible to reduce the service period for eighteen-year-olds, induct part of them for training only, and leave the remainder liable for full service on reaching age nineteen. The president was also to appoint a five-to-eight-man committee to advise him on the UMT program.

The Senate committee asked few questions about these aspects of the plan, but it did modify the proposals somewhat. Paralleling the president's authority, Congress was also to have control over the future adjustment of service and training periods. The advisory committee became a National Security Training Commission, with authority, subject to presidential direction, to designate the departments and agencies to carry out training under such policies and standards as the commission might establish. Men inducted for training only would go into a National Security Training Corps, to be established at the time the commission came into being.

There was little criticism of these details on the Senate floor, but two attempts were made to eliminate all UMT provisions from the act. One, by Senator E. C. Johnson (D., Colo.), prompted a lengthy debate, but was turned down 20-68. The second, by Senator Jenner (R., Ind.), was rejected without a vote.[35]

The House committee, on the other hand, made major revisions in the projected UMT machinery. It altered the composition of the commission slightly and provided that its chairman must be a civilian. The commission was given authority, subject to the president only, to direct and control the training programs of the National Security Training Corps. The latter would come into being only at such time as the active service period for men under age nineteen had been eliminated. Prior to that, the commission was to prepare a plan covering all aspects of training and administration. "In order to assure the establishment of a truly military training program," the commission's plan was to be subject, for a period of sixty days, to a legislative veto in Congress. These recommendations were prepared well before the end of the House hearings; but neither Secretary Marshall nor Mrs. Rosenberg took issue with them in their second public appearance.

Before debate opened in the House, the committee yielded to House critics and proposed still further changes. Under these new committee amendments, the National Security Training Commission was to submit legislative recommendations, rather than an administrative plan, concerning all aspects of the training program, within six months of its appointment. Congress would then have sixty days to pass legislation dealing with all aspects of the commission's recommendations. In the absence of such positive action, no inductions into the National Security Training Corps could take place. The effect of this was to subject the whole matter of UMT to still another complete cycle of legislative action.[36]

Even with this considerable concession to UMT skeptics and opponents, the current fate of UMT remained in doubt. An entire day was set aside for debate of an amendment by Representative Barden (D., N.C.) to substitute a simple extension of Selective Service for the universal training and service proposals of the committee. The test came on April 12, and the Barden substitute was defeated fairly easily—thanks no doubt to heavy pressure from the leadership and the Administration, but even more to the committee's earlier watering-down of the UMT plan.[37]

In conference, the Senate and House versions were compromised in favor of the House. Most important, the requirement for further legislation to implement UMT was made part of the final act.

Two other issues in the congressional debates also affected the long-term nature of the Unversal Military Training and Service Act, one of them only indirectly. This latter was the question of a ceiling on active strengths. The 1948 act had provided such ceilings by service; but these had been suspended until 1953. The Defense Department wanted the individual service ceilings repealed, and the suspension of total active force ceilings extended to 1961. There was little discussion regarding the individual service ceilings. In conference, the House version was accepted, retaining these ceilings (but deleting the authorization for one-year enlistees), and then suspending them for one more year until 1954. In floor debates, however, attempts were made in both houses to set a total ceiling on active strength. The House rejected such attempts, the Senate accepted a ceiling of four million,[38] and the conference committee settled on five million. A final controversy arose over the Defense Department's proposal to eliminate the act's terminal date, an important object of the Department's and Hershey's hopes for establishing a permanent manpower procurement act. The Senate committee accepted this, defended its action vigorously on the floor, and defeated an amendment by Senator Taft limiting the act to four years' duration.[39] In the House, the concept of a limited life for the act had a more powerful friend in Chairman Vinson. In open hearings, he asked the Defense Department to answer why there should not be a three-year limit, and also why there should not be a formal annual report to Congress on the operation of the act. The Department's response is nowhere recorded in the hearings; but the committee wrote both these provisions into its amendments to the Senate bill, the House accepted them, and the conference committee compromised on a terminal date for the induction authority of July 1, 1955.

7. Results of the Legislative Debate

Passage of the Universal Military Training and Service Act of 1951 met one broad manpower procurement policy need—adjustment of Selective Service to fulfill manpower requirements of the active forces during a period of partial mobilization. In asking for ways to meet this need, the Defense Department and the Selective Service System got most of what they wanted—a lengthened term of service, a lower induction age, and authority to continue extending enlistments and calling reservists to active service. Most of these proposals had been amended in committee or on the House and Senate floors, but not to the extent of destroying their effect. Another proposal, elimination of deferments for young National Guard enlistees, was effectively postponed; at the same time large numbers of reservists whose induction had been administratively postponed were made deferrable; for the future, however, Congress indicated it wanted those entering the reserves after age eighteen and one-half to be liable for induction. A final pool-expansion proposal, rehabilitation of Class IV-F service rejects, was not promoted enthusiastically by the Defense Department, and was ignored by Congress. In related actions, however, standards of physical and mental fitness were lowered by statute, and the Defense Department was put on notice that Congress would press for statutory solutions to the imbalance among the services in acquiring the better-qualified men, should the Department not act itself. The Defense Department did act, by interservice agreement on recruiting quotas; the results did not satisfy all the critics, but the threatened congressional action never took shape.

Still to be met were the Defense Department's long-range goals for procurement, training, and control of men for the reserves. The 1951 act went partway toward this goal in two respects. It provided, as had the 1948 act, that men entering military service, active or reserve, voluntarily or by induction, would have a total active and reserve training and service obligation of eight years; for most men, at this point, this would mean a period of active service, twenty-four months or more, followed by reserve service for the remainder of the eight years. But the 1951 act went farther; in the closest approach yet to the Marshall-Palmer concept of mobilizable reserves based on a universally trained male citizenry, it set the stage for enactment and inauguration of a UMT program to train young men primarily for the reserves.

Yet the stage setting was spare. Congress had reserved the right not just to review, but to control as completely as in any other legislative act, the actual creation of UMT. Thus the supply of trained manpower for the reserves contemplated in the Defense proposals was not yet assured. Moreover, there was as yet no agreed system or structure for receiving, controlling, and, if necessary, mobilizing the huge numbers of men to be made available to the reserve forces through the operation of UMT, Selective Service, and active and reserve force recruitment.

III. DEATH OF UMT AND BEGINNINGS
OF A NEW RESERVE POLICY

Two related tasks, reconsideration of UMT and creation of a new reserve forces program, constituted the main agenda for manpower procurement policy development during the first year after passage of the 1951 Universal Military Training and Service Act. These two tasks were dealt with in tandem, though not completely coordinated, legislative actions.

1.   *The Fourth Campaign for UMT*

The first of these actions began immediately after the 1951 act was signed, as President Truman appointed the five-member National Security Training Commission.[40] Within four months of its confirmation the Commission made the legislative recommendations required of it by the act; and early in the new session of Congress bills were introduced and hearings held before the Armed Services Committees.[41]

As the hearings went forward, and the committee reports were being written, two developments pointed toward grave difficulties for UMT in Congress. One was confirmation that UMT had lost none of its old, die-hard opponents. As in years past, church, education, farm, labor, and special citizens' groups appeared before the committees to denounce the program, in general and in specific terms. One of their specific objections, that UMT could not or should not be started while Selective Service was still a major source of active forces manpower, pointed to the second and perhaps more serious development. This was that UMT's friends could not agree among themselves on several important issues.

Several of these remained unresolved even in the committee reports. The two most important were the specific conditions under which UMT inductions would begin, and the question of what would happen to the graduates of UMT.

On the latter question, there were two difficulties. First, given even full-scale operation of UMT, and transfer of its graduates to the reserves, what would assure that these men would fill the ranks of National Guard and Organized Reserve units? The total military obligation imposed on all men entering the active or reserve forces by the 1951 act was eight years. Thus this question was only part of the broader one of how the reserve obligation following active service or training would be fulfilled. Given the fact that this was the subject of another bill, passed by the House but still pending in the

Senate, and that it was also one subject of a struggle between the National Guard Association and representatives of the other reserve components, the two committees decided not to resolve the issue in UMT legislation at all.

The other problem involved in the posttraining obligation of UMT graduates was closely bound up with the question of when and under what conditions UMT could begin. As already noted, some UMT opponents were arguing for delay of legislation until the active force demands for manpower through Selective Service were clearly to be reduced or eliminated. Otherwise, they argued, UMT might well interfere with the current rearmament effort, both by draining the manpower pool and by straining the active forces' training facilities and personnel. The Defense Department's answer to this was that it planned only a small start for UMT, with an initial class of only 60,000. These men would be volunteers; following their training, they would be transferred to the reserve components of their respective services and then called for an additional eighteen months' active duty. This would have the advantages of keeping the program fully within the current strength goals of the three services, and of beginning the build-up of a young, trained reserve for the Air Force and Navy as well as the Army.

This proposal to place UMT graduates, volunteers or not, on active duty following their training proved to be anathema to those most thoroughly indoctrinated in the postwar litany that had carefully distinguished between *training* for the reserves and *service* in the active forces. Representative Kilday (D., Tex.) had, some months before, declared his intent to make active service for UMT graduates a matter of Congressional control.[42] Chairman Vinson apparently supported the Defense Department's proposal at first,[43] but he eventually changed his mind and supported House committee provisions which would prevent the Defense Department from carrying out its intent. The Senate committee took a less adamant stand. It argued that the decision as to when and how the program should start was a military decision, not to be specified in legislation, and therefore placed no special restraints on Defense regarding its plan for 60,000 volunteers.

Both committees urged that UMT be started as soon as possible; and each committee, in its own way, made this a questionable proposition. Beyond placing restrictions on the use of UMT graduates which would effectively remove them from the current pool of men available for active service, the House committee imposed an additional burden by insisting that the entire training establishment for the program (except for extra doctors, dentists and chaplains) would have to come from within the military and civilian personnel strengths already established. The Senate committee also acted to make full-scale inauguration of UMT in the near future a doubtful event. Specifically it proposed to test the claim that UMT, by providing a strong, trained reserve of manpower, would eventually permit reduction of the active armed forces. Its bill required that, after UMT had provided 300,000 graduates to the reserves, the Secretary of Defense was to reduce the active forces by one man for every three new reservists acquired from UMT. This might have, as the committee believed, removed "the guesswork from the matter of whether UMT will cost money or whether it will save money."[44] But it surely must have given Defense planners pause. As Mrs. Rosenberg told the House committee,

> . . . We are neither at peace nor at war. We can't afford the luxury of having a peacetime program or a wartime program. We do know one thing: we can't give you a guarantee of how soon, whether it is 2 years from today or 3 years from today, that we can discontinue selective service and start reducing the size of the Armed Forces.[45]

The two committees submitted their divergent reports within a few days of each other, late in February. At this point there were important procedural advantages in getting a bill through the more hostile House first, and Chairman Vinson marshalled his forces toward this end. Despite the privileged status of his bill (assured in the 1951 act), Vinson followed normal procedures and gave it to the Rules Committee first. This done, general debate began on February 26 and extended, for the allotted twelve hours, through February 29. The next move came on March 4, as reading of the bill for amendments began. Immediately Vinson played his major card, offering an important concession to the opposition: UMT, under his new committee amendment, would not begin until Selective Service inductions ceased; moreover, the program would have a terminal date of July 1, 1958. This amendment was accepted overwhelmingly; given an emotional endorsement by Speaker Rayburn, the bill's chances seemed quite good for a short while.[46] But it failed a crucial test later in the day, as a crippling amendment was adopted by just five votes. The fourth UMT campaign ended as the House voted to recommit the bill to committee.[47]

2. The Armed Forces Reserve Act of 1952

UMT was a dead proposition; and Congress and the Administration were once again faced with the task of piecing together some sort of reserve program without an assured source of trained but nonveteran reservists.

In the six years since World War II, the development and implementation of coordinated policies and programs for the reserves had been the victim of interservice disagreements, conflict between the National Guard and other reserve components, and most importantly, the overriding demand for active forces adequate to immediate needs and as a base for full mobilization. One consequence was the sorry state of the reserves at the outbreak of the Korean War. Another was the vast scope of inequities and incongruities in the recall of reservists during the first year of that war. As to the latter, by mid-April, 1951, the Defense Department had prepared preliminary plans for the early release of veteran reservists; and by the end of July these plans were being carried out at a rate which would release 100,000 Army reservists by the end of the year.[48] What Congress and the Administration had in mind, however, was not the further legislative correction of these inequities, but a full-scale reorganization of the reserves and of the method of bringing them into active service, which might preclude a recurrence of the Korean War problems.[49]

To a greater extent than is usually true of major military policy-making, the initiative and moving energy for new legislation on reserves in this instance came from Congress, specifically from the House Armed Services Committee and a special subcommittee chaired by Representative Brooks (D., La.).[50] Unfortunately, in searching for a long-range reserve policy, the committee, and most witnesses for the Administration, the reserve associations, and the veterans groups who aided its work, made one assumption about the reserves which quickly proved wrong. The assumption was, of course, that there would soon be available a pool of nonveteran UMT graduates who would comprise the larger part of those involuntary reservists to be made most vulnerable to an active service call.

The House bill distinguished between three classes of reserves—Ready, Standby, and Retired—differing essentially in the degree of their vulnerability to such a call. The Ready Reserve would be available for active service on declaration of war or emergency by Congress or declaration of national emergency by the president; the Standby Reserve could be called only after Congress had declared war or a state of emergency; and the Retired Reservists might be called only when no more men with their particular qualifications were available in the Ready and Standby classes. There was an additional restriction added by the House bill: the president, even after declaring an emergency, could call Ready Reserve units and individuals only in the numbers specifically designated by subsequent act of Congress. Thus the distinction between Ready and Standby Reserves, though still intended, was considerably dimmed.

The bill did not alter the total service obligation of eight years. It did provide that men serving four years or more on active duty might serve their entire remaining reserve obligation on Standby status. (Thus the Navy and the Air Force, which required minimum four-year enlistments, would have no discharged veterans obligated to Ready Reserve status.) A man with less than four years of active service would serve his remaining time in Ready Reserve status; he could, however, volunteer to participate in the training program of a Guard or Organized Reserve unit for three years and then request transfer to the Standby Reserve for the remainder of his service obligation.

The House bill also contained extensive provisions defining the Guard and Reserve components of the various services and providing for reasonably uniform rules regarding appointment, enlistment, release from duty, as well as pay, allowances, and other benefits for members of the several reserve components and categories. But the chief purpose of the act lay in its provisions regarding postservice or posttraining obligations, vulnerability for call to active duty, and the authority of Congress and the president in such calls.

Following the hard work of the Brooks subcommittee, the bill met no obstacles either in the full committee or on the House floor.[51] But, given the goal of creating trained reserves for all the military services, reserves that might with some degree of justice and equity be called to active service in a future emergency, the House bill contained two serious flaws. First, although it imposed an obligation on certain trained men to remain for set periods in the most vulnerable reserve class, there was no obligation—only inducement—to participate in further training programs of the Guard and Organized Reserve units. The second flaw became obvious upon the defeat of UMT in early 1952: in the absence of any UMT graduates, only the Army (and to a lesser extent the Marine Corps) would have large numbers of postservice veterans obligated to the Ready Reserve (following three-year enlistments or twenty-four months' inducted service) and thus open to the unit-training-participation inducements of the bill.

Various solutions were offered in the Senate hearings,[52] which were not held until May, 1952; and all of them gave at least tacit recognition to the end of any realistic hopes for UMT. The National Guard Association had suggested, in the earlier House hearings on UMT, that UMT graduates might be required to join National Guard or other Organized Reserve units. The NGA did not raise this proposal again in Senate hearings on the House reserve bill, but suggested instead that Guard and Organized Reserve recruiting be promoted by extending Selective Service deferments to include men enlisting in those units after February 1, 1951.[53] Also, apparently with NGA approval, a representative of the New York National Guard did advocate compulsory Guard or Organized Reserve service. The Senate committee did not seriously entertain either of these proposals.

A second solution was promoted by General Hershey. Under the 1951 act, the Defense and military department secretaries were authorized to permit early release from the twenty-four-months active duty requirement of any man who volunteered for service in an organized unit of the Guard or other reserve components. Hershey proposed inducting all qualified young men, presumably at the minimum age; after six months' training, and depending on active force needs, a small number would be allowed to enlist in reserve units and go off active duty; the remainder would stay in active service, as inductees or volunteer enlistees. The Senate committee ignored this idea, which would have bypassed completely the carefully written restrictions in the 1951 act on inauguration of UMT.

Still a third answer, proposed by the Defense Department, was to manipulate reserve obligations to get the desired result. Men with four years' active service, instead of serving the last four years of their obligation in Standby, would have the choice of serving four years in Ready status or of transferring to Standby after two years of participation in the training program of a Ready Reserve unit. Similarly, men with two or three years' active service could transfer to Standby for the last two years of their total obligation only by active participation in an organized reserve unit; otherwise they would retain Ready Reserve status and recall liability for their total reserve service period. The Senate committee rejected this proposal, too.

Indeed, the committee chose to abandon the whole concept of Ready and Standby Reserve classes, focusing instead on a different aspect of reserve recall vulnerability. There is a difference, it argued, between the procedures required for mobilizing large numbers of nonveteran UMT graduates, and the screening needed for recalling active service veterans. These latter would be the only reservists available, there might eventually be some four to six million of them, and the House bill did not really address itself to this problem. The committee's report hinted at a solution: let the president and the military services have control over recall of a portion of the reserves; but place recall of the majority of individual reservists in the hands of Selective Service or some other nonmilitary agency which would be sensitive to the needs of the civilian economy and communities and the claims of individuals. In face of Defense Department opposition to this, however, the committee simply urged that a complete study be made of the matter so that the next Congress might enact provisions for screening reservists to minimize inequities in any future recall. The committee did include one provision, protecting combat veterans of the Korean conflict from recall ahead of noncombat veterans. The Senate passed its committee's version of the Armed Forces Reserve Act with only minor amendments.[54]

In conference, the Senate managers receded from most of their revisions of the House bill. The distinction between Ready and Standby Reserves was restored, and these classes were subjected to recall under the original House provisions. Transfer to Standby was permitted after a total of five years' active and drilling reserve service, in any combination. The conferees required that the secretary of defense publish regulations for screening Ready Reservists, taking into account the length and nature of previous service, family responsibilities, and the needs of the civil economy; and they further required the secretary to report annually to the Armed Services Committees on this process. The conferees also expanded on rules for recalling the Standby Reservists, to assure that even when their recall was authorized by Congress, the Ready Reservists would be called first. Finally, the conferees set an authorized strength ceiling for the Ready Reserve (including all Guardsmen and those reservists on duty with the active forces) of 1.5 million. The conference report was accepted with little debate, and the Armed Forces Reserve Act of 1952 was quickly signed into law.[55]

IV.   ISSUES OF COLD WAR
MANPOWER POLICY IN 1952

The two years following the outbreak of war in Korea brought marked, though hardly surprising, changes in military manpower procurement policies and programs. In contrast to the frustrations of 1944-47, and the uncertainties of 1948-50, by 1952 the Truman Administration achieved what seemed then an adequate compromise policy to meet cold war demands for military forces. Yet problems remained, some explicit, others muted, regarding every major issue that had affected manpower procurement policy debates over the preceding eight years.

1.   *Military Effectiveness and the Muted Question of Costs*

By mid-1952 there was relatively little concern over the adequacy of the manpower procurement system for meeting active force needs. Through inductions, enlistments, and reserve calls, the system had expanded total active military strength from 1.46 million on June 30, 1950, to 3.64 million two years later;[56] and the June 30, 1952, strength was still well below the congressionally imposed ceiling of five million. The chief worrier was the director of Selective Service, who continued to voice concern over the high rate of physical and mental rejections; but even he would not argue that there was an immediate inability to meet active manpower demands.[57]

Congressional response to the Administration's case for immediate improvements in active force procurement machinery was generous by earlier postwar standards. But response to hopes and proposals for a more permanent solution to the nation's military manpower needs was less than enthusiastic. Congress showed no taste at this point for providing permanent selective service legislation or for long-term suspension of the limits on active force strengths. This reluctance had only minor effects on the Administration's long-range proposals, though, compared to the impact of congressional rejection of UMT. The concept of UMT was indeed woven into the new Selective Service amendments, as Secretary Marshall had hoped; but Congress, especially the House, insisted on still another chance to review and act before the program could become a reality. UMT got its review; but action in the House subjected this last serious attempt to legislate Marshall's postwar dream to the ignominy of recommittal.

By this action, the House also shattered its own committee's painstaking efforts to establish an effective program of procurement for and control of the reserve components. One main intent of the 1952 Armed Forces Reserve Act was to establish some fundamental distinction among reservists on which to base future calls to active service. The most important feature was to have been that those with the least previous service, the UMT graduates, would be most vulnerable to recall. With UMT stillborn, the great majority of future reservists would be veterans. All Congress could do in this situation was to make a dim distinction between Ready and Standby Reserves as classes of differing recall vulnerability, and insist that the Defense Department establish screening standards and procedures for the recall of Ready Reservists which would take into account past service and current dependency and occupational obligations.

A second purpose of the Armed Forces Reserve Act was to provide manpower to the organized, drilling units of the National Guard and other reserve components. From the outset there was reluctance to force anyone into these units, and this hardly diminished with the defeat of UMT. That defeat also removed the greatest recruiting inducement offered in the House bill—a chance for UMT graduates to shorten their Ready Reserve obligations by four and one-half years through participation in a drilling reserve unit. As finally enacted, the inducement was altered to provide transfer to Standby after any five-year combination of active service and reserve training participation; and it was feared this still might not attract enough men to fill out the Guard and Organized Reserve units.

If Congress was unresponsive to Administration hopes for UMT and its potential contribution to well-manned, trained reserves, it was certainly not irresponsible. Charges raised by long-time opponents, that UMT would mean eight years of slavery and the militarization of American youth, that it would disrupt their education and corrupt their morals perhaps beyond repair, certainly had some impact. More to the point during this period of American awakening to practical defense needs, and more influential, was the question of whether UMT was really necessary or would even be a reasonable solution.

The language of UMT supporters was not reassuring. The National Security Training Commission, for example, insisted in its 1951 report that "the American people must be prepared, like their forebears who pushed the frontier westward, to meet a savage and deadly attack at any moment. *The return to frontier conditions demands a frontier response.*"[58] The House committee's latest report on UMT also drew upon traditional preparedness arguments, focusing upon an impending apocalypse to justify the program. Only the Senate committee made any formal attempt to relate UMT to the possibility of recurring conflicts on the scale of the Korean War, and it did this largely in terms of avoiding the injustices committed against veterans in the recent call of reservists.

It remained for outsiders (and unnamed insiders) to question the whole concept of huge reserves embodied in UMT and the Armed Forces Reserve Act. While UMT was still pending before Congress, Hanson Baldwin summarized some current critiques of the proposal. He quoted the late Robert Patterson, long a proponent of UMT, as finally having decided that universal service, rather than training, was the real need in meeting the new demands for military strength. Baldwin also cited critics within the Defense Department who were concerned about the possible effects of UMT, and the large reserve it would produce, on the pool of men available for active service and on Defense budgets. Later, after passage of the Armed Forces Reserve Act, Baldwin offered an even broader critique. He could not accept the argument that changes in military weaponry meant the end of needs for large numbers of well-trained men; but neither could he accept the older argument that these trained men could be kept effectively ready in the reserves. Whether the internal issues of reserve policy had been solved by the new act or not (and he felt they had not), no implementation of these policies should be allowed to detract from the first priority in defense, the strength of the active forces.[59]

There were echoes of these concerns in the public debates over UMT and reserve policy in 1951 and 1952, especially in the Senate Armed Service Committee's insistence that the growth of UMT-trained reserve pools be balanced by reductions in active forces. But the cost efficiency considerations implied in the contrast between mobilizable reserves supported by UMT, and the modified forces-in-being structure suggested by Baldwin and like-minded UMT critics, did not seem to affect the Defense Department's outlook in this period of expanding military strengths and budgets.

Equally muted during the Korean War rearmament were the cost implications of reliance on Selective Service to meet active force needs. Even more in 1952 than in 1948, it was simply assumed that no increase in pay and benefits could produce enough volunteers to preclude conscription; and no one showed any interest in exploring the costs of a purely voluntary system.

2. *Attitudes toward Compulsion*

In 1950, Congress and the public accepted Selective Service as a necessary device for meeting active force needs, virtually in the sense of a declaration of war. By 1952, Selective Service still had three years left of a new four-year lease on life. For twelve years, public attitudes toward the System had alternated between patriotic acceptance in time of national peril and rejection in time of apparent peace. Now, however, national peril had come to be understood in long-range, cold war terms; and the Selective Service System began to blend into the governmental and social scene as a seemingly permanent fact of life.[60]

While Selective Service was becoming more and more accepted, conscription as the sole or even chief means to meeting military manpower demands was not. Recruiting went on during the Korean War, for the services themselves wanted conscription only insofar as volunteers did not meet their needs. The Defense Department did promote universal conscription as a way of producing basically trained reservists; but only the National Guard Association (and finally only its New York chapter) and the American Legion thus far supported compulsion to fill up drilling reserve units. The House, in rejecting UMT, rejected compulsion even for the initial training program. Representative Cox (D., Ga.) could ask: "Does not the young man owe some duty to his country, and if so, when has it become immoral for him to perform it?"[61] The answer, of course, was that the 1951 act did indeed recognize such an obligation, and that American youth stood ready to meet it as called; conscription was not immoral so long as the military need for it was clear. But the military need to give all young men basic training had never been clear. It had always been a hypothesis about the future, and this hypothesis could not be persuasive while a major and popular part of the defense establishment challenged it. Thus even as the nation had begun to accept the need for military forces to meet the perils of the cold war in the late 1940's, Air Force opposition had made adoption of UMT improbable. In 1952, it was argued that current demands for active forces made UMT impracticable, and Marshall's own case in 1951 for broadening the manpower pool lent weight to this view. The military need for UMT remained, then, an often stated but never proved hypothesis. Likewise, the social principle of universal conscription remained a legislative statement without programmatic content.

3.   The Submerged Question of Equity

The one freshly emphasized argument for UMT in 1951 and 1952 was the need for trained, nonveteran reservists as the only sure way to avoid repeating the individual and collective injustices of the Korean War recall of veteran reservists. This was an argument for equity, however, not for military needs. Moreover, no one asked, but some may have wondered, whether UMT itself would really solve this problem. Under the House bills, the Ready Reserve would include both UMT graduates and combat veterans; the latter would surely be more needed in the initial stages of a reserve call, and the Defense Department had already defended the inequities of its Korean War recall on grounds of administrative effectiveness and military needs. In the end, Congress and the public seemed to reject the idea that universal training was needed to establish equity between generations of military-age youth; at the same time, by insisting on careful screening procedures, Congress did show concern that future military needs not be allowed to override individual claims to reasonable and equitable treatment.

Nor was universal conscription, for training or for service, accepted to maintain equity among men in the same military generation. A passion for rationality might easily lead to the principle and practice of seeking equity in compulsion by compelling each man equally; but such a rationalist passion has dominated American politics and policy no more in military conscription than in taxation.

The 1951 amendments to the Selective Service Act gave it a new title implying universal application; but universality went no farther than to establish a general obligation for training and service. Left in the act were the injunctions that "in a free society, the obligations and privileges of serving in the armed forces and the reserve components thereof should be shared generally. . . ." Also retained, however, was the qualification that this sharing should take place "in accordance with a system of selection which is fair and just, and which is consistent with the maintenance of an effective economy." Underscoring the need to recognize nonmilitary demands on manpower was a parallel injunction, also retained from the 1948 act, calling for "maximum effort in the fields of scientific research and development, and the fullest possible utilization of the Nation's technological, scientific, and other critical manpower resources." Underscoring the intent that equity be pursued within the principle of selectivity, rather than through universality, was the requirement that the selection be made "in an impartial manner, under such rules and regulations as the President may prescribe, from the persons who are liable for such training and service and who at the time of selection are registered and classified, but not deferred or exempt. . . ." Equity under the law, then, was to be a matter of impartial administration, not of universally exacted obligation.

In 1951, Congress did require some adjustments in the president's rules and regulations. It continued to allow deferment on grounds of dependency, but forbade extending this generally to childless husbands. It also indirectly reemphasized the induction liability of newly enlisted reservists. These were both moves toward more general sharing of the military obligation. At the same time, though, Congress gave post facto recognition to the postponed induction of reservists enlisted before February 1, 1951; and it passively accepted continued deferment of fathers regardless of hardship. Most importantly, Congress gave added recognition to a major class of deferments—those based on occupation, and especially those granted to students.

The record of congressional intent regarding student deferments is complex. In 1948, the House committee had rejected the idea of a blanket deferment for college students as inequitable, and the issue was left to administrative discretion. In 1951, the Administration asked for a statutory endorsement of a student program limited both in numbers and in time; and the Senate accepted the idea. In rejecting this program, the House committee reaffirmed the president's authority to defer students at his discretion, and it endorsed the Selective Service System's plans. The House moved the level of discretion a little farther toward the local boards, by forbidding imposition on them of any specific national standards for these or other occupational deferments. Still in the act, though, was the intent that these deferments be "necessary to the maintenance of the national health, safety, or interest. . . ." In addition, at House insistence, Congress extended the liability of deferred men to age thirty-five, thus establishing an intent that deferment should not become permanent exemption from service.

Through all the record of justification for student deferments ran the theme that, in a partial mobilization, military needs must not be allowed to shut off the necessary flow of college-trained men into the economy and the armed forces, or to damage seriously the institutions of higher education responsible for this flow. How long student deferments would be necessary to these ends was not clear; but aside from the problem of providing medical and other specialists directly to the armed forces, no one suggested that the general need would exist for more than two, three, or four years.

By mid-1952, the student deferment program had operated for a year, and there were few who still objected to it outright. But serious questions were still being raised about the equity of the program. Dr. Trytten continued to defend it on grounds of national need, but repeated his support for scholarships to enable men to qualify for deferment regardless of financial ability.[62] The National Manpower Council's study joined in this concern, but expressed others as well. In its statement, the Council called for removing dependency alone as grounds for deferment, partly for fear that students might use this means to convert their student deferments into effective exemption from service. Studies published with the Council's statement raised the question of part-time students, for whom no deferments were authorized. The studies questioned, too, the discretionary power granted to local boards in the program, noting that an individual board might, in response to community pressure or its own independent views, grant deferments to students not meeting the standards but engaged in some favored field of study.[63] One answer to this lay in Hershey's philosophy that the local board was in the best position to relate individual cases to national needs. But the Selective Service System also hinted that it was willing to counter community pressures and local board attitudes through the appeals system. Answering an accusation by the American Council on Education that some boards were refusing to defer any college students, the deputy director stated that "the recent test, and the reports on class standing, were designed to be used by local boards as guidelines. The local board which disregards the recommendations of Selective Service and of its advisory board is being arbitrary. Arbitrary action, here or elsewhere, should not be tolerated."[64] This suggests once again that equity in the Selective Service operation was not to be a matter of precisely equal treatment of individuals or of general justice as between groups or generations. Rather, the System concentrated on applying its rules, whatever they might be, reasonably and impartially. Nevertheless, it preferred to let those rules vary according to local views and needs.

Whether because the System's rules and operations were well understood and accepted or because these and the whole problem were just too difficult to contemplate, there was at this time no widespread public or congressional criticism of manpower procurement policy on grounds of equity.

4.   Adapting to Social Goals

As to the major justification for student deferments—the protection of the flow of trained men through the colleges—by mid-1952 there were not quite 200,000 men classified in II-S. In addition, about 23,000 college students were given statutory (I-S) deferments to the end of the 1951-52 academic year, and there were about 200,000 ROTC students classed as reserved for military service (I-D) and deferred from induction.[65] Taking into account other provisions of the law as well (exemption of veterans and deferment for dependency), General Hershey noted that at the end of November, 1951, some 891,000 out of 1,259,000 male college students of draft age (eighteen and one-half to twenty-six years) were exempt or deferred.[66] But the student deferment program itself was protecting only a small part of the college-graduate flow. Nor was the degree of selectivity very high. Applied alone, the standard of class standing would allow only a quarter of the group completing freshman year to remain through their senior year. But some 62 percent of those taking the test in fiscal year 1951 made passing scores,[67] and many who failed could still meet the class-standing requirements. A study of students of twenty-three colleges taking the test during the summer of 1951 showed that, from the previous year's classes, 68 percent of freshmen, 81 percent of sophomores, and 88 percent of juniors remained deferrable for the next year when the two standards were applied cumulatively (see Table 6). Applied together, then, the two standards would allow nearly half of those students surviving their freshman year to remain through their senior year. Noting that the prewar attrition rate for the four undergraduate years was 50 percent, the National Manpower Council background study

TABLE 6

STUDENT DEFERMENT ELIGIBILITY, FALL, 1951
(By Percentage)

Reason for Deferability	College Year Completed		
	Freshman	Sophomore	Junior
Test score only* _____	18	14	13
Test score and			
class standing† _____	35	48	58
Class standing only‡ _____	15	19	17
Total _____	68	81	88

SOURCE: Educational Testing Service Report SR-52-1, *A Summary of Statistics on Selective Service College Qualification Test of May 26, 1951, June 16, 1951, June 30, 1951, July 12, 1951* (Princeton, N. J.: Educational Testing Service, 1952). Reproduced by permission. Percent figures are estimates based on comparison of test scores and college grades of a 10 percent sample of examinees from 23 colleges.

* Percent scoring 70 or higher but standing in bottom portion of class.

† Percent scoring 70 or higher and standing in upper portion of class.

‡ Percent scoring below 70 but standing in upper portion of class.

concluded: "If the freshmen with low test scores or low class standing tend to be the same students who would normally fail to graduate, then it follows that . . . any reduction in the number of college graduates as a result of the present deferment standards will [with high probability] be small."[68] In recognizing the national security and social needs for educated men, then, the Selective Service program seemed more than generous.

Claims for dependency deferment on grounds of general national or social need were not so completely recognized. The National Manpower Council study stated that "deferment of married men, or of fathers, recognizes the importance of maintaining a stable family unit." But the Council noted that this justification had not protected reservists in 1950-52, and that "families and homes were not irreparably injured during World War II because fathers were called into service."[69] For whatever reasons, and they seemed to be a combination of military manpower needs and equity, deferment for childless husbands was cancelled by law in 1951; but deferment for fathers continued for two more years.[70]

A somewhat more compelling claim was advanced by industry and the Department of Labor for industrial apprentices. In the 1951 hearings on universal training and service, both Senator Morse and Senator Johnson urged Secretary Tobin to consider carefully the problem of deferment for apprentices in skilled trades. Although Tobin recognized the problem, he had no solution; but by mid-

1952 an agreement had been worked out between the Selective Service System and the Labor Department for cooperation in setting guidelines by which young men in apprentice programs might qualify for deferment. In all, however, deferments for industrial and agricultural occupations together amounted to little over 130,000.[71]

5. *Unfinished Business*

The Korean War rearmament was the second phase of America's military preparations for the cold war. More successful than the first, it produced active forces larger than those supported by this nation in any earlier time of formal peace. It also produced a manpower procurement system easily able to support those forces. Selective Service had become, in effect, the central feature of manpower policy for the cold war, as it had been in World War II. Its compulsions were accepted as necessary, even inevitable.

There were serious questions to ask of this system and this policy. The general issue of equity seemed especially sharp when the system could select one man to serve and perhaps risk his life, could defer another perhaps permanently, but could offer no clear and generally applicable grounds for distinguishing between the two. Nonetheless, for at least fifteen more years this question did not stir enough concern to threaten major alteration in the system. The general public, Congress, and a new Administration all remained willing, with General Hershey, to let the local boards carry the burden of distinguishing and selecting.

Other questions remained unanswered, too—questions concerning manpower for the reserves and the quality of men in the active forces. With the advent of a new Administration, these soon became objects of renewed debate.

chapter four

The Quiet Triumph of
Selective Service

I. NEW LOOK IN MANPOWER POLICIES

The aims of the Defense Department in manpower procurement policy during the Korean rearmament had been: first, to assure an adequate flow of men into the active forces for a build-up which more than doubled the total in one year and increased it another one-eighth in the second year; second, to assure that this process did not interfere unduly with the civilian and defense support economy, either during the period of build-up or during the longer period of heightened preparedness which was to succeed it; and, finally, to assure the long-term existence of machinery for drawing trained veterans and nonveterans into organized reserve units and pools to be available for active duty should further mobilization be required. The first and second aims had largely been achieved by mid-1952; to the extent that a sense of emergency and crisis was coming to be part of everyday American political and social life, Selective Service seemed to have been accepted as necessary even into the foreseeable future, although Congress had served notice it intended to review the act again in 1955. The third aim had proved more elusive; an orderly process for manning and controlling the reserves was still, for the most part, a pious hope.

These manpower policy aims reflected the dualism in the strategic side of American military policy in the Korean War period: the desire to maintain large forces-in-being to deter all-out and lesser conflicts, and simultaneously to build a base for a total mobilization should we find ourselves at war with the Soviet Union.

In the succeeding eight years, Samuel Huntington has argued, most of the mobilization thinking disappeared from American strategic policy; yet the structural side of military policy, and especially manpower procurement aims, retained much of the older dualism.[1] This is clearly revealed in the two major questions about manpower policy which aroused the most widespread interest and activity in Congress and among public groups: the question of reserve policy implied some future mobilization, presumably to meet a military threat on the scale of the Korean War or larger; the question of manpower quality, however, underlined the need for competent forces-in-being to deter general or lesser conflicts.

A major source of this continued dualism in manpower policies was the very pattern imposed on American military policy by the new Eisenhower Administration. What was new in the New Look was the declaratory policy of relying on nuclear weapons—strategic and, as they became available, tactical—as the major deterrent to all levels of armed challenge to American security and foreign policy aims. Inextricably intertwined with this major change in strategic outlook, however, was a thoroughly traditional emphasis on economy in military defense, growing out of a deep-seated concern that defense expenditures might overstrain and perhaps bankrupt the American economy. This traditional outlook had very nearly controlled military policy as recently as the two years between the abortive attempt at cold war rearmament and the Korean War; and it was given renewed strength by the Republic election victory in 1952 and the nature of the Administration and Congress that election produced.[2] Together these two policy attitudes were succinctly stated in the popular cliché "more bang for a buck."

The New Look emphasis on nuclear weaponry partly stimulated, and certainly symbolized, a further acceleration in the revolution of military technology begun forty years before, loudly proclaimed during World War II, and pursued with ever-increasing intensity in the cold war era. Nuclear weapons were only one aspect of this postwar multiplication of technical complexity in the means of war. As important were Air Force developments in the means of delivering these weapons and in the machines and devices for supporting and controlling these delivery systems; Air Force and Army development of systems to defend against enemy delivery systems; developments in nuclear, aircraft, submarine, and electronic control and detection technologies for naval forces; and the multiplication of new weapons, communications, and transportation for the ground forces.

At the same time, the New Look and later defense budgets forced, indeed were largely built on, levels of active force manpower significantly lower than those achieved during the Korean War rearmament. Some strength reductions had begun even before the advent of the New Look, reflecting mostly the reduced requirements for manpower in the wake of the Korean truce negotiations; and from the beginning of the Eisenhower Administration, the drive for a reduced defense budget was coupled closely with manpower cuts in the active forces. By June, 1954, active strengths totaled a little over 3.3 million (see Table 7); the total fell even more rapidly the next year; and almost annual reductions thereafter brought total active strength down to 2.484 million in June, 1961, the end of the last Eisenhower budget year. These cuts were effected in all services; the Air Force felt them least, the Navy a little more, and the Army and Marine Corps most of all.

The dual impact of military technology and shrinking active forces sharpened the problem of quality in military manpower. In varying forms it became a major concern of the military services during the 1950's; and toward the end of the first Eisenhower Administration it attracted growing congressional and public attention.

In the meantime, partly as a traditional Army response to reduc-

TABLE 7

Active Duty Military Personnel, June 30, 1953–June 30, 1961

(In Thousands)

	Dept. of Defense		Army		Navy		Marine Corps		Air Force	
	Total	% of Officers	Total	% of Officers	Total	% of Officers	Total	% of Officers	Total	% of Officers
1953	3,555	10.6	1,534	9.5	794	10.3	249	7.5	978	13.4
1954	3,302	10.7	1,405	9.1	726	10.6	224	8.3	948	13.7
1955	2,935	12.0	1,109	11.0	661	11.3	205	9.0	960	14.3
1956	2,806	12.5	1,026	11.5	670	10.7	201	8.9	910	15.6
1957	2,796	12.3	998	11.1	677	10.9	201	8.7	920	15.3
1958	2,601	12.5	899	11.6	641	11.2	189	8.8	871	15.3
1959	2,504	12.7	862	11.8	626	11.1	176	9.2	840	15.7
1960	2,476	12.8	873	11.6	618	11.3	171	9.5	815	15.9
1961	2,484	12.7	859	11.6	627	11.2	177	9.1	821	15.7

Source: U.S. Department of Defense, Directorate for Statistical Services, *Selected Manpower Statistics* (Washington: Department of Defense, April 11, 1966), pp. 19, 24.

tions in active strength, partly through congressional response to this problem and to pressure from the reserve associations and veterans groups, and partly as an oddly conceived aspect of the New Look itself, early and continuing attention was given to the problem of manning and controlling the reserve components of the armed forces.

The answers found to these problems were in themselves important aspects of manpower policy development during the New Look years. Their importance was heightened by their not too clearly perceived impact on the total pool of available military manpower. This impact was perhaps best understood by leaders of the Selective Service System. Their responses to newly developing difficulties of managing a growing surplus of available military manpower became heavily dependent on answers to the problems of manpower quality and reserve forces. These Selective Service responses may have been understood, and their significance appreciated, in other parts of the Administration and by some members of the armed services committees; but they were never clearly explained to the rest of Congress and to the public, most of whom remained unaware that there was any such manpower management problem at all.

Some aspects of manpower policy and Selective Service operations did stir public discussion; muted and sporadic attention was given to the nonmilitary issues involved—compulsion, equity, and impact on other social goals. But, given the general lack of public and congressional understanding of the total military manpower picture, the occasional outbursts of criticism and discomfiture which marked consideration of these issues never developed into a consistent and effective critique of policy. The remainder of the 1950's were years of partial answers to narrowly conceived problems. They were also years of the quiet and supremely administrative triumph of Selective Service.

II. MANPOWER PROCUREMENT
FOR THE RESERVES

1. *Slow Development of Administration Proposals*

Ostensibly, an improved reserves program was an integral part of the New Look in military policy. In fact, it was only a poor country cousin—or so it was treated for the first two years of the Eisenhower Administration.

Among some there was hope that the Administration might be persuaded to continue its predecessor's seven-year sponsorship of UMT, at least formally. But President Eisenhower had cooled toward the idea after his nomination in 1952, and the election did not change his attitude. In February, 1953, he told a news conference that he doubted that UMT could be operated at the same time as Selective Service, but said he was awaiting a report on the matter from the National Security Training Commission.[3] Not until August 1 did the president send formal requests to the commission and to the director of defense mobilization for reports on reserve manpower problems. The commission was to examine (1) inequities in the current reserve procurement system; (2) the feasibility of operating Selective Service and a training program to produce nonveteran reservists simultaneously; and (3) the relation of such a training program to the general problems of strength and equity in the reserve systems. The Office of Defense Mobilization was to report on the availability of manpower for such a reserve training program in light of other military and civilian demands for manpower.[4]

The commission set about its work enthusiastically and came up with a report by the deadline of December 1. Predictably, the commission insisted that the 1951 concept of universal military training and service should and could be put into practice at an early date. It based this recommendation on three grounds. First, the current service reserves were largely a veteran force; thus any future call of reserves to active duty would only repeat the inequities experienced by veteran reservists in 1950 and 1951. Second, even these veteran reservists did not constitute a truly ready force; only 610,000 reservists, or 30 percent of the total, were participating in regular reserve unit training programs, and almost a third of these were National Guardsmen, the great majority of whom received no active training; nor were conditions improving with the return of Korean War veterans, only 4 percent of whom were volunteering to shorten their reserve obligations through participation in reserve training. Finally, the commission concluded there was no shortage of manpower to support such a program; given varying assumptions about the future needs of active forces, about 1–1.5 million young men would become available for a six-months National Security Training Program in the fiscal years 1955-60. Moreover, without such a program, some of these men would receive no training at all, and would escape all practical military obligations, active or reserve.

The Office of Defense Mobilization was less confident than the commission about the feasibility of conducting the National Security Training program and simultaneously maintaining active forces totaling 3 million or more. Its report went to the president on January 6, 1954; and, on its recommendation, the president turned over the problem of preparing a new reserve program to the Defense Department, with instructions to report by May 1. He also instructed the Office of Defense Mobilization and the commission to combine efforts in assessing the availability of manpower for the National Security Training Program, and to report to the National Security Council by April 1.[5]

While studies were being piled upon studies of the reserve program, the Administration was presenting its full-blown New Look defense program to Congress and the public in the fiscal year 1955 appropriations hearings. Despite heavy cuts in active ground forces, the Administration showed no real sense of urgency about putting the reserves in order. The only exceptions came in prepared statements by Army Secretary Stevens and General Ridgway, who argued that increased readiness in the reserves might partially affect reductions in active Army strength. Secretary Wilson, when pressed, merely observed, "you have put your finger on a very important matter. . . ." He saw the problem as one of inducing service veterans to participate in reserve training programs.[6]

Through 1954, further studies preceded the Administration's proposals for a National Reserve Plan; and at the end of the year, briefings for congressional leaders revealed this new program would differ in some fundamental fashion both from the current reserve program and from older UMT plans.[7] Despite the exhaustive Administration preparations, however, and perhaps just because they symbolized a lack of urgency in the Executive over repairing the reserves, the new reserve plan was fated to further major revisions, and near extinction, in the next session of Congress.

2. *The Reserve Forces Act of 1955*

The Administration's legislative program for military manpower in 1955 included both the National Plan and extension of the Universal Military Training and Service Act, due to expire on July 1. Though separate bills were offered, the Administration hoped they would be considered simultaneously; but these hopes yielded early in the session to the Armed Services Committees' insistence on dealing with the two programs separately.

The fundamental difference between the proposed National Reserve Plan and older UMT plans turned out to be that the newer plan would not necessarily be universal. Through a variety of obligations and options, it sought to provide a steady annual increment of trained nonveterans to the Ready Reserve; but the Ready Reserve was to be limited in size to specific service mobilization requirements, and its hard core was to consist of active service veterans serving required periods of time in drilling Reserve or Guard units. The Department's bill,[8] consisting of amendments to the Universal Military Training and Service Act, the Armed Forces Reserve Act of 1952, and the National Defense Act, included the following features:

1.   A continued military obligation of eight years for men inducted, enlisted, or appointed in the active services.

2.   Two enlistment programs for the reserves for men under nineteen years old not already ordered for induction: First, a continuation of the program already used extensively by the Navy, allowing reserve enlistment for eight years, to include two years' active service and periods of reserve training to be set by the service secretaries. Second, the major new feature in the National Reserve Plan, allowing reserve enlistment for ten years, to include six months' active duty for training and subsequent periods of reserve training to be set by the service secretaries.

3.   Annual quotas for these two reserve enlistment programs for those under nineteen years, with authority to induct men to fill these quotas.

4.   A Ready Reserve, consisting of those men and units needed in the first six months of a general mobilization, subject to call by Con-

gress for the duration of a war or emergency, or by the president for up to twenty-four months' active duty.

5.   A Standby Reserve, consisting of all other members of the reserves, subject to call only in a congressionally declared war or emergency, and then only upon determination of availability by the Selective Service System.

6.   Screening from Ready to Standby, under service regulations approved by the Secretary of Defense, to assure that the needs of the services and the civilian economy for skilled persons were properly balanced, that individual situations barring sudden recall were taken into account, and that, within the limits of defense needs, credit was given for prior combat service of men with reserve obligations.

7.   Compulsory assignment to drilling Ready Reserve units, including Guard units where permitted by the state governor, under rules established by service secretaries. Penalties for failure to participate in prescribed unit or individual training programs could include, for those enlisted or inducted into the six-months training program, induction into active service for up to eighteen months, or, for any obligated reservist, a discharge other than honorable.

This plan clearly allowed for wide variations in service plans. The Navy, Marine Corps, and Air Force were satisfied with their voluntary reserve programs. Except for token Marine participation of 1,000 annually, they did not intend to use the new six-months training program; nor did they intend to induct men into their reserve components or to enforce postservice reserve training obligations unless and until that seemed necessary. The Army, on the other hand, planned annual quotas of 99,000 for the six-months program, to be filled by induction if there were not enough volunteers. It also intended to enforce the Ready Reserve training obligations of both these men and active service veterans, whether assigned to National Guard or other Ready Reserve units or to the Ready Reserve pool.

Service and Defense Department plans also provided positive incentives to participation in reserve unit training programs, including the usual pay for such duty, and credits toward promotion and retirements. The most important incentive would be reduction in the

Ready Reserve obligation: men entering the six-months program could transfer to Standby after a total of eight years' participation in Ready Reserve unit training; men with two years' active duty could reduce their remaining six-year Ready Reserve obligation to five years by satisfactory participation; and men enlisting for longer periods of active service would automatically reduce their Ready Reserve obligations, and satisfactory reserve unit participation would reduce them even more.

Most subject to attack and revision in the lengthy House subcommittee hearings were the two compulsory features of the NRP—inductions to fill the six-months program, and enforcement of Ready Reserve obligations. The first of these was suspect because it sounded too much like UMT. Secretary Wilson gave these suspicions some substance by arguing that, though the proposal was not for UMT at all, still almost every qualified young man would probably have to fulfill a military obligation of one sort or another. Given this goading, although the NRP bill itself was enough, the usual church, farm, labor, and citizens groups (but no education groups) once more rallied to defeat what they saw as, at best, an entering wedge for UMT; and committee members friendly to the NRP warned Defense representatives that the induction feature would have to be dropped to get support in the House. When it came to rewriting the bill,[9] the House subcommittee did drop the provision. Although this was a major revision, and the Defense Department had wanted this compulsory feature as a backup for meeting the six-months program's quotas, the Administration yielded to what seemed inevitable. Testifying before the full Armed Services Committee on this issue, Secretary Wilson signalled surrender: "We still hope that you would give us the authority. . . . But I think I will have to frankly say it doesn't ruin the bill if you go the other way."[10]

The remaining issues stirred little concern outside the subcommittee, the interested executive agencies, and the National Guard Association. All three of these groups, however, found themselves deeply involved in the complexities of the other compulsory provisions of the plan and in the related problems of widely varying and confusing obligations to Ready Reserve training participation and total service. In the original bill, the Army was still left with the two potentially least popular programs for fulfilling the military obligation—one involving a ten-year training and reserve service obligation, the other involving two years' service in the Army. This was sensible so long as the induction power remained to support the six-months program. But in the absence of that feature, and desiring to reduce the total obligation across the board, tidy up the various Ready Reserve obligations, and still get full reserve value from both service veterans and training graduates, the House subcommittee revised these aspects of the bill extensively. Most of its revisions were in the direction of softening both obligations and compulsions. The total obligation for all men entering military service in any fashion was set at eight years in active service and the Ready Reserves; but for all except six-months program volunteers, transfer to Standby was guaranteed after any combination of five years' active service and satisfactory Ready Reserve training. The subcommittee also softened the penalties for failure to participate in specified minimum Ready Reserve training programs; instead of the threatened less-than-honorable discharge, it provided a penalty call to active duty for training for forty-five days annually. The subcommittee stiffened other provisions, however. What the Defense Department had proposed as normal participation in reserve training (forty-eight drills and seventeen days' active duty for training, or thirty days' active duty, annually) the subcommittee set as the minimum. For the six-months program volunteers, it offered no reduction in subsequent Ready Reserve service below seven and one-half years, and it authorized a penalty induction of up to twenty-four months (instead of eighteen) for failure to participate in minimum reserve training.

The subcommittee also took care of the National Guard Association's major concern. Under the Defense Department bill, the Guard was losing its prime recruiting inducement, deferment from the draft for men enlisting in the Guard before reaching age eighteen and one-half. Instead, it was to receive men from the six-months program, or from active service, just as were other reserve components. The subcommittee wrote into its bill a provision guaranteeing that the flow of men to the Guard would be sufficient "to meet their approved program strengths"; and it put a floor under the six-months program quota of 100,000 annually (and a ceiling of

250,000), in recognition of the association's fears that the program would not be large enough to supply the Guard along with other reserve components.

As to men already in service, the subcommittee recognized that the Department's bill would impose new reserve obligations, or enforce old ones that had not been enforced before. Consequently, while it did not change the programs' effect on their total Ready Reserve obligations, the subcommittee did relieve all men who had been in active service prior to the end of the Korean War (July 27, 1953) of required participation in Ready Reserve training.

In all this, the subcommittee did little to reduce variations among the services in their intended programs, obligations, and penalties for Ready Reservists (the penalty provisions were permissive). Apparently it felt this problem ceased to exist, or to be serious, once the provision for inducting men directly into the reserve components was eliminated. It still remained true, however, that the only men who would have a military obligation actively imposed upon them would be those inducted for two years' Army service; and these men, along with other Army service veterans, were the only ones aside from the six-months trainees for whom there were firm plans to enforce Ready Reserve obligations.

Two other major issues, both involving control of the reserves and both of long-standing interest to Congress, were affected by revisions to the Defense Department's bill. The proposal that the president, on his declaration of a national emergency, could call the Ready Reserves to active duty for up to twenty-four months, was accepted, as the full committee gave recognition to "the changes in the strategic situation that have occurred since enactment of the Armed Forces Reserve Act of 1952."[11] But a ceiling was placed on this presidential recall authority, limiting it to 1 million men. At the same time, contrary to the departmental recommendation, a ceiling on total Ready Reservists was maintained, although it was raised from 1.5 to 2.9 million.

The other reserve control question had to do with the Standby Reserve. In the departmental bill, certain men would be eligible for transfer to Standby at their request, and others could be screened into that category at the services' discretion. These men would be subject to recall only when Congress declared war or a national emergency, and this recall would then be controlled by the Selective Service System. The subcommittee recommended, and the full committee accepted, several changes in these provisions. It made transfer to Standby upon completion of a Ready Reserve obligation automatic (unless the individual volunteered to remain in the Ready Reserves). It left further screening into the Standby Reserves to administrative discretion, but added one more provision—creation of extreme personal or community hardship—to the screening criteria. The committee's report added that "Highest priority in the screening process will be given to combat veterans."[12]

After nearly two months of hearings and mark-up sessions, the Brooks subcommittee forwarded its new bill to the full House Armed Services Committee; and a month later, in late April, the full committee approved a favorable report. The committee's vote was split 31–5; and the one member not voting, Representative Short, stated he still feared the bill was a step toward UMT. This possibility was an issue as debate opened on the bill in the House, and it was suggested that the next step would be a request for power to fill the six-months program quotas by induction. Nevertheless, even such well-accredited UMT opponents as Leo Allen (R., Ill.) found themselves able to support this bill.[13]

When a real threat to the bill did develop, it came from a different, unexpected, but not unprecedented, quarter. Representative Adam Clayton Powell, who had led the fight to amend to death the Selective Service Act of 1948, also offered the chief challenge to the National Reserve Plan. Powell's amendment attacked not the reserve plan itself, but its implications for service segregation. The Korean War had brought down the last formal barriers to integration in the active forces; but National Guard units not called to active service, especially those in the South, remained unaffected by these changes. Powell argued that this was intolerable, especially in view of the authority given by the National Reserve Plan bill to transfer men to National Guard units, and in view of the opportunities for discriminatory selection in enlisting men into the Guard for the six-months program. He proposed prohibiting such discrimination in either the enlistment or transfer of men to Guard units. After a brief debate, the amendment was accepted by an overwhelming vote.[14]

The Powell amendment did not at all damage the National Reserve Plan as a manpower procurement measure for the reserves; but it made the bill anathema to its own sponsors in the southern-dominated House Armed Services Committee. The next day, Vinson offered a major compromise—the deletion of all language in the bill referring to the National Guard. This would make the Powell amendment innocuous; but, as one major purpose of the reserve plan was to assure effective training of newly enlisted Guardsmen, it would mean a major change in the effect of the bill. Vinson's amendment was defeated,[15] and thereafter the bill languished.

The next move was an attempt by the Administration, with public backing from President Eisenhower, to persuade the Senate to attach the reserve plan provisions to a bill extending the Universal Military Training and Service Act. That bill had passed the House early in the session, and was still pending in the Senate committee. Terming the Powell amendment "extraneous," the president expressed his hope that that issue would not be allowed to block a vital military security measure, and urged the Senate to push the reserve plan proposal to a conference. Senator Russell and other members of his committee did not take kindly to the idea; and even though both the majority and the minority leaders (Senators Johnson and Knowland) were amenable, no such attempt was made.[16]

Taking the occasion of his participation in a nation-wide civil defense test, President Eisenhower at last injected the sense of urgency in Administration proposals for reserve reform which had been lacking for over two years. In a radio and television speech to the nation, he linked the creation of effective reserves to civil defense needs in a nuclear attack, and urged early new action on the program. But this pressure, added to that of other administration officials and of veterans organizations, did not move Powell from his position; nor did a conference with the president; nor did a visit by Vice-President Nixon to Harlem to explain to Powell's constituents the needs of national security and the inflexibility of southern members of Congress.[17]

The president's plea nonetheless did move Representative Brooks to introduce a new bill, with all references to the National Guard—and indeed, almost all the National Reserve Plan provisions—carefully excised.[18] Vinson asked his committee for immediate approval of this much-weakened version of a reserve program, but the committee voted 16–14 to refer the bill to the Brooks subcommittee.[19] There, in one session of section-by-section reading, with the help of Defense Department representatives, the new bill was amended extensively. Most of the provisions of the earlier House bill were restored, but the military obligation was reduced to six years, and no reference was made to the National Guard. Following committee approval, and after rejecting another antisegregation amendment by Representative Powell, the House passed the new bill by voice vote.[20]

There were no serious difficulties in securing Senate passage of a reserve bill, although it was amended in a number of important ways. The ensuing conference produced a bill quite close to the House version, with the following major provisions:

1.   The Ready Reserve ceiling was set at 2.9 million, 1 million of whom could be called in a presidentially declared emergency. Obligated members of the Ready Reserve were to be screened into Standby Status according to the criteria in the original committee bill. Standby Reservists were made liable for call only on action by Congress, and then under control of the Selective Service System.

2.   The total military obligation was, with exceptions, set at six years. Men completing two or more years' active service were to be transferred to Standby status after a total of five years' active service and satisfactory participation in the Ready Reserve. The penalty for less than satisfactory reserve training participation (forty-eight drills and seventeen days' active duty for training, or thirty days' active duty for training, annually) was set at recall for forty-five days' active duty annually.

3.   A special program for six-year enlistments in the reserves was provided. Active and reserve obligations were similar to those for men enlisted or inducted in the active forces, except that the required active duty of two years might be postponed for up to two years after enlistment.

4.   A second special reserve enlistment program was set for men under age eighteen and one-half. Enlistees in this program would undergo three to six months' active duty for training, and serve

the next seven and one-half years in the Ready Reserve of the reserve component (other than the Guard) for which enlisted. Draft deferment was guaranteed enlistees in this program. Unsatisfactory post-training reserve participation could restore draft liability up to age twenty-eight, but a total of eight years' satisfactory training and reserve participation would complete the military obligation and remove draft liability. Quotas, set by the service and Defense Department secretaries, were not to exceed 250,000 annually (the 100,000 House floor was omitted), and were further limited by the 2.9 million total Ready Reserve ceiling.

5. Authority for enlistment in the National Guard prior to age eighteen and one-half, with accompanying draft deferment, was retained. Satisfactory participation in weekly and annual Guard training was required up to age twenty-eight, and unsatisfactory participation could restore draft liability. By voluntary participation in three or more months' active duty for training, such Guard enlistees could reduce their total obligation to eight years.

6. Men who had entered active service prior to enactment of the new law were excused from required Ready Reserve training, but retained their old total obligation of eight years. Inducements were offered to such men still on active duty, in the form of reduced Ready Reserve obligations, to get a flow of service veterans started immediately into the drilling units of the Ready Reserve.

With these provisions, the Reserve Forces Act of 1955 attempted solutions to some, but by no means all, of the reserve problems experienced since the 1952 act. Perhaps the chief military value of the new act lay in the provisions requiring regular participation in reserve training programs of all obligated Ready Reservists. This solved a serious problem for the reserve components, other than the Guard, especially the Army and Air Force Reserves. The Guard's problem was not participation but basic training. The bill solved this for the other reserve components, assuring that all men entering their Ready Reserve units would have at least three months' continuous active duty training. For the Guard units, however, this preparation remained voluntary, thus leaving them saddled with the Sisy-

phean task of conducting basic training during weekly drill periods
and in summer camps.

The new act also failed to guarantee a flow of trained nonveterans
into components other than the Guard. It remained to be seen
whether the new six-month training program would prove as successful a recruiting inducement for them as a draft deferment for enlistees under age eighteen and one-half, with no active duty training
requirement, had been for the Guard.

Neither this act nor the original Administration bill proposed to
remove completely one problem which had spurred new legislation
during the Korean War, had stirred much congressional concern,
and had sent the National Security Training Commission report's
authors to heights of emotional prose. This was the continued dependence of the reserve components on service veterans. The Defense Department had proposed to screen combat veterans from
Ready into Standby status, subject to overriding requirements for
their skills. Congress wrote that screening criterion into the law,
and attempted to improve on other criteria, to preclude the sudden
recall of men with large families or with civilian professional or
technical skills essential to their local communities or to national defense. But, as the House committee's report argued, service veterans,
with their higher military skills and greater experience in them, were
to remain the backbone of the reserves.

One little discussed feature of the new reserve program was its
impact on the total available military manpower pool. Opponents of
UMT in 1952, and of the National Security Training Commission's
plan in 1953-54, had argued that there were not enough men in the
pool to support enlistments and inductions into the active forces
and at the same time provide men to a reserve training program.
Despite the fact that the Defense Department never indicated any
intention of letting a UMT program interfere with its immediate
demands for active forces, this argument was not wholly specious.
Inauguration of UMT under provisions of the 1951 act, which required reducing or eliminating the induction threat hanging over
men under age nineteen and provided no firm posttraining obligations other than vulnerability to recall, might have interfered with
a prime source of voluntary enlistments, young men aged seventeen

to twenty. The limitation of the new six-months training program to men under age eighteen and one-half, and the imposition of long Ready Reserve training obligations on those entering the program, were evidence of concern to protect this active service enlistment source.

Public announcement of the studies and restudies of proposed reserve plans through 1953 and 1954 all gave the impression that the fundamental problem of military manpower continued to be one of potential shortages. But by 1955 a new situation was developing, as the New Look promised reduced active force demands on the total manpower pool, and the annual input to that pool was beginning to grow. A manpower surplus was emerging, which created serious problems for Selective Service operations. The new reserve program provided a partial answer to these problems, as well as to reserve needs. As the House report put it: "Regulation of the manpower pool . . . is one of the essential features of the National Reserve Plan."[21]

3.   *Administrative Expansion of the Reserve Program*

The new six-months training program was given a four-year lease on life by the Reserve Forces Act of 1955. In that time it experienced, in succession, near collapse from public indifference, near swamping from newly enthused Selective Service registrants, and, finally, attempts by the Defense Department to regulate the program and its costs in the face of congressional protections.

The National Security Training Commission was given the task, under the 1955 act, of looking out for the welfare of reserve program trainees. Its first report to Congress, in September, summarized the program's progress through mid-1956, not only in regard to welfare but also with respect to recruiting. The commission found that the enlistment rate since the beginning of the year had been about 4,000 a month, about half what was needed to meet an annual quota of 100,000. The commission also noted that the program was competing with regular enlistments, with enlistment into other reserve programs, and with National Guard enlistments; these were taking, from the same group under age eighteen and one-half, about 180,000, 65,000 and 105,000 men annually. Thus, while about

400,000 men between the ages of seventeen and eighteen and one-half were volunteering for the armed forces, only 50,000 of these were electing the special reserve training program, with another 5,000 National Guard enlistees also volunteering for this training. The commission also concluded that the publicity campaign, promoted by the public relations staffs of the Defense Department, the Army, Marine Corps, and Army National Guard, and aided by private individuals and organizations, the radio-television and motion picture industries, and the press, had done its job of acquainting the public with the program. It argued, however, that to meet reserve needs, and to avoid having large numbers of qualified young men escape all service, the special reserve program would have to be doubled or tripled. "If by the end of this year the facts justify it, we should fundamentally revise the program and take steps to provide the necessary manpower."[22] Whether the commission had in mind authorizing inductions to fill out the Reserve Forces Act program's quotas is not clear.

In January, 1957, the Administration acted in a different fashion to expand initial reserve training. The Department of the Army announced that all men enlisting in the Army National Guard on or after April 1 would be required to perform six months of active duty for training. At the same time, enlistments in the other reserve components for the special reserve training program were opened to men between the ages of eighteen and one-half and twenty-five inclusive, and the whole structure of reserve obligations was altered downward. Later in the year, draft deferments for reserve service were also altered to accommodate the new policy.

For several weeks, most public and congressional attention to these moves was focused on the requirement that Guard enlistees undertake an initial six-months' continuous training. There was considerable concern over the general state of training of Guard units, which were having little trouble keeping up to strength, but which lacked an adequate input of basically trained and more experienced men. At a House committee briefing on military posture, Secretary Wilson accused the Guard of dragging its feet on voluntary participation in the RFA training program by its enlistees. Waxing indignant over this, he let slip a comment which suggested still another reason for the move: " . . . You know, the thing was really sort of a scandal during the Korean War. It was a draft-dodging business. A boy 17 to 18½ could enlist in the National Guard and not be drafted and sent to Korea and fight."[23] Wilson went on to say that the current issue was not one of draft-dodging, but of unit effectiveness; but he had touched off a storm of protest. Out of wounded pride, the Guard and those who wished to be its friends sprang to the defense of its wartime record. More important to the Guard's immediate interests, however, was the threat posed to its recruiting by the new training requirement. As the new policy was being developed in late 1956, the Guard, through the Army's National Guard Bureau, had promoted alternative solutions to the training problem. First it asked that the six months be split between two summers; then it promoted a three-month requirement for the Guard. Neither was accepted, and the Army, with Defense backing, stuck to its insistence on six months of continuous training.[24]

Even before this storm broke, Chairman Vinson had set Representative Brooks and his subcommittee to work determining whether the new reserve plans were within the intent of the 1955 Reserve Forces Act. In this Army-National Guard quarrel, Brooks served as less an overseer than a go-between. After his subcommittee's hearings, he entered into negotiations with the two parties, which produced a short-term compromise. As agreed by the parties (and approved by the House Armed Services Committee in a subsequent 27–2 vote), the Guard accepted the requirement of six-months' active duty training for all new enlistees after April 1. Until January 1, 1958, however, Guard enlistees under age eighteen and one-half could satisfy this initial requirement with only eleven weeks' active duty training.[25]

More important in reshaping the reserve program were the new opportunities for enlisting in the six-months program and the changes in reserve obligations and draft deferment policy. Until 1957, the only men over age eighteen and one-half eligible for the Reserve Forces Act program were those few with certain "critical skills," who were allowed to participate in the initial training and then, with some exceptions, were excused from further Ready Reserve participation in order to use these skills, usually in defense research or industry. Under the new directives, the RFA program was opened to all men qualified for military service and accepted for enlistment into the Guard or other reserve components. For those under age eighteen and one-half, the posttraining Ready Reserve obligation was reduced to four and one-half years (later reduced to three years), with the remainder of their eight-year enlistment to be spent in Standby status. For those aged eighteen and one-half to twenty-five, the Ready Reserve obligation would extend through the remainder of a six-year enlistment. To give a final boost to the new program, Selective Service regulations were altered to require deferment of any otherwise eligible member of a Ready Reserve unit, regardless of when or at what age he entered the reserves.[26]

The results of these new inducements to reserve enlistment were soon felt with a vengeance, and by mid-May there was such a large backlog of reserve enlistees awaiting training that enlistments for those under age eighteen and one-half were suspended for six weeks. More serious, the projected production of reservists from this program, plus the reserve accessions of men completing active service, would soon strain and surpass the plans and budget for Ready Reserve training. As Overton Brooks put it, "We are in a harvest season and can't pick the melons."[27]

These problems, and a concurrent squeeze on the whole defense budget, led directly to the Administration's attempts in 1958 and later to cut the strength of both the Guard and the Army Reserve. Despite congressional and Guard resistance, which preserved Army National Guard and Army Reserve unit strengths of 400,000 and 300,000,[28] there still was not room in the Army's Ready Reserve units for all men obligated to Ready Reserve training. This had been expected, and the Army was calling some obligated veteran reservists for thirty days' summer training as an alternative to weekly drills with units; but even as early as 1957 not all these men were being trained every year, and some were not being trained at all. Thus, in 1957 and increasingly in succeeding years, the Army followed the other military services in imposing reserve training requirements selectively rather than universally on those who had acquired Ready Reserve obligations.

In 1959, the special reserve enlistment programs provided in the Reserve Forces Act of 1955 were due to expire on August 1. The Defense Department asked for a four-year extension, and a House Armed Services Committee subcommittee took the occasion to review the entire special training program and other aspects of the Ready Reserves. By that time over 275,000 men had enlisted in the program, of whom only 105,000 had entered under the statutory provisions; the rest were Guard enlistees, and reservists entering after age eighteen and one-half. The subcommittee also learned that all reserve components had been able to raise the qualifications for enlistment in this and other programs. Finally it learned that, although the Ready Reserves had reached a total of nearly 2.5 million, less than 1 million of these were in regularly drilling Ready Reserve units. The general conclusion of the chief Defense witness was that "by reason of this law you have the finest Reserve this country has ever had."[29] No one asked just how much the special program created in the 1955 act, as opposed to those created by Defense and Selective Service regulations, had contributed to this success. Instead, the subcommittee simply approved the bill; and with little discussion in the House and none in the Senate, the expiring portions of the Reserve Forces Act were extended to August 1, 1963.[30]

After a slow start in 1955 and 1956, the Defense Departent had finally solved, indeed over-solved, the long-standing problems of providing basic training for the reserves and of assuring participation of both veteran and nonveteran reservists in Ready Reserve training programs. The screening of veteran and other reservists whose occupation, dependents, or past service made them less vulnerable to recall had begun in 1956, and by 1960 the Selective Service System had records of 1.6 million Standby Reservists classed in varying categories of availability.[31] But important problems and questions remained unanswered, and in some cases unexamined. The military readiness of reserve units and the precision of control over reserve manpower remained to be tested some years later; and that testing and later experiences would raise more sharply than before the question of what need there was, in face of changing strategic demands on the military establishment, for such a large Ready Reserve. The problem of individual quality of reservists was being met partly through tighter enlistment standards; but this problem was considered even more important for the active forces. Finally, the whole question of the relations among reserve manpower procurement, total military obligations, and management of the manpower pool, had by 1960 been submerged under a pile of administrative decisions and regulations, and did not get fresh attention for several years more.

III. CAMPAIGN FOR MANPOWER QUALITY

"Man, the Ultimate Weapon" was an official Army public relations theme in the mid-1950's. As such, it was a defensive reaction to the growing emphasis, both in the popular mind and in Administration budgets, on the highly sophisticated and expensive new weapons, delivery systems, and control complexes of the nuclear age, and to arguments that increased firepower in ground units justified cuts in their manpower. The theme was intended to call attention to the more important truths about manpower needs in modern military forces.

In the armed forces, as in the civilian economy, the new technology was creating new tasks even as it reduced or eliminated old ones. It was not reducing the need for large numbers of men; rather it was requiring more extensive and differentiated training and larger training establishments. Military man was increasingly the tender of machines rather than the bearer of weapons and supplies. But despite the new technology, even partly because of it, he was needed in larger numbers than ever before in peacetime. (Another major reason for this was that the 1950's were not really "peacetime," but the new military technology was partly responsible for that, too.) More than quantity was required, however. Men for the new military forces also had to be better trained and more skilled, competent, and trustworthy than ever before.

There were, generally, three ways to assure that the armed forces' needs for high quality manpower would be met: attract and hold good men with pay, bonuses, other benefits, and good working conditions; support volunteering by maintaining a credible threat of induction for less desirable service; and set entry standards high enough to screen out the less trainable and less dependable men. Again, generally, a balance had to be struck among these means; the first two had to supply enough men to make the choices involved in the third meaningful and effective. The balance, and the results, were different for each service; and attempts were made throughout the 1950's to adjust the balance and improve the results for all the services.

Nowhere were the realities of this complex of procurement goals and policies debated with greater heat, but less cogency and less effect, than in the 1956 election campaign. Up to 1952, the Democrats had been the party of the hard line on manpower procurement: maintain large standing forces in all the services, through induction if necessary; and make military training and service an obligation of citizenship, in peace or war, to be exacted in some form from the vast majority of military-aged young men. The Republicans, when they thought about it, had been the party of volunteerism, to be made adequate by keeping the active forces small, concentrating on machines and new weapons, and, if necessary, improving pay and benefits; military service was accepted as an obligation of citizenship, but was to be compelled on a large scale only in war or other major military crises. After 1952, the Republican Administration seemed to diverge somewhat from this line. To be sure, the New Look emphasized machines and new weapons, and it decreased active strengths; but service strengths remained high, closer to their Korean War peaks than to their 1948-50 postwar low. In promoting new reserve legislation, moreover, the Eisenhower Administration had agreed with its predecessor that wide-spread performance of military service was an obligation, if not in peace, certainly for the indefinite term of the cold war.

By 1956 the draft was well into its latest four-year extension, good into 1959; and there had been no particularly sharp fight over that extension the year before. Nevertheless, speaking before (of all groups) the American Legion, Democratic candidate Adlai Stevenson probably stirred the hopes of a great many Americans when he stated cautiously: "We can now anticipate the possibility that within the foreseeable future we can maintain the military forces we need without the draft." Vice-President Nixon, speaking before the same group the next day, set the tone of Republican response to this claim:

> I realize that in an election it is always tempting to tell the voters that there is an easy way to meet difficult problems. I would like to tell you that we can safely get rid of the draft, cut our defense spending and thereby reduce our taxes. Unfortunately, however, in international affairs, the easy way is seldom the right way.

Senator Knowland was more blunt, calling Stevenson's statement a blatant grab for votes. The president was more bland, saying simply that he saw no hope of ending draft calls in the immediate future. To this, Stevenson replied that he had never asked for an immediate end to the draft, that this could come only when it was consistent with security needs, but that manpower needs could be reduced by concentrating on creation of a hard core of skilled, professional soldiers.[32]

Thus went the debate, if it was that. Stevenson pressed the issue later in the campaign; he argued that the current manpower system produced a huge turnover of men which was wasteful and inefficient, and that new weapons called for professional, highly paid, skilled volunteers, rather than large forces, repeated training, and an unfair, obsolescent reliance on inductions.[33] But he got little hearing for his claims and proposals in the face of a barrage of damnations from his Republican opponents. Probably most deadening to pertinent debate was the series of phrases which turned up in comments by the president himself, as he escalated his characterization of Stevenson's proposals from "loose talk" to "incredible folly" and, finally, "the way to disaster."[34] The vice-president drove home this strategy by suggesting the proposals could lead to another Munich, and that Stevenson was inviting a "ludicrous" contrast between his and President Eisenhower's knowledge of military needs.[35]

Stevenson said later that he did not regret making the draft a campaign issue.[36] But he might have regretted his failure to stir any realistic public discussion of the criticisms he raised—a failure ironically to be repeated by a less astute and even more hopelessly outdistanced Republican candidate in 1964.

1. *Manpower Quality and Military Pay*

Even before 1956, steps had been taken to cut down the heavy turnover of military personnel which resumed with the end of the Korean War. Turnover had, indeed, suddenly become a serious problem. Prior to that war and its consequent rearmament, the reenlistment rate[37] for all services was a respectable 59 percent; and during that war, the rate for regulars (as distinguished from draftees and reservists called to active duty) held at nearly 55 percent. With the end of the war, however, reenlistments fell off drastically to a rate under 24 percent.

As a first step to improve retention, the Defense Department developed proposals roughly doubling the scale of reenlistment bonuses and varying these payments according to the monthly pay attained by the reenlistee and the number of years for which he was to reenlist. These proposals were presented to Congress in mid-1954, and were approved with little discussion.[38] The immediate results were not impressive, as the reenlistment rate for FY 1955 rose to just over 27 percent. Even more disappointing, the rate for men completing their first enlistments, and thus facing a choice of making military service a career, was less than 16 percent.

The Administration and Congress then launched a broader attack on the problem with a general pay measure, the Career Incentive Act of 1955. As with the 1954 increase in bonuses, the pay raise was aimed not so much at attracting new men to the services as at retaining those already in service. Once again, the discouragingly low reenlistment rates, especially among first-termers, were cited; and difficulties in holding junior officers after their period of obligated service were also mentioned. Pay scales in the new act were based on those recommended six years earlier, but modified downward in the 1949 pay act. To those were added a 4 percent cost-of-living increase (pay already had been increased by that flat rate once during the Korean War) and a series of additional increases at certain grade and longevity points in the pay charts thought to be critical for officers and enlisted men in deciding whether to continue or end their military careers. The resulting scales offered an over-all 11 percent raise in pay, with much heavier increases going to junior officers (after three years of service) and to enlisted men in the lower noncommissioned officer grades. In addition, increases were granted in hazardous duty pay (for flyers, submariners, and parachutists), and a new dislocation allowance was added for men with dependents to supplement the long-time practice of paying moving costs.[39]

In FY 1956 the total reenlistment rate jumped impressively to nearly 44 percent. This was probably as much a result of having earlier weeded out most of the one-time volunteers in the Korean War as it was of the new pay scales, as the rate for first-termers rose to only 23 percent. These rates continued to rise slowly through the next two years, but in FY 1958 the armed forces were still losing about three of every four men who had volunteered for a first term and were eligible to stay.

Although the Administration did not feel it necessary or desirable to discuss these matters at the time of Stevenson's campaign challenge, it already had initiated an extensive and detailed study of the whole problem of pay scales and retention of skilled, experienced service men. In May, 1956, Secretary Wilson appointed a special Defense Advisory Committee on Professional and Technical Compensations, chaired by Ralph Cordiner, president of General Electric. A year later, the committee gave its report and recommendations to Secretary Wilson; and within a few weeks Cordiner was publically proclaiming that adoption of his proposals could bring the draft to an end.[40]

The Cordiner Committee had found that the key problem of excessive turnover, while extending across the board, was especially serious among men possessing just those skills requiring a high investment of training time and money. Worse yet, the pay scales themselves, incorporating a longevity principle based on time in service and offering roughly biennial pay increases within each grade or rank, provided little incentive to especially ambitious and talented men, and contributed to their leaving service early. The Cordiner Committee recommended a wholesale revision of the military pay system. For enlisted men, it recommended expanding the number of basic pay grades from seven to nine, periodic raises based on conversion to longevity-in-grade rather than total-service-longevity, elimination of pay inversions, and proficiency pay to supplement basic pay in recognition of outstanding work. For officers, a similar conversion to the longevity-in-grade principle was recommended; in addition, the Cordiner Committee suggested raising pay in the higher ranks to provide real incentives to competition for advancement, with special emphasis on the very top general officer ranks. It also recommended special pay incentives for non-career reserve officers willing to spend part, but not all, of their working lives in service. Cordiner did not attach a precise price tag to his proposals; instead he claimed that in five years the savings in reduced training loads and lower total manpower requirements would more than overbalance the pay increases and produce net savings of about $5 billion a year.

The Defense Department did not wholly agree, or at least it was more responsive to immediate budgetary considerations than to possible savings in later years. It did support a new pay bill in 1958, however, one based on, if not directly reproducing, the Cordiner Committee's recommendations. The major differences in the general pay scales were that the Department proposed stretching out the incentive increases over a four-year period rather than granting them all at once; and it recommended a minimum 6 percent cost-of-living increase for all those not receiving incentive increases, including men still in initial periods of obligated service.

The annual additional cost of the Department's bill was reported at $518 million. The House, on recommendation of its committee, made changes in the pay scales and other benefits, partly in the direction of the Cordiner Committee proposals and partly to reserve longevity advantages for junior officers with prior enlisted service, which raised the cost to an estimated $683 million. The Senate, coming to the rescue of the Administration, cut this to $576 million, and the conference committee held to that level in its report. There were varying estimates on how much the new pay bill might save by reducing manpower turnover; but the House committee warned that its pay proposals would assure neither the $5 billion savings nor the end of the draft by 1959 which Cordiner had predicted.[41]

This was the last pay raise for the military services until 1963. Before and after this, the Administration promoted, often with considerable prodding from one or another of the Armed Services Committees, a number of other measures aimed at making service careers more attractive; these ranged from better systems for managing officer and enlisted promotions to better assurances of medical care and improved housing for dependents. At the same time, steps were taken in quite another direction to improve the quality of military manpower.

2. Recruiting: Enlistment and Reenlistment

Improved pay and other benefits for servicemen were intended primarily as measures to raise reenlistment rates and retain junior and middle-grade officers, and only incidentally to promote initial recruiting. During the late 1950's, reenlistment rates did improve somewhat, with the total rate reaching just under 49 percent in FY 1958 and 1959, and the first-term rate peaking to 30 percent in

1959. But, as the initial effects of proficiency pay and of the 1958 pay increases began to wear off, these rates dropped back in FY 1960 to 41 percent total and 21 percent first-term. By the next year the total rate reached 53 percent; but the crucial first-term reenlistments had recovered only partly to 25 percent. At the same time, only a slightly better balance had been achieved in first-term reenlistment rates among major occupational groups. Comparing FY 1957 and 1961, when the total first-term rates were about 25 percent, first-term reenlistments in the ground combat group improved from 20 to 28 percent; but the electronics group stayed at under 21 percent for both years, and other technical groups rose slightly from 25 to 26 percent. The administrative and clerical, mechanics and repairmen, and crafts groups continued to lead the total rate by a few percent; and the services group, including the least critical skills, led all others in both years, at 31 and 33 percent.

While these adjustments were taking place in internal recruiting, some very significant changes were occurring in the relative importance of this to other sources of enlisted procurement (see Table 8). In the period of the first New Look, as total active strength dropped from 3.3 million in FY 1954 to 2.8 million in FY 1957, inductions as a proportion of total enlisted procurement dropped from 33 percent to 22 percent. By FY 1961, as active strength fell further to under 2.5 million, the induction share was down to 9 percent. By contrast, internal procurement through first-term and career reenlistments, provided only 19 percent of the total in FY 1954, jumped to 29 percent in FY 1957, and further increased to 33 percent in FY 1961. This exchange between inductions and reenlistment as the second and third most important sources of enlisted procurement took place shortly after the Korean War; and, as noted above, reenlistment rates also made their greatest recovery in the period of the first New Look. As total strength and the relative importance of inductions declined still further in FY 1958 and after, initial enlistments served as the major procurement source; in the last three years of the period, this source provided over half of the total manpower required.

There were important differences in this general pattern among the four services. The most obvious was the Army's continued heavy reliance on inductions, which provided one-third to one-half of that

TABLE 8

Active Duty Enlisted Personnel Procurement,
Fiscal Years 1954, 1957, 1961
(In Thousands)

	1954		1957		1961	
	Number	%	Number	%	Number	%
Army						
Inductions _____	265	58.1	179	48.5	60	22.5
First enlistments _	94	20.5	69	18.6	116	43.5
Reenlistments ____	81	17.9	83	22.4	88	33.1
Reservists to						
active duty ____	16	3.6	39	10.5	2	0.9
Total _____	456	100.0	370	100.0	267	100.0
Navy						
Inductions _____	___	____	*	‡	___	____
First enlistments _	55	61.4	80	49.2	94	57.6
Reenlistments ____	19	21.8	56	34.3	47	28.4
Reservists to						
active duty ____	15	16.8	27	16.4	23	13.9
Total _____	89	100.0	163	100.0	163	100.0
Marine Corps						
Inductions _____	___	____	___	____	*	0.2
First enlistments _	72	68.0	30	39.9	30	76.6
Reenlistments ____	12	11.8	19	26.0	8	20.2
Reservists to						
active duty ____	22	20.2	26	34.1	1	3.1
Total _____	107	100.0	76	100.0	40	100.0
Air Force						
Inductions _____	___	____	*	0.1	*	‡
First enlistments _	108	74.6	123	59.8	119	60.3
Reenlistments ____	37	25.4	81	39.4	78	39.6
Reservists to						
active duty ____	†	‡	1	0.7	†	0.1
Total _____	145	100.0	206	100.0	197	100.0
Department of Defense						
Inductions _____	265	33.2	180	22.1	60	9.0
First enlistments _	329	41.3	303	37.1	360	54.0
Reenlistments ____	151	19.0	240	29.4	221	33.1
Reservists to						
active duty ____	53	6.6	93	11.4	26	3.9
Total _____	797	100.0	816	100.0	667	100.0

Source: U.S. Department of Defense, Directorate for Statistical Services, *Selected Manpower Statistics* (Washington: Department of Defense, April 11, 1966), p. 45. N.B. Totals do not add due to rounding. Percent derived from totals given in source.

  * Penalty inductions only, for failure to meet reserve training obligations. Number usually totals less than 100 each year.

  † Less than 500.

  ‡ Less than 0.05 percent.

service's total enlisted procurement in all years of the FY 1954-61 period but the last. (Only one other service inducted men out of necessity—the Navy during part of FY 1957; all other inductions were penalties for failing to participate in required reserve training.) The Navy and Marine Corps depended throughout the period on initial enlistments as their most important source of procurement, and the Navy continued to use the two-year-active-duty reserve enlistment as a third important source of active as well as reserve enlisted procurement. A third pattern is apparent in Air Force procurement, where higher reenlistment rates made that a more important source than in any of the other services. Indeed, in FY 1958 and FY 1959, drops in total strength and procurement put the Air Force, alone among the services, in the position of procuring over half its total intake from reenlistments.

The procurement figures suggest that the Air Force had by far the largest proportion of career enlisted men, the Marine Corps the least, with the Army and Navy falling close to each other in the middle. The figures also suggest, however, the continued reliance of all four services on fresh inputs of manpower to maintain their active strength. While only the Army relied directly on inductions for this input, the other services benefited indirectly.

3. *Rising Entry Standards*

The increased reliance on reenlistment in all services, and the reduced dependence of the Army on Selective Service inductions, no doubt contributed considerably to improving the quality of active force manpower. Probably more important were the steps taken to raise enlistment and induction standards, especially in the area of mental qualifications.

In 1951, Congress forced downward the current mental standards for induction, required that men in Class IV-F be rescreened according to these lower standards, but simultaneously insisted on administrative measures to assure that each service got a reasonable share of both the better and the least qualified men. The Selective Service reexamination program began in January, 1952, and by June, 1953, some 268,000 had been retested, of whom about one-third were found acceptable under the new standards. The Selective Service System was so pleased with the results that it recommended a further lowering of the standards, both physical and mental, and continued retesting.[42]

The services were not so pleased; and not long after the Korean War truce, they asked the Defense Department to lower the quotas for intake of men in the lower mental categories imposed on them in mid-1951. Although this request was rejected, the services apparently did begin to tighten their interpretation of the minimum standards for entry.[43] This practice was extended through the mid-1950's, with both draft and enlistment rejection rates showing marked increases over the Korean War period. Rejections of draftees had run at about 34 percent during the Korean War, and the over-all rejection rate, including volunteers for enlistment, was just under 24 percent. In the period from the Korean truce to July, 1958, these rates rose to 40 percent and 27 percent respectively.[44] Even more spectacular, however, was the impact of a new measure, enacted in 1958 at the request of the Defense Department and especially of the Army.

Despite the decline in inductions, the Army was still taking better than 40 percent of its annual input of enlisted men from that source; and it felt the standards imposed by law, especially the Armed Forces Qualification Test score minimum, were far too low for a period of further cuts in total strength and increased need for men trainable to special skills. It had raised standards for voluntary enlistment (as had the other services), and the examining stations had apparently narrowed their interpretation of the statutory minimums to the limit. Nevertheless, while the proportion of Army volunteers in mental group IV (test score 10-30) had dropped from 28 percent in 1954 to 17 percent in June 1957, the proportion of draftees in this group had risen from 32 to almost 40 percent. Not only were these group IV men less trainable, they also created about twice their share of disciplinary problems.[45]

In 1957, Congress was asked to authorize the president, except in time of war or national emergency declared by Congress, to modify both physical and mental standards for induction. Given this authority, additional tests would be set for those scoring in group IV, tests already being given men actually accepted for service to determine their aptitude for nine different sets of skills; and passing scores in at least two of these would qualify men for induction. All others in group IV and below would be rejected. The Army expected this would exclude about half the group IV inductees, and reduce its total proportion of such men in active service to about 19 percent.

With Chairman Vinson's strong support, and even General Hershey's reluctant blessing, the House committee approved the measure with almost no discussion, and the House quickly followed suit. The Senate committee seemed more doubtful in the beginning, especially Chairman Russell and Senator Stennis.[46] A year later it had somehow been convinced, perhaps by the assurance that the Defense Department intended to change only the mental, not the physical, standards; and the Senate passed the bill with no discussion at all.[47]

The effects were immediate and impressive. The Selective Service preinduction rejection rate jumped from 38 percent in July, 1958, to 44 percent in August, and continued up. For FY 1958 the annual rate was 41 percent; by FY 1961 it was over 46 percent. Among those rejected, the proportion failing to qualify on mental tests alone had also risen, from 40 to 45 percent of total rejections. Moreover, the 1961 figures represented a slight downward trend. The draft rejection rate for all causes between August, 1958, and June, 1960, was 51 percent, and the overall rejection rate, including applicants for enlistment, rose to 32 percent.[48]

As a result of these changes in entry requirements, and of improvements in pay and other benefits, the active forces entered the decade of the 1960's considerably smaller than they had been in 1953, but much better able to retain their experienced men and to be selective in recruiting and inducting new ones. But the reductions in active forces had created new problems for management of the manpower pool, problems for which the emphasis on quality and the concurrent expansion of reserve programs provided only partial and peculiar relief.

IV.   NEW LOOK IN SELECTIVE SERVICE

1.   *Extending the Induction Authority*

In 1951, the Department of Defense asked for permanent authorization of the Selective Service System, but Congress met this request only part way. It made permanent the Selective Service System provisions relating to organization, staffing, and appropriations authorization, and the provisions for registration, classification, and penalties; but it limited the basic authority to induct men to a four-year period ending July 1, 1955. By 1955, two other provisions of the law closely related to the Universal Military Training and Service Act, all enacted at the outset of Korean War, had also been extended to new expiration dates in 1955. One was the Dependents Assistance Act, which supplemented the regular pay scales for the lowest grades of enlisted men with wives and children; this had, in 1953, been given a new expiration date of July 1, 1955. The second was the act providing for special classification and induction of physicians, dentists, and allied specialists—the Doctor Draft Act —which had most recently been extended in 1953 to July 1, 1955.

The opening of the 1955 session thus found Congress faced with Administration requests for four major pieces of legislation relating to manpower procurement. Two of these were a pay raise and the National Reserve Plan proposal, already discussed. The third was a bill to extend the Universal Military Training and Service and Dependents Assistance Acts to July 1, 1959. The fourth was a bill to extend the Doctor Draft Act to July 1, 1957.

The Defense Department and the Selective Service System experienced no important difficulties in securing a four-year extension of the draft.[49] Issues were indeed raised, both in hearings and on the floor, and a few of these resulted in minor changes in the law. One of the more interesting of these ended the Selective Service practice of considering surpluses and shortages of agricultural commodities in deciding on occupational deferments for farmers and farm workers. General Hershey defended that practice in hearings. Noting that national and state circulars to local boards provided only guidelines, not directives, on occupational and other deferments, he also insisted that the local board was bound by law to grant such deferments only in the national, not the individual, interest. If a board could not consider crop surpluses in applying this standard, how could it consider crop shortages? If it could not consider the latter, what justification then remained for any agricultural deferments? Until Congress told him to do otherwise, he felt this advice to local boards was sound. The House committee recommended no change; but over no particular objection from Chairman Vinson, the House adopted a proviso forbidding any consideration of agricultural commodity supply in granting deferments; and this provision received Senate and conference support.

The 1951 proviso extending the induction liability of deferred registrants to age thirty-five was the object of attack from several directions, with varying degrees of success. The broadest of these was launched by the Scientific Manpower Commission, a group formed in 1953 by designated representatives of ten major professional groups of physical and biological scientists. This group argued that despite retitling of the act in 1951, and despite the proviso extending liability to age thirty-five, Congress had not intended the act to lead to universal military service; that the national shortage of scientists and engineers was a critical problem; and that Selective Service was taking these men just at the time they were beginning to be most useful to their callings and to the nation. Although the Scientific Manpower Commission denied it wanted exemptions from the military obligation for scientists and engineers, it did lend support to several proposals which would have had much the same effect.

At committee hearings, General Hershey responded to these criticisms and proposals in several ways. He contended that the 1951 provisions did establish a universal obligation, and he hoped that would not be changed. He wished to retain the extended liability proviso, particularly in order to avoid turning student deferments into exemptions. On the other hand, he claimed to be as interested in having engineers and scientists as the next man, and he cited the broad permissiveness of student deferments as one way of promoting their production. He did admit to problems concerning poststudy employment of these men, but cited the establishment of advisory committees, in twenty-seven states thus far, to assist Selective Service Boards in selecting such men for further occupational deferment in the national interest. His real concern was to assure that men so deferred actually did go to, and remain in, critical occupations related to national defense. He was also interested in assuring that any committees assisting in selecting men for such deferments would be, and would remain, advisory only and would not supplant or override local board jurisdiction and discretion. In addition, Hershey supported a second means of adjusting the military obligation to the defense research and industry needs for highly trained men. This was the Defense Department's proposal to include a special category of men in its six-months reserve training program, men with critical skills who would be eligible for this reserve program even though past age eighteen and one-half.

The Scientific Manpower Commission and others interested in

limiting or eliminating the military obligation for men trained to science and engineering, thus had their wishes met part way; but they could not get favorable consideration for doing away with the extended liability proviso entirely. The broadest limitation on this proviso considered in either house was an amendment proposed on the House floor to restrict the extension of liability to persons deferred for study or research only, and this was defeated easily.[50]

A final attack on the proviso extending liability to age thirty-five met with greater success. Men enlisting in the National Guard before reaching age eighteen and one-half were deferrable so long as they participated in Guard unit drills and training. The Selective Service System, taking a careful view of the act, had applied the extended liability proviso to these men as well as to those deferred for civilian pursuits, thereby effectively establishing a sixteen-and-one-half-year to eighteen-year obligation for Guard service. The National Guard Association, with strong support from House committee counsel John Blandford and Chairman Vinson, argued this had never been Congress's intent; and in the end a balance was struck setting the top age of liability to these men at twenty-eight.

These issues, agricultural deferments and the wide impact of the extended age liability proviso, were the only important ones considered in committee. There was remarkably little debate on them in either house, or on the only other amendment considered, a House proposal to limit extension to two years. With its minor amendments, the extension bill met no difficulty in passing either house. The first House vote was 394–4, and the Senate accepted its version by voice vote. On the conference report, the House agreed 389–5, and the Senate again voiced its acceptance.[51]

The Doctor Draft Act extension proved little more difficult. Enacted in 1950 to provide adequate military medical service for expanding active forces in the Korean War, this program established a special class of Selective Service registrants—men in medical, dental, and allied specialist categories, up to age fifty—and made them liable for induction until age fifty-one. The original act was to have expired in 1953, but had been extended to expire with the Selective Service induction authority in 1955. As General Hershey interpreted and applied it, the intent of the act was not to induct these men, but to persuade them to accept reserve commissions and a call to active duty. In this he had been eminently successful; to meet special calls (all for physicians, dentists, and veterinarians) totaling nearly 16,000 by the end of FY 1955, only 81 had to be inducted, and over half of these were offered and accepted commissions after induction.[52]

By 1955, the American Medical, Dental, and Veterinary Medical associations no longer supported these provisions in their current form. Instead, at the Senate committee's hearings on Selective Service extension, they proposed continuation of special calls for induction, but only from among those otherwise liable under regular Selective Service provisions. As large numbers of students preparing for these professions had been deferred, it was argued that the Defense Department could, by more careful setting of its medical skills requirements, meet its needs from among those special registrants still subject to the extended liability proviso.

The Defense Department answered with Selective Service figures and Defense requirements indicating that, without extension, physicians available over the next two years would fall short of replacement needs by about 15 percent. Moreover, the services still had need for the more experienced and specialized physicians they were acquiring under current procedures. The Department asked for a two-year extension of the doctors' draft to July 1, 1957, and proposed in the meantime to relieve the specialist problem through a special reserve commissioning program; this would permit some medical students to accept reserve commissions on graduation and then complete residency as well as internship before entering active duty. The Senate committee accepted these arguments, as well as a proposal to extend the $100 monthly incentive pay provision to July 1, 1959. It then attached the Doctor Draft extension to the Selective Service extension bill already passed by the House,[53] correctly assuming that the other body would accept both measures in a conference report.

In 1957, the medical profession's 1955 proposals were, by and large, adopted; and the Doctor Draft Act as such was allowed to expire. But the provisions allowing induction of persons in special categories outside the normal order and quotas for Selective Service registrants within regular ages of liability were made an integral part of the Universal Military Training and Service Act. This was accomplished with the somewhat reluctant concurrence of the American Medical and Dental Associations and the Association of American Medical Colleges. In consideration of their views, and with the acceptance of the inevitable by General Hershey, Congress also retained the structure of medical advisory committees at state and national levels of the Selective Service System to guide the selection, and especially the deferment, of special registrants. Once rewritten by the House committee, the bill passed easily in both houses.[54]

In 1959, the Defense Department presented a bill to extend the induction authority, and other related and expiring authorities, for another four years to July 1, 1963. Chairman Vinson, opening House committee hearings early in the session, set the tone for the remainder of the congressional review proceedings: "As far as I am concerned, we have no choice in the matter but to extend the draft. It is the right and proper thing to do. I hope there will be no hesitancy on the part of any member of the committee to meet his responsibility in this regard."[55]

There followed the by now familiar line-up of witnesses and printed statements: from the Administration, from veterans and other groups supporting extension, and from church and peace groups opposing it. (Indeed, there were more witnesses from the last category than from the other two together.) The Senate committee listened to almost the same witnesses. In addition, it heard out a proposal by the Scientific Manpower Commission that authority be given to assign men with critical skills to essential defense research and industries through Selective Service. It also listened, without great interest, to a proposal by the National Student Association that the universality of the service obligation might be preserved by crediting alternate service in teaching, foreign service, scientific research and development, technical assistance programs and the like, in lieu of active or reserve military service.[56]

In the floor debates, only one important amendment was considered: the substitution of a two-year extension for the four years being asked. In the House, this was defeated on a voice vote, and in the Senate, it went down 24–67. In House debate, the five hours granted by the Rules Committee were not fully used; and the bill passed easily, on a 381–20 roll call. Senate debate was not much more sparkling; after defeat of the two-year extension, the bill passed 90–1. The following day, the House accepted the Senate version without discussion. The entire process, from the opening of the hearings to final passage, stretched over just a little more than six weeks, from January 26 to March 12.[57]

The extension acts of 1955 and 1959 provide a marked contrast with earlier considerations of military manpower procurement policies. One major ingredient of earlier hearings had been the presence of groups representing, or seeming to represent, large sectors of the American public opposed in principle to peacetime conscription. Spokesmen for almost the same groups appeared again in 1955 and 1959; but gone was the sense that, on this issue, they represented any important forces in the electorate, and committee members seemed far less patient with them than before. Conscription had receded from its former position as a major issue of public conscience, and now presented merely a series of technical manpower procurement and management issues. A few of these, already noted, were handled through the cumbersome process of legislation; but during the 1950's, most problems of military manpower procurement were met in the equally cumbersome, but less visible, administrative process. As far as Congress and the public were concerned, most accepted without much question the standard arguments offered by the Administration for continuing in force the power to induct men for military service: first, the armed forces rely on this authority to maintain their strengths required for security, the active Army directly, and the other services and reserves indirectly; and second, our allies and our potential enemies might misunderstand our intentions were we to abandon the draft and accept the consequent force reductions.

2. *Managing the Manpower Pool*

Most of the problems facing the Selective Service System during the Eisenhower years stemmed not, as earlier, from manpower shortages, but from a growing military manpower surplus. There was an absolute decline of inductions during this period—from 265,000 in FY 1954 to a low of 60,000 in FY 1961. Active force procurement from other sources also responded to strength reductions during this period, though not so sharply as inductions (see

Table 8). As annual withdrawals for service from the military-age manpower pool shrank, the total pool grew.[58] In mid-1953, there were over 9.1 million men registered with Selective Service who were within the liable ages for induction (eighteen and one-half to twenty-six in most cases) and another 434,000 between ages eighteen and eighteen and one-half. By mid-1957, this pool had grown to 10.9 million in the liable age groups, plus 420,000 who were eighteen to eighteen and one-half. Growth in the next four years was even more rapid; by mid-1961, the liable age group stood at 13.9 million, and there were almost 561,000 between ages eighteen and eighteen and one-half. Thus the average annual growth of the total pool had increased from about 450,000 in each of the first four years to over 770,000 during the years of the second period. Consequently, the pool of available manpower not already in service also grew, though not in parallel with the total pool. A rough index of this growth is the number of registrants classified I-A plus those unclassified of liable age. This pool of "working sources" stood at a little over one million at mid-1953, grew to nearly 2.9 million at mid-1957, and grew further to just over four million at mid-1961. Thus the average annual growth in this working pool was about 460,000 per year in the period 1953-57, but only about 290,000 for the period 1957-61. A final index of the manpower surplus which the Selective Service System had to face is the average age of induction. In early 1953, most states were dipping into their supply of nineteen-year-olds to meet current induction calls. But by 1955, 74 percent of involuntary inductees were aged twenty-three or over; in May, 1956, this grew to 81 percent. In mid-1961 the average age of involuntary inductees was still rising slowly.[59]

Faced with the task of selecting fewer men each year, from a growing pool of manpower, for involuntary service in a shrinking Army, the Selective Service System might have moved in any of several directions. The most extreme, and one clearly unacceptable to it, to the Services, and to the Administration, would have been to abandon Selective Service inductions entirely. The reaction to a suggestion only bordering on this, made by Adlai Stevenson in 1956, has already been discussed. Nevertheless, there did remain those few groups, opposed to conscription in principle, who contended but could not prove that the armed forces could get by on voluntary recruiting alone. Despite its work to improve recruiting, which had Congress's eager cooperation, the Eisenhower Administration contended throughout the 1950's that even the reduced active forces it thought necessary could not be maintained without inductions or the threat of them. The evidence offered was slight: the Senate report on extension in 1955 cited the experience of 1947-48, when active strength fell below 1.4 million despite short enlistment terms and lower quality of intake, and concluded this was as much as could be hoped for from volunteering alone; in House hearings that year, an Air Force witness told of a recent survey of enlistees, in which 40 percent of a sample of new enlistees cited the service obligation as their prime motive for enlisting; and in 1959, Assistant Secretary Finucane told the House committee that the Army's strength would drop to 580,000, from the current 870,000, in the absence of inductions and induction pressure. Aside from these, there were no studies or figures cited; there was only the bald fact that the Army was taking a sizable number of inductees each year, and the common-sense assumption that the other services, as well as the Army, owed a large proportion of their voluntary recruits to the pressure of inductions. The latter was a believable assumption which no one could disprove; and few were willing to risk the consequences of a negative test. Even the arguments of industrialist Ralph Cordiner—that adoption of his committee's pay proposals could put the services on a voluntary basis, and by reducing turnover actually save money—did not prove persuasive. The Administration did not accept all of his proposals, and Congress did not take seriously his prediction of savings and relief from the draft.

The task assumed by Selective Service, then, was to adjust the supply of manpower to military demand administratively, or in a few instances by legislation. It was a series of such adjustments which, fortuitously or not, enabled the Selective Service System to keep its manpower supply from hopelessly outstripping the armed forces' needs. These same actions produced a pattern of Selective Service operations at the end of the decade very different from that existing at the end of the Korean War.

Two major adjustments in manpower supply and demand resulted, at least in part, from the legislation on reserves and entry standards discussed above.

The Reserve Forces Act of 1955 worked eventually to increase the demand for reserve military manpower. Most of this effect was not felt, however, until after the 1957 expansion of the special reserve training program, which was accomplished without legislation.[60] In mid-1955, Class I-D registrants (including ROTC students as well as deferred reservists) numbered 300,000, and stood at 303,000 in mid-1957. During the next year, this class increased to 518,000, and by mid-1961 it totalled 849,000. The new reserve programs, then, besides providing trained nonveterans to the Ready Reserve, also drained a net of almost 550,000 from the pool of manpower who would otherwise have been available for induction. The Selective Service System strongly supported this approach to manpower management. As early as 1954, the System cited the growing "untrained reserve" as a major defect in manpower policy, and coupled this with the observation that "the manner in which the country's manpower reserves are disposed is of greater significance than the adminstrative stability often striven for by 'career' Armed Forces." In 1955 it hoped that new reserve program could correct this growing pool of untrained manpower. It met early disappointment in 1956 with the conclusion that the only alternative to filling the Ready Reserve with volunteers would be inductions for that purpose, and stated the System stood ready to implement such legislation. The post-1957 expansion of reserve training was no doubt gratifying; but in 1961 the System still worried over the "millions" of untrained men of military age.[61]

The Selective Service System's disdain for the "administrative stability" of career forces, and its concern for the millions untrained, were also reflected in its initial attitudes toward rising entry standards. The System vigorously cooperated with the lowering of standards during the Korean War, and it wished to lower them still further. In 1954 Hershey explained his attitude toward emphasis on high-quality, professional active forces:

> The Armed Forces says, "You can run the Armed Forces cheaper if you run them for long periods of time with very smart men." That is fine. But if you ever have to mobilize for all-out war, the more people you have that have served 20 years, the more people you have prevented from being in that might have served 3 or 2 years, and therefore you will have to defend yourself with far less people. . . . [62]

Hershey's major concern was the rising rate of disqualification for failure to pass the mental tests. Never a great believer in those tests, he was generally critical of the armed forces' system of screening. He would have preferred instead the application of "functional" standards for qualification—involving initial acceptance of all but the obviously disqualified, followed by screening out of those who actually could not absorb training.[63]

Nevertheless, in 1956 Hershey was beginning to face the reality of high selectivity in the System's operations: "It provides Selective Service," his report concluded, "continually with the problem of how to insure, during a time when few are forwarded for induction, that the registrants selected shall be the ones who can be used to the best advantage by the Armed Forces."[64] By 1957, he was willing to support the Defense proposed bill to allow raising entry standards for inductees, and he explained his change of mind (if not of heart) to the House committee:

> . . . Even as a person who is trying to get everybody into the service, I find myself in embarrassment when we have sufficient people of a higher grade than we are using in the surplus. I don't like the word "surplus" because I have a feeling that if we had our Reserve forces filled up . . . they wouldn't have a surplus. But that is a separate question. As long as we are running this alleged surplus, I don't see how you can justify compelling the Government to use less than the best.[65]

The impact of this legislation on the manpower pool is difficult to trace, as low induction calls were met in part by allowing the number of unclassified men in the younger age groups to increase. A reasonable estimate, however, would be that the number in the pool aged nineteen to twenty-five who were rejected or rejectable rose from 1,760,000 in mid-1953 to 2,670,000 in mid-1957, and more rapidly to 3,850,000 in mid-1961; thus the annual growth of this group was a little over 225,000 in the period 1953-57, and jumped to nearly 300,000 in the period 1957-61.[66]

Reserve enlistments and higher rejection rates both acted, especially in 1957-61, to drain the manpower pool (or reduce its rate of growth) and thus restrict the number of men "available" for service in the face of declining active force manpower demands. Other measures also played an important role in this process, and these were all administrative in conception and application.

The first such administrative measure was a response to problems arising from the proviso extending the liability of deferred men to age thirty-five. In 1953, to meet an incipient danger that students, by fathering children, might convert their draft deferments into effective exemptions despite the proviso, fatherhood alone, in the absence of hardship, had been eliminated as grounds for deferment.[67] Given the Selective Service System's careful interpretation of the age proviso,[68] this in turn had created new problems for the System and its older registrants. Evidence for these can be found in the complaints voiced during the 1955 extension hearings. Men deferred initally for reasons of occupation or family hardship, as well as to attend college and graduate school, and even some initially rejected for service, were being reclassified I-A in later years, just as they acquired small families of their own and were opening businesses, successfully managing small farms, or rising to more important career positions. The number of these could not have been large, but even a few anguished cries from constituents served to rouse a number of senators and representatives. A House amendment relieving certain IV-F's from the proviso disappeared in conference, and nothing was done legislatively to resolve the issue (except for National Guard enlistees). Instead, the Selective Service System met the problem with new regulations which effectively exempted fathers and men aged twenty-six and over from induction.

These regulations were put in operation tentatively in July, 1955, through the device of postponing induction; they were made formal by an executive order in February, 1956.[69] The new regulations amended the order of inductions, rather than establishing new deferments. Priorities within Class I-A for each local board were ordered as follows:

1. Delinquents aged nineteen or older, oldest first.
2. Volunteers for induction under age twenty-six, in order of volunteering.
3. Nonvolunteer nonfathers aged nineteen to twenty-five inclusive, oldest first.
4. Nonvolunteer fathers aged nineteen to twenty-five, oldest first.

5. Nonvolunteers aged twenty-six or older, youngest first.

6. Nonvolunteers aged eighteen and one-half to nineteen, oldest first.

Selective Service practice had long recognized the first two of these priorities, and the last was fixed by law. Priority three became the major source of inductees. Priorities four and five, without adding to the formal deferment rolls, effectively restored deferment for all fathers, and returned to the even earlier practice of not inducting those past their twenty-sixth birthdays.

Beyond halting the induction of fathers and older men, these regulations had a number of other effects. The Selective Service System stated two reasons for the new order of induction, the principle one being to provide younger inductees to the Armed Forces. The exclusion of men over twenty-six and fathers in the nineteen to twenty-five age group (most of whom were in the older part of that bracket) tended in this direction; but these groups were so small that the effect on average induction age was short-lived. It dropped somewhat in late spring and summer, 1956, and then resumed its gradual upward trend. A secondary reason was "to strengthen the Nation's civilian economy by inducting nonfathers in preference to fathers." This preference was defended, in that it "fosters the family life of the Nation"; and the System suggested this provision might be stimulating marriages, citing growth in the group of I-A fathers from 151,000 to 370,000 in that single fiscal year. Still another effect, reinforced by the continuing decline of inductions, was a sharp reduction in appeals from classification.[70] The impact of these new rules on the pool of men most "available" for induction was less spectacular, but impressive (see Table 9). By redefining this group after 1955 to include only those men in priority three of Class I-A, it was possible to keep the available pool below the 1955 level (until 1961), despite a 35 percent increase in the total of Class I-A.

The new order of induction was only one indicator of an important change in the Selective Service System's conception of its manpower procurement functions. As late as the 1955 extension hearings, General Hershey had pleaded intent-of-Congress and letter-of-the-law in his strict interpretation of the proviso extending

TABLE 9

SELECTIVE SERVICE REGISTRANTS IN CLASSES I-A AND I-A-O, JUNE 30, 1953–JUNE 30, 1961

	1953	1954	1955	1956	1957	1958	1959	1960	1961
				Number (in Thousands)					
By Priority*									
Non-fathers, 19-25	---	---	---	1,470	1,430	1,373	1,533	1,685	1,760
Fathers, 19-25	---	---	---	151	370	472	424	369	342
Registrants, 26 and over	---	---	---	25	51	67	75	90	110
Registrants, 18½-19	---	---	---	166	224	241	241	173	162
Total I-A, I-A-O	938	1,408	1,758	1,812	2,075	2,153	2,273	2,317	2,374
				Percent of Total					
By Priority*									
Non-fathers, 19-25	---	---	---	81.0	68.9	63.8	67.4	72.7	74.2
Fathers, 19-25	---	---	---	8.3	17.8	21.9	18.7	15.9	14.4
Registrants, 26 and over	---	---	---	1.4	2.5	3.1	3.3	3.9	4.6
Registrants, 18½-19	---	---	---	9.2	10.8	11.2	10.6	7.5	6.8
Total I-A, I-A-O	100.0	100.0	100.0	100.0	100.0	100.0	100.0	100.0	100.0

SOURCE: U.S. Selective Service System, *Annual Report of the Director of Selective Service, Fiscal Years 1953-61* (Washington: U.S. Government Printing Office, 1954-62). N.B. Percent figures derived from totals. Men in Class I-A-O, not tabulated separately, are those in Class I-A who object to combatant service.

* Priorities within Class I-A, I-A-O were established by Executive Order No. 10659, on February 15, 1956.

liability to age thirty-five; but the System's 1955 report emphasized the virtues and uses of local board flexibility, and stated that "a freer deferment trend would seem to be in order." For the future, it predicted that "an attitude of continued facility with respect to deferments, especially in the case of older registrants, may be expected from the local boards of the System." The 1957 report expanded in this new direction, calling the System a "storekeeper of manpower," and noting that the System's function was not only to procure manpower for the armed forces, but also to defer them to train for and perform important tasks in civil life. In the 1958 report, this aspect of deferment got a new name: "Through its constant classification actions, the System has not only selected men for induction, but by the incentive of deferments has *channeled* others into essential activities. . . ." From that time forward, the thrust of the reports, and of General Hershey's public testimony, was that the System, as a storekeeper, not only procured manpower for military service, but channeled much of the remainder into important nonmilitary tasks.[71]

The Selective Service local boards did indeed adopt "an attitude of continued facility with respect to deferments." The total deferred (see Table 10) other than reservists and IV-F's, actually de-

TABLE 10

SELECTIVE SERVICE DEFERMENTS,
1953, 1957, 1961.
(In Thousands)

	1953	1957	1961
I-S, high school student _____	69	27	15
I-S, college student _____	41	8	2
II-A, non-agricultural occupation _____	33	32	72
II-C, agricultural occupation _____	87	25	18
II-S, college student _____	162	144	180
III-A, hardship to dependents _____	1,143	1,123	1,773
IV-B, government official _____	*	*	*
Total _____	1,535	1,359	2,060

SOURCE: U.S. Selective Service System, *Annual Report of the Director of Selective Service, Fiscal Years 1953, 1957, 1961* (Washington: U.S. Government Printing Office, 1954, 1958, 1962). N.B. Statistics are valid as of June 30 of each year. Those deferred for service in the reserves or disqualified for service are not included in this tabulation.
* Less than 50 total.

clined by 176,000 between June, 1953, and June, 1957; but it rose by 701,000 during the next four years. Not all these deferments fit the System's stated concept of channeling, which it eventually defined as ". . . that process through which registrants are influenced to enter and remain in study, in critical occupations, and in many other activities in the national health, safety, and interest by deferment or prospect for deferment from military service."[72] Those fitting this definition best were Class II-A, nonagricultural occupation (including apprentices), and Class II-S, college students; but a more questionable class—III-A, hardship to dependents—accounted for 93 percent of the total increase in deferments in the period 1957-61. The difference between the concept and the classification picture is partly explained by the Selective Service practice of classifying "from the bottom up"; only those not eligible for III-A deferment were considered for Classes II-S and II-A. Yet it also suggests that protecting family life was considered by local boards to be as much in the national interest as college studies, or training and work at critical tasks in essential industries.

A general view of the changes in Selective Service classifications between 1957 and 1961 is shown in Table 11, where each classification is shown by total and as a proportion of the total classified. Among those classified, the proportion available for service declined slightly, and the proportion really likely to be inducted (I-A, I-A-O nonfathers, aged nineteen to twenty-five) rose only a little—all as the total number classified increased by 20 percent, and the total within liable ages increased nearly 30 percent. This stability in the priority three group stands in contrast to the decline of over 9 percent (from 38.2 to 29) in the proportion of age-eligible classified registrants inducted, enlisted, commissioned, or completed service, and the counterbalancing rise of more than 10 percent (from 40.6 to 50.8) in the total proportion of these registrants in reserve programs, disqualified for service, or deferred for occupation, study or dependency.

One might conclude that the newly conceived channeling function of the Selective Service System consisted of roughly equal parts irrigation of the reserves, drainage of the less qualified, and floating of family life, with the promotion of study, research, and other critical occupations accounting for much smaller flows. The System itself offered a somewhat more cheerful summary, concluding in its 1960 report:

TABLE 11

SELECTIVE SERVICE REGISTRANTS BY CLASSIFICATION STATUS, 1957, 1959, 1961

	1957		1959		1961	
	Number*	%	Number*	%	Number*	%
Total available for service	2,081	20.5	2,281	20.1	2,383	19.5
I-A, I-A-O, non-fathers, 19-25	1,430	14.1	1,533	13.5	1,760	14.4
I-A, I-A-O, fathers, 19-25	370	3.6	424	3.7	342	2.8
I-A, I-A-O, over 26	51	0.5	75	0.7	110	0.9
I-A, I-A-O, under 19	224	2.2	241	2.1	162	1.3
I-O, conscientious objector	6	0.1	8	0.1	9	0.1
Total in Service	1,912	18.8	2,016	17.8	2,228	18.2
I-C, inducted	317	3.2	216	1.9	146	1.2
I-C, enlisted or commissioned	1,290	12.6	1,189	10.5	1,231	10.1
I-D, reserves	303	3.0	609	5.4	849	6.9
I-W, conscientious objector at work	2	‡	2	‡	2	‡
Total who have completed service	2,276	22.4	2,223	19.6	2,170	17.7
IV-A, veteran (or sole surviving son)	2,271	22.4	2,217	19.5	2,164	17.7
I-W, conscientious objector released	5	‡	6	0.1	6	‡
Total deferred for physical, mental. or moral reasons, IV-F	2,453	24.2	3,057	26.9	3,322	27.2
Total deferred for other reasons	1,359	13.4	1,704	15.0	2,060	16.8
I-S, high school student (statutory)	27	0.3	24	0.2	15	0.1
I-S, college student (statutory)	8	0.1	5	‡	2	‡
II-A, non-agricultural occupation	32	0.3	49	0.4	72	0.6
II-C, agricultural occupation	25	0.2	21	0.2	18	0.1
II-S, college student	144	1.4	160	1.4	180	1.5
III-A, hardship to dependents	1,123	11.1	1,445	12.8	1,773	14.5
IV-B, governmental official	†	‡	†	‡	†	‡
Total with original exemptions	64	0.6	67	0.6	70	0.5
IV-C, alien	7	0.1	7	0.1	7	0.1
IV-D, minister or divinity student	57	0.5	60	0.5	63	0.5
Total classified within liable ages	10,145	100.0	11,348	100.0	12,233	100.0

SOURCE: U.S. Selective Service System, *Annual Report of the Director of Selective Service, Fiscal Years 1957, 1959, 1961* (Washington: U.S. Government Printing Office, 1958, 1960, 1962). N.B. Statistics are valid as of June 30 of each year. Percent figures derived from numerical totals. Details do not add to totals due to rounding.

* In thousands.

† Less than 50.

‡ Less than 0.05 percent.

At the moment, the delivery of manpower for induction into the Armed Forces is a collateral product of the System's operation. The process of providing inductees and enlistees to the various services and their reserve training programs is a task in itself. However, it is in dealing with the other millions of registrants within the Selective Service System jurisdiction that the program is likewise occupied, developing more effective men in the national interest through channeling.[73]

Looked at in either way, channeling had become a vital feature of the New Look in Selective Service.

V. MANPOWER PROCUREMENT POLICY IN 1960

1. *Meeting Military and Social Goals for Manpower*

By the end of 1960, of the three major problems facing the procurers and users of military manpower at the end of the Korean rearmament, one had been met with perhaps too much success, one remained an open difficulty, and the third was being quietly swept into the corners of local board offices.

The quantitative problem of reserve manpower had been over-solved, at least from the Administration's point of view. Congress (and the Selective Service System) did not entirely agree; hence the Administration was under considerable pressure to maintain a Ready Reserve which was certainly larger and better trained than at any other time in American history, but which also had grown larger than the Administration was willing to support with enthusiasm. The difficulties this posed for relating the size, cost, and readiness of reserve forces to current and reasonably prospective military needs would be revealed only a few months later, as the nation undertook its first partial mobilization since the Korean War. In 1960, however, it did seem that existing manpower procurement inducements and compulsions were more than able to fill the required reserves with an acceptable balance of experienced and new men. The recall mechanism remained untested, but no one was worrying about that in public.

In 1960, there was no concern, as there had not really been since 1950, over the ability of the active forces to maintain the strengths set for them by the Administration. There were worries, to be sure, set forth in the unpublished Gaither Report and in a public report of the Rockefeller Brothers Fund, and voiced particularly by Army leaders, that the Administration's force requirements were set too low. But this was a problem for operational, budgetary and strategic planners, not for personnel staffs and the manpower procurement machinery. There was little doubt that the procurement system— a complex of inductions, threat of inductions, and enlistment and re-enlistment inducements, of local boards and recruiting sergeants, of draft laws and pay raises—could meet whatever quantitative strength goals the armed forces might reasonably set for it.

There was still open concern for the quality of manpower in and entering the active forces. With the inducements of steady, if not luxurious, pay and in-service training, the military services sought to attract large numbers of well-qualified young men to train for and perform their increasingly technical tasks; and with the attractions of better pay and other personal benefits, and of a sense of belonging to an important enterprise, they sought to keep the best of these new men for longer periods, perhaps a full career. Yet to get enough men to apply for enlistment, so that the services could make some reasonable selections, something more was required. This was supplied by the Selective Service System, whose active operations indirectly persuaded tens of thousands of men to visit recruiting stations of all the services each year, many of whom would otherwise probably not have come. The questions remained open, however, whether even these added applicants gave the services the choice they needed to assure high enough quality in their ranks, whether the inductees themselves were of high enough quality to fill the Army's needs, and whether the inducements were high enough to retain the quantity and quality of longer-service and career personnel desired. The answer to these questions in the mid-1950's was no. By the end of 1960 a series of pay increases and improvements in other benefits had been enacted, and induction standards were higher. Nevertheless, reenlistment rates for first-termers, especially in the critical occupational groups, which had reached a post–Korean War peak in late 1958, fell off sharply thereafter, and recovered only to mid-1957 levels during FY 1961. Moreover, although the general educational level in enlisted ranks had improved markedly since the Korean War, more than a third of all active ser-

vice enlisted men in 1960 had not completed a high school education.[74]

As Congress, the Administration, and the services developed responses to reserve and active force manpower problems, they also
assisted the Selective Service System in meeting its less publicized
difficulties. The rise in reserve enlistments and in rejections for service created two major channels for draining off the surplus of the
System's manpower supply as the demands upon it declined.

A secondary goal of cold war manpower procurement policy,
vaguely conceived in 1948 and more vigorously pursued in 1951,
was that the procurement of men for active service should not interfere unduly with other essential activities. During the Korean rearmament, this goal had been pursued through a generous program of
student deferments, and smaller programs deferring men for apprentice training and critical tasks in industry. Deferments in Classes II-S and II-A fell off somewhat after the Korean truce, but between 1957 and 1961 the former increased 25 percent and the latter
more than doubled. Coupled with these rises was the new Selective
Service conception of its function as a channeler of manpower. The
older view of deferments was that they protected certain vital civil
interests against military demands for manpower. The new concept,
developed after 1957, saw deferments, especially in these two categories, as a means to active pursuit of nonmilitary goals for manpower development and use.

The difference between these concepts is well-illustrated by the
change in attitudes toward, and the fate of, the 1951 extended
liability proviso. In 1955, at hearings and in congressional debate,
the proviso was defended as a way of assuring that those deferred,
especially for college study, would eventually serve. Except for altering its impact on National Guard enlistees, Congress preserved
the proviso intact, resisting even the House-approved relief for those
deferred by rejection. Within weeks, however, the Selective Service
System introduced, and later gained the president's approval of, a
new order of induction which effectively exempted all men in Class
I-A over age twenty-six. By 1959, General Hershey was still defending the extended liability proviso, but on very different grounds. No
longer did he regard it as assurance of eventual service. Rather, he
told the House committee, he now construed the intent of Congress

to have been, even in 1951, that those deferred to prepare themselves for better service to society should remain at the tasks they were deferred for.

One of the Selective Service System's chief claims for its newly conceived function of channeling was that "thousands of young men would not have continued their education at the college level if there had not been a Selective Service program of student deferment."[75] This assertion is, at best, impossible to disprove. Certainly many other factors must also be included in accounting for the enormous growth in college population since the reenactment of Selective Service in 1948 and inauguration of a formal student deferment program in 1951 (see Table 12). From June, 1953, to June, 1957, college student deferments declined about 24 percent, while fall

TABLE 12

COLLEGE STUDENT ENROLLMENTS AND DEFERMENTS,
1953, 1957, 1961, 1964
(In Thousands)

	1953	1957	1961	1964
Class I-S and II-S				
College students*	203	152	182	1,175
Men enrolled in college†	1,423	2,003	2,424	3,936
Women enrolled in college†	808	1,065	1,467	1,936

* SOURCE: U.S. Selective Service System, *Annual Report of the Director of Selective Service, Fiscal Years 1953, 1957, 1961, 1964* (Washington: U.S. Government Printing Office, 1954, 1958, 1962, 1965). Figures are for June 30 of year shown.

† SOURCE: U.S. Department of Commerce, Bureau of the Census, *Statistical Abstract of the United States, 1954, 1958, 1962, 1965* (Washington: U.S. Government Printing Office, 1954, 1958, 1962, 1965).

male enrollment in colleges and universities rose nearly 41 percent. Between 1957 and 1961, as the Selective Service System promoted student deferments, Classes I-S (College) and II-S rose 20 percent, and college male enrollment rose 21 percent. But enrollment of women rose 38 percent in this same period. The explanation for these enrollment increases probably lies at least as much in rising college-age population, increasing availability of scholarships, and changing social attitudes toward, and hiring policy demands for, college education, as it does in the benignity of Selective Service local boards. Considering the rise in average induction age to over twenty-three, a better case might be made for the specific influence of student deferments on graduate enrollments; but here, too, other factors played an important part. In sum, although those deferred certainly were able to continue their education, it is not at all clear that others would not have been found to take the place of drafted students had there been no such deferments after 1953.

Through reserve programs and induction standards, Congress and the Administration were assisting Selective Service in managing its manpower pool; through deferments in pursuit of nonmilitary goals for manpower, the System was helping itself. If the channeling of men into studies and important civilian tasks had a relatively minor quantitative impact on the pool, the same could not be said of the System's increasing regard for the integrity of family life. Deferments in Class III-A, plus I-A priority four for fathers, constituted the second-widest channel (after rejections and ahead of reserve enlistments) for draining down the pool of availables. In addition, thanks to low induction calls, the System was not wrenching immature boys from the shelter of home and community and exposing them, unwilling, to the evils and temptations of military life. The recruiting system, to be sure, was attracting large numbers of youths aged seventeen to twenty; but these were volunteers, in the American tradition, and they made it possible for others to delay their service. Thus, in managing its manpower pool, the Selective Service System was at the same time achieving most of the standard nonmilitary goals of manpower procurement policy. That it was not too clear on priorities between these two aims—management of the pool or pursuit of social goals—concerned very few people in 1960.

2. *Acceptance of Compulsion*

The liberality of Selective Service deferments probably also contributed to continued acceptance of the idea of compulsion to military service. Gone were the days of postwar innocence about the United Nations' precluding America's need for military forces, and faded too was the apparent power of traditional American sentiments against conscription (which had done so much to defeat UMT). The 1950's had started with a major war in Korea, and if later years in the decade brought the fleeting spirits of Geneva and Camp David, the death of Stalin, and the thaw, they also brought crises in the Formosa Straits, in Hungary, at Suez, in Lebanon, in Berlin. The 1950's brought a United Nations army into being, but it was manned mostly by Americans and South Koreans; they also brought a NATO armed force into being, again manned mostly by Americans. There was some resentment, but more generally acceptance, of these and other needs for American military manpower. Whether out of active commitment to the goals of cold war deterrence and acceptance of its burdens, or out of resignation to these, or simply out of a sense that "I won't be called anyway," few Americans complained much about the existence of Selective Service and its compulsions. Apparently most Americans were satisfied in 1960 that manpower needs were being met with the least necessary imposition on individual freedoms.

3. The Question of Equity

Usually associated with this acceptance of compulsion, as necessary if not entirely desirable, was a sense that the obligations imposed were being shared by all. As Carl Vinson put it in 1951: "People say 'We have no objection to whatever draft if it is fair and equitable and everyone has to do his part.' " Vinson, for one, was not convinced that the pre-1951 Selective Service law had measured up to this standard, for he went on to say, "As it is written today, there are only a few lines in the draft about who is being inducted, but page after page as to who is being deferred. It is written almost like members of a State assembly would write a sales tax just before the election." By 1955, however, Vinson had become more than reconciled to the even more complex, and doubtfully more equitable, Universal Military Training and Service Act. "The strength of Selective Service," he insisted, "is its uniformity. It applies to everybody equally and alike. As long as we keep that as the fundamental basis, we are on sound ground." His counterpart in the Senate, Richard Russell, took a rather different view of the matter. "There is discrimination in all fields of living," he concluded, "and until human institutions achieve perfection and there is nothing in human history to cause us to believe they ever will, we will have some. . . . Some people will be compelled to contribute more to their country than others in military service, taxation, and other fields."[76]

Senator Russell's view was probably the more representative of those most concerned with making and executing manpower procurement policy. It certainly paralleled General Hershey's philosophy, and probably reflected more or less closely the feelings of a majority of the Armed Services Committees' members, including Carl Vinson. Nevertheless there was, in 1959, an elaborate effort by the Defense Department to show that few if any were escaping their military obligations.

Based on Census Bureau population estimates by age group, and on armed forces and Selective Service records of the age distribution of men entering active and reserve service, Defense studies concluded that the great majority of young men were fulfilling these obligations in one fashion or another. The estimated population of the group aged twenty-six (plus or minus six months) was 1.1 million in June, 1958; and a total of 770,000, or 70 percent, of these were in or had completed military service. Given a disqualification rate of 21.8 percent (based on the older standards under which most men this age were examined), nearly 90 percent of those qualified were fulfilling, or had completed, their obligations. Moreover, given that only 5,000 men in this group remained in Class I-A (the remainder were deferred for dependency or other reasons), and given the Selective Service policy of inducting first those most closely approaching their twenty-sixth birthdays, it could be argued that practically no qualified nonfather reaching age twenty-six and not deferred would escape service. Much the same was true for the June, 1963, projections of these figures: although only 54.6 percent of the group aged twenty-six would have entered service, rejection rates in examinations of these men would have risen since 1958; hence 78 percent of those qualified would have entered service; given deferments for dependency and other reasons, only about 5,000 of this group would still be in Class I-A; most of these would be inducted, and once again "virtually no I-A nonfather who is qualified and available for service will be in a position to escape his military service obligation."[77]

This very careful argument certainly took care of any claims that a man could evade his obligation by simply waiting out his local board, but no one was seriously claiming this. For the few who were worried about the equity of the total system and its various parts, however, this argument only begged the question.

The reserve program itself was vulnerable to criticism; six months' active duty for training, followed by a (steadily reduced) number of years in Ready Reserve training was not really equivalent in burden to two years' active service followed also by a Ready Reserve obligation. The original concept of universal military training sought equity through calling all, or almost all, to train, and then allowing those who so desired to go on with active service. In practice the compulsions were reversed, with some forced into active and reserve service and others allowed to volunteer for that or for reserve service alone; and the idea of universality had really been abandoned. But equity through universality had never been a popular American practice (though it approached this status in World War II). Moreover, at least the reserve enlistees were performing some military service, and they remained liable for active service if needed.

What then of other drains on the manpower pool? The greatest was rejections for physical, moral, or, mostly, mental shortcomings. Was this fair? General Hershey worried quite a bit about the high rejection rate, but his concern, at least in public, was for the dangers to national security of allowing such large numbers to go untrained, not for equity. Only one witness voiced any strong criticism of entry standards on grounds of equity during hearings on the 1958 change in standards. His argument was not that this discriminated against those selected for service, however, but that it unfairly denied large numbers of men the opportunities and benefits of such service.[78] There was some repetition of this point in hearings on the 1959 extension, but it roused no great interest.

Apparently Congress and the public at large accepted the discriminations of the arbitrary "equalization" of reserve and active service obligations, and of the exemption and exclusion from service of the less qualified. They accepted, too, the deferment of students and fathers, which meant effective exemption of many students and almost all fathers. The Defense Department's argument, that nearly all men "qualified and available" would eventually serve, may not have been a wholly candid answer to potential doubts about the equity of the system; but very few were asking the penetrating questions which might have raised these doubts.

4. Unexamined Questions of Cost

Fiscal, that is budgetary, restraints were more or less openly implied, and sometimes even explicit, in most manpower procurement programs of the 1950's. The New Look's emphasis on ground force reserves was billed as an effort to keep defense costs down without lowering deterrent effectiveness. The Administration's reaction, if not Congress's response, to the overabundant success of the new reserve program was an equally clear recognition that all these reserves might cost more than their military worth. The Administration's emphasis on higher quality in the active forces, through higher entry standards, stemmed at least partly from a desire to cut or hold down the costs of training, turnover, and discipline. The Administration's reluctance to couple this emphasis on quality with a wholehearted endorsement of the Cordiner pay proposals was openly based on budget cost considerations. And, more clearly than ever since World War II, the continuation of Selective Service support for both active and reserve forces implied a reluctance to accept, or even consider, the costs of manning the armed services solely with volunteers.

The full cost implications of these responses to budgetary restraints nonetheless remained almost as thoroughly unexplored by 1960 as did the problems of equity in military manpower procurement. Everyone knew, of course, that given numbers of reserves were cheaper to raise and maintain than equal numbers of active forces; but no one knew, and no one even asked, at least in public, whether a given dollar expenditure on reserves would buy more or less military effectiveness than the same dollar expenditure on active forces. Everyone knew, too, that it would be more costly to raise and maintain military forces of given effectiveness through voluntary recruiting than to procure and sustain the same military effectiveness with the direct and indirect help of Selective Service; but only the Cordiner Report assayed any estimate at all of the extra cost involved. Moreover, the assertion that it was feasible to raise adequate forces voluntarily was so contradicted by entrenched assumptions about past infeasibility (based on the 1947-48 experience) that the Administration was easily able to convince Congress and the public of the fiscal unwisdom of testing Cordiner's claims. Finally, given that few questioned the impact of current procurement programs on the problem of spreading the burden of military service among military-age youth, it is hardly surprising that, again with few exceptions, the financial impact on individuals of obliged service also went unexamined.

5. Selective Service Channeling:
Critique and Response

There were, during the 1950's, a few critiques of the manpower procurement system which took as their starting point the many anomolies, if not inequities, which this system imposed on various groups and classes. The more interesting of these attacked, not the need for strong forces (except, perhaps, the reserves), but the way in which the procurement system went about manning those forces.

Among these critiques, the most thorough was a short study written for the Fund for the Republic by John Graham, a Washington lawyer. Graham's report was highly critical, not only of the increasingly complex set of reserve and enlistment options, but of the whole system of Selective Service classification, deferment, and effective exemption. His premise was that "no compulsory system which is not universal and non-discriminatory can long survive in a free society"; and he concluded that: "If it is true that the military must be more selective, that only a minority can be absorbed and used productively by the armed forces, that the obligation is neither universal in scope nor uniform in application, then the present system, with the heavy civil and financial restrictions it imposes, must be changed."[79] Graham's preferred alternative to the current system was an all-volunteer force, and he suggested the Cordiner pay proposals, increased reliance on civilian manpower for support functions, and raises of initial pay, as possible means to this end. The military services might have joined in much of this; but the Administration had already found the Cordiner proposals alone too expensive to introduce all at once; and the Defense Department took great pains during hearings on utilization of manpower to show there was not much more room for replacing military men with civilians.[80]

Moreover, the question of just what it would cost in additional pay and benefits to support the required active and reserve forces with volunteers alone was moot, for no one had thoroughly studied it.

Short of this, Graham suggested another change, the reintroduction of the Selective Service lottery. Coupled with this, he urged elimination of all deferments, and limitation of exemptions to clear cases of physical or mental disability. He suggested a flat compensation of $200 a month, plus dependents' allowances, for all those called to involuntary service; the increased cost could be met, he argued, by a special tax on the incomes of those not required to serve. The intent of this scheme was to reinforce the universality of the military service obligation and to reduce discrimination in imposing the liability for service as much as possible, while continuing to recognize the military services' inability to absorb all obligated youths.[81] This very inventive proposal received no attention in the 1959 extension hearings; but it did perhaps inspire this comment in the Selective Service System's 1958 report: "The problem [of rising induction age] cannot be solved by taking the youngest liable and available registrants first. With over 100,000 a month becoming 18½ and draft calls only 10,000 to 15,000 a month, a lottery system would be required, and that is totally undesirable."[82]

No reasons were given for the System's out-of-hand rejection of a lottery solution.[83] It may have had something to do with preserving operational flexibility at local board and higher levels, which the system considered very desirable indeed. This flexibility, arising from the considerable grant of discretionary authority under the law to the president and, by delegation, to the director and the local boards, was another object of Graham's critique. Recalling the many important administrative changes in Selective Service policy between 1955 and 1958, he suggested that "the laws should be openly amended and not perverted *sub silentio* by administrative action."[84] This same flexibility was, on the other hand, the object of constant emphasis and praise from the System and its director. As General Hershey put it in the 1959 hearings: "This bill has so many more things in it than we even implemented—that is why I want to keep it. But most of the things that everybody has ever asked for we have been able to do with this bill. First, because it is general and, second because it is not too specific."[85]

Although Graham's was the most extensive nonpacifist critique of the existing manpower procurement system, he was not the only one with alternatives to offer. The 1959 hearings brought suggestions that non-military volunteer service, especially abroad, might properly be credited in lieu of a military obligation. The proposal got little attention at the time; but through early 1960 it gained further currency. It did not become a live public issue, however, until late in the 1960 election campaign, when John Kennedy suggested at Michigan University that a volunteer "peace corps" ought to be established to serve overseas with technical aid missions. Draft exemption, he felt, might properly be given to those so serving. Vice-President Nixon attacked the idea, especially its alternative service aspect, predicting this would only promote draft evasion. The peace corps idea itself was an immediate public success (though some had reservations); but postelection discussions soon led to the conclusion that attaching a draft exemption to it might be impolitic, and perhaps inherently undesirable; and the idea of alternative service was dropped when the Peace Corps bill was acted on in 1961. Nevertheless, this idea did strike a harmonious, if faint, responsive chord in the Selective Service System. Its 1960 report concluded that "the concept that 'duty' is best exemplified by service in the Armed Forces is now under some degree of analysis and evolution and may eventually be interpreted somewhat more broadly." Thus the System demonstrated that its responses to criticism and proposals for change, just as its day to day operations, could be selective and flexible.[86]

During the eight years after the Korean War, Administration and congressional attention to military manpower procurement policies was focused predominantly on the needs of the active and reserve forces, on the costs of meeting these needs, to a lesser extent on non-military social goals, and very little at all on the relation of these to the more abstract issues of compulsion and equity. Given Adlai Stevenson's experience in 1956, it would seem that the general public also accepted these priorities. This pattern also survived the election of 1960. Even as the Kennedy Administration took office and began charting new courses in military policy, abstract issues of compulsion and equity in military manpower procurement remained relatively dormant, while more concrete problems of military needs and social goals for the development and use of manpower continued dominant. At the center of the military manpower procurement machinery stood the Selective Service System, accepting, promoting, and benefiting from this pattern of priorities. In its twenty-year existence, the System had often been the object of strong criticism and public protest; but for now, it could enjoy its quiet triumph.

chapter five

New Challenges to Selective Service

In 1960, the Selective Service System operated largely unchallenged as the central engine of the nation's military manpower procurement programs. Six years later, Selective Service was once again the object of heated debate and criticism; and by 1970, a new Administration was seriously entertaining the idea of mothballing the System, in a fashion reminiscent of that proposed in the pre–Korean War debate over Selective Service extension.

This shift in fortunes for Selective Service, and the current debate over military manpower procurement, have their roots in three partly overlapping stages of policy change and debate during the 1960's. The first stage involved partially successful attempts at adapting policy and programs to a variety of internal and external pressures for change. The second stage brought sharp readjustments in procurement programs to meet military manpower needs for war in Vietnam. The third stage, marked by intensified public and congressional interest in military manpower procurement, began before the first stage ended, continued through the second stage of military build-up, and produced an unsuccessful campaign for major policy and program reforms; reactions to that failure are still in progress.

I.   MILITARY MANPOWER PROCUREMENT ON THE NEW FRONTIER

Three major influences pressed directly upon military manpower procurement policies and programs during the first half of the 1960's. The first was a shift in Defense Department planning from a strategy of massive retaliation to one of flexible deterrence, which put a new premium on conventional forces in relation to nuclear capabilities, and on active forces in preference to reserves. The second was the McNamara regime's injection of economic analysis into defense calculations. These two influences originated largely from within the defense community, both tended toward downward reappraisals of total manpower procurement demands, and they reinforced each other in stimulating the changes in reserve and recruiting programs discussed in the first subsection below. A third influence, reflecting the coming of age of the postwar "baby boom" generation, was an inexorable increase in the potential supply of military manpower. All three of these influences, moreover, operated in the context of a general shift in public policy priorities— away from fixation on cold war imperatives, and toward intensified interest in domestic problems. The second subsection below recounts the Selective Service System's responses to a changing environment of military strategy and programs, of manpower supply and demand, and of relevant domestic priorities.

1.   *Manpower for a Strategy of Flexible Deterrence*

The advent of the Kennedy Administration in 1961 brought the important shift in defense strategy, away from reliance on threatened massive retaliation, and toward recognition that the variety of military threats required multiple deterrent capabilities and a more flexible deterrent strategy. This shift was reflected in a general increase of defense spending; part of this went toward improving the main nuclear deterrent and nuclear firepower of the ground forces; but an even greater share went to rebuilding conventional active force capabilities. Much of the new defense funds thus went toward providing new infantry, artillery and armor weapons, new battlefield air and ground transport, increased strategic airlift, and stepped-up training; and some of them were used to increase active force manpower strengths. This emphasis on conventional forces continued, with some modifications, in the Johnson Administration after 1963. Between 1961 and 1965, the flexible deterrence strategy was complemented by a net active force strength increase of 171,000, with the major part (123,000) going to the Army and Marine Corps (see Table 13).

This increase in active, and especially ground, force strengths was not spread evenly over the early 1960's. Instead, the net increase represented a tapering off from higher levels achieved by mid-1962. The initial increases were the result of the first significant mobilization since the Korean War, involving large calls of Army and Air Force Ready Reservists to active duty, and more than doubled calls for Selective Service inductions. This mobilization experience had important impacts of its own on manpower plans and programs. Thus the net increases in active strengths by mid-1965 reflected both the new emphasis on conventional forces for flexible deterrence and, less directly, shifts in force structure planning and attitudes toward reserve forces' roles.

In the years since World War II, two kinds of reserves have been sought: *pools* of trained men, available in emergency to fill out existing active units and to help in creating new ones, were wanted by all the services; but only the Army and Air Force, especially the former, planned to rely heavily on reserve *units*, to be mobilized intact, brought up to active strength and equipment levels, and used alongside regular units. There has never been much dispute over the need for reserve pools. But arguments over the need for and feasibility of reserve units, mobilizable as such for use on short notice, and the related congressional interest in the dual structure of these units, part federal and part National Guard, have been the core of most postwar debates over reserve policy. These features

TABLE 13

Active Duty Military Personnel, June 30, 1961–June 30, 1965

(In Thousands)

Year	Dept. of Defense		Army		Navy		Marine Corps		Air Force	
	Total	% of Officers	Total	% of Officers	Total	% of Officers	Total	% of Officers	Total	% of Officers
1961 -------	2,484	12.7	859	11.6	627	11.2	177	9.1	821	15.7
1962 -------	2,808	12.2	1,066	10.9	666	11.3	191	8.8	884	15.3
1963 -------	2,700	12.4	976	11.1	665	11.4	190	8.8	869	15.4
1964 -------	2,687	12.6	973	11.4	667	11.4	190	8.9	857	15.6
1965 -------	2,655	12.8	969	11.6	671	11.6	190	9.1	825	16.0

Source: U.S. Department of Defense, Directorate for Statistical Services, *Selected Manpower Statistics* (Washington: Department of Defense, April 11, 1966), pp. 19, 24.

have also made the reserves problem peculiarly an Army problem; and it was primarily the Army's reserve units which were the focus of major changes in reserve structure and planning in the early 1960's.

A few years before, almost as soon as it had solved the bulk manpower problems of the reserve components, the Eisenhower Administration had begun to regret the huge structure it had created through liberal interpretation of the 1955 Reserve Forces Act. This regret, largely budgetary, was not shared by Congress and its interested committees, which succeeded in placing mandatory floors under the drill-pay strengths of the Army Reserve and National Guard Components of 300,000 and 400,000 respectively (see Chapter Four, section II). In early 1961, the outgoing Administration again recommended a 10 percent cut in the minimum strengths; but the new Kennedy Administration decided not to press this issue at once.

On July 25, in a nationwide broadcast faintly reminiscent of President Truman's 1948 response to the crisis in Europe, President Kennedy announced he would seek to build up the active forces, especially their conventional warfare capabilities, both as a response to renewed Soviet pressure on Berlin and in preparation for future threats. Draft calls would be doubled, perhaps tripled, and a number of National Guard and other reserve units would be called to active duty, to add more than 200,000 men to active force strengths.[1]

In 1948, the need had been to create new machinery to procure military manpower; in 1961, the task was to use the machinery which had been put together over the past thirteen years. The president decided not to use existing authority for calling reservists to active duty; this would have required a formal declaration of national emergency, and few in the government wished to take such a serious step. Instead, he asked for a joint resolution of Congress authorizing the call of 250,000 Ready Reservists for up to twelve months of active duty, and authorizing extensions of up to twelve months in the service terms of men already on active duty. This was readily granted and the stage was set for the first test of reserves mobilization in over a decade.[2]

The actual call was not that large; in all, about 148,000 reservists were ordered to active duty in October and November, 1961. Nearly 90 percent of these were Army reservists; and about two-thirds of those were in organized National Guard and Army Reserve drill-pay units, with the remainder coming from the Ready Reserve pool.[3]

The immediate military purpose of this reserve recall was quite limited. It was simply to support an increase in effective active force strengths more rapidly than could be accomplished by taking in only untrained men. Measured by this standard, the exercise was a success. By April, 1962, three active establishment training divisions, two National Guard divisions, and a number of lesser reserve units had been filled, trained, and added to the Army's contingency forces based in the United States; this met the goal of increasing the Army's total combat-ready force from eleven to sixteen divisions plus support units. At this point the Army was ready to use an increased inflow of recruits and inductees to create new regular divisions and other units; when these were ready, the reserve divisions and units were to be released.

This limited success was very nearly obscured by a storm of protest and debate during the winter of 1961–62.[4] As might have been expected, this first large-scale recall of reservists in more than ten years revealed quite a number of technical weaknesses, in screening of individuals from the Ready Reserve on grounds of occupation or dependency, in records of reserve unit strengths and training status, and in availability of equipment and active training facilities. In 1940 and 1950, similar difficulties had been submerged in the patriotic response of a nation at, or about to be at, war. This time, however, as President Kennedy was forced to repeat several times, the reserve recall was not for the purpose of fighting a war, but to prevent one.[5] The relative subtlety of this political-military goal was difficult to convey to reservists conceived in the traditional "Minuteman" image, and that difficulty was a major contributor to the widespread, though far from universal, problems of morale and discipline in the activated units.

The 1961 mobilization used reserves for an unusually limited purpose; it also accelerated reassessment of the long-run role of reserve forces and their usefulness in preventing war. The 1961 crisis in United States–Soviet relations came at a time when the Administration had already decided that the nation's conventional military forces, especially the Army, had to be expanded. The 1961 mobilization was not so much for the purpose of deterring the enemy in any specific crisis as it was for expanding the active forces' ability to deter or otherwise deal with a multiplicity of existing and potential threats. The reserves were called, not as a direct supplement to the Army's combat capability, but as a shield behind which the Army could build its own strategic reserve into its active-duty structure. That same expansion also gave the Army the ability to absorb additional training loads within its existing active structure; now it could recruit and induct fresh manpower and train it to create additional units in a major mobilization about as quickly as the reserve units could be activated, filled to strength, trained, and equipped. Thus the 1961 callup of reserves, by achieving its active force structural goals, simultaneously served to weaken arguments for maintaining large ready reserves against minor crisis contingencies, and called into question the usefulness of yet larger, less ready, reserves to meet major war threats.

Such, at least, were the Army and Defense Department conclusions. From these they developed new plans for the Army's reserve components: to concentrate a greater proportion of drill funds, paid drill manpower, and equipment on high priority Army Reserve and National Guard units; to eliminate a large number of low priority units and allow others to decline in strength and capabilities; and to cut total paid drill manpower strengths.

The ensuing struggle, extending over several years, among the Army and Defense Departments, the Armed Services Committees and Defense Appropriations Subcommittees, and the Reserve Officers and National Guard Associations, is amply recounted elsewhere.[6] Congress and its committees continued to regard the reserves as their special responsibility and concern within the total military force structure; and reservists and their organizations continued to depend upon and encourage this special concern. In a move widely regarded as an attempt to split the reserve associations' opposition, the Defense Department eventually proposed merging all the high priority Army reserve units under management of the National Guard, and converting the Army Reserve to its pre–World War II status as simply a reserve pool. The Reserve Officers Association and its congressional allies successfully resisted this move; but they could not, either alone or in combination with the National Guard Association and a broader base of congressional support, defeat the major thrust of the new reserve plans.

Between 1961 and mid-1965, much was accomplished in reorganizing the Army's reserves. Authorized paid drill strength was cut from 700,000 to 650,000; at the same time, achieving that strength was made more difficult by tightening reserve enlistment criteria and unit strength limits. As a consequence, actual paid drill strength for Army reserve components fell below 600,000. A 150,-000-man Select Reserve Force was identified, including three divisions, six separate brigades, and nearly a thousand smaller units, all programed for expansion to 100 percent strength and an intensified training schedule; the combat readiness goals for this force were set at eight weeks from activation to deployment for the full divisions, and four weeks for the smaller units. All members of this force were authorized drill pay, as were members of the remaining lower priority units. Marked for elimination were about 750 low priority Army Reserve units.

The manpower results of force structure changes during the early 1960's, then, were a net expansion of active forces, but a sharp reduction in demand for trained, combat-ready reservists. Accompanying these changes, considerable attention was also given to problems of quality and careerism in the active forces.

The pattern of active force enlisted procurement in this period was similar to that of the late 1950's, except for increased reliance on reservists and inductees in FY 1962, and the echo effect of this build-up on inductions in FY 1964 (see Table 14). Especially disappointing and disturbing to defense planners was the continued weakness in reenlistments. Only the Air Force consistently obtained 40 to 50 percent of its annual input from this internal source; the other services did no better than 20 to 30 percent.

Reenlistment rates[7] showed minor changes from the patterns of the late 1950's, reflecting the receding effects of the 1958 pay raise, the temporary impact of the 1961–62 build-up, and changes in unemployment rates. Crucial first-term reenlistment rates remained well below those for enlisted careerists who had completed at least two service terms. First-term rates were particularly low among men with technical skills in all services, and across all occupational groups in the Marine Corps.

TABLE 14

ACTIVE DUTY ENLISTED PERSONNEL PROCUREMENT, FISCAL YEARS 1962-1965

(In Thousands)

	1962		1963		1964		1965	
	Number	%	Number	%	Number	%	Number	%
Army								
Inductions ———————	158	31.5	74	27.5	151	41.8	102	34.8
First enlistments ———	127	25.4	112	41.3	116	32.2	102	34.7
Reenlistments ———————	104	20.8	83	30.8	93	25.7	88	30.1
Reservists to active duty ———	111	22.2	1	0.4	1	0.3	1	0.4
Total ———————	499	100.0	270	100.0	361	100.0	294	100.0
Navy								
Inductions ———————	—	—	—	—	—	—	—	—
First enlistments ———	107	54.2	85	50.6	95	56.2	94	55.5
Reenlistments ———————	56	28.2	53	31.4	45	26.6	44	25.9
Reservists to active duty ———	35	17.6	30	18.0	29	17.2	31	18.6
Total ———————	198	100.0	169	100.0	169	100.0	170	100.0
Marine Corps								
Inductions ———————	*	0.1	*	0.1	*	0.1	*	0.1
First enlistments ———	37	73.5	28	68.2	39	75.0	34	74.7
Reenlistments ———————	11	20.5	12	27.8	12	23.0	11	22.6
Reservists to active duty ———	3	5.9	2	3.9	1	1.9	1	2.6
Total ———————	51	100.0	42	100.0	52	100.0	46	100.0

TABLE 14 (Continued)

ACTIVE DUTY ENLISTED PERSONNEL PROCUREMENT, FISCAL YEARS 1962-1965

(In Thousands)

	1962		1963		1964		1965	
	Number	%	Number	%	Number	%	Number	%
Air Force								
Inductions	*	‡	*	‡	--	--	--	--
First enlistments	113	48.6	102	55.3	95	54.6	88	45.7
Reenlistments	96	41.3	71	38.2	79	45.3	104	54.2
Reservists to active duty	23	10.1	12	6.5	†	0.1	†	0.1
Total	233	100.0	185	100.0	174	100.0	192	100.0
Department of Defense								
Inductions	158	16.1	74	11.1	151	19.9	103	14.6
First enlistments	385	39.2	328	49.3	345	45.6	318	45.4
Reenlistments	266	27.2	218	32.7	229	30.3	247	35.2
Reservists to active duty	172	17.5	45	6.8	32	4.2	34	4.9
Total	981	100.0	666	100.0	757	100.0	702	100.0

Source: Derived from U.S. Department of Defense, Directorate for Statistical Services, *Selected Manpower Statistics* (Washington: Department of Defense, April 11, 1966), p. 45. N.B. Details do not add to totals due to rounding. Percent derived from totals given in source.

* Penalty inductions only, for failure to meet reserve training obligations. Number usually totals less than 100 each year.

† Less than 500.

‡ Less than 0.05 percent.

Attempts to improve the quality of active manpower continued through this period. There was no major raising of entry standards comparable to the 1958 change in induction minimums; but both induction and enlistment standards were adjusted in minor ways, mostly upward, between 1959 and 1963. Much more important, however, were the attempts to improve retention rates and raise the average quality of enlistment applicants through a series of military pay increases.

Pay raises in 1963 and 1964 proved relatively noncontroversial. The 1963 raise was the more important, entailing an annual cost of $1.2 billion, or more than twice that of the 1958 increase. The average pay increase provided was 14.4 percent. The new scales continued the 1958 emphasis on proportionately larger increases for those just completing a first term of service; but they omitted any increase for men with less than two years' service.[8]

In 1965, as Representative Mendel Rivers (D., S.C.) replaced the retiring Carl Vinson as chairman of the House Armed Services Committee, a considerable debate erupted between that committee and Defense Secretary McNamara over the character of the next pay raise.[9] Total annual cost was one issue: the House committee led off with a $1 billion proposal, an average increase of a little over 10 percent; McNamara countered with a more modest 5 percent proposal; in the end, after the Senate committee had compromised other differences between the Rivers committee and McNamara, the total cost of the 1965 pay raise came to $1.05 billion. Other differences, however, were more crucial for the character of this and future pay raises, and for the impact of these on active force recruiting and retention.

One of these differences was resolved almost wholly to the House committee's satisfaction. In 1963, the Defense Department had promised to undertake annual reviews of military pay scales and to make recommendations for adjusting these to changes in federal civil salary rates and increases in the cost of living; a small raise in 1964 was the first result of this process. In 1965, McNamara proposed a second adjustment; he also asked for authority to make such annual adjustments administratively, subject to legislative veto; and he promised in-depth reviews of the pay structure quadrennially, to be followed by formal recommendations for statutory changes. Rejecting the legislative veto proposal, the House committee supported Chairman Rivers in calling for mandatory annual reviews, softening the distinction between these and the more thorough quadrennial studies, and requiring annual reports by the president to Congress on military pay. Despite Defense Department objections that mandatory annual reports would build in artificial pressures for large annual pay increases, the House committee's views prevailed in the Senate committee's compromise.

Still other differences went to the heart of the pay scales themselves. McNamara admitted that the existing strucutre of the pay scales probably would not solve the services' recruiting and retention problems. But, he argued, retention was no longer a problem susceptible to the general remedies applied in 1958 and 1963. Rather, it was one of identifying critical officer and enlisted skills, and applying special inducements to retain men possessing them; and so far only the Air Force, he contended, knew enough about its career goals in each skill to begin solving the problem this way. Consequently, he wanted only minor adjustments to pay scales in 1965; but he also asked for authority to devise and apply a variable reenlistment bonus scheme, as a supplement to the proficiency pay in use since 1958, as a means of retaining outstanding enlisted men in identifiable critical skills. The House committee accepted the variable bonus idea, but disputed McNamara's analysis on two other points.

One was the general scope of an appropriate pay raise in 1965. Citing evidence piling up in congressional mail, and reports of moonlighting by noncommissioned officers and of service dependents on relief, Rivers contended that minor adjustments of the 1963 pay structure would not be adequate. Instead, he proposed going all the way back to the 1952 scales, and adjusting them for subsequent cost-of-living increases. McNamara insisted that this approach would undo all the work of 1958 and 1963 aimed at making the pay structure a generally attractive inducement to choosing a military career; but the House committee followed Rivers's lead.

A final dispute marked an important shift away from the traditional view that men serving under obligation ought to receive much lower pay than those who had chosen military service as a career. This attitude had been expressed much earlier in an almost perfect chain of proposals that UMT trainees be paid less than volunteer recruits. By the mid-1950's, its chief expression was the very low pay rates for officers and enlisted men having less than two years of service, rates justified as underlining the obligated character of their service. In 1965, McNamara and several military witnesses admitted that pay of these men was so low as to raise a serious question of equity; but McNamara argued that the justification for the low pay had been reaffirmed by Congress as recently as 1963. Rivers, proposing steep pay raises for these men, contended that this might aid in recruiting. McNamara disputed this, citing survey studies predicting poor responses to even very large increases in starting pay; but the House committee again followed its chairman.

The Senate committee compromised these last two Rivers-McNamara differences. It provided increases of 6 and 11 percent respectively for officers and enlisted men with more than two years' service, and 22 and 17 percent in officer and enlisted starting pay. Otherwise, it preserved the 1963 pay structure within officer and enlisted grades.

By mid-1965, the Kennedy and Johnson Administrations had negotiated a number of important changes in military manpower programs. The 1961–62 reserve recall had generated a rethinking of reserve roles, resulting in a new goal for the Army's reserves: creation of a fast-reaction force of reserve units much smaller than ever contemplated in pre-1962 plans, but also much better manned, equipped, and trained. Moreover, the 1961-62 build-up had given the active forces new capacity to meet crises without resort to reserves. Thus the precise circumstances in which such a reserve force might be mobilized and deployed were not at all clear, leaving room for later argument. It was clear, though, that the Defense Department, if not Congress, was committed to a major departure from the old assumptions about broad mobilization that had in one way or another dominated the active-reserve force structure, contingency planning, and general manpower goals during the fifteen years after World War II. At the same time, under continual if not cogent prodding from the Armed Services Committees, the Defense Department had also committed itself to a search for more sophisticated ways of employing military pay and benefits to improve retention of skilled men in the active forces. And it had accepted, reluctantly, a modification to the traditional attitude that obligated military service deserved only minimal pay and benefit compensation.

All these changes had important implications for the concept of compulsions in support of military manpower procurement, and for related problems of equity and impact on nonmilitary social goals. But, as a peripheral member of the defense policy community, the Selective Service System was not a party to these changes; nor did it really absorb the rethinking and redefinition of manpower problems and goals that produced them. Instead, as will be seen in the next subsection, Selective Service responded to the new policy environment of the 1960's in ways that were logical extensions of its administrative triumph after the Korean War, but ways that threatened the long-range viability of the System as the chief engine of manpower procurement.

2. *Selective Service Channeling and the Manpower Flood*

In 1963, the Administration and Congress once again extended the expiring Selective Service induction authority and related provisions of the Universal Military Training and Service Act. House hearings began on March 1, and concluded on the second day with a 36-0 committee vote for extension. After a brief debate on March 11, the House rejected three amendments, and passed the bill on a 388-3 vote. The Senate committee held even briefer hearings on March 12; and on March 15 the Senate passed the bill with almost no discussion. The bill was signed on March 28. Just four weeks were needed to extend the once controversial peacetime draft act for another four years, to July 1, 1967, setting a new speed record. Most members of Congress voting for the measure probably agreed with Senator Russell's observation:

> With all its faults and imperfections, the present system is the only way we can get the manpower we require. It is somewhat like the seniority system in the Congress in selecting committee chairmen. You can always find something wrong with it, but when it comes to getting some alternative, the alternative has more objections than you have.[10]

The Administration clearly agreed, for the short term at least. Inductions during the early 1960's fluctuated widely from year to year, largely due to the 1961–62 build-up and the echo effect of this in 1963–64. After this smoothed out, though, the Defense Department expected to call for about 90,000 inductions during each year of the extension period.

As in the late 1950's, so also in the early 1960's: emphasis on quality and careerism in the active forces, various adjustments in reserve policy, the growing supply of military-age young men, and the self-conceived function of Selective Service as a storekeeper and channeler of manpower all contributed to the pattern of manpower pool management. Until mid-1965, this pattern was mostly an extension and refinement of that existing in 1960. General Hershey no doubt wished that more men were being taken for military service; but the Selective Service System, in its own way, faced the reality of low inductions. As Hershey explained it to a university audience: "we deferred practically everybody. If they had a reason, we preferred it. But if they didn't, we made them hunt one."[11]

Changes in numbers and proportions of Selective Service registrants (see Table 15) reflected this attitude. Specifically, these changes were consequences of mostly administrative responses to new manpower supply and demand conditions, affecting each of the major channels already operating in 1960: disqualification, dependency, reserve service, and student and occupational deferment.

Between 1961 and 1965, the total number of registrants found disqualified for service rose by nearly a third, although this group declined slightly as a proportion of all classified registrants. These changes reflected, not a marked rise of induction standards, but a stepped-up process of classification and examination. This came in response to the deep concern expressed by Presidents Kennedy and Johnson, and others, about the relation between draft rejections and hard core youth unemployment. In 1961 a pilot program began, referring medical rejectees to the Public Health Service. In early 1964, President Johnson approved a plan expanding that program, adding referral services for men failing the mental examination, and requiring the earliest possible examination of all youths after they registered at age eighteen. Like many other War on Poverty programs, this one was only a partial success; but it did give Selective Service and other agencies a new sense of social mission. And, as Selective Service changed from its older practice of delaying examination until close to time for induction, the program added millions of youths to the roles of classified registrants, and over a million of these to the disqualified group.[12]

TABLE 15

Selective Service Registrants by Classification Status, 1961, 1963, 1965

(In Thousands)

	1961		1963		1965	
	Number	%	Number	%	Number	%
Total available for service	2,383	19.5	2,043	15.3	1,977	11.5
I-A, I-A-O, priority three*	1,760	14.4	1,720	12.9	876	5.1
I-A, I-A-O, priority four	342	2.8	70	0.5	555	3.2
I-A, I-A-O, priority five, over 26	110	0.9	85	0.6	69	0.4
I-A, I-A-O, priority six, under 19	162	1.3	159	1.2	465	2.7
I-O, conscientious objector	9	0.1	9	0.1	12	0.1
Total in service	2,228	18.2	2,572	19.2	2,872	16.7
I-C, inducted	146	1.2	210	1.6	240	1.4
I-C, enlisted or commissioned	1,231	10.1	1,465	10.9	1,610	9.4
I-D, reserves	849	6.9	895	6.7	1,020	5.9
I-W, conscientious objector at work	2	#	2	#	2	#
Total who have completed service	2,170	17.7	2,186	16.3	2,339	13.6
IV-A, veteran (or sole surviving son)	2,164	17.7	2,180	16.3	2,333	13.6
I-W, conscientious objector released	6	#	6	#	6	#
Total deferred for physical, mental, or moral reasons	3,322	27.2	3,515	26.2	4,353	25.4
IV-F, not qualified for military service	3,322	27.2	2,517	18.8	2,425	14.1
I-Y, qualified only in war or national emergency‡	---	---	998	7.5	1,928	11.2

TABLE 15 (Continued)

SELECTIVE SERVICE REGISTRANTS BY CLASSIFICATION STATUS, 1961, 1963, 1965

(In Thousands)

	1961		1963		1965	
	Number	%	Number	%	Number	%
Total deferred for other reasons	2,060	16.8	3,003	22.4	5,505	32.1
I-S, high school student (statutory)	15	0.1	15	#	550	3.2
I-S, college student (statutory)	2	#	2	#	2	#
II-A, non-agricultural occupation	72	0.6	118	0.9	193	1.1
II-C, agricultural occupation	18	0.1	16	0.1	19	0.1
II-S, college student	180	1.5	372	2.8	1,656	9.7
III-A, hardship to dependents§	1,773	14.5	2,480	18.5	3,085	18.0
IV-B, government official	‖	#	‖	#	‖	#
Total with original exemptions	70	0.5	80	0.6	96	0.6
IV-C, alien	7	0.1	9	0.1	10	0.1
IV-D, minister or divinity student	63	0.5	71	0.5	86	0.5
Total classified within liable ages	12,233	100.0	13,399	100.0	17,142	100.0

SOURCE: U.S. Selective Service System, *Annual Report of the Director of Selective Service, Fiscal Years 1961, 1963, 1965* (Washington: U.S. Government Printing Office, 1962, 1964, 1966). N.B. Figures are valid as of June 30 of each year. Percent figure derived from totals. Details do not add to totals due to rounding.

* For 1961 and 1963, includes non-fathers, 19-25; for 1965, includes single men, 19-25.

† For 1961 and 1963, includes fathers, 19-25; for 1965, includes married non-fathers, 19-25.

‡ Category established in January, 1962.

§ For 1965, includes all fathers.

‖ Less than 50.

Less than 0.05 percent.

A second change among this group was primarily a matter of bookkeeping. In January, 1962, a new Class I-Y was created for men rejected under the post-1958 peacetime standards but still able to meet wartime requirements;[13] and by 1965 most of the screening of older records to separate I-Y's from IV-F's was complete. The large numbers in this new class, over two-fifths of the total disqualified in 1965, show clearly the continuing impact of the 1958 decision on Selective Service rejection rates.

This new identification of the not-quite-fit, plus increasing concern over the impact of draft rejection on hard-to-employ youths, led General Hershey to propose and the Defense Department to accept yet another program; this one would take men from Class I-Y into military service for rehabilitative medical treatment, physical training, and education, the costs to be charged to the War on Poverty rather than the Defense budget. An initially reluctant Army, once charged with managing the program, eventually took an interest in making it a success. Countering press and congressional criticism that this was just a small-scale duplication of the Job Corps, the Army named it the Special Training Enlistment Program (STEP), emphasized its goal of bringing men up to peacetime Army enlistment standards, and suggested it might result in reducing draft pressures. Although it did get approval from the House, the Army could not overcome objections in the Senate Defense Appropriations Subcommittee; and the conference report on 1966 Defense Appropriations specifically disapproved the program.[14]

Reserve programs also continued to absorb larger numbers, though a slightly declining proportion, of classified registrants between 1961 and 1965. For a variety of reasons, this deferment channel did not widen so spectacularly as it had in the previous four years. There was no major expansion of reserve enlistment opportunities, as there had been after 1957; the average annual number of enlistments in the six-months reserve program increased only a little, from 112,000 in 1957–61, to 125,000 in 1961–65. College ROTC enrollments increased about 7 percent, to just under 240,000 during the years 1961–65.[15] A major inhibition on expansion of reserve enlistments after 1962 was, of course, the Defense Department's renewed drive to cut paid drill strengths in the Army's reserve units; but congressional insistence on maintaining strength floors partly counteracted this trend.

There were some statutory modifications made to the reserve enlistment programs during this period. In 1961, Congress rewrote the provisions for penalty induction of men failing to participate satisfactorily in obligatory reserve drills; but it still failed to insist on uniform application of these penalties among the military services. In 1963, Congress and the Defense Department quietly undertook a major statutory overhaul of reserve enlistment options and obligations, allowing the Reserve Forces Act to expire, and incorporating relevant provisions into the Selective Service statutes: the military obligation was set at a uniform maximum of six years' active duty and Ready Reserve service; this was reducible, through reserve participation, only for men with two or more years' active duty; and the active training period for special reserve enlistees was made flexible, the minimum being four months.[16]

Dependency deferments and their equivalent continued through the early 1960's to be a major tool in the Selective Service System's manpower pool management. They were, moreover, the subject of one of the more spectacular shifts in Selective Service policy during the Kennedy Administration. In two orders during 1963, the president shifted all fathers classified I-A, priority four, to Class III-A, deferred for dependency, and then moved all Class I-A married men from priority three to priority four. The first merely confirmed and accelerated what Selective Service had been urging local boards to do on their own. The second shift, however, effectively exempted a whole new group from induction, despite the statutory bar to deferment on grounds of marriage alone. Answering criticism, General Hershey accepted full responsibility for the new treatment of married men. It was convenient for the services, he said: married servicemen, with their special allotments, were more expensive, and were responsible for most of the hardship discharge actions; and concentrating inductions on the smaller group of unmarried men would reduce the induction age. It was convenient for Selective Service, too, because "we have got more people than we can induct unless the inductions go up."[17] By mid-1965, dependency deferments and priorities provided a 70 percent larger drain on the manpower supply than in 1961; and the proportion of classified registrants benefiting from this channel also increased.

Major increases also occurred in deferments for study and occupations, the heart of the Selective Service System's claims to be a channeler of manpower in the national interest. Occupational deferments remained a minor group, but they roughly doubled in numbers and as a proportion of those classified. The major rise came in deferments for college students, Class II-S. Increased nervousness among college students during the 1961–62 build-up contributed to a near doubling of that class in that year alone. More important was a 1963 presidential order eliminating the detailed 1951 guidelines for student deferments. Local boards were permitted to continue using information on class standing and test scores; but the qualification test was suspended in August, 1963; and boards were encouraged to use additional evidence in a general loosening of college deferment standards.[18] As a result, by 1965 Class II-S was nine times its 1961 size.

In sum, the total proportion of classified registrants accounted for by disqualification, reserve programs, dependency, and student and occupational deferments climbed from 53.5 percent in 1961 to 63.3 percent in 1965. Defined in its loosest sense, then, channeling seemed a successful approach to manpower pool management in this period of growing supply and declining induction demand.

The difficulty with this channeling, or drainage, approach was that it had limits. By early 1965, the Selective Service System was running out of reasons to defer men, even while sending registrants out to hunt for them. There were limits to this approach implicit in each major channel, but nowhere were these explored openly and explicitly in terms of their possible future impact on Selective Service. High rates of disqualification conflicted with new social goals of the War on Poverty, but the military services continued to stress their need for active force quality. New concepts of reserve roles weakened the older justification for huge reserves, but Congress continued to view reserve programs as its special military preserve. The Selective Service System spoke for the Administration in brushing aside criticism of the protected priority for married men with arguments of convenience, but there were no more categories left for expanding dependency deferments. Occupational and student deferments remained potential growth categories, but expansion of this channel now depended on local boards' assessments of what the traffic would bear. In short, there were growing gaps between the Selective Service System's management policies and its policy environment. Yet the more that policy environment changed, the more Selective Service tried to stay the same.

One segment of the Defense Department did try to project the consequences of this approach. Anticipating congressional interest in declining inductions at the time of the 1963 extension, the department's manpower office undertook a study of the impact channeling would have on the distribution of military service burdens among successive age classes.[19] Assuming that active force strengths would remain at levels authorized for mid-1963, and assuming that induction pressure would remain focused on Class I-A nonfathers up to age twenty-six, the study concluded that, by mid-1968, the number of these men reaching the end of their liability would be too large to be wholly absorbed by induction calls (see Table 16).

TABLE 16

KEY MANPOWER POOL INDICATORS,
JUNE 30, 1962– JUNE 30, 1968

| | Non-father Pool by Ages (In Thousands) | | Percent Entering Military Service Aged 25½-26 | Median Age at Induction‡ |
	18½-26	25½-26		
1962 _____	940	†	58	23.5§
1963* _____	1,040	†	57	23.5
1964* _____	1,100	†	54	23.6
1965* _____	1,260	†	53	24.4
1966* _____	1,450	†	51	24.5
1967* _____	1,690	20	49	25.6
1968* _____	1,880	60	46	25.9

SOURCE: U.S. Department of Defense, Office of the Assistant Secretary of Defense (Manpower), *Project 61* (unpublished staff study, October, 1962) Table 6, following p. 17.
* Projected figures.
† Less than 5,000.
‡ Of involuntary inductees.
§ Preliminary.

The study also examined the impact of removing married men from priority three of Class I-A (as was done later in 1963). It found that this would postpone for a few years the problem of large numbers escaping induction merely by passing their twenty-sixth birthdays. By the early 1970's, however, with the "baby boom" generation approaching that birthday, well over half of each age class would perform no military service at all, active or reserve. Most of those not serving would be disqualified or deferred. But, with increasing numbers escaping induction merely by passing their twenty-sixth birthdays, it would no longer be possible to say even that all those "qualified and available" were being compelled to serve. (This could be said for the 1962 results, and these were the only part of the study presented and discussed in the 1963 extension hearings.)

This prospect could not have been pleasant, for Selective Service or for the military services dependent on it. The older channels for avoiding active service were all vulnerable to criticism on grounds that compulsions were not applied evenly among military-age youths. Selective Service and its supporters had successfully resisted such criticism for many years, on grounds of variously defined national interests. By mid-1965, though, time was running out for this defense.

Between 1963 and 1965, there were increasing signs that Congress and the Administration might be willing to re-study and alter the state of Selective Service, even though the System itself was not. Meantime, the spring and summer of 1965 brought a decision for major American military engagement in the Vietnam War. The impact of this adventure on manpower procurement is examined in the next section, before turning, in section III, to the growing policy debate over Selective Service and other military manpower programs.

II. MILITARY MANPOWER FOR WAR IN VIETNAM

1. *Active Force Expansion and Reserve Force Roles*

The expansion of active military forces to meet the demands of a heavy military engagement in Vietnam was the largest increase of military forces-in-being since the Korean War. The size and pace of this expansion are shown in Table 17, and Table 18 shows the sources of enlisted personnel procurement during this period. The growth of the Army and Marine Corps accounted for nearly 69 percent of the first year's expansion, and nearly 79 percent of the total two-year increase.

In 1965, the Administration's reluctance to declare a formal emergency, much less seek a formal declaration of war, was even greater than it was in 1950. At that earlier time, external events,

TABLE 17

ACTIVE FORCES EXPANSION, JUNE 30, 1965–JUNE 30, 1967

	1965	1966		1967		
	Strength*	Strength*	Annual Increase %	Strength*	Annual Increase %	Biannual Increase %
Army _____	969	1,200	23.8	1,442	20.2	48.8
Navy _____	671	745	11.0	752	0.9	12.1
Marine Corps ____	190	262	37.9	285	8.8	50.0
Air Force _____	825	887	7.5	897	1.1	8.7
Department of Defense _____	2,655	3,094	16.5	3,377	9.1	27.2

SOURCE: U.S. Department of Defense, Directorate for Statistical Services, *Selected Manpower Statistics* (Washington: Department of Defense, April 15, 1968), p. 19. N.B. Details do not add to totals due to rounding. Percent increases derived from totals given in source.

* In thousands.

primarily the intervention of the Chinese army, forced a formalization of the war effort. No such external pressures were felt in the mid-1960's.

Two crucial differences between the Korean and Vietnam expansions had important effects on manpower procurement policies and programs. For one, the demand for additional active manpower was much smaller in the Vietnam expansion; active forces grew from 1.46 to 3.64 million in 1950–52, but only from 2.65 to 3.38 million in 1965–67. The other difference was the decision in mid-1965, unlike that of mid-1950, to rely almost wholly on stepped-up inductions, recruiting, and involuntary retention for this new manpower, and to avoid any massive recall of reserves, especially of organized reserve units.

The Administration reached that decision by early July, 1965. There was strong resistance from the Army staff, whose contingency planning for a major commitment in Vietnam had been built around the assumption of a large-scale reserve recall. Nonetheless, President Johnson reconfirmed the decision in late July. The consequence was that the Army had to expand itself by nearly 24 percent in the first year, and another 20 percent in the second year, mostly by taking in new enlistees, inductees and second lieutenants. All of these required extensive training, drawing on the same manpower base that was providing a five-fold increase of combat and support forces in Vietnam and one division in the Dominican Republic. Some earlier commitments of Army forces had to yield, and the training

TABLE 18

Active Duty Enlisted Personnel Procurement,
Fiscal Years 1966-1968
(In Thousands)

	1966		1967		1968	
	Number	%	Number	%	Number	%
Army						
Inductions _____	318	55.4	299	51.9	334	52.5
First enlistments __	170	29.7	190	33.0	199	31.2
Reenlistments ____	84	14.6	85	14.6	85	13.3
Reservists to						
active duty ____	2	0.3	2	0.4	19	3.0
Total _____	573	100.0	576	100.0	637	100.0
Navy						
Inductions _____	3	1.2	---	---	---	---
First enlistments __	143	64.3	101	53.8	123	62.8
Reenlistments ____	41	18.8	44	23.4	40	20.2
Reservists to						
active duty ____	35	15.7	43	22.9	33	17.0
Total _____	223	100.0	188	100.0	195	100.0
Marine Corps						
Inductions _____	20	17.3	*	0.2	5	4.9
First enlistments __	69	60.7	71	84.3	93	84.1
Reenlistments ____	11	9.9	9	10.3	10	8.5
Reservists to						
active duty ____	14	12.1	4	5.3	3	2.6
Total _____	113	100.0	85	100.0	111	100.0
Air Force						
Inductions _____	*	‡	---	---	---	---
First enlistments __	166	65.7	121	64.8	98	54.2
Reenlistments ____	87	34.2	65	35.1	69	38.0
Reservists to						
active duty ____	†	0.1	†	0.1	14	7.8
Total _____	253	100.0	186	100.0	182	100.0
Department of Defense						
Inductions _____	340	29.2	299	28.9	340	30.2
First enlistments __	548	47.2	483	46.7	513	45.6
Reenlistments ____	223	19.2	202	19.6	203	18.1
Reservists to						
active duty ____	51	4.4	50	4.8	69	6.1
Total _____	1,162	100.0	1,035	100.0	1,124	100.0

Source: Directorate for Statistical Services, Office of the Secretary of Defense (P27.3, September 17, 1968). N.B. Details do not add to totals due to rounding. Percent derived from totals given in source.

* Penalty inductions only, for failure to meet reserve training obligations.

† Less than 500.

‡ Less than 0.05 percent.

base for this expansion was augmented by converting three other stateside divisions into training units and drawing down the quality, and to a lesser extent the quantity, of forces committed to Europe;

this in turn resulted in extensive reassignment turbulence for those sent to new training and cadre duties, and for their families. Equipment and supplies for the expansion came partly from new procurement and depot stocks on hand, but part of it also came from reserve and low priority active units. Despite the realities of, and public complaints about severe shortages of basic supplies, equipment, and trained personnel of all kinds, the Administration stuck with its decision not to call reserve units. The Marine Corps, which underwent an expansion proportionately a little greater than the Army's, did rely fairly heavily on recalled reservists in the first year; like the Army, however, the Marine Corps did not call up reserve units as such.[20]

A number of reasons have been suggested for this decision. There were reports at the time that the Administration feared a major recall of reserves would prove too provocative to the Russians and Chinese, and thus out of keeping with a policy of gradual escalation of the war effort in Vietnam. This has been discounted as a reason for not calling reserve units, although that same reasoning surely played a part in the decision not to declare war or a national emergency. It was also suggested that the organized reserve units were viewed as a perishable asset; once released they would have to be rebuilt almost from scratch, a lesson learned after the Korean War and once again following the Berlin Crisis callup.[21] The official reasons, provided in later testimony before the Senate Preparedness Investigating Subcommittee, were two: first, a reserve recall would simply transfer the burdens of reassignment turbulence from members of the active forces and their families to members of the reserves and, through them, to thousands of civilian communities and enterprises; second, and more important, the necessary expansion could be accomplished just as quickly, perhaps more so, by relying on existing forces plus inductions and recruitment to create new units.

Whatever the real priority of reasons, and despite heavy criticism from some members of Congress, the Administration kept to this decision throughout the escalated war in Vietnam—the one exception being a fairly small call of reserve units in early 1968, ostensibly in response to the *Pueblo* incident. The military services had varying recourse to their pools of individual reservists. The Marine

Corps, as noted above, used its pool as an important source for first-year expansion, though not the major one; but the Navy's increase in callup of reservists was mostly the result of a stepup in its long-standing practice of active force recruitment through reserve programs. The Vietnam expansion thus confirmed and extended the change in concept of reserve roles since 1961. Reserve units were not maintained in anticipation of a broad, general mobilization, as they had been before and after the Korean War. Nor were even the more ready reserve units to be used in achieving a rapid expansion of deterrent capabilities, as in the Berlin Crisis, if that expansion could be accomplished by other means. Indeed, it was difficult to prophesy just what conditions might occasion a major recall of reserve units.

While defending and maintaining its decision not to use reserves extensively in the Vietnam expansion, the Administration also was embroiled with Congress on two legislative proposals originating in Congress and affecting reserve policy. One stemmed from the increasing popularity of the Reserve Enlistment Program in this period of high inductions, and raised issues of equity considered below. The other was a response to the Defense Department's 1965 move to merge the management of the Army's organized reserve units under the National Guard. To quiet their own and others' fears that the Defense Department might yet find existing statutory authority and administrative audacity to make the proposal a fait accompli, Representative Hebert, chairman of the House Armed Services Committee subcommittee overseeing reserve affairs, and Senator Stennis, chairman of the Senate Preparedness Investigating Subcommittee, successfully sponsored a "Reserve Bill of Rights."[22] Their bills spelled out the existence and character of the various reserve components in greater detail than had earlier acts, prohibited the administrative merger of the Army Reserve and National Guard, established permanent floors under the strengths of these components, required annual authorization of Selected Reserve strengths in all reserve components, and created new statutory supervisors of reserve affairs in the Department of Defense and the military departments at the assistant secretary level. The major impact of this act on reserve structure was its guarantee of the continued existence of, and congressional interest in, organized reserve units. Quite aside from what cost efficiency and military effectiveness considerations might suggest about the reserves' usefulness, the military services—especially the Army—still had to take these units into account in their contingency planning; and they had to continue providing them with adequate sources for trained manpower.

2. Inductions, Recruiting, and Retention

Much more important than reserve recalls as a source of additional new manpower were initial enlistments, which ran 72 percent higher in FY 1966 and 62 percent higher in FY 1967 than the same source in FY 1965 (see Tables 14 and 18), and remained the major procurement source for all services except the Army. Inductions were the second largest source of procurement in the expansion years; and compared with FY 1965, inductions increased more than did initial enlistments in each of the two expansion years. The great majority of inductees went to the Army, as that service's draft calls rose higher than any since FY 1954; the Marine Corps also took inductees for the first time since the Korean War; and the Navy took a few thousand as well. At the same time, reenlistment fell from its position as second and most important procurement source in FY 1965 to third place, as reenlistments declined absolutely in the expansion years.

Reenlistment rates for the two expansion years did not decline nearly so sharply as did the absolute numbers, suggesting that many men who would have been eligible for reenlistment had their terms of service involuntarily extended instead.[23] Nonetheless, overall enlistment rates were lower in most categories in the expansion years than in FY 1965. The declines in both first and career reenlistment rates were especially sharp in the Marine Corps, where rates already tended to be lower than in other services, and in the Air Force, which had generally enjoyed the highest rates. Among occupational groupings, reenlistments rates fell most sharply among service and supply handlers, craftsmen, and clerks, and least sharply among electronics equipment repairmen, medical and dental specialists, and communications specialists; rates for infantry, gun crew and allied specialists fell only a little more than the average for all occupations. Perhaps the least explicable movement in these rates was a rise in reenlistment by inductees, from 8.4 percent in FY 1965 to 20.8 percent in FY 1967.

If much of the decline in total enlistments can be accounted for by involuntary retention, much of the decline in reenlistment rates among those eligible must be attributed to the special burdens and risks of military service during this period. Countering these, of course, were the pay and reenlistment bonus inducements of the 1965 pay act. Moreover, the military services gained still further pay raises for 1966 and 1967, amounting to nearly a 6 percent increase over 1965 rates.[24]

Despite these recent increases in pay and benefits, and Secretary McNamara's talk in 1965 of a more selective effort at retaining skilled personnel, the heavy influx of first-term officers and men, and the accompanying reductions in enlistment and induction standards, produced a temporary setback in the long-standing drive for quality and careerism in the active forces. Nonetheless, the active forces of the late 1960's were the highest paid and best educated ever to fight in an American war; and numerous reports testify that they were also the best trained, the most professional.[25]

The 1965 pay act marked an important departure from past attitudes toward pay and benefits for men serving obligated tours, although subsequent pay changes did not immediately strengthen this trend. Another move toward raising the compensation of these men came in 1966, with passage of a "Cold War G.I. Bill of Rights" providing limited education and housing benefits to persons serving since the cut-off date for Korean War benefits in 1955. This legislation had been pushed for seven years by Senator Yarborough (D., Tex.), and opposed for almost as long by successive Defense secretaries. Opposition was based on fears that such benefits would induce men to leave service early, and thus offset the post-1958 gains in career retention. The new act met this objection in part, by providing education benefits to men remaining in service as well as to veterans. Although the Administration proposed a very limited bill, benefiting only veterans of such specific "hot spots" as Berlin, the Dominican Republic and Vetnam, the House and Senate passed the much broader bill originating in the Senate, by the usual margins accorded veterans' legislation when it is allowed to reach the floor.[26]

Yet another, and broader, trend in military pay implicit in the

1965 increase was confirmed in later legislation. One title in the 1966 authorization for military procurement granted a small pay raise, tying it to a planned increase in pay for civil officials; further increases were implied for later years, with military-civil pay parity to be achieved in 1968 and maintained thereafter.[27]

3. *Widening the Manpower Pool*

In mid-1965, the decision to expand active forces for major participation in the Vietnam war brought at least temporary relief from any concern the Selective Service System may have had over the growing surplus of available manpower. The System, which had responded so flexibly to the need to drain down the manpower pool during the late 1950's and early 1960's, began reversing direction in an equally flexible response to a markedly increased demand for military manpower in 1965–67 (see Table 19).

One of the earliest draft policy changes, following announcement of the Vietnam build-up, affected the order of induction priorities within Class I-A. An executive order in August, 1965, instructed local boards to discontinue placing men married after that time in priority four. The consequent increase in the priority three pool meant that very few boards had to dip into priority four to fill rising draft calls.[28]

Another major change came in November, 1965, as the Defense Department began lowering standards for induction. Although the size of Class I-Y continued to increase, many men previously in this group were reclassified I-A and subsequently inducted.[29]

This trend toward lower induction standards took on a new tone in the fall of 1966, as Secretary McNamara announced that all services would participate in a new program intended to absorb large numbers of young men currently being rejected. The goal was to take in 40,000 of these during FY 1967, and 100,000 annually thereafter—hence the tag "Project 100,000." By FY 1968, the program was in full operation, and seemed to be creating new difficulties for the military services. Each service was assigned a quota of men qualifying under new, and lower, mental standards announced in October, 1966, expressed as a percent of total enlisted procurement by quarter. The quota could be met by recruitment or

TABLE 19

Selective Service Registrants by Classification Status, June 30, 1966–June 30, 1968

(In Thousands)

	1966		1967		1968	
	Number	%	Number	%	Number	%
Total available for service	1,121	6.2	1,428	7.5	1,294	6.5
I-A, I-A-O, priority three*	451	2.5	769	4.0	708	3.5
I-A, I-A-O, priority four	147	0.8	61	0.3	28	0.1
I-A, I-A-O, priority five, over 26	68	0.4	72	0.4	104	0.5
I-A, I-A-O, priority six, under 19	446	2.5	516	2.7	442	2.2
I-O, conscientious objector	9	§	10	0.1	12	0.1
Total in service	3,513	19.3	3,741	19.6	3,927	19.6
I-C, inducted	422	2.3	589	3.1	581	2.9
I-C, enlisted or commissioned	1,880	10.4	2,128	11.1	2,366	11.8
I-D, reserves	1,207	6.6	1,018	5.3	974	4.9
I-W, conscientious objector at work	4	§	6	§	6	§
Total who have completed service	2,434	13.4	2,558	13.4	2,762	13.8
IV-A, veteran (or sole surviving son)	2,428	13.4	2,552	13.4	2,754	13.8
I-W, conscientious objector released	6	§	6	§	8	§
Total deferred for physical, mental, or moral reasons	4,854	26.7	4,867	25.5	5,070	25.3
IV-F, not qualified for military service	2,500	13.8	2,450	12.8	2,390	11.9
I-Y, qualified only in war or national emergency	2,354	13.0	2,417	12.7	2,680	13.4

TABLE 19 (Continued)

SELECTIVE SERVICE REGISTRANTS BY CLASSIFICATION STATUS, JUNE 30, 1966–JUNE 30, 1968

(In Thousands)

	1966		1967		1968	
	Number	%	Number	%	Number	%
Total deferred for other reasons	6,130	33.8	6,376	33.4	6,828	34.1
I-S, high school student (statutory)	492	2.7	526	2.8	572	2.9
I-S, college student (statutory)	19	0.1	49	0.3	29	0.1
II-A, non-agricultural occupation	233	1.3	263	1.4	372	1.9
II-C, agricultural occupation	22	0.1	23	0.1	24	0.1
II-S, college student	1,783	9.8	1,655	8.7	1,764	8.8
III-A, fatherhood or hardship	3,581	19.7	3,860	20.2	4,067	20.3
IV-B, government official	‡	§	‡	§	‡	§
Total with original exemptions	108	0.6	117	0.6	122	0.6
IV-C, alien	12	0.1	15	0.1	17	0.1
IV-D, minister or divinity student	96	0.5	102	0.5	105	0.5
Total classified within liable ages	18,160	100.0	19,087	100.0	20,003	100.0

Source: U.S. Selective Service System, *Annual Report of the Director of Selective Service, Fiscal Years 1966, 1967, 1968* (Washington: U.S. Government Printing Office, 1967, 1968, 1969). N.B. Percent figures derived from totals. Details do not add to totals due to rounding.

* Age 19-25, single or married after August 26, 1965.

† Age 19-25, married on or before August 26, 1965.

‡ Less than 50.

§ Less than 0.05 percent.

induction, but only the Army took inductees for Project 100,000. Some 85,000 men were to enter annually under the new mental standards, plus 15,000 volunteers having minor physical defects. Although the latter were given remedial treatment, men entering service through this program were fully integrated into the services' various training programs rather than being given special training. Project 100,000 had several purposes. For one, it widened the pool of manpower considered available and qualified. It also gave each of the military services experience in training and employing recruits or inductees who could not meet peacetime standards; large numbers of such men might have to be absorbed in some future active force expansion larger than, say, those of 1950–52 and 1965–67. Finally, Project 100,000 was viewed as the Defense Department's major contribution to the War on Poverty, in that it absorbed thousands of youths who otherwise would have been denied the armed forces' training and post-service benefits, and who probably would have had great difficulty in the civilian manpower market.[30]

A third major channel of active service avoidance, the reserve enlistment program, was the object of considerable public and congressional criticism; this resulted in some important, but not fundamental, changes. A series of scandals, involving a recruiter who solicited bribes for quick enlistment in the National Guard and fathers who bought forged reserve membership papers for their sons, spurred the Selective Service System to a thorough rescreening of records of men in Class I-D by mid-1966. Two other problems were beyond Selective Service control, however. One was that, in the process of holding down paid drill strengths, the Defense Department had allowed large numbers of obligated reserve enlistees to transfer out of overstrength drilling units into the Ready Reserve pool. Many organized units, however, were not at full strength, and it was not feasible to fill them from overstrength units. So, still under pressure to meet statutory floors for paid drill strengths, these units were accepting many thousands of new reserve enlistees. This, and the priority use of training facilities given to active force expansion demands, led to the second problem: many of the new reserve enlistees could not be trained immediately, and the backlog of these grew from about 74,000 on June 30, 1965, to over 185,000 a year later. The issue of equity implicit in these problems came to a head in the late summer and fall of 1966; and it promptly became entangled with attempts to pressure the Administration to call up reserve units, to protect the Army Reserve from the Defense Department's proposed merger of that component with the Army National Guard, and to protect the integrity of organized reserve units from piecemeal calls for individual reservists to fill the active forces. In October, 1966, pending later approval of the "Reserve Bill of Rights" (see subsection 1 above), the Senate and House finally agreed on an appropriations proviso intended to shift all responsibility for preferential treatment of reserve enlistees to the Defense Department.[31]

This proviso authorized the call to active duty, as individuals, of obligated Ready Reservists not in drilling units who had not completed twenty-four months on active duty, and the call of those, in units or not, who had not undergone their initial months of active training; the proviso also authorized the call of whole Ready Reserve units, and removed the requirement for a presidential declaration of a national emergency prior to calling these or the individual reservists; this authority was to terminate on July 1, 1968. The Defense Department promptly announced it had no intention of using this new authority, but pressure to do so continued both from outside the Department and from within. Late in 1966, the Department announced that a sharp cut in future draft calls would open more training facilities for the backlog of reserve enlistees. Induction calls for the whole first half of 1967 remained well below those for the preceding eighteen months, and by mid-1967 the backlog of untrained reservists had been cut to the mid-1965 level. Moreover, by May, 1967, the Department was ready to proceed with a program to call up, or have reported for induction, some 30,000 trained reserve enlistees who had let their drilling unit participation lapse without the Defense Department's permission.[32] These actions were only marginal to the whole question of relative military service burdens for reserve enlistees and active service inductees and enlistees; but they did serve to dampen criticism in Congress and the press.

Of much greater public interest were the Selective Service System's changes in the student deferment program (Class II-S). In late summer of 1965, a number of local boards began to exercise their large discretionary powers over student deferments; and early in the 1965–66 school year many students previously deferred, especially graduate and law school students, received ominous notices of reclassification to I-A and imminent examination for induction. Some boards also clamped down on part-time students and those taking time off to work or to study abroad, and many schools experienced sharp enrollment increases as a result of these pressures. National Headquarters of the System finally responded to the need for firmer guidelines, and decided to reinstate the college qualification test and return to the 1951 standards, with minor modifications, beginning in fall, 1966. The increased pressure on students to seek deferment produced an expansion of this class during 1965–66; but by mid-1967 the stiffer attitude of the boards, and application of new guidelines, brought the class back to its 1965 size.[33]

During the Vietnam expansion, the cold war manpower procurement system, which had undergone so much quiet change since the Korean War, nonetheless proved to be a very flexible and responsive machine for meeting suddenly expanded military manpower demands. Most of this flexibility must be attributed to the Selective Service System, which had converted itself to quite different purposes between 1953 and 1965, but was able to carry the heaviest burden of the 1965–67 build-up of active forces for war in Vietnam.

Nevertheless, had not the Vietnam conflict and expansion intervened, it is doubtful that the procurement system existing in 1965 could have found ways to cope with a continuation of pre-Vietnam military manpower trends—rising manpower pools, increasing emphasis on active forces at the expense of reserves, and increasing pay and other career attractions for the active forces. As will be seen in section III, renewed interest in the Selective Service System's problems began to appear even before 1965. The Vietnam War expansion provided only temporary relief from the earlier exhaustion of administrative devices for draining down the manpower pool. Moreover, the very actions taken to widen the manpower pool after mid-1965—especially the change in policy on married men, the rescreening of men in Class I-Y, and the mild restrictions on student deferments—rather than restoring faith in Selective Service channeling, instead served to spur public and congressional doubts about the draft; and these doubts were reinforced by a rising tide of vigorous and bitter criticism of the Administration's war efforts in Vietnam. In addition to offering a temporary reprieve, then, the Vietnam War expansion also assured that the Selective Service System would soon be embroiled in the first great national debate over military manpower procurement policy since the restoration of Selective Service in 1948.

III.   MANPOWER POLICY FOR THE GREAT SOCIETY

Commenting on congressional and public apathy toward the extension of Selective Service in 1959, Hanson Baldwin wrote: "the debate, or rather lack of it, is, in view of the history of the principle of compulsion for military service, one of the more unusual political-psychological phenomena of our time."[34] The same apathy permitted a speed-record extension in 1963. As one member of the House committee expressed it during the hearings, there were no new issues, no new arguments to consider. But this was true only for one reason: all parties to that decision chose to treat it on the narrowest possible grounds. In the absence of strongly expressed objections to the current manpower procurement system, no one asked whether this was the best system available, or even whether it might be improved. All anyone asked at the time was: does the system deliver enough manpower at reasonable cost? And even the cost question was implicit, not expressed as a careful calculation.

Events in 1963 and 1964 served to unsettle the apathetic public and congressional acceptance of Selective Service. Renewed interest in the draft was stirred by the manipulation of draft regulations for purposes not very closely related to national security, nor even to equitable management of Selective Service registrants. This was not a new practice; it began with the nondecision in 1953 to continue large-scale student deferments even after returning Korean War veterans were available to keep the college population in balance; and it continued with the 1955–56 decision establishing priorities within Class I-A that protected fathers and older men from induction. Both of these actions had some substantive policy justifications; yet both were major administrative departures from the 1951–52 legislative compromise on cold war manpower policy, and both were directed in part at mere manipulation of the manpower pool for the government's convenience. The easy acceptance of these actions finally met with sharp questioning and criticism in the wake of the almost wholly manipulative order shifting all married men to a protected priority.

This order, and the apparently cavalier attitude of General Hershey and the Administration toward criticism of it, touched off a flurry of congressional responses; and the approaching presidential campaign provided additional impetus. On nearly two dozen occasions during the 1964 session of Congress, one or another member addressed himself to a critique of the draft—just about equalling the sum of such occasions (aside from the extension actions) in the preceding ten years. Several bills were introduced, some to create a study commission for comprehensive review of the deferment-induction system, and one to require a plan for ending the draft by mid-1967. The latter approach took on the color of a Republican party position, as Senator Goldwater (who had been a minor critic of Adlai Stevenson's ill-fated assault on the draft in 1956) asserted that the draft could end almost immediately without hurting military strength. "Republicans will end the draft altogether," he promised in his opening campaign speech, "and as soon as possible!"[35]

Given another candidate, or a different campaign, this promise might have stirred considerable excitement in 1964. But most of its political value had already been discounted some five months earlier; and, at the same time, much of the impetus for congressional criticism had been effectively countered when President Johnson himself ordered a formal draft study.[36]

The Defense Manpower Study had its origins in the summer of 1963; after briefings by Selective Service and the Defense Department that resulted in the decision on married men, President Kennedy asked for a more extensive review of manpower needs and policies; and by late February, 1964, the study became a formal project for a special group in the Defense Department's manpower office. This group sought much of its basic data from within the department and the military services; it also hired academic consultants, and employed the services of the National Opinion Research Corporation and the Research Analysis Corporation; and it went to the Selective Service System for data and analysis, to the Census Bureau for additional data, and to other agencies for opinions and assistance on selected parts of the study. The report resulting from this study reached Secretary McNamara's office by July 1, 1965; but the simultaneous decision to escalate the Vietnam War meant that some of the study had to be rewritten, to reflect higher assumptions of military strength needs. In the end, the full report was not published, ostensibly because it contained too much classified information, but also, probably, because its recommendations were not acceptable to many others in the Defense and military service staffs and in Selective Service, and because events had outrun many of its details.[37]

Selected findings and conclusions from the Defense Manpower Study were made public in June, 1966, at hearings by the House Armed Services Committee. These hearings marked the first extensive public review of Selective Service since the Korean War, and the first ever conducted without some specific legislative proposal at hand.[38]

After the House hearings closed, with the promise of more to come in the next session, President Johnson ordered yet another study, appointing a twenty-member Natonal Advisory Commission on Selective Service, chaired by Burke Marshall, and instructing it to make a report by January 1, 1967. This Marshall Commission was given access to the Defense Manpower Study's materials, and received other assistance from the Defense Department, the Selective Service System, and other interested agencies; and it also sought opinions and information from interested private groups and individuals.[39]

Responding to the president's move, and apparently wanting a rather different set of views on Selective Service and related subjects, the House Armed Services Committee appointed its own Civilian Advisory Panel on Military Manpower Procurement, chaired by retired General Mark Clark. The Clark Panel was to review the forthcoming report of the Marshall Commission for the House committee, was to undertake an independent review of those provisions in the Universal Military Training and Service Act that had become objects of public criticism, and was to report no later than March 1, 1967.[40]

While these formal studies were underway, several unofficial public conferences were held, bringing together critics and defenders of Selective Service, though mostly critics. In May, 1966, a group met in New York to explore and promote ideas for a system of national service, as an explicit alternative to the military draft; out of this meeting came the creation of the National Service Secretariat, organized to study and publicize that concept. Much more press attention was given two other important meetings: the National Collegiate Conference on Selective Service Reform, held at Antioch College in November, 1966; and the more ambitious University of Chicago Conference on the Draft, held in December.[41]

In March, 1967, just after the Marshall Commission (reporting late) and the Clark Panel published their findings, President Johnson made a formal request for another four-year extension of Selective Service induction authority beyond July 1. The Senate and House Armed Services Committees held their hearings in mid-April and in May. Before that, two other congressional groups held their own investigations: in March and April, a subcommittee of the Senate Committee on Labor and Public Welfare, chaired temporarily by Senator Edward Kennedy (D., Mass.), examined the impact of military manpower policies on general welfare and anti-poverty goals; and later in April, four members of the Joint Economic Committee heard testimony from two economists and a Defense Department manpower expert on the question of shifting to an all-volunteer military manpower system.[42]

The national debate over military manpower procurement in the last half of the 1960's, reflected in these various forums and elsewhere, considered two major sets of alternatives. One half of this dual debate concerned the possibilities of replacing the existing mixed voluntary compulsory procurement system, either with an all-volunteer system, or with some scheme of more or less universal conscription; issues in this part of the debate are examined in subsection III-1. The second half of the debate considered the possibilities of specific reforms to the current system; issues in this reform debate are explored in subsection III-2. The climax of this dual debate came as the deadline for extending the Selective Service induction authority approached; at this point the debate narrowed, focusing mainly on issues of specific reforms rather than on the larger alternatives to Selective Service; the failure of the reform movement is discussed in subsection III-3.

1.   *Selective Service, Volunteer Forces, or Universal Conscription*

One part of the dual debate over manpower procurement in the late 1960's was an updated version of older, pre–Korean War arguments, recast in light of experience with the draft since 1950, and reflecting, too, various attitudes toward the Vietnam War and Great Society domestic programs. It resembled the older debate, in that its central issues were military needs and the problem of compulsions, and in that the major program alternatives were, once again, no conscription, selective conscription, or universal conscription. It differed from the older debate, in that the burden of proof now lay upon those who would abandon Selective Service, and in that issues of cost, equity, and impact on nonmilitary social goals were more important, and more explicit. This part of the debate is explored below in terms of the same major issues that shaped earlier debates: military effectiveness and the question of costs, which mostly affected arguments between defenders of the existing system and proponents of all-volunteer forces; and compulsions, equity, and impact on nonmilitary goals, which were involved in arguments about all three program alternatives.

Military Effectiveness and Cost Analyses

As the Defense Manpower Study began work in early 1965, it seemed to many that only a little more effort might be required to close the gap between military demands for and voluntary supply of manpower. The total supply was rising each year. The average annual intake of new men for both active and reserve forces was then projected at 610,000, for fiscal year 1965–68, with inductions supplying less than 11 percent of each year's total.[48] Defenders and critics of the existing system both viewed the Vietnam War's effect on these projections as only temporary. Nonetheless, there was considerable disagreement over the future feasibility of providing adequate military forces by relying only on volunteers, and over the impact this would have on military effectiveness.

The Defense study explored three possible ways of closing the gap between demand and volunteer supply. One was the possibility of reducing military demand by hiring civilians to fill jobs currently performed by uniformed servicemen. In its survey of military manpower requirements, the study agreed that all jobs in those parts of the military forces requiring a high state of operational readiness—that is, forces assigned to potential or actual operations overseas or at home, or held at home to cover overseas contingencies—had to be manned with military personnel. It found that other traditional justifications—providing a rotational base for overseas forces, and maintaining opportunities for career advancement —actually required very few additional military job positions. Important additions to the hard core had to be accepted, however, to staff and operate training establishments, and to allow for noneffectives (men in transit, in hospitals, and the like). Altogether, the study concluded, comparing these requirements to actual numbers of men in service did leave some room for civilian substitution.[44] In September, 1965, *Army Times* reported that more than 300,000 military jobs had been identified for possible substitution; but a cautious Defense Department program, which began soon after, had a two-year goal of only a little over one-third that number. The military services voiced considerable opposition to the program from the outset; their arguments, and congressional and budgetary reluctance to increase civil payrolls, seemed likely to keep civilian substitution a very minor contributor to narrowing the gap between voluntary supply and military manpower demands.[45] A second approach explored in the Defense study was to increase the voluntary supply by lowering service entry standards. No details on the study's findings were published, but some conclusions may be inferred from later events. The most obvious limitation to closing the gap in this way was the danger that reducing the quality of manpower in the military services wholesale could seriously affect their operational readiness. Reducing quality by smaller degrees could also be nonproductive; it might simply increase total manpower requirements by lengthening training periods or increasing the number of noneffective men undergoing medical or, more likely, disciplinary treatment. Nevertheless, the Defense Department proved willing to experiment with men at or just below normal recruiting or induction standards, as evidenced by its unsuccessful proposal for the Special Training and Enlistment Program in 1965, the lowering of induction standards during 1965–66, and the later inauguration of Project 100,000.

A third possibility, increasing the supply of volunteers by raising pay and otherwise improving career attractiveness, received major attention in the Defense study. The problem was not simply one of determining how rates of voluntary enlistment might respond to increases in pay, but also one of more precisely defining the gap between military demand for manpower and the current voluntary supply.

Supporters of the draft had argued ever since 1945 that the threat of inductions was an important factor in producing military service enlistments, but very little had been done to quantify this assertion. Regularly cited in extension hearings was the fact that, even with lower standards, active service strength had fallen below 1.4 million only a year after termination of Selective Service in 1947; but almost nothing had been done to project potential strengths of all-volunteer forces under changing conditions of pay, civilian unemployment, and gross manpower supply. Some sample surveys had been taken to discover the extent of draft-motivated enlistments; but the wide range of their answers was not satisfactory for use in further analysis.[46]

The Defense study's own survey of draft motivations yielded the results shown in Table 20. These in turn were applied to projections

TABLE 20

PERCENTAGE OF VOLUNTEERS AFFECTED BY INDUCTION PRESSURE

Group Queried	All Services	Army	Navy	Marine Corps	Air Force
Regular enlistees _____	38	43	33	30	43
Officers _____	41	48	40	27	39
Reserve enlistees (including National Guard) _	71	72	75	50	80

SOURCE: U.S. Congress, House, Committee on Armed Services, *Review of the Administration and Operation of the Selected Service System,* Hearings, 89th Cong., 2d sess., 1966, chart titled "Percent who would not have volunteered without the draft," p. 9936.

of future enlistments, based on experience in the period 1957–64 and taking into account future increases in military-age population, under varying assumptions of civilian employment. This yielded estimated rates of enlistment that would support an all-volunteer active force of only 2 to 2.2 million men, compared with a pre-Vietnam total strength of about 2.65 million. The study also concluded that absence of the draft would have an even more drastic impact on enlistment of men with above-average education and mental aptitude, who are the major source of trainees for high-skill tasks, and still more so on procurement of officer specialists, especially medical personnel.

Having defined the voluntary supply-demand gap with some degree of precision, the study went on to estimate the costs, in terms of higher pay, of maintaining mid-1965 force strengths in the absence of the draft. These estimates ranged from increases of 20 to 50 percent in officers' entry pay to increases of 80 to 280 percent in enlisted entry pay, or annual pay cost increases of $4 billion to $17 billion to sustain the active forces and an additional $1 billion for the reserves; the dollar costs took into account the savings resulting from reduced turnover and training loads. The study also considered the possible effects on recruiting of improving other military career benefits. It found that most fringe benefits helped to keep men in service, but not to attract new men. An exception was the possibility that improved educational benefits, especially before or during service, might attract more volunteers. In the end, though, the Defense Manpower Study concluded that costs of maintaining adequate forces on an all-volunteer basis would be prohibitive, and that no end to the draft could be seen even for the 1970's.[47]

No one objected to the conclusion that, whatever reasonable moves might be made toward greater civilian substitution and lower entry standards, an effective all-volunteer procurement system was sure to cost more than the current system. But there were some strong counterarguments to the Defense Department's conclusion that the added cost would be prohibitive. The most effective challenge came from professional economists. One important critic of the Defense study's estimates was Walter Oi,[48] who had directed the study's analysis of costs. He argued that the Defense Department was stressing the most pessimistic end of a range of estimates, that a different interpretation of the data would yield a $4 billion annual cost in added pay to support a 2.65 million-man active force, and that savings in training and other costs from reduced turnover would cut that figure even more. Another critic, Thomas Schelling,[49] offered no estimate of his own. Rather, he emphasized the difficulty in predicting responses to higher pay, given the sparsity of experience in recruiting without the aid of draft pressures: "All estimates are bound to be indirect, based on interpretations of dubious evidence in a changing world. . . . I can have no great confidence that my interpretation is correct or that the original evidence is adequate to permit an estimate, or that, if it was at the time, it will remain pertinent in the aftermath of Vietnamese hostilities." A third critic, Milton Friedman,[50] seemed quite confident of the ease with which an all-volunteer force might be achieved. But Schelling and Oi took a minimalist position; they suggested that pay scales, especially at entry levels, be raised significantly, though not so high as the Defense Department felt would be required, and that the results be studied for further evidence on the feasibility of ending the draft.

In addition to arguing that an all-volunteer system would be feasible, some proponents also argued that it would be economically desirable. They pointed out that, by requiring inductees to serve at very low pay levels, the draft acted to obscure the real costs, as distinct from the budgetary costs, of military manpower. Schelling offered the very pertinent observation that paying these men something closer to their real economic value would cut total real costs, by forcing better manpower management practices on the military services. Bordering on the specious, however, were Friedman's and Oi's contentions that the current system added to real costs by conscripting some men who could otherwise earn far more than even the amount needed to induce adequate volunteering. (Pay high enough to attract enough volunteers still would not attract, for example, the highly paid star athlete. But the hidden real cost of conscripting the star athlete is the same as that of conscripting the unemployed man; it is the difference between the pay of draftees and the higher level of pay that would be required to recruit sufficient volunteers. The additional differential, between the volunteer forces pay level and the athlete's civilian salary, would be chargeable to the real cost of military manpower only if there were zero unemployment or if the supply of star athletes were rigidly fixed.) Defenders of the existing system generally ignored these arguments about real costs; their concern always had been, and would continue to be, with the budgetary impact of the military pay bill rather than its broader economic effects.

Aside from arguments over the feasibility and economic desirability of closing the gap between voluntary supply and military demand for manpower, the debate between proponents of all-volunteer forces and defenders of continued Selective Service raised two other considerations of military effectiveness. One defense of Selective Service was given short shrift by critics. This was the contention that, without the turnover resulting from low entry pay and draft pressures, the active forces would eventually experience rising age levels and stagnation in the lower officer and enlisted ranks. It took little imagination, critics suggested, to conceive personnel management devices which could assure future turnover rates as high as desired.[51]

A more serious defense of continued conscription was the argument that, even if voluntary enlistments could meet all normal manpower needs, still that system would not be flexible enough to meet sudden emergencies with a rapid and efficient expansion of active forces. This argument was far from new, but the ongoing expansion for the Vietnam War made it especially pertinent. As one Defense manpower expert pointed out, even an annual increase in total strength as low as 10 percent would require a 50 percent increase of annual procurement.[52]

Proponents of an all-volunteer system argued that high enough pay scales could enable the military services to meet limited, emergency needs even without statutory authority to adjust pay scales on short notice. This argument, as stated by Professor Friedman, rested on an analogy with the civilian industry practice of setting wages high enough to produce hiring queues; when labor demands rise, the queues merely shorten without any increase in wages. Defenders of Selective Service never addressed themselves to this especially sophisticated attack on their position, probably because they were already convinced that pay raises just to support normal force levels would be prohibitively expensive. Being so convinced, they neglected to stress two major weaknesses in Friedman's queuing hypothesis when applied to the military manpower market. One is that the intrinsic attractions of military life vanish for many men just at the time of suddenly expanded manpower demands. (Arthur Smithies has suggested the civilian analogy, a manufacturing plant where danger to workers' lives increases as operations are expanded.) Patriotic appeals, and special pay and recognition for combat and other hazardous duties, can overcome this decline in service attractiveness only in part, and on a large scale only in an overwhelmingly obvious national emergency. Second, and more important, the impact on national security of a failure to meet emergency military manpower needs could be far more immediate and disastrous than any delay of increased production due to labor shortages.

A second argument against the contention that only continued conscription could provide the flexibility needed in an emergency was that this need could be met through reliance on reserves.[53] Those making this argument generally overlooked the central contribution of Selective Service in providing both new recruits and trained manpower to the reserves. Moreover, despite the Administration's clear reluctance to use reserves for even so large a military emergency as the Vietnam War, only once was it suggested that "the worth of continuing the present reserve and National Guard system ought to be brought into question."[54] And no one, on any side of the debate, offered any analysis of relative costs in providing flexibility through reserves, large active forces, or a mixture of both.

For the first time since 1950, some critics of the existing manpower procurement system questioned whether the responsiveness of Selective Service did not afford the president and the military services too much flexibility in meeting sudden increases in manpower demands. Just as the Vietnam war expansion reconfirmed the Selective Service System's basic operational capacity, so also did doubts about American participation in that war underscore the very slight degree to which Congress could affect current military policy by controlling the extent and sources of military manpower procurement. Congress had once come close to establishing such controls, during the 1950 debate over Selective Service extension, but abandoned the idea in the wake of Korean War military needs. Since then it had never really considered imposing direct control over conscription for the active forces, and had steadily loosened its control over recall of reservists. Now, as critics of several persuasions pressed the argument for all-volunteer forces, some of these same critics suggested that requiring the military services to rely on volunteers during periods of normal manpower demand would permit Congress to reclaim a voice in decisions for unusual expansions of active forces. This possibility was only suggested, not pressed; and neither the Administration, nor Congress, nor their commissioned advisory groups, gave it much attention.[55]

For the time being, the Administration and Congress accepted the Defense Department's contention that there were severe limits to adjustments in procurement policy that could be made reasonably and prudently. The draft still seemed a necessary part of that policy for the foreseeable future, even though it might benefit from some reforms; in its absence, the costs of meeting quantitative manpower requirements would be prohibitive, qualitative requirements would suffer seriously, and the flexibility inherent in the existing classification and induction processes would be lost. On the last point, even most critics of continued Selective Service admitted there was a need to maintain the rudiments of registration and classification for possible use in some future emergency.

Arguments over budgetary and real costs of draft-supported and all-volunteer forces thus had little immediate impact on policy. Nevertheless, the pioneering work of the Defense Manpower Study, and the responses of professional economists, did have an important impact on the continuing policy debate. They represented a major shift away from the traditional reliance on bald assertion, and made a first step toward educating policy-makers to the practice of careful analysis in assessing the military cost effectiveness of alternative manpower procurement systems.

Recasting the Issue of Compulsion

In the early postwar years, the issue of compulsion, together with problems of meeting military requirements for manpower, dominated debate over military manpower procurement policy. Fears for the consequences of peacetime conscription frustrated Administration hopes for a permanent military establishment relying on UMT-produced reserves; until the shocks of early 1948, these same fears made it impossible to support the active forces with a consistent and effective program of Selective Service; and two years later, as the Administration seemed headed for a renewed build-up of active forces, these fears were still strong enough to very nearly eviscerate the Selective Service System on which such a build-up would have to rely. The Korean War brought with it general acceptance of the need to maintain sizeable active forces, and the cold war outlook of the 1950's further eroded public reluctance to use conscription. But the older fears were still potent enough to preclude direct application of conscription to maintaining and increasing the reserve forces, even though Selective Service, at one and two removes, was used to these ends. By 1956, it was possible to denounce opponents of conscription as irresponsible vote-seekers or worse; in 1963, questioning the continued existence of Selective Service was still distinctly unfashionable.

In the later 1960's, conscription was once more a matter of debate and the subject of a number of issues. These new issues grew out of several more general trends in American political thinking: an increasing perception of thaw in the cold war, growing concern for the rights and welfare of individuals and disadvantaged social groups, and, after mid-1965, the increasing unpopularity of American participation in the Vietnam War. These trends underlay a variety of questions raised in the debate involving the use of compulsion in military manpower procurement. Is conscription necessary to continued support of military forces which are adequate and appropriate to national defense needs? Is it justifiable, or even possible, to maintain military conscription in the face of strong objections by a sizeable minority to forced participation in an unpopular war? Does military conscription serve some important function in maintaining proper civil-military relations? And, ought not the principle of compulsory service, if applied at all, be applied universally, for both military and other national service?

Even more than some other aspects of America's response to the cold war—foreign aid programs and military-political alliances, for example—the maintenance of large active military forces and the accompanying use of Selective Service were most often spoken of as unhappy necessities, not part of the natural order of things and certainly not good in themselves. By 1963 the need for large forces-in-being as guarantees of national security was widely accepted. Yet, not surprisingly, when it seemed that these forces might be supportable by voluntary recruiting alone in the near or more distant future, one early reaction was a widespread questioning of continued Selective Service operations. This reaction was no doubt spurred by the decision to exempt married men from the draft, which underlined and brought to public attention the arbitrary side of the selection process. But the fundamental question was: is Selective Service still needed? If the answer were no, then most would agree that inductions for military service should end.

Necessity had always been an important factor in the issue of compulsion, and in the early stages of the renewed debate it was the dominant one. Even as questions about the continued need for Selective Service surged strongly in 1964, and as they were dampened by the Johnson Administration's promise to examine the problem thoroughly, there was little early revival of older fears for the untoward effects of peacetime conscription on American society and its youth. Perhaps this was because the program at issue was Selective Service, not universal conscription; the former had been treated throughout the postwar debate as a practical question, while the ideological attack on conscription had generally focused on UMT.

After 1965, however, the issue of compulsions once again began to take on ideological overtones. The widespread, though hardly universal, unpopularity of escalating American involvement in Vietnam led many to question not only the need for conscription to maintain large standing forces, but also the desirability of such large forces themselves. Statements like the relatively mild one of the Antioch Conference clearly echoed older postwar attitudes toward conscription and the need for military forces; and the new ideological tone was apparent in many other expressions of favor for all-volunteer forces, and of mistrust of the military flexibility accorded the Administration by current manpower procurement policy. Perhaps the most interesting aspect of these arguments was not their content, but their reflection of an incipient reunion of right and left on questions of manpower procurement and of military policy generally, a union shattered nearly two decades earlier by the right's acceptance of cold war imperatives.

If antidraft sentiment aided a reunion of right and left critics of military policy, antiwar sentiment on the left certainly limited that reunion. A major manifestation of the antiwar position was the growing "we-won't-go" attitude, a phenomenon almost exclusively associated with the strong political pacifism of the New Left allied with the traditional position of older pacifist religious groups. This resurgent American pacifism, religious and political, expressed itself most spectacularly in the demonstrations celebrating burning or turning-in of draft cards, in various sit-ins, and in even more disruptive demonstrations against Selective Service and more purely military operations. At first it seemed to many that there might be a good-humored tolerance of these activities by the Administration, the courts, and those large segments of the public who supported American involvement in Vietnam with varying degrees of reluctance. But soon there were arrests and convictions for violations of new legislation protecting draft cards; and before long hundreds of young men who were reluctant or unwilling to support an unpopular war, the Administration, Congress, and the courts became both participants and victims in a war of symbols between the government and some of its constituent citizens.

At the heart of this symbolic war lay a new critique of compulsory military service, one quite different from the older fears that conscription would militarize and undermine the morals of American youth. For the first time, at least in this century, the right of Americans to abstain from military service on grounds of conscientious objection to a particular war was asserted against the general power of government to conscript.

The unique aspect of this assertion deserves some explanation. The legal power of the government to conscript for military service has been challenged a number of times, under each of the three conscription acts passed in this century (1917, 1940, 1948), each time without success. Nonetheless, the current statute respected certain kinds of unwillingness to serve (section 6(j)):

> Nothing contained in this title shall be construed to require any person to be subject to combatant training and service in the armed forces of the United States who, by reason of religious training and belief, is conscientiously opposed to participation in war in any form. Religious training and belief in this connection means an individual's belief in a relation to a Supreme Being involving duties superior to those arising

from any human relation, but does not include essentially political, sociological, or philosophical views or a merely personal moral code.

The law and Selective Service regulations provided for induction and restriction to noncombatant service of those opposed only to combatant service, and for deferment (Class I-O) and assignment to civilian work (Class I-W) of those opposed even to noncombatant service.

Before 1965 these provisions had come under increasing scrutiny by the courts; and in that year a Supreme Court decision concluded that "the test of belief 'in a relation to a Supreme Being' is whether a given belief that is sincere and meaningful occupies in the life of its possessor a place parallel to that filled by the orthodox belief in God of one who clearly qualifies for the exemption."[56]

The challenge of many new pacifists was two-pronged: they sought to erase the limitation of qualification for conscientious objector status to those professing religious scruples (even as broadly defined) against war; and they sought to broaden the interpretation of opposition "to participation in war in any form" to include objection to particular wars as well as general opposition to all war. Given the 1965 Supreme Court decision loosening the religious test, it seemed possible that the concept of conscientious objection would eventually be broadened to include atheist objectors. But how far such decisions might go toward permitting men to opt out of a military obligation on grounds of selective objection to particular military policy goals, or to particular military actions in pursuit of those goals, was not at all clear. Even dimmer was the prospect that the Administration might propose, much less Congress accept, a legislative broadening of the conscientious objection concept.[57]

Almost all the congressional sentiment expressed in committee hearings on this and related matters was in the direction of tighter definitions and stricter enforcement of Selective Service administrative decisions. Indeed, committee members voiced considerable alarm at the implications of the whole "we-won't-go" movement, and at the trend of recent court actions interposing their judgments between the Selective Service System and claimants to a variety of deferments and exemptions. Some House committee members were especially agitated over the Justice Department's failure, up to then, to prosecute persons allegedly counseling defiance of the draft law. When Assistant Attorney General Fred Vinson defended the department's caution, citing the court's attitudes toward intruding on free speech, Representative Hebert (D., La.) exploded: "Let's forget the first amendment, I know that will be the refuge of the Supreme Court. . . . This begging the question of the first amendment continuously . . . upsets not only me but millions of Americans. They want to know . . . why can the Carmichaels and why can the Kings, and other individuals of that ilk stand before the American people and institute riot, incite defiance of the law, while the Justice Department stands idly by and the Congress takes no action to strengthen that law?" Vinson could only reply that "any law that deals with utterances has to be read in the light of the first amendment."[58]

The renewed ideological critique of military conscription in the mid-1960's was accompanied, indeed preceded, by resurgent arguments that conscription might have positive social and military values quite aside from its direct contribution to national security. This was a favorite contention of many who supported UMT in the early postwar years; but it was generally avoided by UMT's military sponsors. Selective Service, however, was usually considered by these same groups and persons as a regretful necessity, to be ended as soon as practicable. This accorded well with the Marshall-Palmer vision of a postwar military establishment, and most military leaders then probably were convinced that conscription for the active forces over the long term was neither politic nor productive of good regular military units. In later years, however, military men as well as veterans groups came to argue that, beyond providing men for the military services (or for other important activities), Selective Service was a guarantee that the military services would not become a mercenary force completely apart from society. This guarantee arose not only from the direct operation of Selective Service, but even more from its indirect promotion of military recruiting efforts, both enlisted and officer, across a broader spectrum of society than seemed likely were recruiting wholly voluntary. Added to these results was the constant turnover of military personnel that accompanied short-term conscripted or semi-voluntary service, assuring an intermixed society of soldiers who were civilians at heart with civilians who had the experience of being soldiers. A number of answers to this argument were suggested, ranging from the older ones that conscripts do not make good soldiers and that forced service may not be the best sort of public relations for the armed forces, to a cogently reasoned view that Selective Service is not essential to assuring the desired turnover of military personnel.[59]

Not all the echoes of earlier debates over military manpower procurement were products of a newly revived distaste for and mistrust of military conscription. In a lead article for the *Reader's Digest*, General Eisenhower sponsored universal military training as an alternative preferable to the current system. The Defense Department's draft study group looked at the idea briefly, and concluded that it would cost about $2.5 billion annually in added operational expenses alone, that it could offer no increase in military effectiveness under current concepts of reserves' roles, and that therefore all this added cost would have to be charged to UMT's enhancement of equity and other social values. Aware of this, Eisenhower promoted UMT as a means of restoring social unity and national morality among the nation's youth.[60]

Similar motives, less simply expressed, inspired much of the enthusiasm for some scheme of universal national service, promoted by the National Service Secretariat, Morris Janowitz, and Labor Secretary Willard Wirtz, among others. At least one enthusiast argued that the universal compulsion implied in such schemes would be nothing more than an extension of traditional American attitudes toward compulsory education. Even the more devoted proponents of universal national service recognized, however, that the program would probably have to start on a voluntary basis; and some opponents of compulsory military service suggested programs of national service rooted in the voluntary principle.[61]

Both the Marshall Commission and the Clark Panel offered answers to the four major questions raised in this renewed debate over compulsion in military manpower procurement. Both groups agreed with the Administration's position that continued Selective Service was necessary to support military service strengths and provide needed flexibility for expansion; but the Clark Panel also recommended further study of the prospects for making the reserve training system wholly voluntary, while the Marshall Commission recommended new authority for direct inductions into the reserves.

A majority of the Marshall Commission opposed broadening the concept of conscientious objection, and the Clark Panel's view was similar. The latter group also recommended vigorous prosecution of youths evading the draft or demonstrating illegally against it. The Marshall Commission noted, and the Clark Panel emphasized, the asserted value of continued conscription to promoting a healthier relation between the military services and society at large. Both groups rejected UMT as not justified by military need, though; and the Marshall Commission suggested that neither the precise needs nor the constitutional basis were yet apparent in arguments for universal national service.

In sum, renewed debate over military effectiveness and cost efficiency implications of the existing manpower procurement system opened the door to reconsidering the use of compulsions. Resurgent interest in this issue reflected a more general move toward reassessing the nation's roles abroad and concentrating on domestic difficulties. With some exceptions, there was an increasingly explicit consensus on returning to the position of the late 1940's that compulsory service be limited to meeting clear military needs. This position had been passively accepted during the Korean War, but not carefully guarded thereafter. Renewal of debate on this issue suggested, then, that henceforth neither military needs nor the propriety of compulsions would be taken for granted.

Equity and Manpower Development Goals

Concern for problems of equity, and for the impact of military programs on nonmilitary goals for youth development, ran high in the renewed debate; indeed, interest in these issues was greater than ever before in the postwar period. This new interest stemmed largely from the same trends in American political thinking that inspired resurgent questioning of the need for and propriety of compulsions; and debate over issues of equity and social impact focused on three different kinds of proposals reflecting varying attitudes toward compulsions: voluntary military service, more or less universal service, and reformed selective service. (The last is treated in subsection III-2 below.)

Proponents of all-volunteer military forces argued that true

equity could be achieved only by allowing each individual the freedom to serve or not to serve. Among the professional economists,
Schelling was especially eloquent in condemning the injustice done
those men selected to give involuntary service to the nation at very
low pay levels, pointing out that this amounted to a huge, hidden
tax in kind on their earning capacity. Friedman and Oi noted that
this tax was also exacted from those serving voluntarily; and Oi estimated that this tax in kind burdened first-term enlisted men at
rates some four to five times heavier than the average federal income tax burden on adults over age eighteen. Only the higher pay
required to attract truly volunteer forces, it was argued, could overcome this injustice. The major objection raised against this view, in
terms of equity and social impact, was that an all-volunteer system
would concentrate the burdens and risks of defending the nation
on the poor generally and on Negroes in particular. To these fears,
proponents answered that there would never be enough qualified
Negroes to form a majority of servicemen, that the necessarily higher
pay levels of voluntary forces would attract more than Negroes and
others of society's disadvantaged youths, and that at least those
serving would be fairly compensated for the risks and burdens they
undertook.

These views reflected a new questioning of high entry standards
for military service, by enthusiasts for a wholly voluntary system
and by other critics of existing programs as well. Earlier critics had
argued that high standards artificially limited the supply of manpower to the armed forces, and hence postponed the day when compulsion might be eliminated. But in the years of the New Frontier
and the Great Society, national attention to the problems of urban
and rural slum dwellers increased manyfold. Criticism of entry
standards concurrently shifted to emphasize their impact on already disadvantaged sectors of society.

The military services' demands for high quality manpower clearly
resulted in excluding the physically and mentally less fit from the
opportunities and benefits of military service. These benefits, as suggested in an earlier study by Professor Eli Ginzberg, were extensive: the principle benefit of short-term military service was a broadening of occupational horizons through exposure to a wider range
of possibilities than might occur to those staying at home, through

training in convertible skills, and through encouragement and assistance toward advanced education in off-duty hours; in addition there were the advantages of veterans' benefits, of regimented diets and personal hygiene, of free medical and dental care, and of learning to live in a heterogeneous social environment. For those who stayed beyond an obligated service term, of course, there were further advantages of steady employment, adequate pay and benefits, and early retirement with pay. Youths from middle to lower-middle-class homes and communities, and even those from more comfortable backgrounds, might well gain from at least some of these benefits, if only as supplements to the advantages already offered them as sons of an affluent society. But for many thousands of youths from disadvantaged homes and communities, military service was often the best road out of an otherwise impoverished, perhaps hopeless, future. It was among the very groups and individuals who might benefit most from military service, however, that rates of disqualification were highest.[62]

The Defense Department's new Project 100,000 went some distance toward meeting this criticism, but it was aimed at absorbing men who would require a minimum of special instruction and attention by the military services. The Marshall Commission recommended that the Department initiate legislation for a program which would accept any volunteer who, though unable to meet induction standards, could be brought up to minimum standards through special in-service education and training. The Clark Panel was not so favorable to expanding the military services' role in educational rehabilitation, but it did recommend consideration be given to increasing the numbers of youths accepted for service providing they agreed to in-service correction of physical defects. Project 100,000, moreover, was aimed both at volunteers and at potential inductees; and this raised an unanswered question of the extent to which the government might apply compulsions, beyond those of public education, to improve the quality of its citizens' skills and way of life.

The problem of distributing the benefits of military service equitably was a fairly new one in the debate over military manpower procurement. Much older was the question, raised by many opponents of all-volunteer forces, of how to distribute the burdens and risks of service more fairly. These critics of current manpower procurement programs either argued for, or assumed the necessity of, continued conscription in some form. Some went so far as to argue that compulsion could be equitable only if made universal; and they proposed schemes of universal national service which would, they hoped, also meet certain nonmilitary youth development needs. Others would not go so far, but did propose widening the number of those fulfilling some national service obligation by recognizing certain nonmilitary programs as formal alternatives to military service.

The argument that compulsion must be universal to achieve equity had always been implicit in the case for UMT, and it was again in these proposals for some system of universal national service. The assertion that UMT would be equitable had never been seriously challenged, although its weaknesses were apparent: the difficulty of balancing burdens among training options and of assuring that the incidence of UMT would in fact be universal. These same weaknesses afflicted the new claims of universal service enthusiasts even more seriously. There was no clear assurance that sufficient manpower needs could be identified to absorb each annual class of eligibles; nor was it at all clear that the various options for national service could be made to carry burdens and risks equivalent to those of military service. Especially for this last reason, most proponents of UNS granted the need to include measures for distributing the burden of those special compulsions required to meet specific military manpower demands.[63]

Similar problems arose in considering various schemes for recognizing alternatives to military service without requiring universal compulsion, including proposals for voluntary national service. The idea of nonmilitary alternatives to fulfilling either a selectively imposed or a voluntarily accepted obligation to national service had roots deep in the experience with Selective Service since 1940. However, aside from conscientious objection, none of the many grounds for deferment "in the national interest" had ever been recognized as a formal alternative to military service. The idea of expanding such formal alternatives beyond the work programs for conscientious objectors was first broached to the armed services committees in the 1959 hearings, but it attracted very little attention. It was the 1960 proposal for a peace corps, actually an adaptation of suggestions made in 1959, which first brought this idea into the wide arena of public debate. As the Peace Corps came into being following the 1960 election, its friends generally agreed that support in Congress for the program was doubtful enough without tying it to the even more doubtfully acceptable concept of alternative service. Thus Peace Corps volunteers were declared deferrable from induction, but not exempt from the military obligation by reason of their service.

One major inspiration for the Defense Manpower Study was concern that the declining incidence of military service might eventually undermine the principle of universal obligation. Thus the study group considered the idea of recognizing service in nonmilitary programs as alternative ways of fulfilling that obligation. The activitives explored included the Peace Corps and possible public or private domestic counterparts; teachers in public and private elementary and secondary schools; scientists and engineers in government, universities, foundations or other nonprofit activities; and civil defense workers. Consideration of these "equivalent service" alternatives to the current military obligation was abandoned, or at least suspended, late in 1964. By then, the Defense study had concluded that a number of objections made the idea distinctly unpromising. Specifically, the Peace Corps administration was still not at all interested in tying its organization to such an idea; not only might it be impolitic, it might also lower the quality of applicants and increase the motivational screening problem. Civil Defense officials stated that they had no large-scale program in mind at the time, and certainly not one which could absorb large numbers of military-age young men. This last limitation also applied to nonprofit employers of teachers, scientists, and engineers. Thus the study concluded that, by any reasonably rigorous standards, the "equivalent service" concept would involve too few persons to be of much help in broadening the incidence of national service. Moreover, there were serious questions raised whether such service, even tightly defined, could really be considered the equivalent of military service, especially in regard to discipline, separation from family, reserve recall vulnerability, and other hardships and risks of military life.[64]

The Defense study's foreclosure of the alternative service idea was never announced; and proponents of that idea, and of even more elaborate schemes of national service, took heart from later hints that the Administration might still be interested. There was, for one, Secretary McNamara's suggestion that inequities in Selective Service might be remedied "by asking every young person to give two years of service to his country—whether in one of the military services, in the Peace Corps or in some other volunteer developmental work at home or abroad." And President Johnson authorized the Marshall Commission to evaluate proposals for national service. Neither the Marshall Commission nor the Clark Panel found the concept of national service a viable alternative to the military obligation. Moreover, the Marshall Commission specifically rejected the idea of recognizing such nonmilitary programs as the Peace Corps or VISTA as alternatives to obligated military service. Such programs, it argued, were not equivalent in burdens to military service; recognizing them as alternatives would therefore provide those qualified with a privileged avenue of military service avoidance; and the whole concept would serve to confuse the distinct functions of obligated military service and civilian voluntary service.[65]

2. Equity, Social Goals, and Selective Service Reform

Many critics rejected both the voluntary principle and the more or less universalist approach as viable ways of solving the problems of the existing manpower procurement system. Nonetheless, they faulted the current operation of Selective Service both for being inequitable and for having undesirable social effects; and they promoted extensive changes in the policy and process of classification and induction and in the organizational machinery of Selective Service. It was from this area of the renewed debate that there came the most important of the Administration's initiatives for change in military manpower procurement policies.

The Defense Department's summary report of conclusions from its draft study, made public in mid-1966, was the first substantive and official recognition of charges that Selective Service operated inequitably and with questionable social impact. The most comprehensive support for this view came from the Marshall Commission Report in 1967. Simultaneously, the Selective Service System defended itself in congressional committee hearings and public conferences; and it gained partial support for its views from the report of the Clark Panel. This multisided debate ranged over almost every aspect of Selective Service policy and procedures, and some aspects of Defense Department policy and practice as well; but the most important subjects of reform proposals were: channeling and the whole process of classification and deferment; the order of induction for those men declared available; local board autonomy and standards for decision; and organization of the Selective Service System.

Channeling

In reviewing the complex debate over issues of equity and social impact raised by the various classifications, by deferments in general, and by the whole concept of channeling, it will be helpful to consider Selective Service classifications (as do the local boards in classifying registrants) from the bottom up.

The criticism and proposals concerning the impact of military service entry standards on rates of disqualification (Classes IV-F and I-Y) have already been considered (see subsection III-1).

Hardship and dependency deferments (Classes III-A and I-A, priority four) came in for little direct criticism, although one initial spur to renewed debate was the 1963 order giving low induction priority to Class I-A married men. Rising draft calls in 1965 gave the Administration a welcome opportunity to relieve itself of the embarrassment this action had created. The Defense Manpower Study concluded that twenty- and twenty-one-year old men had accelerated their marriage plans during the two years after the order; that continuation of the policy had by 1965 proved undesirable on grounds of manpower supply, social considerations, and equity; and that the policy should not be resumed in the future. The study did not take any stand on automatic deferment for fathers; the Marshall Commission merely implied criticism of that policy in recommending that hardship deferments be judged on their individual merits; and the Clark Panel did not consider any questions of dependency classification.

Most criticisms of classification policy and practice focused on student deferments (Class II-S) and deferments for critical occupa-

tions (Class II-A), and the relation of these to the group of registrants aged twenty-six to thirty-five, technically liable for induction
by reason of earlier deferment, but effectively protected by low induction priority (Class I-A, priority five). There were two questions
involved: what was the impact of these classifications on the incidence of military service; and were there military or other social
grounds for continuing these classifications? The Marshall Commission was highly critical of student and occupational deferments,
concluding that they led to an inequitable distribution of military
service among socioeconomic groups; a majority of the commission
also found no national interest to be served in continuing these
deferments, although a minority disagreed. The Selective Service
System and the Clark Panel did not accept the conclusion that these
deferments were inequitable, and stressed the continued need for
them. The Defense Department agreed with the Marshall Commission on the impact of these deferments on military service incidence,
and by 1967 it converted an earlier defense of continued deferments into a neutral position.

Much of the debate over these questions involved a confusing
variety of figures purporting to show the incidence of military service among men of different educational attainments. In the 1966
House committee hearings, General Hershey reported that only 43
to 46 percent of men never deferred for college eventually entered
service, while 56 to 57 percent of those deferred later did serve.
Defense Department witnesses countered with figures on service
incidence among men reaching age twenty-six in 1964: among those
never reaching college, the incidence was 53 percent, while among
those entering college it was only 49 percent; further breakdown
showed that among the non-college group, 50 percent of those not
finishing high school served, compared to a 57 percent incidence
among the high school graduates; and among the college group,
service incidence for those not getting degrees was 60 percent,
while only 40 percent of those getting a bachelor's degree eventually served. The Clark Panel, taking Hershey's side in the argument, reported a service incidence of 60 percent for "the college
student group" and 57 percent for "the non-college students," figures remarkably similar to those for the Defense Department's
categories of college dropouts and high school graduates. The Mar-

shall Commission Report relied on surveys of men reaching ages twenty-seven through thirty-four in 1964, and reported the results in different categories; it concluded that service incidence among these men was lowest for those not reaching high school (41 percent) and those entering graduate school (27 percent), and highest among high school graduates not entering college (74 percent) and college graduates not entering graduate school (70 percent). Later Defense Department testimony, relying on the same studies but reporting results in slightly altered categories, nonetheless confirmed the Marshall Commission's general conclusions. Further confirmation came from yet another set of Defense Department figures, reported late in the 1967 House committee hearings by Representative Stratton (D., N.Y.), based on the same age groups, but excluding men found physically or mentally unqualified for service; among those qualified, the service incidence was again lowest for men not reaching high school (73 percent) and those entering graduate school (37 percent), and highest among high school graduates not entering college (84 percent) and college graduates not entering graduate school (85 percent).[66]

Despite the confusion in figures, it seemed clear that at least some college students, mostly those also attending graduate school, did have opportunities to avoid military service not available to youths with lesser educational attainments. The major reason seen for this was the greater opportunity for the college graduate to extend his deferred status, by means of graduate school, fatherhood, or occupation, past age twenty-six; after this he would at worst be eligible only for priority five of Class I-A. The Defense Department backed up this reasoning by noting that 11 percent of college graduates who were age twenty-six in 1964 had occupational deferments, while only 1 percent of nongraduates in that age class had such deferments. Even General Hershey seemed to admit the possibility of manipulating deferments into service avoidance; he stated in 1966 that he wanted authority (which was never granted) for a special call of men from priority five, and later explained that he hoped this would persuade many of these protected registrants to seek or return to deferrable occupations.[67]

Evidence was harder to come by that this pattern of service avoidance by some college students also meant there was a differential incidence of military service among socioeconomic groups. The initial plans for the Defense Department's draft study called for surveys of service incidence, past and current, among men grouped by educational level, marital status, race, and urban/rural residence; but the only data from these studies produced in the public debate were the figures on incidence by educational level, noted above, and some tables in the Marshall Commission's report showing 1964 service incidence by race (white/nonwhite) among men aged twenty-six to thirty-four. The latter showed that, although only 34.1 percent of whites in this age group had not served, compared to 50.8 percent of nonwhites, still 12.7 percent of whites had avoided service for reasons other than unfitness, compared to only 8.4 percent of nonwhites. Despite the paucity of hard evidence, however, it was difficult to avoid the conclusion that opportunities for avoiding service through student and occupational deferments were greater for youths in the higher socioeconomic strata than for relatively disadvantaged youths.

One other aspect of student deferment impact on military service incidence was the object of debate between a Marshall Commission majority, on the one hand, and a commission minority and the Clark Panel on the other (with other participants choosing sides, or not, largely according to their general views on student deferment). This was the fact that, no matter what his later eligibility for service, the young man able to qualify for a student deferment could choose at least to delay his service. At House committee hearings in 1967, General Clark said his panel found no particular inequity here, especially when so few were needed to fight in the Vietnam War; and George Reedy, speaking for the Marshall Commission minority view on student deferments, pointed out that those exercising their deferment option in the early 1960's had managed to delay their service right into the middle of a hot war. Nonetheless, a majority of the commission thought it more important that "the chance to postpone service right now might mean the difference between the obligation to serve in a shooting war and the possibility of serving later when the war might have come to an end."[68]

What the various parties to the debate made of this evidence in terms of policy recommendations depended very much on whether they felt other policy goals justified ignoring any inequities which student and occupational deferments might produce. The original justification for student deferments in the early 1950's had rested narrowly on military requirements for college educated personnel, and more broadly on fears that the Korean War mobilization might so disrupt individuals' educations, and so reduce university enrollments, as to damage both the institutions of higher education and the flow of skilled men into the economy; and occupational deferments had been similarly defended on grounds of national interest. The question was, then, whether these or newer needs justified a continuation of the disputed deferments.

Answering no, the Marshall Commission's majority cited official statements by the Departments of Defense and of Health, Education, and Welfare, indicating that the older justifications no longer amounted to a compelling demand for student deferments; and it noted that about half the registrants granted occupational deferments by local boards were not in any officially designated critical occupation or essential industry. Later testimony[69] by the Commissioner of Education and the Secretary of Labor confirmed the commission majority's conclusion that no national interest would be damaged by abolishing undergraduate and occupational deferments. Supporting this conclusion, moreover, was the view of many professional educators, and even some students, that the policy guidelines and procedures governing student deferments were positively harmful to the educational integrity of the universities and their relations with students. These critics emphasized the distorting impact of student deferments on individual students' decisions about their programs, and on university faculty and administrators who were forced to make distinctions among students which might not otherwise be justified.[70]

Against this conclusion was the finding of a minority of the Marshall Commission that there were still good reasons for continuing undergraduate student deferments. This group argued there were ways of assuring that college students would return to the pool of men eligible for induction, by eliminating most graduate study and all occupational deferments, and by denying those accepting undergraduate deferments and opportunity for later dependency deferment except in cases of extreme hardship. This minority position stressed the difficulties which would result from abolishing deferments for college undergraduates. For one, the Defense Department stated it depended on civilian college graduates for 80 to 90 percent of its annual officer procurement; and it would have to admit much larger numbers of college freshmen to its ROTC programs in order to maintain an adequate flow of graduates into reserve and active officer ranks. Even more difficult, the Defense Department would have to devise some scheme of identifying potential medical and allied professionals in their college freshman year, and provide for special deferment of these in order to have sufficient men in these professions liable for later service. Although the Defense Department declined to defend or condemn current policy, the commission's minority felt these potential difficulties justified continuing student deferments in some form. Recognizing the criticism of current student deferment guidelines, the minority recommended instead: a blanket deferment for undergraduates; graduate student deferments limited to those preparing for medical or other critical professions, providing they committed themselves to subsequent military service; and other policy changes to eliminate manipulation of these deferments into service avoidance.

The most obviously self-interested support for continued student and occupational deferments came from the American Council on Education and from spokesmen for the Scientific Manpower Commission and some of its member organizations. Their testimony stressed, as it had in the past, the growing demand for men with scientific, engineering and other technical skills, both for defense and for the civilian economy. But they could only assert, not demonstrate, that abolishing Class II deferments would have serious long-range effects on the flow of such men through the universities and into teaching, research, and industry. Moreover, when pressed on the question of equity involved, their answers were ambiguous. Said Dr. M. H. Trytten, prime author of the Korean War student deferment plan, "If the military services had the need for these people in their professions, certainly. Then they ought to be drafted."[71] But neither he nor his colleagues were pressed hard on the question of what should be done with those who had been deferred and were not needed by the services in their professional capacities.

The Clark Panel saw no fundamental change in military and

civilian needs since the 1950's that would justify eliminating student and occupational deferments; but it did recommend some changes in these policies. For undergraduate students, it recommended blanket deferment until age twenty-four (or until completion or interruption of a bachelor's degree program if that occurred earlier), and return of most students at this point to the pool of men eligible for induction. The panel further recommended establishment of a special manpower board, reporting to the National Security Council, to determine guidelines for deferment of graduate students preparing for, or men working in, a limited group of critically-needed occupations and professions. And it recommended deferment of all full-time students preparing for medical and allied professions.

It is not possible to trace all the subtleties of the Selective Service System's defense of continued student and occupational deferments. Despite the assertions of others, General Hershey admitted he had no hard evidence to show that student deferments were essential to the national interest, or even that Selective Service channeling had helped produce larger numbers of educated men than would otherwise have come through the universities. In a paper for the Chicago Conference, Hershey came close to admitting that student deferments in periods of low military demand were simply a matter of manipulating the Class I-A pool, not of national needs, nor even of channeling. An exchange during one session of that conference underscored the point. Colonel Ingold, of the Selective Service System, took the floor to emphasize that the military services simply could not absorb all the college students. "So if they can't be inducted," he said, "they're going to be deferred in class 1A. Which do you prefer, the honest 2S or the dishonesty of class 1A and being deferred?" Bruce Chapman, of the Ripon Society, replied: "I don't see how it's honest to defer just because you don't need them and then give as your rationale that they're 'essential.'" "How," he asked, "does their not being needed make them 'essential'?" No answer was given, perhaps because there was none. Even so, the Selective Service System pressed for retaining the broadest possible authority to defer both students and men with "essential" skills and in "critical" industries.[72]

A final major channel of deferments was also the object of considerable criticism. This was the Class I-D status accorded all Reserve Enlistment Program enlistees. Concern over the opportunities for active service avoidance afforded by this program was at least as much a reason for the 1966 congressional attempts to give the president additional reserve recall authority as was any more general belief in the military need to mobilize the reserves.

The Marshall Commission was especially critical. It agreed that the decision whether to commit the reserves in the Vietnam war should be left to the Administration, and it recognized favorably the Defense Department's efforts to assure all reserve program enlistees were given active duty training shortly after enlisting. But it also saw justice in the complaint that reserve recruitment imposed qualifications beyond those applied by the active forces, a complaint supported by charges of favoritism, and by the low proportion of Negroes, compared to whites, entering service through reserve programs. The commission commended Defense Department plans to correct reserve recruiting practices, and it offered two further recommendations. One was to limit deferment for reserve enlistees to those entering before being classified I-A; and the second was to provide standby authority to meet Reserve and National Guard unit manpower needs through direct induction.

The Clark Panel was no less concerned over charges that deferments for reserve program enlistees resulted in some inequities. It recommended that the president be given permanent authority to call reserves to active duty without a declaration of national emergency, and that the president exercise this authority. The panel also urged that the service secretaries order to twenty-four months' active duty any enlistee in the special reserve program who was not participating satisfactorily in reserve unit training. To preclude further suspicions and charges of favoritism in reserve recruitment, the panel suggested that the Defense Department amend its recent directives on the subject to specifically forbid any exceptions to standard policy for professional athletes. Going beyond these issues, the Clark Panel was the only important participant in the debate to recognize a further problem of equity in the reserve programs, a problem arising from the statutory reserve obligation imposed on those volunteering for or inducted into active service. It noted that the Army was the only service requiring significant numbers of active duty veterans to meet this obligation by reserve unit training participation, and that even that service imposed this heavier requirement on only 14 percent of those inductees who became available for involuntary assignment to reserve units. To avoid this inequity, the panel recommended special reserve enlistment bonuses to attract postservice volunteers into reserve units.

Not only did most of the various channels for deferment from active military service come in for criticism; so also did the way in which the Selective Service System handled the pool of men in Class I-A, specifically its practice of inducting men by priority group, oldest first. This criticism reflected concern for operations in the past and expectations for the future more than any general dissatisfaction with the existing situation. Part of the criticism was directed at the tendency for the median age of inductees to rise in periods of low military demand. The median age of involuntary inductees was twenty years in 1966-67, having declined since 1963 as a result, first, of the order protecting married men, and then of the Vietnam expansion. But that age could be expected to rise in later years as calls declined and the military age classes grew larger. The Defense Department argued, and the Marshall Commission and the Clark Panel agreed, that this would be undesirable on both military and social grounds. The military services had a long-standing preference for younger inductees; more men in the older liable age groups had family responsibilities; and surveys by the Defense and Labor Departments in 1964 had indicated men ages twenty-two to twenty-five in Class I-A, priority three, especially those with some college education, experienced greater difficulty in getting jobs because of their draft status than did younger men in that liable group. Coupled with these criticisms was a recognition that the oldest-first induction-order procedure would be unable to cope with the growing number of eligible youths; eventually, as the Defense Department had predicted some years earlier, significant numbers of men would escape to exempt status, past age twenty-five, simply by virtue of their being no military need for them and of the inability of the system to find reasons for deferring them. The Defense Department and the two advisory groups all recommended schemes for remedying these potential defects in the current induction-order procedure, each focusing prime draft liability on the younger men, ages nineteen or twenty. General Hershey did not strongly object to this particular aim of the schemes, at least after 1966; but he did suggest such moves might make recruiting more difficult; and he once again suggested that the burden on registrants of draft uncertainty could be avoided by their volunteering for induction or enlistment. None of the other participants was much concerned about the impact of a lower draft age on recruitment; and the Defense Department pointed out that most voluntary enlistments came from age nineteen or younger.

In addition to these specific criticisms of Selective Service channeling, the mid-1960's brought growing recognition that the whole pattern of selection and military service incidence was creating a much more general problem in equity and social impact for the military manpower procurement system. Older arguments against conscription had pointed to the dangers of militarizing American youths. Now it was recognized that Selective Service practices might be dangerously reinforcing the traditional American distaste for military service, and doing so in an especially unfortunate way. By providing broad channels for escaping military service, it was argued, current policies were eroding any sense of military service obligation among the nation's youth and substituting for it an attitude of avoidance. This problem was first publicized widely in reports by the Columbia University Conservation of Human Resources Project, directed by Professor Eli Ginzberg. "Military service," he wrote, "instead of being an obligation which all young men recognize, has become more of a gamble in which certain players hold marked cards." The consequence, he argued, is that "the young man who gets caught and who serves for two or more years on active duty is likely to consider himself a 'sucker,' for that is how his friends who escape military service regard him."[73] The conditions leading to such attitudes did not really change with the step-up of draft calls in mid-1965; indeed the general distaste for the war in Vietnam, especially among many college students, reinforced the urge toward avoidance. Kingman Brewster, president of Yale University, spoke to this problem in his 1966 baccalaureate address. He blamed the combination of current Vietnam War policy and the long-term failure of Selective Service to adapt to new conditions and demands for encouraging ". . . a cynical avoidance of service, a corruption of the aims of education, and a tarnishing of the national spirit"; and he called for a new ". . . manpower policy which would rationally relate individual privilege and national duty."[74] Some, of course, sought solutions to this problem in the various schemes for universal or alternative service discussed earlier. Others, however, especially the Marshall Commission, felt the answer lay in more specific reforms of Selective Service.

Order of Induction: Selection by Age or by Random Lottery?

Criticism of Selective Service channeling in its various aspects, and especially proposals for minimizing deferments and focusing induction on younger registrants, led to a variety of proposals for spreading the risk of having service burdens imposed without increasing the total incidence of these burdens. The Marshall Commission's recommendations on deferments, to a lesser extent the Defense Department's, and even less the Clark Panel's, all would have the effect of increasing the number of youths classified I-A. But projections of population growth in military age groups and of military manpower demands already pointed to a future excess of availables over military needs, and these changes would increase that excess even more. To cope with this, both the Defense Department and the Marshall Commission proposed replacing the current date-of-birth, oldest-first sequence of induction among availables in each local board pool with a random lottery among the national pool of nineteen- or twenty-year-olds in Class I-A. The Clark Panel also recommended inducting first from the younger age classes, but rejected the need for and desirability of a lottery. The Selective Service System at first vigorously opposed any suggestion of a lottery; later, however, it was willing to discuss possible variations, but favored one which would retain the current system of quotas for induction from state and local pools.

When the Defense Department first offered an "illustrative" plan for reforming Selective Service, at the 1966 hearings, the idea of a lottery seemed a simple one. At that time the Defense plan called for retaining the current system of Selective Service classification and deferments. Priority for induction within Class I-A would continue to be accorded draft delinquents and volunteers.

Priority three would consist of men in the nineteen- or twenty-year age class, plus students completing their education and others losing temporary deferments in the past year. Those not inducted during their year of prime eligibility would remain liable for induction in an emergency up to age twenty-six (or to age thirty-five if previously deferred); but they would be in a lower priority, behind the succeeding prime age classes. As initially presented, the proposal did not even mention the word "lottery"; but under questioning it developed that some device would be required to select inductees from a potentially excessive number of men in priority three; and Assistant Secretary Thomas Morris stated a random lottery was the best of various possible techniques.

The Selective Service System had been aware by the end of 1964 that the Defense Department was interested in a lottery scheme, for the Defense Manpower Study had solicited the System's comments on that and a number of other ways of changing Selective Service policy and procedures. The System's response to this attempt at coordination was almost entirely negative, the theme throughout being that all was well with things the way they were.[75]

By the time of the 1966 hearings, even stronger lottery schemes were in the air, such as one presented to the House committee by Senator Edward Kennedy which called for minimizing deferments and for random selection by lottery from a national pool of I-A's. In those hearings, General Hershey rejected the Defense Department approach, the Kennedy approach, indeed all suggestions for using a lottery in any fashion at all. In so doing, he pursued three major themes emphasizing the lottery's shortcomings. One was that any lottery would replace human judgment with machine stupidity, and in this vein he stressed the potential absurdities: "In the Armed Forces I can see them, by the time we drew a one-legged man as No. 1 and say 'Here is your first boy,' you immediately know what would happen."[76] His second theme was that, if the Selective Service were to apply its human judgment on classification prior to a lottery, this would select out enough eligibles to make a lottery among the remainder redundant. Finally, Hershey constantly asserted that a lottery was administratively cumbersome, even infeasible. The first theme was irrelevant to any lottery scheme thus far seriously proposed; the second overlooked future difficulties facing the System in draining off the pool of eligibles; and the third rested on experience with a very different kind of lottery from those proposed, applied under the very different conditions of peak manpower demand in World War II. Nonetheless, Hershey's prestige as *the* expert on Selective Service, and the attitude of his friends among senior committee members, made it impossible for even the Defense Department's mild proposal to get a rational hearing.

One major task of the Marshall Commission, then, was to explore and resolve this interagency quarrel. In so doing, the commission reduced the problem to simple arithmetic: of some two million men reaching draft age each year (a figure to be reached and exceeded in the early 1970's), about three-quarters would qualify under current induction standards; the military services would require annual intakes of only 600,000 to 1 million, most of whom would be volunteers; how, then, should the needed 100,000 to 300,000 inductees be selected from the excess of nonvolunteers? Opting for minimal deferments rather than selection-out through channeling, the commission concluded a random lottery would be the fairest system. Endorsing this feature of the commission's proposals, President Johnson labeled it a "fair and impartial random (FAIR) system of selection"; and the Defense Department supported his endorsement enthusiastically.

Establishing the order of induction was, under terms of the existing law, a matter for Executive decision. Rather than break openly with the president on this point, something he had never done in the past, General Hershey simply reversed his public position on random selection. Testifying before Senator Kennedy's subcommittee, Hershey said: "You have the problem of trying to decide if some are going to escape. Who should it be? I think there, a random choice may satisfy better than what we have been doing in the past in the choosing of those who will not have to serve."[77] He even admitted that his earlier objection to replacing human judgment with a mechanical lottery did not really apply to the Defense Department and Marshal Commission proposals. But Hershey made it clear that his reversal stemmed from the president's decision, not a change of heart.

Thereafter, debate over the lottery focused on questions about its detailed operation. Neither the Marshall Commission, nor the Defense Department, nor the Clark Panel had explained precisely, ahead of the congressional hearings, just how they envisioned selection for induction from the young age classes would work. This failure accounted for much of the confused, sometimes exasperated and exasperating, questioning and testimony in the committee hearings. By the time of the House hearings in May, however, mostly thanks to the efforts of committee counsel Frank Slatinshek, much had been done to narrow the debate to two proposals, one built on the Defense Department's and Marshall Commission's approach, and the other constructed by Slatinshek in consultation with Selective Service officials, based on the Clark Panel's report.

By confining himself mostly to comments on other people's proposals, and restraining his enthusiasm for any single scheme, General Hershey managed both to stress the failure of others to do their homework before the hearing and to enhance his image as the expert. He used this advantage to promote two propositions, not inherently necessary in either scheme, that made him appear the judicious compromiser. One, a philosophy-saving proposition, was Hershey's insistence on maintaining the system of state and local quotas for induction. No one could show that this was working any real inequities; but spokesmen for the Defense Department and the Marshall Commission argued that military service was an individual's obligation to the nation, and ought to be imposed in a fashion reflecting that fact. Hershey's desire to preserve the existing quota system stemmed from his philosophy of making selection for service a matter of community decision. The other, a face-saver, was Hershey's suggestion that local boards could be given a randomized list of birthdays, and a randomized alphabet, changed perhaps once a year, to determine the order of picking men for induction. As presented, this seemed no more than a means of stressing how useful birth dates had always been to easy administration of the System.

Throughout the debate, Hershey carefully avoided coming to grips with the main argument of lottery proponents. Asked by committee counsel Slatinshek what inequity would be cured by the lottery, Hershey answered: "Well, because you are saying to people, if you have a chance to draw, it gives you justice." "May I interpret what you say?" asked Slatinshek. "You are saying that it gives the impression of greater equity but it does not in fact result in any greater equity?" Hershey responded: "I can see a lot of people reading things into that, but my answer is 'Yes.' "[78] This answer, however, construed the lottery proposal in the narrowest possible terms —as the substitution of a random sequence for date-of-birth sequence in determining who, among those not already selected out, would nonetheless escape induction merely because they were unneeded by the military service. So long as Selective Service channeling could keep the numbers of such men very small, Hershey could accept the lottery, or some form of it, and at the same time characterize it as redundant. Proponents of the lottery expected it to operate under very different circumstances; they saw it, not as an end in itself, but as a device to accommodate drastic reductions in the scope of channeling, as part of a larger pursuit of equity in the whole selection process. Hershey never responded to this lottery rationale, but he clearly could not and did not accept it. To do so would give away, not only his case for channeling, but also most of his argument for decentralizing Selective Service decisions to the local boards.

Local Board Autonomy and Organization for Selection

In mid-1966, a group of thirty House Republicans issued a series of statements on Selective Service, one of them containing the first attack by any sizeable group in Congress on the wide grant of discretionary powers to local boards: "National standards [for deferment and induction] are so imprecise," these members argued, "that neighboring boards will apply different criteria to identical cases, and that the drafting practices of a local board in one state may be almost entirely different from those of a local board in another." Even differences in local board work priorities for applying revisions in regulations could mean the difference, for men approaching age twenty-six, between induction or escape to priority five of Class I-A, as in the 1965-66 tightening of student deferments and lowering of induction standards.[79] The Marshall Commission examined these and similar charges, undertaking an extensive study of Selective Service operations in the field; and it produced hard evidence of wide variations in performance, among local and appeal boards and from state to state, amounting to a strong case for reorganization of the System.

Much of the variability, the commission noted, arose from variations in the socioeconomic characteristics of registrants in different board areas, a situation it granted the Selective Service System could not control. But it also found, in a survey of local board attitudes, evidence of wide variations in the way local board members viewed matters of classification and deferment: differences over the relative difficulty of making specific kinds of decisions; and differences over the relative importance of such factors in student deferment decisions as field and level of study and degree of student self-support (none of these factors was included in the publicized national guidelines). The commission found 40 percent of the boards wanted more specific guidance on student deferments, and 46 percent wanted more specific guidance on occupational deferments.

The commission also studied, by sampling, local board performance in specified classification and reclassification decisions. It concluded there were significant variations in performance, not attributable to socioeconomic characteristics of the registrants, both intrastate and interstate; and it found significant differences from state to state in the amount of intrastate variability. These conclusions strongly suggested that the performance of local boards was affected significantly both by interboard differences in attitudes, and by interstate differences in the amount of guidance given to local boards; and the suggestion of these effects was reinforced both by a sample study of individual registrants' records and by direct analysis of guidance issued by various state headquarters.

The commission also concluded that autonomy of boards and decentralization in the System had important impacts on the appeals procedures; it found wide differences among appeal boards, within and between states, in workloads, in proportion of local board decisions reversed by reclassification, and in the relative proportions of in-state and out-of-state appellants granted reclassification; and it found significant differences between local and appeal boards in their attitudes toward the relative difficulty of various classification decisions, the importance of various factors in making student and hardship deferment decisions, and the desirability of more specific guidance for such decisions. Moreover, despite the existence of some 8,000 advisors and 4,000 appeal agents (volunteers formally attached to the local boards), the commission concluded that most registrants were unaware of their appeal rights.

The Marshall Commission also examined critically the character-istics of the volunteer local board members. The all-male boards (as required by current regulations) were staffed almost exclusively by whites, two-thirds of them veterans; the median age was fifty-eight, with more than one-fifth over age seventy and some in their eighties and nineties; about a third had college educations; more than a fifth were professional men, part of the 73 percent in white collar occupations, while about 17 percent were farmers, and in-dustrial, service and other workers accounted for less than 10 per-cent. The commission also noted that, especially in metropolitan areas, board members neither knew nor were known by their reg-istrants, quite contrary to the Selective Service System's picture of the boards as "little groups of neighbors." And the commission sug-gested this anonymity promoted the tendency of registrants to exag-gerate the importance and power of board clerks. The Marshall Commission recommended measures to increase the turnover and reduce the average age of board members, as did the Clark Panel; the commission further emphasized the need to make the boards more representative of the population, expecially of ethnic groups, and called for opening membership to women; finally, the com-mission recommended that the president not be limited, as under current law, to appointing board candidates recommended by state governors.

Given all these findings concerning the characteristics and per-formance of local boards and the performance of the appeals sys-tem, the Marshall Commission nonetheless found no evidence that the variability in Selective Service procedures led to systematic bi-ases against Negroes or the poor in general. But the commission did conclude there was a strong need to impose greater uniformity and consistency on Selective Service operations.

In response, the Selective Service System never denied any of the Marshall Commission's specific findings on performance variability. But it did deny the critical need for, indeed even the possibility and desirability of, achieving policy uniformity through consistent appli-cation of clearly defined regulations. General Hershey argued that uniformity in selection for military service, as in any other aspect of life, simply did not and could not exist; he suggested that critics who used the term really meant that "If I am going into service, it is not uniform; if you are going in, I can tolerate it."[80] Even after publication of the Marshall Commission's findings, Hershey continued to resist the idea of uniform national standards, specifically in student and occupational deferments; so long as there is no nation-wide uniformity in the standards and practices of institutions of higher education, so long as the essentiality of an employee is a matter of specific local demand for his talents, and so long as no two cases are ever exactly alike, Hershey insisted, then the best place to make the decisions is local boards which can adapt to local and individual conditions. Moreover, he suggested, there was positive advantage in diverting much of the administrative decision-making from a single, central authority to groups of volunteers in local communities: "When things go right it is all right to be the fellow who presses the key, but when it goes wrong it is better to let somebody else have something to do with the decisions, too."[81]

In response to its conclusions on performance variability and the need for national standards—indeed, following naturally from its recommendations on channeling and the use of a lottery—the Marshal Commission also proposed what it felt were necessary organizational remedies to the current impact of Selective Service on equity and social goals. In treating a subject ventured by no other official report since that of the First Hoover Commission (which recommended transferring Selective Service to the Labor Department), the Marshall Commission urged a major consolidation of the System's administration. It called for replacing the state headquarters with eight regional offices; reducing the number of appeal boards from ninety-seven (one for each judicial district) to eight; reducing the more than four thousand local boards (roughly one per county) to some three to five hundred; and locating these boards with an equal number of area offices, allocated on a population basis with at least one in each state. Under this new structure, registration and initial classification would be the task of System employees in the area offices, operating under binding policy directives from National Headquarters and under the immediate supervision of the regional offices. The local boards would in effect become the first level of appeal from area office decisions, and they would be required to render written decisions for possible review by the regional appeal boards (appeal boards currently considered each case *de novo*). As noted earlier, although it recommended retaining the principle of voluntary and uncompensated service on Selective Service boards, the commission suggested measures for making the boards more representative of the public, for enforcing rotation of membership, and for increasing the president's discretion in appointing board members.

The relation between these sweeping organizational reforms and proposals for operational reforms was never far below the surface of the debate. The System's opposition to proposals for minimizing its channeling function sprang at least in part from realization that this would also minimize the need, as the System had expressed it, for local board discretion and autonomy. The System's opposition to reorganization was also reflected in its visceral reaction to the Defense Department's lottery proposal and its continuing reluctance to endorse any real change in the order of induction currently employed by local boards. And the same point of view was apparent in the System's rejection of the feasibility and desirability of imposing national standards. Nevertheless, given President Johnson's decision to postpone any recommendations on Selective System organization, the subject of organizational reforms was never fully developed in public and congressional debate.

A Question of Priorities

The whole debate over channeling, order of induction, local board autonomy, and organization of the Selective Service System, can be viewed in summary as a clash between the System, seeking to defend its record and protect the existing mode of operation, and the Marshall Commission, the participant most consistently promoting Selective Service reform and seeking hard grounds for altering priorities on issues of equity and social impact.

The Marshall Commission found that Selective Service operations produced two kinds of inequities in the distribution of military service among military-age youths. First, certain aspects of the classification process resulted in differential opportunities for avoiding military service among different socioeconomic groups. Deferment and exemption for unfitness weighted the incidence of service toward the relatively healthier and brighter youths and excluded many of the disadvantaged from service benefits. On the other hand,

and of greater concern to the commission, deferment for study and occupation, often convertible to exemption, weighted the chances of service avoidance in favor of the most highly educated (and presumably best-off) youths. Second, the deliberate promotion of decentralization and local board autonomy produced variations in deferments for study, occupation, and hardship, and thus presumably in service incidence, among youths in similar circumstances living in different parts of the country or simply registered with different local boards. The appeals system at best provided only limited correction of these differences, and may actually have aggravated some of them. At worst, as other critics suggested, the operation of Selective Service since the Korean War promoted an evasion mentality, and thus eroded the concept of military obligation, especially among the nation's future leaders, its college students.

The Selective Service System defended the results of its operations on two general grounds. First, differential opportunities for service and service avoidance, insofar as these really existed, were fully justifiable in terms of military or other social goals. After all, not even the Marshall Commission was suggesting radical changes in the fitness standards for military service. Any inter-group inequities arising from student and occupational deferments, and the conversion of these into exemptions, were surely justified by the nation's interest in and demand for the products of higher education. Second, the System insisted that a national program for procuring and channeling manpower had to be adapted to local and individual circumstances. All the evidence for variations in local and appeal boards' performance simply proved this adaptation was indeed taking place.

These differences over channeling, order of induction, and performance variability led to very different conclusions about the proper organization, as well as the operation, of the Selective Service System. To the System itself, the current decentralized and locally autonomous organization was ideal for pursuing its operational policy of granting as many deferments as military manpower demands allowed. The Marshall Commission, given its desire for minimal deferments and exemptions based on clearly defined and enforced national guidelines, wanted a streamlined organization more directly controlled by National Headquarters.

Underlying these differences were two quite different sets of attitudes toward the importance of distributing military service burdens equitably and toward the kinds of substantive policy goals which might justify deviations from a perfectly even distribution. Neither side, of course, favored achieving equity or social goals through universal imposition of military or other service obligations. But the Marshall Commission did favor distributing as evenly as possible the risk of having military service imposed; the only deviations it found justifiable were those clearly related to identifiable national, mostly military, needs. The Selective Service System, by contrast, favored recognizing many nonmilitary social needs as possible grounds for avoiding military service, adapting these to national, local, and individual circumstances as far as current demands for military manpower would allow, and thereby assuring that all those serving involuntarily were needed more by the military services than they were "needed" elsewhere; equity, being unattainable anyway, took second place to meeting these other goals. These two sets of attitudes really amounted to differing priorities for responding to problems of equity and social impact in military manpower procurement. Nowhere was this more clear than in the contrast between the Selective Service System's self-conceived function of channeling, and the Marshall Commission's choice of a report title—"In Pursuit of Equity: Who Serves When Not All Serve?"

3. *Defeat of the Reform Movement*

By spring of 1967, when the Armed Services committees opened hearings on the extension of Selective Service, debate in the preceding two years had probed all the fundamental issues of military manpower procurement policy and had raised a variety of proposals for change ranging from wholly voluntary procurement to universally compulsory systems. At this point, however, the debate narrowed to consider mostly proposals to revise, rather than replace, the current mixed voluntary-compulsory procurement system.

The basic agenda for legislative debate was set by President Johnson's message of March 6.[82] In that message, the Administration justified its call for a four-year extension of Selective Service on familiar grounds. President Johnson noted the steps already taken to strengthen volunteering, including an average pay raise of 33 percent in the past four years and both in-service and veteran's benefits; he stressed the steps taken to reduce military manpower demand through civilian substitution, and to increase supply through Project 100,000; and he promised to recommend a program of medical scholarships to reduce the pressures of the doctors' draft. Nonetheless, the president rejected the possibility of relying on volunteers alone, arguing that the costs would be too high and that the system would lose essential flexibility. In congressional floor debate there were limited challenges to this position, as some members sought moves in the direction of a voluntary system. In effect, however, legislative debate over issues of military effectiveness, cost efficiency, and compulsions was limited to considering minor variations in the pattern of military manpower procurement policy suggested in 1948, confirmed in 1951 and 1952, and followed ever since.

The rest of the agenda for legislative debate, however, raised the possibility of major departures from that pattern of policy. The old pattern, most clearly set in 1951, had sought to allocate a limited manpower supply between military and civilian needs during a partial mobilization of the nation's security forces and its economy; and these goals had dominated policy then and in the decade and a half following the Korean War. In 1967, however, the Administration adopted the theme of the Marshall Commission: who serves when not all serve? In pursuit of this theme, the president's message proposed a number of legislative and administrative changes in Selective Service channeling, order of induction, local board autonomy, and some aspects of the System's organization. The thrust of these proposals was toward changing the older pattern of policy, through a new emphasis on the goal of equity and an altered view of the relation between military manpower procurement and nonmilitary social goals.

Recognizing inequities inherent in the current process of channeling, President Johnson endorsed some, though not all, the changes recommended by the Marshall Commission. He agreed that Project 100,000 was an important step toward wider opportunities for disadvantaged youths to benefit from military service, and promised it would be continued. He made no recommendations on dependency or occupational deferments, but he did note that lowering the age at induction would reduce the numbers eligible for them. He did propose using his authority to eliminate future deferments for all graduate students except those pursuing medical and dental courses (this would also have an effect on occupational deferments). Noting the sharp difference of opinion within the commission on undergraduate deferments, the president said he wanted further debate of this question before making any decision; but he did criticize existing opportunities to compound these deferments into exemptions. On deferments for reservists, the president noted steps already taken to standardize reserve recruiting, and promised to give youths under draft age priority in reserve enlistment; he noted actions taken to call up those reservists not satisfactorily fulfilling their obligations, and recommended that legislative authority for such calls be made permanent, and he asked for standby authority to supplement recruiting for Reserve and National Guard units by direct induction.

President Johnson also noted the Marshall Commission's critique of the current order of induction among men in Class I-A, stressing the uncertainty this created for both those youths and their employers, the proliferation of applications for dependency and occupational deferment, and the military services' desire for younger men. He stated he would issue an order focusing inductions on youths age nineteen. Moreover, he instructed General Hershey, in collaboration with the Defense Secretary, to develop a "Fair and Impartial Random (FAIR) system of selection to become fully operational before January 1, 1969."

The president was much more cautious in dealing with the Marshall Commission's recommendations concerning local board autonomy, the appeals system, and organization of the Selective Service System. "We cannot lightly discard an institution with so valuable a record of effectiveness and integrity. Neither can we afford to preserve it, if we find that in practice it cannot adapt to the new controlling concept of equal and uniform treatment." The president directed the secretary of defense, the director of the Selective Service System, and the director of the Bureau of the Budget to create a special task force to compare the cost effectiveness of the current structure with that of the reorganized system proposed by the commission. In the meantime, he directed General Hershey to assure that advice and assistance were readily available to all registrants in making appeals, to assure that appellants' rights were being fully protected, to improve the System's public information programs, and to work with the governors (through Farris Bryant, director of the Office of Emergency Planning) to assure that local boards were "truly representative of the communities they serve"; and he requested periodic progress reports on the last subject.

One recommendation to Congress, not mentioned in the president's message, was directed at reducing the autonomy of local boards in making decisions on occupational and student deferments. This was a call for deleting the proviso, added in 1951, that local boards could not be required to make such decisions solely on the basis of criteria provided by the national government.

To these proposals, Congress added two more subjects—congressional oversight of the System, and enforcement of Selective Service law.

The 1967 agenda for debate over military manpower procurement was, in the variety of specific proposals, long and complicated. But the fundamental alternatives at stake were simple. One was to preserve existing policy and programs more or less intact; defenders of this alternative continued to emphasize the principle of a universal military obligation selectively applied to meet both military and civilian needs for manpower in a partially mobilized economy. The other alternative involved important changes in the principle and process of selection; those seeking reform urged greater concern for equity and an altered vision of nonmilitary needs.

Congressional debate over the president's recommendations and plans for Selective Service reform was extensive and, at least in the House, heated. The Administration sought to alter the older pattern of manpower procurement policy in some important ways; but opponents in Congress managed to stay that effort, at least for the time being, and in some ways even hardened the older pattern of policy.[83]

Prospects for reform were still good at the end of Senate deliberations. The Senate committee's report was not very enthusiastic about the reforms the president proposed to undertake on his own authority, especially the limitation of student deferments and introduction of a random lottery. Rather than restrict that authority, though, the committee's bill simply refused the president's request for deletion

of the proviso protecting local board autonomy in student and occupational deferment decisions. Otherwise, the bill gave the president most of what he asked for. On the Senate floor, managers of the
bill had little difficulty in defeating the several amendments proposed (five of these would have increased reliance on voluntary recruiting or otherwise limited the impact of compulsions, another
would have given registrants the right to counsel in appearances before local boards, and another would have deleted the proviso protecting the local board autonomy). In accepting that bill, then, the
Senate left the president in a position to undertake most of the reforms he had already endorsed.[84]

The House Armed Services Committee proved much less easily
satisfied. Its reported amendments, reflecting schizoid tendencies
rare in the committee's public record, sought both to blunt and to
strengthen the president's authority to reform Selective Service; and
it added measures of its own seeking to strengthen enforcement of
Selective Service law.[85]

In the matter of deferments, the committee mostly followed
recommendations of the Clark Panel. It provided a blanket peacetime deferment of full-time college students until graduation, drop-
out, or age twenty-four; and it forbad further deferment of such
students except in cases of extreme hardship or for graduate study
in limited fields. It proposed establishment of a National Manpower
Resource Board to advise the Selective Service director, after consultation with the National Security Council, on what limited fields
should be considered for graduate study and occupational deferments.

The House committee reacted strongly to the president's announced plans for random selection of nineteen-year-olds for induction. In revising the provision of existing law giving the president
authority to establish the order of induction among qualified registrants, the committee bill did leave him with authority to induct first
from that age class; and it recommended a scheme of induction much
like that developed by the Clark Panel and the committee counsel.
Its version also left the president with authority to substitute random
selection for the birth date order of induction; but it provided that
no such change could go into effect until Congress had been given
sixty days in which to reject it by resolution of both houses.

Contrary to the Clark Panel's recommendations, and reflecting pressure within the committee for some reforms along lines of the Marshall Commission's recommendations, the committee's bill deleted the local-board-autonomy proviso and required the president to establish, wherever practicable, firm national criteria for classification, and to require uniform application of these criteria by all local boards. But the committee rejected another reform move to replace local board quotas with induction from a national pool.

The committee recommended some changes in Selective Service organization, but these were minor. It repeated a Senate provision allowing inactive reserve officers to serve as appeal agents and advisors; it prohibited service on local or appeal boards for more than twenty-five years or past age seventy-five; it changed the title of "chief clerk" of local boards to "executive secretary" and limited service in this position to ten years; and it established a new position of deputy director of Selective Service for public affairs. As did its Senate counterpart, the House committee declared its opposition to any major reorganization of the System.

Seeking to tighten oversight of the Selective Service System, the bill provided for quarterly reports by the director on the System's operations, in addition to the annual report already required. This was a response to the Clark Panel's recommendation that the two Armed Services Committees monitor the System more closely than in the past.

The House committee's bill pushed strongly in the area of law enforcement. It provided that any registrant who prolonged litigation of his draft classification until he reached age twenty-six should nonetheless remain liable for induction if found qualified. It reinforced the provision in existing law attempting to forbid judicial review of local board and appeals system decisions on classification until the individual classified has accepted or refused an induction order. It required trial and appellate courts to give precedence on their dockets to criminal cases arising under the act, removing the attorney general's existing discretion in requesting such precedence. And it required the attorney general either to comply with requests of the director of Selective Service for prosecution of cases or to submit an explanatory report to Congress.

In much the same spirit, the committee's bill sought to tighten provisions for recognizing conscientious objection to military service. It struck out the 1948 clause defining "religious training and belief," on the theory that this might reverse the effect of the Supreme Court's *Seeger* decision (which had widened the concept of religious objection) by removing the basis for it. It eliminated all provisions for Justice Department hearings in conscientious objector cases. Further, it revised the procedures distinguishing between those objecting to combatant service only, and those objecting to any military service; instead, all persons classed as conscientious objectors by the System would, if otherwise qualified, be inducted for noncombatant military service; thereafter, those considered by the System to be conscientiously opposed to any military service would be furloughed by the appropriate military department secretary, without pay and allowances, to perform two years of civilian service.

Reaction on the House floor was vigorous, but ineffective. In order to confine debate to a single day, consideration of most proposed amendments was restricted far more severely than is usual when a significant minority, including members of the sponsoring committee, opposes a bill. Later, one House member reflected the general bitterness of reform proponents over their treatment: "We are asking young men to give up 2 years of their lives, and we will not give them 2 days of our time to consider this matter."[86] Several proposed amendments attracted visible support from one or another of two sources: first, those who were not satisfied with the committee bill's scant inclusion of some reforms and strict limitations on others, including some junior members of the committee from both parties; and second, those supporting stronger moves toward reliance on volunteers, including both conservative midwestern Republicans and members who were dovish or otherwise disgruntled over the Vietnam War. The strongest show of opposition, and the longest discussion of a single proposal, came on an amendment by Representative Rumsfeld (R., Ill.), to limit extension of Selective Service to two years. This lost, 77-160. Rumsfeld had already declared his intent, if that amendment failed, to make a two-year limitation the formal issue in a motion to recommit. This might have been a final rallying point for the opposition, but it was denied them by a quick parliamentary maneuver. Representative O'Konski (R., Wis.), who had been inactive in both hearings and debate, served the interests of other senior committee members by offering an unqualified recommital motion that had no appeal for either group of opponents; and Rumsfeld was unable even to get a roll call vote. The House bill then passed, 362-69.

Reform proponents were bitter not only over the conduct of floor debate, but also over the general antireform tone of the House bill. That bill did contain two important reforms—the narrowing of opportunities for students to compound deferments into exemptions, and the requirement that the president enforce national standards for classification. And, in floor debate, the committee had retreated from its proposal to induct all conscientious objectors prior to assigning those eligible to alternative work programs. But the bill's general tone, supported by committee leaders of both parties, favored preservation of the older policy pattern and more rigorous action against those resisting the draft.

The bill that emerged from conference was even less satisfactory to the reformers.[87] It included several noncontroversial policy and program changes: permission for a registrant to enlist in the reserves up to his date of induction (instead of the date of his induction notice); permanent authority to call up reservists not satisfactorily meeting their training obligations; limitation of local and appeal board service to twenty-five years or age seventy-five, and opening of such service to women; limitation of service as chief board clerk, now titled "executive secretary," to ten years; and requirement of semiannual Selective Service reports to Congress. The conference version retained all the new enforcement provisions added by the House committee. It also preserved the effect of House attempts to redefine conscientious objection; although it restored the 1948 clause excluding political, sociological, philosophical, or personal views from the meaning of "religious training and belief," it continued to pursue reversal of the *Seeger* decision by striking out reference to a "Supreme Being." But the conference committee's treatments of channeling, local board autonomy, and order of induction were the most objectionable retreats from what might have been a reasonably reformist compromise of House and Senate provisions.

Accepting the House committee's approach to channeling, the conference bill required deferment of all full-time undergraduate students, restricted further deferment of those students to cases of hardship (excluding both marriage and paternity as *prima facie* grounds) or for graduate study or work in limited fields, and required that those fields be established on advice of the National Security Council. But the conference bill severely limited the potential effects of this approach: instead of requiring the president to set and enforce national criteria for classification, it simply stated that he might set such criteria; more importantly, it reaffirmed the 1951 proviso protecting local board autonomy from imposition of national criteria. The requirement for national standards was the sole reform proposal among several promoted by Representative Schweiker (R., Pa.), a junior committee member, to survive even this far; and he and others on the committee felt their conference managers, all senior committee members unhappy with this reform, did not fight very hard for it.[88] Finally, the conference accepted a House provision limiting the president's discretion on order of induction to a narrowing of the prime age class; and it strengthened the House restriction on random selection by requiring new statutory authority for any change in the current date-of-birth induction order. The conference report attributed this change to Senate conferees' doubts about the propriety of a legislative veto; in fact, Senate committee chairman Russell did promote such doubts (to the surprise of those familiar with his past record on the subject); but the result could not have displeased the House conferees.[89]

Enthusiasts for reform later noted there was no real White House pressure to promote the president's program at the committee and floor stages, or even to protect parts of it in conference. Neither Secretary McNamara nor any service secretary testified at committee hearings. Moreover, the content and wording of the conference report suggest either that the conferees listened only to officials of the Selective Service System, or that they and their staffers had absorbed thoroughly the philosophy and rhetoric of the System. In the end, after brief protests, the conference report was accepted by the Senate (72-23) and House (377-29); and the president signed the new four-year extension act on June 30, 1967, just ahead of the deadline.[90]

The narrowed legislative debate over Selective Service resulted, substantively, in defeat for the reformers. Their efforts to inject greater concern for equity into policy and programs met with small success, and there were no firm indications that the procurement system might soon be revised to reflect social needs different from those of the early cold war years. There was symbolic evidence that Congress might be rethinking the pattern of policy followed during and since the Korean War: then the Selective Service Act had been retitled the Universal Military Training and Service Act, reflecting hopes for a policy never fulfilled; now a third title, The Military Selective Service Act, was adopted to emphasize its fundamental purpose of meeting military manpower needs. What this and other revisions meant in terms of shifting priorities for future policy, though, was ambiguous at best.

Renewed debates since 1965 had, nonetheless, reshaped most issues of military manpower procurement policy. This, and a wide range of proposals for policy change, raised too much ferment to be settled in a single, narrow, ambiguous legislative response. In the wider debate over Selective Service reform, and even more sweeping changes, the defeat of 1967 proved only a temporary setback.

IV.   RENEWED CHALLENGES

The ambiguous outcome of the attempt at Selective Service reform in 1967 was not altogether the fault of the policy-makers. In 1965, the paths to reform and possible replacement of Selective Service seemed clear and simple: close, or narrow, the gap between voluntary supply and military demand for manpower through civilian substitution, more flexible service entry standards, and increased pay and benefits; adopt a more skeptical attitude toward Selective Service channeling as a means for adjusting military and nonmilitary needs for manpower; and revise Selective Service procedures and organization to meet head on the inequities inherent in selective imposition of a universal military obligation. In the next two years, though, escalated fighting in Vietnam, and increasingly vigorous protests against that war and against the draft machinery supporting it, infected every major issue of military manpower procurement policy with ambiguity, and obscured the simple paths to reform and change.

Despite the ambiguities, developments after 1967 indicated that challenges to the older pattern of manpower procurement policy, and to Selective Service's central role in that pattern, remained very much alive. These changes and challenges pointed in two different, though not contradictory, directions: increased reliance on volunteers, perhaps to the point of limiting Selective Service to stand-by status; and reform of Selective Service along lines proposed in 1967.

1.   *Moves toward All-Volunteer Forces*

The successful response of Selective Service after mid-1965, providing manpower for an escalated war in Vietnam, illustrated the System's usefulness to a strategy of flexible deterrence. To most members of Congress, 1967 was just not an appropriate year for replacing, or even seriously reforming, so responsive a manpower procurement machine. At the same time, critics of the war and of Selective Service were inspired by their experience to suggest that too much procurement flexibility could be dangerous: it had in 1965, and might in the future, enable an Administration to translate a strategy of flexible deterrence into political-military responses easily escalated but agonizingly difficult to reverse.

Several developments after 1967 altered the content, but did not shift the character, of arguments over the all-volunteer proposition. The most dramatic of these was the beginning of deescalation in Vietnam. This had a spectacular impact on presidential politics in 1968, and an equally visible impact on troop levels in Vietnam after mid-1969. Less visible, but highly relevant to manpower procurement planning, were reductions in active force strength goals, from 3.46 million in mid-1969, to 3.16 million for mid-1970, and 2.91 million for mid-1971.[91] As in the 1965–67 expansion, most of this reduction was aimed at ground force, especially Army, strengths; and these reductions were accompanied by declining draft calls, already down from the 1966–67 peaks .

As gross demand for military manpower declined, several other developments had uncertain effects on the demand-supply balance. The small but significant trend toward civilian substitution, begun in 1965, faltered as the new Nixon Administration pressed for cuts in the federal civil work force.[92] Project 100,000 was also trimmed somewhat, to a goal of accepting about 75,000 marginally qualified (New Standards) youths in 1970–71; but this paralled cuts in total intake. (There was no official disenchantment with the program; but follow-up studies on those accepted showed results close to what might have been predicted, given earlier arguments in 1957–58 for raising entry standards: among New Standards men, rates of failure to complete basic training and more advanced skill courses, and of courts-martial convictions, were over twice those for fully qualified servicemen; even so, over 90 percent of the former finished their first service tours.)[93] Pay raises after 1967, including a 12.6 percent basic pay increase in 1969, continued to emphasize cost-of-living parity and retention, as reenlistment rates continued weak. Major pay reform proposals, growing out of an in-depth study in 1967, and calling for an annual active service pay increase of more than $5 billion, were postponed indefinitely. On the other hand, a pay raise proposed for early 1971 included major increases for men with less than two years' service. Finally, in 1969 and 1970, the Army began experimenting with selective lateral-entry recruiting; it offered enlistment at corporal and sergeant levels to civilian medical technicians and construction workers, and announced plans to expand such recruiting to other skills, focusing on junior college graduates in a wide range of vocational and technical programs.[94] (The Navy has used lateral-entry recruiting to acquire skilled construction workers off and on beginning in World War II.)

All these developments, and the doubtful chance of early and rapid reversal of American military commitments in Southeast Asia, left in considerable doubt the prospects for all-volunteer forces. In early 1969, President Nixon fulfilled a cautious campaign promise by appointing a commission, chaired by former Defense Secretary Thomas Gates, to advise him on that subject. In February, 1970, the Gates Commission turned in a report notable for its optimism, but effectively silent on the question of introducing such a system while fighting continued in Vietnam.[95]

The Gates Commission attempted answers to many doubts about an all-volunteer system. Its estimates of total annual cost were markedly lower than those of the 1965 Defense Manpower Study, reflecting intervening pay increases, more careful economic analyses, and a fundamentally more favorable attitude as well. It estimated a first-year cost of $3.24 billion, including increases in basic pay, proficiency (special skills) pay, reserve pay, Medical Corps expenses, and recruiting and ROTC costs; it noted that about $540 million of this increase would be recovered in income taxes; and it estimated long-term annual cost, net of savings through reduced turnover and recovery of taxes, of $2.1 billion to support a 2.5 million-man active force (slightly less than pre-Vietnam strength). The commission rejected notions that an all-volunteer system would further isolate the military services from civil society, noting that most enlisted men and officers already were volunteers. And it estimated that Negroes, currently 10.6 percent of the active enlisted forces, would constitute about 15 percent of an all-volunteer force, a proportion only slightly larger than that projected for a mixed volunteer-draftee force. For flexibility in emergencies, the commission argued, first recourse should be to the Ready Reserves, also to be recruited voluntarily; but it gave scant attention to analyzing the relative costs and military value of active forces and truly ready reserves. The commission also recommended a standby draft, requiring congressional action for activation, a proposal reminiscent of Carl Vinson's in 1950.

Understandably, given its sponsor, the Gates Commission only hinted at more radical arguments for abandoning the draft. Specifically, it did not view presidential flexibility in committing military forces as dangerous to liberty and peace. It did emphasize traditional American reliance on volunteers in peacetime, and the responsiveness of Congress in the past to emergency requests for draft authority. It argued that a generation's experience with the draft had proved costly, in real economic terms, in the unequal burdens and uncertainties imposed on many youths, and in damage to "the political fabric of our society and . . . the delicate web of shared values that alone enables a free society to exist."[96]

In sum, the Gates Commission offered probably the best case possible for an all-volunteer system. Whether its case would prove persuasive, in enactment and in implementation, remained to be seen. In April, 1970, President Nixon endorsed the commission's goal, stressed the proposed 1971 pay raise as a step in that direction, but stated neither he nor anyone else could predict when an all-volunteer system might be achieved.[97]

2. Moves toward Selective Service Reform

After 1967, residual hopes for constructing a Selective Service reform victory out of the aftermath of legislative defeat were not quickly met. An important setback, easily anticipated, was the failure of President Johnson's inter-agency task force, assigned to review the Selective Service System's organization, to come up with any significant changes. The task force viewed its charter in very limited terms: it was to advise on the specific organizational reforms proposed by the Marshall Commission, especially in terms of budget costs relative to those of the existing organization; but it was to leave any advice on the selection system itself to the Selective Service System. This ignored, of course, the close connection between organizational autonomy of the local boards and the channeling and order-of-induction aspects of selection procedure; but, as one task force consultant put it, he could see no need to alter the System's organization if all that was wanted was new policy.[98] The result was a foregone conclusion: the task force endorsed the current organization, stressing the need for local boards to adapt policy to local conditions and to absorb some of the pressure against inductions that an unpopular war produced. Although it recommended a few measures toward increasing uniformity in the guidance given local boards, and stepping up the System's own audit of classification decisions, the Selective Service System found most of these measures too expensive. Commenting on these results, General Hershey also criticized the original recommendations of the Marshall Commission as having ignored past experience: "I've wondered what they'd been eating to come to the conclusions they did. . . . Maybe they're the wave of the future—I couldn't say—it hasn't come in yet."[99]

Other events suggested there were grounds for doubting the value of local boards in deflecting antidraft pressures. Partly in response to stepped-up draft protests on a nation-wide scale, the Justice Department brought to trial several of the more prominent spokesmen for the antidraft cause, including Dr. Benjamin Spock and the Reverend William S. Coffin. The government won conviction of all but one man charged with conspiracy to promote draft resistance; but an appeals court later acquitted Spock and one other defendant, and required new trials for the others should the government decide to pursue its case. Later the Justice Department dropped the whole case. In the meantime, annual prosecutions for draft violations increased ten-fold over the pre-Vietnam level, to some 3,500 in 1968–69, despite increasingly stiff sentences given those convicted. Legal attacks on the Selective Service System's enforcement powers met with considerable success, though; and in 1970 the Supreme Court struck down the System's practice of moving draft delinquents up to top priority for induction, and ruled the 1967 congressional limitation on pre-induction suits did not preclude suits against punitive reclassification.[100]

Several post-1967 moves did amount to partial, piecemeal reform of Selective Service. In mid-1967, President Johnson implemented the new statutory provision for blanket deferment of undergraduates; he continued deferments for graduate students in medical and allied fields and for other students beginning their second or later year of graduate study before that fall; and he allowed one-year-only deferments for first-year graduate students.[101] These initial moves had little effect on the existing pattern of deferments. In early 1968, the National Security Council concluded that deferment of graduate students in other than medical and related fields, and occupational deferments, were no longer essential to the national interest; and the Selective Service System so notified its local boards. The boards still retained, and exercised, their discretion in these deferments; but even partial compliance with the new guidelines had two kinds of consequences: one was sharp, but far from disastrous, reductions in graduate student enrollments, beginning in fall, 1968; the other was a three- to four-fold increase in the proportion of college graduates among new draftees after mid-1968, as graduating seniors and graduate students losing their deferments found themselves among the oldest in the available group of men in Class I-A.[102]

These consequences reinforced the running antiwar, antidraft critique of and legal attack on Selective Service (a national draft resistance more apparent than real in its effect on current inductions), producing pressures for further reform. The Nixon Administration responded with two measures, both of which stirred ineffective counter-resistance in Congress.

In May, 1969, the president asked for authority to inaugurate a random lottery that would, in turn, make it feasible to focus draft pressure on the younger men in Class I-A. Both the Senate and House Armed Services Committees stalled for several months, partly because there was no firm presidential pressure for the change, and partly because this measure might reopen the whole range of Selective Service policies to attack by reformist blocs seeking wider changes. In late September, President Nixon focused his and the nation's attention on the lottery proposal; but it took two more months for him and the committee leaders to assuage the reformers sufficiently with promises of more to come in 1970.[103]

Congressional action merely removed the 1967 ban on changes to the oldest-first induction order. Once authorized to move, the Administration immediately introduced its scheme, assigning lottery numbers to registrants in a random drawing of 366 birth dates, with secondary numbers determined by matching registrants' last initials with a randomly drawn alphabet. The first drawing affected all registrants reaching age nineteen, but not age twenty-six, by December 31, 1969; later drawings will assign lottery numbers to men reaching age nineteen in successive calendar years. A registrant's lottery number set the order in which he might be inducted during his calendar year of prime liability; that year being either the one following his receiving a lottery number (the year he reaches age twenty) or the year in which he loses his deferment. (Registrants not inducted during their calendar year of prime liability drop to a lower priority in subsequent years, and lose all liability for induction at age twenty-six, or age thirty-five if previously deferred.) Despite evidence that the first drawing was not truly random, no one seriously questioned its impartiality; and use of the new lottery-based order of induction began with the call for January, 1970.[104]

Given plans to place calls on Selective Service for about one-third the number expected to become available during 1970, the Administration at first predicted that men with lottery numbers in the lower third of the drawing could expect to be inducted, those in the upper third would probably escape, and those in the middle third would have to remain uncertain for the rest of the year. This calculation reckoned without several factors the System should have anticipated: many men with low numbers did not become eligible, through loss of deferment, until late in the calendar year; any man in Class I-A with a low number had a strong inducement to seek enlistment in the reserves, or even in the active forces, or to find a job his board considered deferable; and these and other individual changes had differential effects on each local board's pool of eligibles. To avoid the worst effects of this situation, in which men with high numbers might be called by mid-year in some board areas, but not called at all in others, the Selective Service System introduced a modification in its local quota procedure: it limited boards to calling men with lottery numbers 30 or lower in January, 60 or lower in February, and so forth, even if this meant not meeting a monthly local quota; in this way, no one with a number higher than 150 could be inducted before the end of May, after which large numbers of graduating students would enter the local pools and relieve the pressure. Estimates were that the top lottery number reached by any board during 1970 would be 240.[105]

In early October, 1969, President Nixon announced a second reform move: General Hershey would be replaced as director of Selective Service in mid-February. Some news reports suggested Hershey was sacrificed to the looming "moratorium" demonstrations against the Vietnam War, but he had been losing friends within government for years. Some Defense Department manpower officials no doubt remembered his successful resistance to their reform proposals in 1966–67; and his endorsement of early induction for draft delinquents continued to discomfit the legal consciences of some Justice Department officials, including Solicitor General Erwin Griswold. (Within two weeks of the announcement that Hershey would be replaced, Griswold refused to sign two Justice Department briefs to the Supreme Court defending the delinquency concept and procedure; later, as noted above, the court found against the government in both cases.) Also working against Hershey were his age, seventy-six, and his long failing eyesight. (In 1968, Hershey jokingly referred to Representative Hebert, chairman of a new House subcommittee monitoring Selective Service performance, as a "blind watchdog" set to watch over a blind administrator.) Finding a successor to Hershey proved difficult. By mid-February, several candidates had refused the job; another had withdrawn after informal rejection by the Senate Armed Services Committee's chairman and ranking minority member; and Hershey was replaced temporarily by a long-time aide. Not until mid-March was the new director appointed and confirmed—Curtis W. Tarr, an Air Force assistant secretary and, earlier, president of Lawrence University.[106]

Congressional interest in Selective Service reform revived considerably by early 1970. In October, 1969, Senator Kennedy initiated hearings before his subcommittee of the Senate Judiciary Committee. One witness, former Attorney General Ramsey Clark, offered a strong critique of the Selective Service System's delinquency procedures. Other witnesses included spokesmen for a group of reform-minded House Republicans, and two political scientists who summarized and commented on their own incisive examination of Selective Service operations. One of the latter was James Davis, whose preliminary work with Kenneth Dolbeare led both of them to positions on the Marshall Commission's staff in 1966; their published work assembled data on Selective Service activities and surveys of public attitudes into a damaging attack on the System's case for local board autonomy. The other, Gary Wamsley, reviewed his study of local boards in Pittsburgh and the Pennsylvania state headquarters, based on interviews and direct observations; he strongly reinforced the conclusion that local boards neither truly represented their localities nor made consistent decisions on deferments "in the national interest." In February, 1970, the Kennedy subcommittee recommended major changes in Selective Service deferments and the System's organization, similar to those suggested by the Marshall Commission.[107]

In April, in his message endorsing the goal of an all-volunteer force, President Nixon cautioned that the draft would have to be phased out gradually, not abandoned or put on stand-by status immediately. In the meantime, he also endorsed several major draft reform measures. He announced an immediate end to new deferments for occupation or fatherhood. He asked Congress to remove the 1967 provision for mandatory deferment of undergraduate students; if discretionary authority were restored in this area, he said, then he would end new deferments for undergraduates and for youths in apprentice training programs. He asked Congress for authority to suspend the statutory requirement that draft calls be subdivided into local board quotas; this would allow application of the lottery system to a national pool, each board calling men with the same sequence numbers each month. Soon after, draft director Curtis Tarr publicly reviewed his own efforts to revamp Selective Service procedures and personnel. State directors, he said, were being urged to recommend that their governors nominate younger, more racially representative replacements for the 12 to 15 percent of board members who leave annually. He was also considering a reduction in the number of local boards. Most important, he announced the appointment of a new general counsel, whose first major task would be to review all the regulations, memoranda, and directives currently guiding the work of state and local draft officials; improvements in this area, Tarr hoped, would lead to more uniform decisions by local boards.[108]

As with the proposal for all-volunteer forces, the prospects for draft reform remained uncertain in mid-1970. In general outline, and in many details, the Nixon Administration was promoting changes close to those recommended three years earlier by the Marshall Commission. Whether President Nixon's interest in reform would prove more active and more successful than President Johnson's remained to be seen. Much would depend on the energy of, and the backing given, the new draft director. Even at best, the Administration would find it difficult to reshape the thinking of Selective Service officials and congressional leaders, tutored for years in General Hershey's philosophy of local board autonomy in making national manpower decisions. Nor would it be easy to disentangle Selective Service policy and practice from the many direct beneficiaries of channeling—young fathers and their families, reservists and the reserves, students and universities, school teachers and school systems, engineers and industries. If the draft had, especially in recent years, torn at the nation's "web of shared values," it had also created a complex net of disparate interests; these interests would at least make the reform of Selective Service a noisier business than had been its administrative triumph a decade earlier.

chapter six

Military Manpower Policy, Past and Future

I. POLICY ISSUES AND POLICY CHANGE, 1945–1970

Over the past quarter-century, five major sets of issues shaped debates and decisions on military manpower procurement. Support of national security was the predominant goal, but policy evolved only partly in response to changing perceptions of what constitutes an effective military establishment. Policy and programs also responded to shifting attitudes toward questions of costs, compulsions, equity, and impact on nonmilitary social goals. The content of debate shifted several times, reflecting changes in the relative importance accorded one or another issue, changing perceptions of how programs affect policy goals, and growing or waning influence of parties to the debates.

1. *Military Needs versus Traditional Resistance to Conscription*

In the early postwar years, the central issues of manpower procurement were framed in fairly simple terms of voluntary versus universal versus selective military training and service; and the dominant considerations were those of meeting military manpower requirements within narrowly perceived budget limits and of the need and desirability of doing so through compulsions. At the outset, the Administration hoped that the public and Congress would recognize a need for greater military strength in the postwar years than they had been willing or asked to provide before the war, assumed that they would not support large active forces, but expected that they would accept Universal Military Training as a means of providing military strength through large, trained reserves. Underlying these hopes were two assumptions: that the proper course for postwar military policy was an orderly transition to a peacetime establishment; and that the proper goal for this transition was small active forces, manned by volunteers and backed by large, well-trained reserves. The chief proponents of UMT and of arguments for reliance on mobilizable reserves were General Marshall and the ground Army. The Navy, traditionally the proponent of a fleet-in-being and a less than secondary role for reserves, did not oppose UMT, but did not promote it enthusiastically. The Army Air Forces dissented from some of the assumptions behind UMT, arguing that the chief reliance for defense must be on powerful air forces; but its dissent was not formally heard, and even outside support for the air power argument had little effect on the early debates over postwar policy.

The major opposition came instead from persons and groups who agreed that the wartime armed forces should be transformed into a small peacetime establishment as quickly as possible, and that those peacetime forces should be recruited, not conscripted. But these opponents—chiefly church, labor, farm, education, and peace-group leaders—challenged the Administration's proposals by arguing that peacetime conscription in any form, whether for service or only for training, was a contradiction of all that was best in American political and social traditions.

The result until 1948 was stalemate. After three years' debate UMT supporters had little more to show than two favorable committee reports and a bill pending before an unfriendly House Rules Committee. Selective Service barely survived a precipitous demobilization, saved only by the obvious need for occupation troops and wide agreement that veterans should be relieved of such duties as early as possible. Nine months after a last-minute postwar extension, Selective Service was abandoned in March, 1947, as economy-inspired force cuts lowered manpower demands to the point where an already unfriendly Congress could hardly be expected to extend it again. A year later, the United States had the largest active military forces it had ever achieved by voluntary means alone; but, despite a pay raise, lowered standards, and intensive recruiting efforts, those forces were neither at their budgeted levels nor strong enough to support American aims during what was being thought of less as a transition to peace and more as a cold war.

The Czech coup of early 1948, and the Berlin blockade a few months later, brought a new phase in the debate over manpower procurement. These crises did not create the need for stronger military forces than the country had been able to raise voluntarily; up to a point, this need was already implicit in the nation's commitment to postwar collective security through the United Nations. But the crises of early 1948 did make the logic of cold war clear and compelling to a majority of Americans; they helped overcome, for the moment at least, traditional attitudes toward the distinction between peace and war, toward the nation's international responsibilities, and toward the role of military forces in carrying these burdens of foreign policy. They did not, on the other hand, make the Administration any more single-minded in its perceptions of cold war military needs than it had been earlier. The consequence was a refocused debate over military policy and its military manpower procurement elements, a debate in which the dominant issues were still those of meeting military requirements and of using compulsions to do so, but in which the programmatic content of those issues was altered.

The Administration proposed a return to Selective Service as a means of supporting the active forces; but it was not clear whether Selective Service was to be simply a temporary measure, still based on the earlier transition-to-peace assumption, or conscription was to become a more or less permanent element of cold war military policy. This ambiguity was reinforced by the Administration's restated support for UMT as an essential element of a permanent military program, in which the chief reliance for defense would be upon mobilizable reserves, not large active forces. This time the Air Force's dissent from UMT was heard in public. Arguments for the dominance of air power in any future war had great attractions for a public entranced by technology and mindful that the United States alone had the atomic bomb; indeed these arguments affected not only public sentiments, but military planning as well. The Air Force did not openly quarrel with Army and Navy arguments for their own forces-in-being, arguments cast in terms of the support ground and naval forces could give the Air Force in an all-out war; but it did openly challenge the argument that military defense could in the long term rely chiefly on mobilizable reserves, and the proposal that UMT be instituted to supply these reserves. Outside the Administration, roughly the same public groups which had helped frustrate earlier manpower procurement policy proposals lined up against both Selective Service and UMT, on much the same grounds. Their arguments might have lost in both cases, against rising public and congressional sentiment that peacetime conscription was a lesser evil than international Communism. But air power enthusiasts in Congress were joined by die-hard ideological opponents of UMT in preventing that proposal from reaching either house floor, and in eviscerating even the modest, and far from universal, reserve training program which did come to a vote.

The immediate outcome of this phase in the debate was passage of the two-year Selective Service Act of 1948 to supplement voluntary recruiting in supporting larger active forces, and further postponement of decisions on the general structure of the postwar military establishment and the sources of trained reserves. In the following year, active force strength goals were once again cut back, though not to pre-1948 levels; and inductions, barely begun, were halted. At the same time the quarrel over the relative virtues of UMT and a seventy-group Air Force went through one more round, resulting in no action on the former and little net gain for the latter.

In early 1950 the Administration dropped UMT from its agenda of immediately necessary legislation, and concentrated its military manpower efforts on extending Selective Service past a mid-year deadline. Given the halt of inductions and economy-induced cuts in active strengths, it was impossible to argue that Selective Service was necessary as a currently operating procurement device; but the Administration made a case for it as an indirect guarantee of active and reserve strength, as a vital part of the nation's international image, and as an essential element of standby mobilization machinery. The public evinced little interest, and only the last justification attracted any widespread support in Congress for extension. Congress moved to prevent the use of Selective Service except in a major national emergency, and the Administration seemed unwilling or unable to prevent this crucial alteration in its 1948 plans for a cold war manpower procurement policy.

In that same period, the Administration began a major revision and rationalization of its general cold war military strategy. The first stage was the production of NSC-68, which called for creation and maintenance of much larger active forces than those on hand, larger even than the top goals of the 1948 rearmament proposals. The implications for manpower procurement were that UMT-supplied reserves could not become the main underpinning of defense in the foreseeable future, and that Selective Service inductions would probably have to be resumed under conditions rather short of the sort of emergency which Congress felt might justify such action. Had these goals been converted into formal legislative proposals, the result would undoubtedly have been yet another extended, perhaps frustrating, but possibly instructive debate over military manpower procurement. As it turned out, however, the Administration was spared the burden of such a debate, and Congress and the public were denied the opportunity for it, by the outbreak of war in Korea. Selective Service was extended, not as a calculated act of cold war manpower policy, but as an immediate response to the needs of a hot war.

2. *Adapting Policy to Cold War Military and Civilian Needs*

When debate over manpower procurement resumed in 1951, the assumptions and goals of NSC-68 had crept unheralded into the

Administration's justifications for its military policy and into congressional and public responses as well. The dominant issue from the Administration's point of view was still that of meeting military requirements at reasonable cost, but its now united and firm emphasis on creating strong active forces for the long term meant a shift in program priorities. Thus, the Administration's proposals stressed retention and reshaping of Selective Service to meet both immediate and long-term manpower needs. Authority for UMT was still desired; but the trained reserves it might eventually supply were pictured as at most a supplement to active forces, rather than the central feature of a postwar military establishment. The Administration also stressed the problems of adapting military manpower procurement to the immediate and long-term needs of a partially mobilized civilian economy. Congress and the public likewise accepted these two general issues, meeting military requirements and the impact of doing so on other manpower goals and demands, as the dominant ones calling for policy resolution. At least this was true where the reshaping of Selective Service was concerned. The debate focused mostly on details of length and service, ages of liability, and deferment policies, rather than on the question of whether Selective Service should exist at all. Long-standing objections to conscription played little part in this aspect of the debate; but the issue of compulsion remained visible in the treatment accorded UMT and other proposals for creating more effective reserve forces. Congress accepted the outlines of a UMT program in 1951; but inauguration of this program under the newly styled Universal Military Training and Service Act was postponed, pending yet another round of congressional and public debate. The final outcome was a humiliating defeat for UMT on the House floor early in 1952. The Korean War rearmament phase of debate over military manpower procurement policies thus left unresolved the problem of supplying trained reserve forces. Its positive achievement was the initial adaptation of Selective Service to meeting long-term bulk procurement needs of the active forces and to sharing a relatively small supply of military-age manpower between military and nonmilitary demands.

During the next ten years, the closest approach to a full-scale debate over military manpower procurement came as the Eisenhower Administration sought resolution of the reserves' problems. The

New Look's strategic doctrines, as had those of NSC-68 and the Korean War rearmament, implied at most a secondary role for reserves in the total national defense effort. But their emphasis on the nuclear deterrent and atomic weapons for the battlefield pointed to major reductions in ground force strengths; and these made large and effective reserves seem almost as important to Army plans as they had in the early postwar years. The Administration delayed making its proposals until 1955, and then eschewed UMT for reasons of both principle and tactics. Instead, it proposed to supply the reserves with trained nonveterans in much the same way the active forces were being supplied, through a mixture of voluntary recruiting and selective conscription. The House Armed Services Committee, anticipating repetition of earlier objections to conscription for the reserves, decided that voluntary recruiting alone, with only indirect support from Selective Service deferments, would have to be tried first; but it also agreed to adjust the reserve obligations of post-Korean active service veterans to induce a better supply of these men to the organized reserve units. The whole program was almost lost in a quarrel arising from sharp congressional divisions over segregation in the National Guard; and the Administration was able to obtain part of its program only by stressing the demands of national security, and by exempting the National Guard from the training standards imposed on nonveteran volunteers in the other reserve components. The Defense Department regarded this as a major shortcoming in the reserve programs; but in 1957 it found that, with some adjustments, it could impose the desired training standards on the National Guard administratively. At the same time, it opened the possibility of draft deferment through reserve enlistment and training to the whole span of military age classes; this administrative decision made the recruiting program for nonveteran reservists, which had been a failure among eighteen-year-olds, an overnight and oversubscribed success. Partly as a consequence of these successes, the Eisenhower Administration turned to a series of futile proposals for cutting back the strength of the organized reserve units, and finally handed on this problem of reserve manpower oversupply to its successors.

Although rejecting criticism in 1956 of the relation between Selective Service and the needs of the active forces for skilled and experienced men, the Eisenhower Administration undertook a number of moves aimed at improving the quality of active force manpower. Pay raises and other improvements in money and money-equivalent benefits, including a sharp rise in reenlistment bonuses, were major features of this drive to improve manpower quality by strengthening career elements in all the armed forces. They were all aimed, as had been the second major postwar pay raise in 1949, at increasing rates of retention among officers and enlisted men completing their initial obligated tours of duty, and at enhancing the financial attractiveness of military service for those in the middle and higher officer and enlisted grades; the incalculable, or at least uncalculated, cost of raising entry pay rates high enough to avoid the need for conscription remained, to most, simply beyond reason. Each of these actions had some immediate effect on retention rates; but in the end, after an early general improvement over the low rates of the years immediately after the Korean War, these efforts tended merely to keep the services from falling farther behind their retention goals. The other major thrust toward manpower quality was a general tightening of entry standards for all the services. This process began soon after the close of the Korean War; but the Army, remaining dependent on Selective Service for a large portion of its annual intake, did not enjoy the full fruits of these moves until Congress was persuaded, in 1958, to allow important upward adjustments of the induction standards. Most of this effort was concentrated on mental, or training aptitude, standards. The consequence was a rise in overall rejection rates among potential enlistees and inductees from about one in five during the Korean War to almost one in three by the early 1960's.

Selective Service, viewed in the early postwar years as a second-best choice of manpower procurement systems, became entrenched as the heart of military manpower procurement, for both the active and the reserve forces, in the decade following the Korean War. Only the Army, the largest and least popular of the services, regularly called on the Selective Service System for inductees to fill out its active enlisted ranks; but the threat of induction was also an important supplement to other motives—patriotism, enjoyment of service life, career ambitions, financial security—inducing volunteers to meet the enlisted and officer needs of all the services. The reserve components also relied on Selective Service pressures, both for direct volunteers who preferred reserve to active service and for active service veterans who still had reserve service obligations. Military pay scales also took into account the existence of Selective Service and the military obligation imposed by the act; these scales were adjusted with an eye to retaining men already in service, and entry rates underwent only occasional cost-of-living increases.

In 1951 the Universal Military Training and Service Act became permanent legislation in all important respects save the crucial power to order induction of men into the armed forces. Given the character of early postwar debates over military manpower procurement, the need to renew this authority at the end of four years might easily have occasioned a resumption of debate over the propriety of peacetime conscription. In fact, no such debate developed in 1955, although anticipation of traditional objections to conscription persuaded the Administration to abandon attempts to authorize direct inductions into the reserves. Indeed, in 1955, and in 1959 and 1963 as well, organized opposition to Selective Service extension on grounds that military conscription was destructive of American traditions faded to a nearly inaudible echo of its earlier vigor. Nor, in the absence of this opposition, were any other persuasive objections raised against continued Selective Service operations. The need for large active military forces as well as sizable and trained reserves, both to be maintained over an indefinite period, was no longer the challengeable hypothesis it had seemed to be in the early postwar years. Instead this need had become an almost undebatable premise of national military policy for the cold war; and conscription, at least on a limited scale, gained acceptance as the inevitable if unfortunate consequence of this military need.

What little debate did develop over Selective Service in the post–Korean War decade focused mostly on the specific impact of military manpower procurement on various groups of young men and on the relation of military needs to other goals for the development and use of manpower. After 1955, however, even these questions receded from the agenda of legislative decision-making and review; and consideration of them was absorbed into the general administrative management of the military manpower pool. Thus, what had been a major political debate over the appropriateness of conscription to military needs and to American traditions gave way to a largely bureaucratic process of adapting the Selective Service System to changing conditions of manpower supply and demand.

During this period, the Selective Service System conceived for itself a major new function beyond that of directly or indirectly supplying the armed forces with manpower. It became, in its own eyes, the storekeeper and channeler of the nation's manpower. This new function had its roots in the long recognized need to dampen the disruptive effects of military manpower procurement on civilian, especially defense-oriented, production and services, and on family and community social patterns.

The limited scale of the Korean War mobilization, and the general assumption that fairly high levels of military strength would be required over a long period, made possible and desirable a more extensive adaptation of Selective Service to nonmilitary demands than had been attempted in World War II. Indeed, the need for adapting Selective Service to a period of low demand for active service manpower had been recognized in 1948; but, while specifying the conditions for deferment of reservists, Congress had left decisions on deferments in two other major areas—occupation, including schooling, and dependency—to the discretion of the president and the Selective Service System. In 1951, Congress slightly altered this wide grant of discretionary powers. It expressed interest in a relatively large-scale program of student deferments, and forbad imposition of uniform standards for local board decisions on these or other occupational deferments; it also forbad granting dependency deferments on grounds of marriage alone; and, by extending the liability of deferred men to age thirty-five, it sought to assure that deferments, especially those for students, would not become de facto exemptions.

After 1951, Congress made no important changes in the law regarding deferments, other than to adjust reserve service deferments to administrative changes in the reserve programs. The Selective Service system, subject to the president's approval, was left free to adapt its selection and deferment policies to changing military and nonmilitary demands, and to the general supply of manpower, pretty much as it saw fit.

In the post–Korean War decade, as the supply of military-age manpower began to grow, and as the demand for active military manpower declined, the Selective Service System might have decided that low inductions reduced the need for special protection of selected groups by deferment. Instead, it used deferment powers as a device for taking up the slack between manpower supply and demand; and it defended this decision on grounds that a universal obligation to military service justified channeling those not needed by the armed forces into other activities deemed to further the national interest. Thus, a variety of decisions, expanding deferments, establishing special induction priorities, and offering effective exemptions, had the common result of so redefining and narrowing the group of truly liable men that the supply of "availables" did not outrun the armed forces' demands for them. Until the 1960's, student and other occupational deferments played a small part in this process; yet the Selective Service System increasingly emphasized its role as a channeler of manpower into socially important activities. This function was never specifically endorsed by either the president or Congress, nor did it become part of the accepted public image of the Selective Service System. As a self-conceived function, channeling was really little more than self-justification. Nevertheless, the general broadening of student and dependency deferments was not simply an arbitrary response to manpower supply and demand conditions. Both had at least passive support from public attitudes and from the groups specifically benefited, and student deferments had the active support of various scientific, engineering and academic professional groups.

The Department of Defense also contributed to the process of taking up slack between manpower supply and demand. At least this was one result, intended or not, of both the broadening of reserve enlistment programs and the tightening of entry standards. Partially countering this effect, however, were the emphasis on career retention, which tended to reduce turnover, and the fact that active strength levels were held below Korean War levels, even after the 1961–62 build-up.

3. The Unexamined Issue of Equity

Throughout the postwar period, military requirements and the goal of national security in the insecure world of cold war dominated both debate and policy in military manpower procurement. Up to 1948, and to a lesser extent up to the outbreak of war in Korea, the inability of the military services and the Administration to define manpower requirements clearly and persuasively, and the impact of traditional objections to peacetime conscription, made settled policy difficult to achieve. With the Korean War rearmament came a degree of agreement within the Administration on manpower requirements, and widespread acceptance of cold war logic made these demands seem inevitable to Congress and the public. Traditional resistance to peacetime conscription was still strong enough to defeat UMT; but given widely agreed upon assumptions about costs and budgetary constraints, this resistance faded into general acceptance of selective conscription. Thereafter, the major pressure for modification of conscription came not from resistance to it on principle but from a series of not very throughly examined nonmilitary claims on the manpower pool.

During all of this time, yet a fifth major issue, that of equity, played a part in the debates and decisions on military manpower procurement policy; but until the mid-1960's, the impact of this issue was only minor and sporadic.

In the early postwar years, equity through universal conscription was an unquestioned premise of UMT supporters; and this premise, probably more than any other aspect of UMT, seems to account for the highly favorable attitude of unorganized public opinion. UMT's organized opponents did not meet the issue head on; but it is reasonable to construct from their arguments the answer that all-volunteer forces would avoid the dangers of conscription and provide an equally good answer to the problem of equity. In the pursuit of cold war national security goals, manpower procurement policy took neither direction. Conscription was accepted as necessary, but universal conscription could not meet this test and eventually was abandoned.

The question of equity occasioned some debate over student deferments in 1951; but then and thereafter, policy in this area was dominated by desires to protect colleges and universities, the students in them, and numbers of their graduates from the disruptions of military conscription. Considerations of interracial equity played a part in temporarily limiting the effectiveness of reserve manpower policy in 1955, but the Administration held these considerations to be irrelevant to national security goals, and it soon found ways of overcoming the limitations without resolving that problem of equity. The executive order in 1956 that effectively exempted men over age twenty-five from induction came partly in response to protests over the injustice of taking men already settled in family and career when younger men with fewer commitments were not being called; but few gave much thought at the time to whether this decision might not create more inequities than it prevented. In 1958, the Administration, Congress, and the public all turned a deaf ear to suggestions that a sharp rise in entry standards might discriminate unduly against disadvantaged youths. Some congressional and public criticism was directed at the large number of reservists without prior service who were not called in the 1961 partial mobilization; but this did not develop into any general questioning of the fairness of allowing some men to discharge their military obligation with only six months' active duty while requiring others to serve two years. Much stronger than this criticism was the pressure in Congress to preserve the reserve programs in the face of Administration desires to redefine the military requirements for reserve forces and cut back their strengths.

Presumably, a limited sort of equity was built into the operations of the Selective Service System; but it was not clear, either in the law or in its interpretation and implementation, just how this was to be achieved. The statute demanded a fair and impartial system of selection, suggesting the impersonal equity of uniformly applied rules; but it did not spell out any requirement for uniformity, and indeed included provisions contradicting that goal. The Selective Service System's operational philosophy stressed the attention given by local boards to individual cases and local conditions. At times, the System argued that any injustices created by decentralizing decisions could be corrected through the appeals system; but more often it stressed the value of decentralization and the undesirability of imposing uniform standards on some four thousand local boards in fifty states. It could, moreover, point to the general lack of public protest as proof that inequities, though they might exist, were not very strongly felt.

4. *Revival of Debate*

After mid-1963, long-standing political apathy toward problems of military manpower procurement began to fade. Attention of the Administration, of members of Congress, and of private groups and individuals increasingly focused on two aspects of existing programs and policies: the various inequities alleged to exist in both the protective and the exclusionary features of the selection and recruitment processes; and the implications of current manpower practices for newly perceived problems and possibilities in the development and use of manpower. The Defense Department's study of Selective Service explored various approaches to narrowing the gap between voluntary supply and military demand for manpower, and reinforced skepticism toward the value of Selective Service channeling in meeting military and nonmilitary needs for college-educated manpower. Predictably, the Selective Service System's reaction to this study was negative and highly defensive. Nonetheless, by early 1965 it seemed probable that the Johnson Administration would promote revisions in policy, including higher pay, more flexible entry standards, and reformed deferment and induction procedures, as part of its Great Society programs. And it seemed that the new policy proposals would reflect a higher priority for equity and an altered view of the social needs to which military policy ought to adapt.

After mid-1965, though, the opportunity for new policy directions was obscured by demands for military manpower to meet the needs of an escalated war in Vietnam, and by the Selective Service System's quick and effective response to those demands. At the same time, related antiwar and antidraft movements intensified both pressures for and resistance to policy change. Proponents of voluntary forces argued that manpower procurement flexibility could be achieved without permanent conscription, and some suggested that too much flexibility had proved dangerous. In answer, defenders of the existing system, and of the war, made much of the Selective Service System's unique adaptability to changing conditions. Draft reformers, on the other hand, pointed out that Selective Service channeling had only been redirected, not reversed. By 1967 there were still large numbers of reservists, students, young husbands and fathers, and marginally disqualified youths deferred from active service, most of whom would never be called; and assignment of draftees to combat, and rising casualty figures, sharpened public perception of anomalies and inequities in this situation. Vigorous protests against both the American role in Vietnam and the draft machinery supporting that role heightened the reformers' sense of urgency; they called for changes that would spread the risk of involuntary service more equitably in war and peace and would provide answers to charges that war burdens were borne unfairly by less advantaged youths. The result was different for those already committed to preserving the existing policy, especially the Selective Service System and its allies among senior members of the Armed Services Committees; they pointed out that disproportionate numbers of Negroes and other disadvantaged youths were already better protected against the draft, in Class IV-F, than many college students; and some suggested that antiwar, antidraft movements on campus ought to be met by inducting the dissenters. Adamant resistance and counterattack by those favoring the status quo probably swayed many who might otherwise have supported reforms. In the event, 1967, the year for quadrennial extension of Selective Service induction authority, did not prove the occasion for reform, much less abandonment, of this central engine of manpower procurement.

Pressure for reform faded after the 1967 defeat, and had little impact before 1970. Then, as the Vietnam War deescalated, and as the Nixon Administration sought to give flesh to its ambiguous campaign promises, prospects for policy change brightened. Lottery induction of youths aged nineteen to twenty was introduced early in the year. The Selective Service System acquired a new director, the first in over twenty-eight years, who proved friendly to further changes. A presidential commission produced an optimistic report on prospects for all-volunteer forces. And, late in April, the Administration proposed new changes in both directions: extensive reform of Selective Service, and greater reliance on voluntary recruiting.

Public and congressional reaction to these proposals was not yet clear by mid-1970. It was clear, though, that these two directions for policy change summed up the most important thrusts of policy debate since the mid-1960's. That debate reopened and refined every major issue suggested in the long postwar development of military manpower procurement policy, and it raised fundamental questions about priorities among policy goals. Analysis of these latest proposals, then, in terms of the major issues, should suggest guidelines for both policy-making and policy change in the foreseeable future.

II. POLICY AND POLICY-MAKING FOR THE 1970'S

Throughout this study, a simplified framework of policy issues and goals has served to organize the examination of specific policies, programs, and practices that were adopted or proposed in the past twenty-five years. These same issues—military force effectiveness, costs, compulsions, equity, and nonmilitary social impacts —are all present in current debates as well, debates focusing on proposals to further reform Selective Service and to rely more heavily on voluntary recruiting. Even so, the content and context of debate in the 1970's differ from the consideration given military manpower procurement policy in earlier periods.

The most marked change is the widened scope of debate, especially in contrast to the post–Korean War decade. After 1952, certain aspects of policy—compulsions, equity, nonmilitary impacts— were assumed to be settled; and decisions on military effectiveness and costs were mostly matters for executive formulation, congressional ratification, and passive public acceptance. After 1963, though, new challenges arose, at first focusing on the question of equity and on the possibilities of adapting military manpower programs to the active pursuit of nonmilitary social goals. This renewed interest in equity and social impacts, and the failure in 1967 of reform proposals intended to make the draft more equitable, inevitably spurred interest in the possibility of avoiding these difficult questions by ending the use of compulsions. Simultaneously, the Vietnam War, and the visible connection between it and the draft, encouraged widespread reconsideration of military needs, and hence of the propriety of using compulsions to meet those needs. Consequently, in the 1970's, the whole range of military manpower procurement issues is open to debate.

This wider debate is reminiscent of the struggle over policy in the early postwar years, before the reenactment of Selective Service; but there are important differences, too, stemming from experiences affecting each of the general issues. In the earlier period, it was assumed that large military forces, however acquired, were a more or less temporary response to special conditions marking the postwar transition to a small peacetime military establishment. Today, debate over the nation's international responsibilities rages anew; but few would argue that these responsibilities, however defined, will permit the wealthiest nation to act in a chaotic world without sizeable military forces-in-being at its command. In the 1940's, it was assumed that budgetary constraints put severe limits on the funds available to support military forces. Now, in the context of vastly increased defense spending, an added expense of a few billion dollars annually is at least a debatable proposition. Earlier opposition to peacetime conscription was emotional, ideological, based on a traditionalist reading of American history, and promoted by important, organized interests. Today, resurgent opposition to conscription is again partly emotional and ideological, but is not well organized, and is based on a revisionist interpretation of the nation's postwar experiences. In the 1940's, with attention focused on the conflict between military needs and resistance to conscription, questions of equity and social impacts were generally overlooked. Today, more than two decades' experience with a highly selective draft forces attention to problems of social impact, and especially of equity, inherent in that selectivity. Finally, new and sophisticated analyses have added a dimension of economic rationalism to debate over all these issues, but particularly to relations among military effectiveness, costs, and compulsions.

Four discussions below conclude this study. The first reviews major linkages among military manpower procurement programs and goals, and ends with a statement of preferences to guide the remaining discussions. The second and third review potential impacts of currently proposed changes on the various policy goals. The final discussion reviews possible improvements in the process of translating military manpower procurement goals into satisfactory public policy results.

1. *Programs, Goals, and Preferences*

Manpower procurement programs are related to the structural effectiveness of military forces through their impacts on the size of the active forces, the size and readiness of the reserves, and the responsiveness of mechanisms for active force expansion in emergencies. They are related to military force quality through entry standards and the length of training and experience of men in service.

Short of a major mobilization, the primary constraint on military demand for manpower is budget cost; and the main restraint on the military manpower budget is competition from other budget programs, military and nonmilitary. Economists may argue that the underlying constraint is real cost, that is, the impact of military manpower on total national product; but budget cost is more relevant to most program decisions, for a number of reasons. Because government revenues are limited, and because the relation between total government expenditure and revenue has a major impact on national economic policy, competing programs must be analyzed primarily in budget cost terms. More important, consideration of budget cost, usually to the exclusion of other real cost elements, is built into the central policy-making processes of authorization and appropriation; thus budget cost is important and relevant, because policy-makers and the public think it is important.

There are other manpower program constraints on military force effectiveness, limitations imposed by the dual federal-state control over part of the reserve forces, by legal and political limits on rapid force expansion in emergencies, by statutory ceilings on minimum entry standards, and by various nonmaterial aspects of military career attractiveness that affect turnover rates. (Statutory ceilings on active and reserve forces have had no practical constraining effect since 1948.)

During most of the postwar period, military manpower procurement programs have employed the powers of government to compel as well as persuade men to military service. Conscription is an important means of relieving budgetary constraints on military manpower. It is also an aid in overcoming some other restraints on military effectiveness: it helps to strengthen those elements of reserve forces under direct federal control; more important, it provides a mechanism for rapid expansion of active forces in emergencies.

Conscription also has disadvantages, but not all of these operate as continuous constraints on military manpower procurement. An obvious disadvantage is that it obscures elements of real manpower cost, and thus permits resource allocations to military manpower larger than might be considered prudent if total real cost was taken into account. In practice, this economic disadvantage of conscription operates, not as a constraint, but as an inducement to relieve budget constraints by employing conscription.

Another disadvantage of conscription is that it brings more or less unwilling men into service. This does not operate as a major constraint, though; none of the services has serious difficulties in absorbing these men—draftees and unwilling volunteers in the Army, mostly the latter in the other services—into the active forces. On the other hand, the presence of unwilling men in the reserves, where control over rewards and punishments is less complete, probably does have negative impacts on the readiness of these forces.

The most important disadvantage of conscription, of course, is its cost in terms of restrictions on individual liberties. Taken in sum, and if perceived to be too high, this cost can lead to abandonment of, or refusal to adopt, conscription. In turn, this can reduce military effectiveness, through budgetary constraints on quantitative and qualitative manpower demands, and through reduced flexibility for meeting emergency demands.

One approach to keeping the perceived costs of compulsions relatively low is the use of selective conscription, but this has limits. Although some forms of selective conscription may be more equitable than others, all involve some felt cost in equity (in contrast to the alternatives of no compulsions at all or universal conscription). Some of this felt inequity may be offset by apparent gains for other goals, as selection is employed to protect or promote family life, community services, defense and other industries, and education. When manpower demands are low relative to total supply, though, selectivity increases but simultaneously becomes less relevant to these nonmilitary social goals; under these circumstances, the cost in felt inequities rises.

Whether selective or not, conscription also affects equity by imposing a huge tax on those compelled to serve, a tax related to the hidden differential between budgeted and real costs of conscripted forces.

Aspects of manpower procurement other than conscription also affect equity and nonmilitary social goals for manpower. Entry standards and manpower turnover affect the distribution of opportunities to benefit from military service; they also affect the military services' contributions to increasing skills in the civilian labor market, and to upward mobility of socially disadvantaged youths. These opportunities and social contributions are further affected, of course, by the existence of conscription and the selectivity with which it is imposed.

A final and important social goal affected by manpower procurement programs is the sense of obligation felt by individuals toward the security and well-being of the nation and of their communities. This sense of obligation may be eroded through widespread perception of inequities in the selective imposition of compulsions; or it may be eroded when this and other costs of manpower procurement —in budget terms, in restrictions on individual liberty, and in impact on other social goals—seems out of proportion to military needs for manpower. Conversely, erosion of the sense of obligation may occur when the burdens of national defense seem to be shifted onto a small group of career military men, comprised largely of the poor and willing.

This review of linkages among military manpower procurement programs and policy goals suggests the complexity of the total problem. Indeed, military manpower procurement is not so much a problem, solvable in some optimal or efficient way, as it is a continuing challenge to search for better policy. The remaining discussions below are offered as contributions to that search.

These remaining discussions are intended as reasoned guides to policy debate, resolution, and review. Underlying them is an ordering of policy preferences, as follows: The fundamental objectives of military manpower procurement policy are to meet the structural and qualitative needs of effective military forces, to meet them under varying and not wholly predictable conditions of demand and supply, and to meet them within a budget for military manpower that is not unlimited. In meeting these objectives, the use of conscription ought to be governed by carefully defined needs for military manpower, not by simple convenience or by unexamined "worst possible" projections of demand; and it ought to be limited by a reasonably generous approach to the military manpower budget. If compulsions are employed, considerations of equity call for spreading the risk of compulsory service as broadly as possible among nonvolunteers, within reasonable limits imposed by military needs. Finally, all these goals are more important, in setting military manpower procurement policy, than are any additional adaptations to improve distribution of military service benefits or to promote nonmilitary goals for the development of manpower.

2. The Case for Selective Service Reforms

The preceding review of linkages among manpower procurement programs and goals, considered together with the expressed policy preferences, suggests an impressive case for one direction of policy change—the further reform of Selective Service along lines proposed by the Marshall Commission and now being promoted by the Nixon Administration.

Negatively, this case is an indictment of the mixed voluntary-compulsory system employed during most of the past twenty-five years. That system has met the fundamental objectives of military manpower procurement policy fairly well, but it has given all too little attention to other policy goals. As the prime engine of manpower procurement, the Selective Service System has accepted or encouraged, and benefited from, various administrative manipulations of deferments that kept the manpower pool down to manageable size. Until recently, little attention has been given to inequities inherent in selective imposition of a universal military obligation. Instead, policies and programs have been mostly responsive to military and social goals conceived in terms of cold war or convenience.

The changes in Selective Service currently proposed offer a moderate program of reform. If conscription continues, and continues to be selective, then a preference for equity over pursuit of nonmilitary social goals supports all these reforms and possibly more. At the same time, the impact of these reforms on military effectiveness and budget costs can probably be kept to acceptable levels.

The recent adoption of a lottery is only a small step toward increasing equity by spreading the risk of compulsory service among nonvolunteers. A second step would be conversion to inducting from a national pool, rather than parceling out induction quotas to local board areas. The latter system was sensible during World

War II, and would be again in a large-scale mobilization; for it protected those communities that produced large numbers of volunteers from untoward additional impacts of military manpower demands. But the local quota system makes little sense in periods of relatively low manpower demand, when the question of selecting inductees should be one of fairness to individual nonvolunteers, not of fairness to communities.

Further progress toward equitable distribution of induction risks requires broadening the proportion of youths eligible for selection; and there are opportunities for doing so by narrowing or eliminating several of the major channels of deferment. (Two of these, deferment for reservists and for men disqualified from service, are more closely related to proposals for all-volunteer forces; they are examined in the next subsection.)

Easily the most defensible such reform is the recent elimination of new deferments for fatherhood alone and limitation of further dependency deferments to hardship cases. The major social justification for deferring fathers, other than convenience to the government, seems to have been that they were needed more at home than in military service; but not since 1946 did this argument lead in practice, as it does in logic, to discharging from the armed forces all those nonvolunteers who become fathers after entering service. Considerations of equity suggest that standards of hardship ought to be the same, regardless of when the child is born; and they suggest that dependents' benefits for men performing obligated service should be raised to the minimum considered adequate for career service personnel. Induction by lottery suggests two more arguments for dropping blanket deferment of fathers: first, very few youths age nineteen to twenty-one are fathers; and second, existence of a deferment for fathers could have the undesirable effect of inducing a higher rate of fatherhood at that age. This leaves the political justification for fatherhood deferments to be considered. In two periods, pressures of constituents on congressmen or of communities on local boards made the costs of continuing to induct fathers seem so high as to make a blanket deferment or exemption seem preferable. One was 1946, when the general demobilization made it difficult to hold the line against such pressures; and the second was the decade 1955–65, when declining inductions and rising manpower supply made the Selective Service System only too willing to adopt a low priority for fathers, and to let local draft boards extend the concept of dependency hardship to the point where blanket deferment of fathers only gave a new label to a long-standing administrative fact. It does not seem likely that such pressures will again become particularly strong, so long as inductions are limited largely to youths of ages nineteen or twenty. In sum, adoption of the lottery makes it both possible and desirable to limit dependency deferments to true hardship cases.

Similar reasoning supports the recent ban on future occupational deferments. This will create some initial problems where draft boards have given extensive recognition to local community needs for teachers, policemen, or other service employment; but these will disappear in succeeding years as the lottery focuses more and more on youths in the youngest draft-age classes. The National Security Council does not recognize any special industry or skill claims to indirect support from selectively compelled military service, and it seems unlikely that local community needs have any better claim. One class of current occupational deferments probably does deserve further attention, though. It would seem realistic and fair, if not altogether politic, to incorporate agricultural deferments with those for dependency, applying hardship standards to both.

The proposed abandonment of student deferments raises more difficult problems. Past experience suggests no clear general argument on social grounds for continuing these deferments in peacetime: there is no evidence they are necessary to maintain college populations over more than the short run, if even that; and lack of a case for occupational deferments removes any argument that overriding civil demands for specially educated men require general deferment of graduate students. Equity would probably be better served by eliminating student deferments than by postponing the lottery liability of all undergraduates; and this would also avoid future pressures for restoring dependency or occupational deferments. Unfortunately, there are two special difficulties that cloud this general case for abandoning student deferments.

One is the fact that the armed forces rely on college graduates for the bulk of their officer procurement. Unless this can be put on a wholly voluntary basis, some form of student deferment system remains a requirement. This might be limited to ROTC students only, with those not completing the program becoming eligible for lottery induction; but even this would require absorption of other college graduate officer-procurement programs into ROTC, and ought to include expansion of ROTC programs to a much larger number of schools. Given current pressures against ROTC on many campuses, this latter might prove very difficult indeed; and the military services would probably have to rely more heavily than in the past on their academies and internal recruitment of officer candidates. Even so, these possible costs in military effectiveness hardly seem large enough to justify blanket deferment of undergraduates.

The second difficulty lies in the services' reliance on special induction pressures in procuring medical and dental officers. In times of low inductions, there is no serious obstacle to maintaining the special obligation to military service for men trained to these professions; but if inductions rise sharply, as in the Vietnam expansion, then the absence of a general deferment for students may force a choice between shortfalls in military procurement of medical and dental officers or double service for some professionals. A better solution to this than blanket deferment of undergraduates would be higher military investment in recruiting potential medical officers and paying for their professional training.

In sum, abandoning student deferments offers some opportunity for equalizing the risk of induction among youths in each age class, especially in periods of low induction pressure. At a minimum, the preference for equity ahead of nonmilitary social goals calls for reversing the practice, followed since 1953, of tightening the rules for student deferment in periods of high inductions and loosening them when manpower demands are low.

If the foregoing reforms in deferment and induction are adopted, and there are no compelling arguments against them, then there is also a strong case for reorganizing the Selective Service System along lines proposed by the Marshall Commission in 1967. The existing local board pattern served quite well in World War II, when the problem was one of extracting large numbers of men across a broad range of ages from civilian life without too seriously disrupting local communities and industry. Today, manpower demands are lower and are focused on relatively young age groups, suggesting a rather different central role for the boards. If the selection process becomes a routine matter of spreading the risk of compulsion across the largest possible proportion of military-age youths in each successive age class, the local boards could more logically and effectively serve as reviewers of that process, empowered to alter its decisions only where individual hardship can be clearly demonstrated. Relieved of the tasks of allocating manpower to national needs on the basis of locally improvised standards, and of meeting monthly quotas for military manpower, local boards that are truly representative of their communities should be able to perform this limited review task quite well.

Had these reforms been adopted earlier, even as late as the mid-1960's, they might have done much to counter widespread erosion among the nation's youth, especially its college students, in their sense of obligation to military service and national security. Instead, reform was delayed; and reaction to the Vietnam War compounded the perceived inequities in Selective Service channeling. The result has been even stronger resistance to conscription, and spreading cynicism toward individual obligations and national security needs. In the 1970's, reform of Selective Service, no matter how much devoted to equity, may not be enough to save that engine of manpower procurement from pressure to abandon conscription. Whether it is worth saving is examined in the next subsection.

3. *The Case for All-Volunteer Forces*

—— The nation may now be on the verge of the public debate over uses of conscription in peacetime that it avoided in 1950. Unease over the impacts of selective conscription on equity and social goals, and spreading mistrust of presidential discretion on military operations, make abandonment of conscription and imposition of congressional control over its resumption a tempting alternative to the manpower policy of the past twenty years. Such a change would bring clear gains in one manpower policy goal, by eliminating compulsions. But the losses and gains in other respects—military effectiveness, budget and real costs, equity, and impact on other social goals— must also be assessed. These considerations make abandonment of conscription a much more debatable proposition than is reform of Selective Service.

Any shift in manpower policy to, or toward, all-volunteer forces would employ elements of four general approaches to closing the gap between voluntary supply of and military demand for manpower: force reductions, lower entry standards, civilian substitution, and competitive pay and benefits. (A fifth approach, more vigorous recruiting activity, would also be employed; it would have no important side effects, other than a relatively minor increase in budget costs for recruiters, overhead, and advertising.) All of these approaches would, by reducing compulsions to zero, obviate concern for equity in spreading the risk of conscription. Only one approach, though, the reduction of minimum entry standards, would improve very much on equity in distributing opportunities to benefit from military service. This particular approach would also increase the total skills available in the economy, by focusing military recruitment on those men least likely to get special training in civil life; but other approaches to voluntary forces, by reducing military personnel turnover, would have an opposite social impact. Two approaches, lower standards and competitive pay, would enhance upward mobility of less advantaged youths, the one by widening opportunities, the other by increasing the economic returns to each recruit; but, again through reduced turnover, the other two approaches would have a reverse impact on social mobility. All of these approaches would also run the risk of further eroding citizens' sense of obligation to national defense.

Given the preferences stated earlier, there are more important effects of an all-volunteer policy to be considered than its impacts on equity and nonmilitary social goals. All four approaches also have serious implications for military effectiveness and dollar costs. The approach that would best preserve military effectiveness, competitive pay, is also the one most stressed by proponents of all-volunteer forces. This approach would have the added effect of equating real and budget costs, from which several consequences would flow. In the long run, reflecting real costs of military manpower in the government budget should have a salutary impact on rational allocation of resources among elements of military cost and between military and other governmental objectives. In the short run, though, the likely result would be lagging adaptation of policy-makers and the public, long used to making manpower deci-

sions based on artificially low budget costs, and consequently an un-
der-allocation of funds to military manpower. In these circumstances,
civilian substitution would probably not be pushed very hard, because of its impact on other military budget elements. More likely
would be force reductions and lower entry standards. In sum, the
probable outcome of immediate, rapid conversion to an all-volunteer
system would be increased budget cost, for smaller forces, filled with
lower quality manpower.

An all-volunteer system would also reduce military force effectiveness by losing the flexibility conscription gives to meeting emergency demands for active force manpower. Reliance on flexible pay
scales or hiring queues would be unrealistic. More likely, and supported by most all-volunteer force proponents, would be standby
authority to restore the draft and call up reserves. As was suggested
in the debate over Selective Service extension in 1950, lodging this
emergency authority in the president might not preclude his resorting to inductions merely to supplement regular recruiting measures;
the alternative, of course, would be to require a congressional resolution. Either form of restriction, but especially the latter, carries two
kinds of risk.

One risk is the obvious possibility that military forces might not
be expanded in time, even at considerable cost to military security
and the credibility of our foreign policy. It was this risk that concerned the Truman Administration in 1950. Given this nation's
long history of unpreparedness for national emergencies, and considering the many rigidities and resistances that make our political
system slow in responding to changes in a dangerous and chaotic
world, this is not a risk to be undertaken lightly.

Recognizing that risk, and faced with an apparent emergency not
well-perceived by Congress and the public, an Administration bent
on expanding military forces would probably resort to promoting
its request, or decision, to restore the draft in the strongest, most
dramatic terms possible. This suggests a second kind of risk that
ought to be pondered carefully by those who decry the flexibility
now given a president in responding to military emergencies. This
is the risk of a far greater presidential, congressional, and public
commitment to military action than the particular situation, realistically assessed, could possibly justify. Had President Johnson, for

example, needed his own or a congressional declaration of emergency for authority to resume inductions and expand forces in 1965, he would very likely have been successful; but the resulting commitment to an American military solution in Vietnam might well have taken even more than three years of costly war, and a threatened defeat at the polls, to reverse.

One remedy to the inflexibility of an all-volunteer system, hopefully suggested by many proponents, is reliance on reserves. This answer begs the question in several ways. For one, it poses the same problems of control, and the same risks of under- or over-responsiveness, as would a stand-by draft authority. Indeed, these problems would be somewhat intensified by reliance on reserves, given the greater difficulty of distributing the burdens of a reserve recall. Worse, this answer begs the question of the military cost-effectiveness of reserve forces relative to that of readily expansible active forces. Finally, it does not answer how, in an all-volunteer system, reserve forces would be manned and kept truly ready.

None of the foregoing arguments necessarily precludes a choice for all-volunteer forces. Indeed, some of the effects of an immediate conversion might be avoided by a gradualist approach; and several measures in that direction commend themselves whether they would lead to an all-volunteer result or not.

Future incremental pay increases, beyond those maintaining cost-of-living parity, might well be focused on several objectives other than the one pursued for the past fifteen years—retention of experienced men. First priority ought to go to increasing pay and benefits for men in their first two years of service, as a matter of equity as well as prudent experimentation in the currently weakest area of recruiting inducements. A second priority for future increases might be to put officer procurement on an all-volunteer basis; at least this would reduce pressure for broad college deferments, thus making a more equitable draft easier to attain. Yet another priority objective for pay increases might be to promote creation of a carefully evaluated, truly ready, volunteer reserve. Even if active forces continue to rely on conscription, this would avoid serious inequities resulting from current draft deferments for short-active-service reserve enlistees and from arbitrary reliance by some reserve components on obligated veterans of active service.

⌐ Continued emphasis on accepting and training marginally qualified men commends itself as good social policy, as well as another
incremental approach to increasing the supply of volunteers. Given
continued conscription, this would also broaden the distribution of
induction risk; but equity imposes a limit, too—the point at which
large numbers of men are accepted who simply cannot cope with
the requirements of military technology and discipline. Whether
attached to conscription or not, successful programs for the marginally qualified will also require careful enforcement of service quotas
for accepting such men.

⌐ Even if broad reductions in force are considered unwise, lesser
measures toward reducing military manpower demand might prove
acceptable. An obvious move in this direction would be sharp reductions in low-priority reserve forces and training programs. This,
along with the various thrusts of pay increases, should be accompanied by increasingly sophisticated analyses of requirements for
military forces, active and reserve, and by strengthened insistence on
substituting civilians for military men wherever possible. This last
might be aided by including military personnel, along with civilians,
within the framework of command responsibilities for program and
financial management throughout the military services.

These gradualist moves toward an all-volunteer system may help
preserve, or even enhance, real military effectiveness, while at the
same time promoting more rational assessment of military security
needs against their true economic and social costs. Should they also
prove successful in leading to an all-volunteer system, though, there
remains the problem of flexibility for emergency expansion.

If cost-effective ready reserves can indeed be provided, these offer
a partial solution. A more difficult part of the problem is deciding
what circumstances would justify their call-up or a resort to standby induction authority. These circumstances ought not be too narrowly defined; the Senate's formula in 1950, requiring a finding of
"national necessity," is probably as far as any legal restriction on a
presidential decision ought to go. This conclusion derives less from
an interpretation of constitutional prerogatives than from a judgment that further restrictions would entail high risks of weak, or
over-vigorous, response to military emergencies. A compromise
with those who deeply mistrust presidential authority might be

found, however, in a form of legislative veto. If so, the special demands of military security ought still to be recognized by requiring unusual majorities, perhaps a two-thirds vote in both houses, to overrule a presidential decision; and, to avoid delays, such a veto ought to operate after the fact rather than require a waiting period.

4. Translating Goals into Policy

Military manpower procurement is a political problem, and thus a continuing challenge to search for better solutions. The results at any given time reflect, not a rationalistic assessment of military, economic, and social costs and benefits, but partial analyses, negotiations, and bargaining in an inherently sequential decision process. Changes in the substance of policy, such as those discussed above, may not be possible without accompanying changes in the process of translating goals into public policy.

Since 1950, and even earlier, setting military effectiveness and cost goals for manpower policy has been a matter largely internal to the Administration, and it seems likely to remain so. Much has been accomplished in the past few years toward analyzing these two objectives in relation to each other, reflected in the Defense Manpower study of the mid-1960's and the recent report of the Gates Commission. It is probably gratuitous to urge further efforts in this vein; these are likely to be forthcoming. But so long as the Administration's analyses are cast only in terms of military effectiveness and dollar costs, neither Congress and its committees nor the public at large can feel much incentive, or competence, to reject or amend the policy conclusions.

Beginning in the mid-1960's, these analyses have been undertaken with yet other policy goals in mind. Specifically, they have given new attention to the point at which the most awkward problems of public policy arise, the application of compulsions to ease the difficulties in making choices between budget costs and military effectiveness. When the manpower problem is understood to involve considerations of compulsions, equity, and social impact, then both Congress and the public will wish to be heard. Thus, not only should the Administration's efforts to rationalize manpower policy analyses be continued and extended, but also their results and the supporting data should be made available to congressional committees and the public. It is their deliberations that offer the best chance of deciding how far military effectiveness and cost-efficiency goals can be acceptably modified to accomodate those additional considerations. At the same time, the quality of congressional and public debate depends heavily on analyses and data that only the Administration is equipped to supply.

Probably the more difficult part of solving military manpower procurement problems lies not in setting policy goals and standards, but in assuring some continuing review of both goals and performance. The recently established requirement for periodic reviews of military pay may focus attention on some of the goals of manpower procurement, as the quadrennial extension of the induction authority has not. Of course there are dangers in too frequent review of policy goals, stemming from the pressures which this can itself create for frequent changes in a system which must, in the end, be understood to be accepted. It is reasonable to assume, though, that the review of goals will take care of itself if there exists some fairly thorough process of continually reviewing performance.

Current devices are not adequate to this task. The process of military personnel appropriations only looks at part of the problem, chiefly performance with regard to cost and military effectiveness; and even this review focuses more on internal management of personnel in the armed forces than on procurement programs. The annual review of Selective Service appropriations accomplishes even less; although both selection policies and internal management are reviewed, the appropriations process really has leverage against only the latter. The Selective Service System is required to give Congress a semiannual report on its operations; but the Armed Services Committees, which are in the best position to review this and the totality of manpower procurement performance, have shown little more interest in these than in the quadrennial reviews of policy. Thus, it seems that not only are the opportunities for review inadequate, but also the will to review has been lacking where it could count most.

Little can be done, beyond exhortation, about congressional unwillingness to undertake periodic and reasonably comprehensive reviews of performance in the military manpower procurement system. But exhortation ought to be accompanied by some specific suggestions for improving the opportunities for review. Probably no fixed system of reporting and congressional review could meet the need for all time. What is needed now is reporting which focuses atten- √ tion on important but neglected aspects of the procurement system, and the most obvious of these is the relation between compulsory service and equity. Assuming that the approach to equity is to be one of spreading the risk of conscription across a broader proportion of military-age youth, as urged above, a number of kinds of information would be useful in assessing performance. The Defense Department could be required to keep up to date, and report periodically, its analyses of relations among pay and benefits, entry standards, civilian-military substitutability, costs, force-effectiveness, and the need for compulsory procurement. It could also be required to report on the more specific manpower needs of the armed forces for officers and for medical and dental professionals, and the extent to which these needs might justify student deferments. The Selective Service System could be required to include in its reports, in addition to data on the scope of deferments, summaries of sample surveys of local board performance in granting discretionary deferments. If information of these kinds were available, to the public as well as to congressional committees, fairly little exhortation might be needed to induce annual or biennial reviews of administrative performance in military manpower procurement.

The debate over military manpower procurement policies is far from being finished business. As with most governmental policies and programs, military manpower procurement affects both very concrete national and private interests and much more abstract national aspirations; but in few other policy areas are the interests so vital and the aspirations so difficult to translate into governmental action.

The military manpower procurement system that finally emerged in the midst of the Korean War was neither achieved with undue haste nor ill-suited to the time. But this setting for policy development induced a subsequent lack of political will and opportunity for review; and this led to administrative overemphasis on concrete national needs and a concommitant disregard for abstract aspirations. If Selective Service survives into the 1970's, the extent of its reform will depend on how thoroughly the policy-makers' interests in nonmilitary impacts of conscription is recast from cold war to domestic welfare terms, and on the extent to which this shift encourages explicit attention to problems of equity. But the survival of Selective Service depends on more than its reform. Whether an all-volunteer system will replace it will also depend on how and how much the Vietnam experience affects policy-makers' attitudes toward military security needs and toward trade-offs among military manpower demands, budget costs, and resistance to conscription. Whatever the substantive results, it does seem that military manpower procurement policies have escaped their rigid mid-century framework, and that those rigidities and oversimplifications should not and need not occur again.

Notes

CHAPTER ONE

1. U.S. Congress, House, *The State of the Union*, H. Doc. No. 1, A message from the President of the United States, 79th Cong., 1st sess., 1945, p. 13.

2. John C. Sparrow, *History of Personnel Demobilization in the United States Army* (Washington: Office of the Chief of Military History, Department of the Army, 1951), p. 57.

3. U.S. Department of Defense, Office of the Secretary of Defense, Directorate for Statistical Services, *Selected Manpower Statistics* (Washington: Department of Defense, 11 April 1966) (short reference: Department of Defense, *Selected Manpower Statistics*, 1966), p. 7.

4. For a detailed legislative history of the Selective Training and Service Act of 1940, see U.S. Selective Service System, *The Selective Service Act, Its Legislative History, Amendments, Appropriations, Cognates and Prior Instruments of Security*, Special Monograph No. 2, vols. 1-5 (Washington: U.S. Government Printing Office, 1945). For an account of congressional and public debate over the act, and of the roles of Grenville Clark, Robert Patterson, and their associates in its initiation and enactment, see Samuel Reid Spencer, Jr., *A History of the Selective Training and Service Act of 1940, from Inception to Enactment* (unpublished doctoral dissertation, Harvard University, 1951).

5. U.S. Congress, House, Select Committee on Postwar Military Policy, *Universal Military Training*, Hearings, 79th Cong., 1st sess., 1945 (short reference: HCPMP, *UMT*, Hearings, 79C1).

6. Ibid., pp. 489, 491-92.

7. Ibid., p. 493.

8. Ibid., pp. 568, 571.

9. Ibid., pp. 483-84.

10. Sparrow, op. cit., pp. 82-84, 86-88.

11. HCPMP, *UMT*, Hearings, 79C1, pp. 566 (King), 576 (Marshall).

12. *New York Times*, April 30, 1943, p. 1; August 19, 1944, p. 1; September 9, 1944, p. 18.

13. HCPMP, *UMT*, Hearings, 79C1, p. 404.

14. Ibid., p. 177.

15. Ibid., pp. 526 (Forrestal), 569 (Marshall).

16. Walter Millis, ed., *The Forrestal Diaries* (New York: The Viking Press, 1951), pp. 59-60.

17. HCPMP, *UMT*, Hearings, 79C1, p. 302.

18. See Hanson W. Baldwin, "Conscription for Peacetime?", *Harper's Magazine*, March, 1945, pp. 289-300.

19.   See also John Fischer, "The Future Defense of the U.S.A.," *Harper's Magazine*, January, 1945, p. 161.

20.   HCPMP, *UMT*, Hearings, 79C1, p. 571.

21.   Ibid., pp. 532 (Fitch), 547 (Eaker).

22.   Ibid., p. 481 (Stimson).

23.   Ibid., p. 548 (Eaker).

24.   Baldwin, op. cit., pp. 298-99.

25.   HCPMP, *UMT*, Hearings, 79C1, p. 194.

26.   For a record of these early statutes see U.S. Selective Service System, *Backgrounds of Selective Service*, Special Monograph No. 1, vol. II, parts 1-14 (Washington: U.S. Government Printing Office, 1947).

27.   Denis S. Philipps, *The American People and Compulsory Military Service* (unpublished doctoral dissertation, New York University, 1956), p. 82.

28.   HCPMP, *UMT*, Hearings, 79C1, pp. 489-90. For the content of the Washington-Knox militia plan, see Washington's "Sentiments on a Peace Establishment," a 1783 treatise which remained in manuscript form until it was published in John McAuley Palmer, *Washington, Lincoln, Wilson, Three War Statesmen* (New York: Doubleday, Doran and Co., Inc., 1930).

29.   Philipps, op. cit., pp. 256, 304.

30.   See Enoch H. Crowder, *The Spirit of Selective Service* (New York: The Century Company, 1920), for extended discussion of the contrast between World War I and earlier experiences with draft laws.

31.   HCPMP, *UMT*, Hearings, 79C1, p. 558.

32.   Baldwin, op. cit., p. 293.

33.   HCPMP, *UMT*, Hearings, 79C1, pp. 193 (Compton), 325 (Marsh).

34.   U.S. Congress, House, Select Committee on Postwar Military Policy, *Universal Military Training*, H. Rept. No. 857, 79th Cong., 1st sess., 1945, pp. 3, 4.

35.   The record of pre-V-J Day House hearings appears in U.S. Congress, House, Committee on Military Affairs, *Demobilization of the Army*, Hearings, 79th Cong., 1st sess., 1945; the committee continued its review in September and October, *Demobilization*, 79th Cong., 1st sess., 1945; and in January, *Demobilization*, 79th Cong., 2d sess., 1946. Senate hearings in August, October, and January appear in U.S. Congress, Senate, Committee on Military Affairs, *Demobilization of the Armed Forces*, Hearings, 79th Cong., 1st and 2d sess., 1945-46 (short reference: SCMA, *Demobilization*, Hearings, 79C1,2).

36.   Sparrow, op. cit., pp. 329-31.

37.   *Congressional Record*, vol. 92, pp. A91-A92.

38.   Sparrow, op. cit., p. 361; SCMA, *Demobilization*, Hearings, 79C1,2, p. 223.

39.   Millis, op. cit., pp. 89-90, 102.

40.   Harry S. Truman, *Memoirs*, vol. 1, *Year of Decisions* (Garden City, New York: Doubleday & Co., Inc., 1955), p. 509.

41.   Sparrow, op. cit., p. 340.

42.   Truman, op. cit., p. 510.

43. U.S. Congress, House, *Universal Military Training*, H. Doc. No. 359, Address of the President of the United States, 79th Cong., 1st sess., 1945.

44. U.S. Congress, House, Committee on Military Affairs, *Universal Military Training*, Hearings 79th Cong., 1st and 2d sess., 1945-46 (short reference: HCMA, *UMT*, Hearings, 79C1,2).

45. Ibid., pp. 3, 5.

46. Ibid., p. 11.

47. Ibid., p. 359.

48. H. Res. 325, 79th Cong.; introduced by Representative Joseph W. Martin (R., Mass.).

49. Details of the Legion plan are drawn from HCMA, *UMT*, Hearings, 79C1,2, pp. 770-802; and from The American Legion, National Defense Division, *The American Legion Plan for Universal Training and National Security* (Indianapolis: The American Legion, 1945).

50. HCMA, *UMT*, Hearings, 79C1,2, p. 652.

51. U.S. Congress, House, Committee on Military Affairs, *International Abolition of Conscription*, Hearings, 79th Cong., 2d sess., 1946.

52. See U.S. Congress, House, Committee on Military Affairs, *Extension of Selective Training and Service Act*, Hearings, 79th Cong., 1st sess., 1945; H. Rept. No. 362, report to accompany H.R. 2625, 79th Cong., 1st sess., 1945; *Congressional Record*, vol. 91, pp. 2264, 3558-70, 3603-11, 3640-58, 3708-33, 3906; *New York Times*, March 23, 1945, p. 32; March 28, 1945, p. 1; April 20, 1945, p. 1; April 24, 1945, p. 17; May 10, 1945, p. 17; Sparrow, op. cit., p. 151.

53. *New York Times*, August 15, 1945, p. 13; September 3, 1945, p. 25; September 22, 1945, p. 1.

54. SCMA, *Demobilization*, Hearings, 79C1,2, pp. 350-51, 359, 360, 379-80. It is not possible to compare these estimates by category with the V-J Day estimates for strengths on July 1, 1946; the figure for inductees since V-E Day remaining involuntarily in service has been calculated residually.

55. Executive Order 9605, August 29, 1945.

56. P.L. 190, 79th Cong., October 6, 1945.

57. SCMA, *Demobilization*, Hearings, 79C1,2, pp. 350-51, 380-81.

58. Ibid., p. 362.

59. *New York Times*, February 14, 1946, p. 22.

60. Ibid., February 15, 1946, p. 11.

61. Ibid., March 1, 1946, p. 1; March 14, 1946, p. 1.

62. U.S. Congress, House, Committee on Military Affairs, *Extension of the Selective Training and Service Act*, Hearings, 79th Cong., 2d sess., 1946 (short reference: HCMA, *Extension of Selective Service*, Hearings, 79C2); same title, H. Rept. No. 1922, Report to accompany H.R. 6064, 79th Cong., 2d sess., 1946; Senate, Committee on Military Affairs, *Selective Service Extension*, Hearings, 79th Cong., 2d sess., 1946 (short reference: SCMA, *Selective Service Extension*, Hearings, 79C2); same title, S. Rept. No. 1167, Report to accompany S. 2057, 79th Cong., 2d sess., 1946.

63. HCMA, *Extension of Selective Service*, Hearings, 79C2, pp. 15-16.

64. Ibid., pp. 261-62.

65. U.S. Congress, House, *Extension of Selective Training and Service Act*, H. Rept. No. 2319, Conference report to accompany H.R. 6064, 79th Cong., 2d sess., 1946.

66. *Congressional Record*, vol. 92, pp. 3660, 3663, 3665, 3667-69, 6244, 6341.

67. Ibid., p. 6126.

68. U.S. Congress, House, *Pay Increases for Personnel of the Army, Navy, Marine Corps, Coast Guard, Coast and Geodetic Survey, and Public Health Service*, H. Rept. No. 2318, Conference report to accompany H.R. 6084, 79th Cong., 2d sess., 1946.

69. SCMA, *Selective Service Extension*, Hearings, 79C2, p. 221.

70. HCMA, *Extension of Selective Service*, Hearings, 79C2, p. 83.

71. SCMA, *Selective Service Extension*, Hearings, 79C2, p. 243.

72. HCMA, *Extension of Selective Service*, Hearings, 79C2, p. 27.

73. *Congressional Record*, vol. 92, pp. 3585-86, 3649, 4963-64, 4995.

74. *New York Times*, May 15, 1946, p. 1; May 17, 1946, p. 1; May 28, 1946, p. 1; May 30, 1946, p. 3.

75. *Congressional Record*, vol. 92, p. 6223.

76. SCMA, *Selective Service Extension*, Hearings, 79C2, p. 42.

77. *Congressional Record*, vol. 92, pp. 3668, 6239.

78. Ibid., pp. 3660, 3665, 3667, 6242.

79. SCMA, *Selective Service Extension*, Hearings, 79C2, pp. 205-6; the words were Roscoe Conkling's, for the New York Committee Against Peacetime Conscription.

80. *Congressional Record*, vol. 92, pp. 6121, 6123.

81. *New York Times*, June 26, 1946, p. 1.

82. Ibid., October 20, 1946, p. E-8; all Army enlistment figures cited below, through September, 1946, are drawn from this source.

83. Advertisement in ibid., June 4, 1946, p. 17.

84. Ibid., August 6. 1946, p. 23.

85. Ibid., October 1, 1946, p. 23; October 11, 1946, p. E-8; October 12, 1946, p. 1.

86. Ibid., October 12, 1946, p. 1; October 20, 1946, p. E-8; January 7, 1947, p. 16; Sparrow, op. cit., p. 352.

87. *New York Times*, December 3, 1946, p. 33; January 28, 1947, p. 2; March 4, 1947, p. 1.

88. Sparrow, op. cit., p. 353.

89. U.S. Congress, House, *No Extension of the Selective Service Act at this Time*, H. Doc. No. 162, Message from the President of the United States, 80th Cong., 1st sess., 1947; *New York Times*, March 4, 1947, p. 15; U.S. Congress, House, *Office of Selective Service Records*, H. Doc. No. 168, Message from the President of the United States, 80th Cong., 1st sess., 1947.

90. *New York Times*, September 19, 1946, p. 15; October 3, 1946, p. 1. U.S. War Department, Public Relations Division, *A Plan for Universal Military Training*, 1946 (short reference: War Department UMT Plan, 1946).

91. *New York Times*, November 29, 1946, p. 27.

92. A great amount of information about this UMT experiment was published at the time in newspapers, magazines, and special pamphlets. A representative example is "A Report on Universal Military Training," *Army Information Digest*, June, 1947, pp. 9-44; for a much more skeptical view, see Alexander Stewart, "Is 'Umtee' the Answer?", *The Christian Century*, May 28, 1947, pp. 680-82.

93. U.S. Congress, House, Committee on Expenditures in the Executive Department, Publicity and Propaganda Subcommittee, *Investigation of Participation of Federal Officials of the War Department in Publicity and Propaganda as It Relates to Universal Military Training*, H. Rept. No. 1073, 80th Cong., 1st sess., 1947.

94. U.S. President's Advisory Commission on Universal Training, *A Program for National Security*, Report, May 29, 1947 (Washington: U.S. Government Printing Office, 1947) (short reference: Compton Report, 1947).

95. Truman, *Year of Decisions*, pp. 511-12; *New York Times*, December 21, 1946, pp. 1, 5.

96. Compton Report, 1947, p. 2.

97. Ibid., pp. 3, 5, 90.

98. Ibid., p. 29.

99. Ibid., pp. 12, 13, 18.

100. Ibid., p. 39.

101. Ibid., p. 42.

102. U.S. Congress, House, Committee on Armed Services, *Universal Military Training*, Hearings on sundry legislation No. 178, 80th Cong., 1st sess., 1947 (short reference: HCAS, *UMT*, Hearings, 80C1); Committee on Armed Services, Subcommittee No. 2, Education and Training, *Universal Military Training*, Hearings on sundry legislation No. 186, 80th Cong., 1st sess., 1947.

103. U.S. Congress, House, Committee on Armed Services, *Universal Military Training*, H. Rept. No. 1107, Report to accompany H.R. 4278, 80th Cong., 1st sess., 1946, p. 7.

104. *New York Times*, May 4, 1947, p. 24.

105. *Congressional Record*, vol. 93, pp. 5775-77.

106. U.S. Congress, House, Committee on Armed Services, *H.R. 4278 and H.R. 612*, Hearings on sundry legislation No. 169, 80th Cong., 1st sess., 1947; Committee on Armed Services, Subcommittee No. 2, Education and Training, *H.R. 4278*, Hearings on sundry legislation No. 190, 80th Cong., 1st sess., 1947; *New York Times*, July 26, 1947, p. 11.

107. *New York Times*, December 24, 1946, p. 9 (Johnson); June 27, 1947, p. 5 (Taft).

108. See Compton Report, 1947, pp. 222-42, for summaries of opinion polls on this and related subjects.

109. *New York Times*, November 11, 1946, p. 3.

110. Millis, op. cit., p. 243.

111. *New York Times*, August 28, 1947, p. 1; August 29, 1947, p. 1; October 2, 1947, p. 19; December 28, 1947, p. 14; December 20, 1947, p. 15; November 22, 1947, p. 8.

112. Ibid., January 8, 1948, p. 3; January 13, 1948, p. 17; February 3, 1948, p. 9; February 2, 1948, p. 13.

113. Ibid., January 5, 1948, p. 9; January 8, 1948, p. 2; January 29, 1948, p. 1; January 30, 1948, p. 16; February 19, 1948, p. 27; February 26, 1948, p. 12.

114. HCAS, *UMT*, Hearings, 80C1, p. 4476.

115. Ibid., p. 4213.

116. Robert M. Hutchins, quoted in *New York Times*, August 13, 1945, p. 13.

117. Elias Huzar, *The Purse and the Sword* (Ithaca: Cornell University Press, 1950), pp. 175-76.

CHAPTER TWO

1. U.S. Congress, House, *Foreign Policy and National Security*, H. Doc. No. 569, Address of the President of the United States before a Joint Session of the Senate and House of Representatives, 80th Cong., 2d sess., 1948 (short reference: H. Doc. No. 569, 80C2), pp. 3-4.

2. *New York Times*, August 20, 1946, p. 9.

3. Walter Millis, ed., *The Forrestal Diaries* (New York: The Viking Press, 1951), pp. 375-76.

4. Ibid., pp. 370, 373.

5. U.S., *The Budget of the United States Government, Fiscal Year 1949* (Washington: U.S. Government Printing Office, 1948), pp. 11-15.

6. *New York Times*, January 16, 1948, p. 1.

7. U.S. Congress, House, Committee on Armed Services, *Selective Service Act of 1948*, H. Rept. No. 1881, Report to accompany H. R. 6401, 80th Cong., 2d sess. (short reference: H. Rept. No. 1881, 80C2), p. 4. Figures are rounded to nearest 100, and refer to enlisted strength only.

8. Millis, op. cit., pp. 369, 377.

9. *New York Times*, January 1, 1948, p. 5.

10. Ibid., March 3, 1948, p. 1; March 9, 1948, p. 1; see also Millis, op. cit., p. 384.

11. *New York Times*, January 16, 1948, p. 1.

12. Millis, op. cit., pp. 377, 386, 390.

13. Ibid., pp. 393-94.

14. H. Doc. No. 569, pp. 4-5.

15. *New York Times*, March 18, 1948, p. 7.

16. Ibid., January 16, 1948, p. 1; February 15, 1948, p. 1.

17. The first of these was the product of a civilian Air Policy Committee, appointed in 1947 by President Truman and chaired by Thomas K. Finletter; the second was produced by the Joint Congressional Aviation Policy Board under Senator Owen Brewster; Millis, op. cit., pp. 373-74.

18. Ibid., p. 374.

19. U.S. Congress, Senate, Committee on Armed Services, *Universal Military*

Training, Hearings, 80th Cong., 2d sess., 1948 (short reference: SCAS, *UMT*, Hearings, 80C2), p. 5.

20. U.S. Office of Selective Service Records, *Report of the Director, 1947-1948* (Washington: U. S. Government Printing Office, 1950) (short reference: OSSR, *Report, 1947-1948*), p. 95.

21. SCAS, *UMT*, Hearings, 80C2, pp. 34, 39.

22. Ibid., pp. 330-32.

23. Ibid., pp. 331, 332, 337, 398.

24. Ibid., pp. 350, 354-55, 358, 375, 377, 379, 392-93.

25. Ibid., p. 331; emphasis added.

26. Ibid., p. 382.

27. Ibid., pp. 382-87, 389, 390, 392.

28. Ibid., pp. 396-97.

29. Parts of this memorandum were reprinted in U.S. Congress, House, Committee on Armed Services, *Selective Service*, Hearings on sundry legislation, No. 265, 80th Cong., 2d sess., 1948 (short reference: HCAS, *Selective Service*, Hearings 80C2), p. 6127.

30. *Congressional Record*, vol. 94, p. D238.

31. HCAS, *Selective Service*, Hearings, 80C2, pp. 6127-28.

32. Ibid., pp. 6128-29.

33. Ibid., p. 6138.

34. Quoted by Forrestal in a formal statement to an executive session of the Senate Armed Services Committee on April 21, which was released to the press and printed in *New York Times*, April 22, 1948, p. 13.

35. HCAS, *Selective Service*, Hearings, 80C2, pp. 6209, 6211, 6214, 6216.

36. Ibid., p. 6228.

37. Millis, op. cit., pp. 345-46, 370-73, 405-6, 410-11.

38. *Congressional Record*, vol. 94, p. 4542.

39. Millis, op. cit., pp. 418-19.

40. Ibid., p. 420.

41. Ibid., pp. 416-17, 420.

42. U.S. Congress, Senate, Committee on Armed Services, *Selective Service Act of 1948*, S. Rept. No. 1268, Report to accompany S. 2655, 80th Cong., 2d sess., 1948; U.S. Congress, House, Committee on Armed Services, *Selective Service Act of 1948*, H. Rept. No. 1881, Report to accompany H. R. 6401, 80th Cong., 2d sess., 1948 (short reference: H. Rept. No. 1881, 80C2); U.S. Congress, House, *Selective Service Act of 1948*, H. Rept. No. 2438, Conference report to accompany S. 2655, 80th Cong., 2d sess., 1948.

43. H. Rept. No. 1881, 80C2, p. 28.

44. Millis, op. cit., pp. 421, 425-28.

45. Ltr. from Forrestal to Chairman Gurney, recording his response to suggestions by Senators Baldwin (R., Conn.) and Tydings (D., Md.); included in Forrestal's later testimony to the House Committee, HCAS, *Selective Service*, Hearings 80C2, pp. 6637-8.

46. *Congressional Record*, vol. 94, p. 7553.

47. HCAS, *Selective Service*, Hearings, 80C2, pp. 6081, 6100, 6119-20.

48. H. Rept. No. 1881, 80C2, pp. 21, 28.

49. *Congressional Record*, vol. 94, pp. 8701, 8703, 8355, 9273.

50. Ibid., pp. 7570, 8510.

51. Ibid., p. 8559; the teller vote was 135-90.

52. Ibid., pp. 7325-26.

53. Ibid., pp. 8663, 8667.

54. Ibid., pp. 7302, 8676.

55. New York Times, May 5, 1948, p. 1; May 7, 1948, p. 7; May 15, 1948, p. 7.

56. *Congressional Record*, vol. 94, pp. 8343, 8354, 8704, 8999.

57. Ibid., p. 7001.

58. Ibid., p. 7525.

59. Ibid., pp. 7589, 7594-95, 7679, 8344, 8351, 8523; in the Senate, the amendment was defeated by voice vote, reconsidered, and defeated again, 22-66; in the House, the vote was 156-88.

60. Ibid., pp. 8398, 9668.

61. Ibid., p. 8682.

62. Ibid., p. 8700.

63. SCAS, *UMT*, Hearings, 80C2, p. 668.

64. *Congressional Record*, vol. 94, p. 8995.

65. *New York Times*, June 13, 1948, p. E-10.

66. See Millis, op. cit., pp. 435-39, 449-50, 492-530, 538; and Warner R. Schilling, "The Politics of National Defense, Fiscal 1950," in Warner R. Schilling, Paul Y. Hammond, and Glenn H. Snyder, *Strategy, Politics, and Defense Budgets* (New York: Columbia University Press, 1962), pp. 1-266.

67. Millis, op. cit., pp. 437-38.

68. U.S. Selective Service System, *Selective Service under the 1948 Act*, Report of the Director, 1948-1950 (Washington: U.S. Government Printing Office, 1951) (short reference: SSS, *Report*, 1948-50), p. 137.

69. OSSR, *Report, 1947-1948*, pp. 20, 23-29, 61, 67-68, 85, 93.

70. SSS, *Report*, 1948-50, pp. 16, 35-53, 57.

71. *New York Times*, June 27, 1948, p. 35; July 17, 1948, p. 6; July 20, 1948, p. 26 (Hershey); July 27, 1948, p. 1; July 31, 1948, p. 16; August 8, 1948, p. 18; August 9, 1948, p. 1; September 1, 1948, p. 15.

72. *New York Times*, August 17, 1948, p. 10; August 28, 1948, p. 2; September 23, 1948, p. 21; October 26, 1948, p. 1.

73. Ibid., December 1, 1948, p. 1; January 9, 1949, p. 25; January 14, 1949, p. 16; SSS, *Report*, 1948-50, pp. 15-16, 248.

74. *New York Times*, October 15, 1949, p. 5; SSS, *Report*, 1948-50, pp. 16-17.

75. SSS, *Report*, 1948-50, pp. 87-88, 117, 267; U.S., *The Budget of the United States Government, Fiscal Year 1951* (Washington: U.S. Government Printing Office, 1950), p. 116.

76. U.S., *The Budget of the United States Government, Fiscal Year 1950* (Washington: U.S. Government Printing Office, 1949), pp. M-18, M-29, M-22.

77. U.S. Congress, House, Committee on Armed Services, *Composition of the Army and Air Force*, Hearings and papers No. 12, 81st Cong., 1st sess., 1949, pp. 156, 164-65, 168, 315-16.

78. Millis, op. cit., p. 546.

79. Paul Y. Hammond, "Super Carriers and B-36 Bombers: Appropriations, Strategy, and Politics," in Harold Stein, ed., *American Civil-Military Decisions* (Birmingham: University of Alabama Press, 1963), pp. 465-564.

80. *New York Times*, October 29, 1948, p. 12 (Bradley quotation); November 12, 1949, p. 3; December 15, 1949, p. 5; December 18, 1949, p. 5; U.S. Congress, House, *The State of the Union*, H. Doc. No. 389, Address of the President of the United States, 81st Cong., 2d sess., 1950, p. 3.

81. U.S. Congress, House, Committee on Armed Services, *Selective Service Act Extension*, Hearings and papers No. 169, 81st Cong., 2d sess., 1950 (short reference: HCAS, *Selective Service Act Extension*, Hearings 1, 81C2); U.S. Congress, House, Committee on Armed Services, *To Extend the Selective Service Act of 1948 (H. R. 6826)*, vol. 2, Hearings and papers No. 190, 81st Cong., 2d sess., 1950 (short reference: HCAS, *Selective Service Act Extension*, Hearings 2, 81C2); U.S. Congress, House, Committee on Armed Services, *Selective Service Extension Act of 1950*, H. Rept. No. 2018, Report to accompany H. R. 6826, 81st Cong., 2d sess., 1950 (short reference: H. Rept. No. 2018, 81C2); *Congressional Record*, vol. 96, p. 7686. The vote for the bill, on division, was 216-11.

82. U.S. Congress, Senate, Committee on Armed Services, *Selective Service Extension Act of 1950*, Hearings, 81st Cong., 2d sess., 1950; U.S. Congress, Senate, Committee on Armed Services, *Providing for the Common Defense through the Registration and Classification of Certain Male Persons, and for Other Purposes*, S. Rept., No. 1784, Report to accompany H. R. 6826, 81st Cong., 2d sess., 1950 (short reference: S. Rept. No. 1784, 81C2); *Congressional Record*, vol. 96, pp. 9072, 9077.

83. *Congressional Record*, vol. 96, pp. 9065, 9108. S. J. Res. 190, 81st Cong.

84. U.S. Congress, House, *Extension of Selective Service Act of 1948*, H. Rept. No. 2345, Conference report to accompany H. R. 6826, 81st Cong., 2d sess., 1950; *Congressional Record*, vol. 96, pp. 9292, 9316, 9631.

85. HCAS, *Selective Service Act Extension*, Hearings 1, 81C2, p. 5108.

86. Ibid., p. 5157.

87. Ibid., pp. 5127 (Gray), 5154 (Collins), 5159 (Bradley).

88. Ibid., p. 5162.

89. *New York Times*, April 27, 1950, p. 24.

90. *Congressional Record*, vol. 96, pp. 7673, 7674 (Havenner), 7677.

91. H. Rept. No. 2018, 81C2, p. 12.

92. S. Rept. No. 1784, 81C2, p. 9.

93. *Congressional Record*, vol. 96, pp. 9069-71.

94. *Congressional Record*, vol. 96, pp. 9291-92, 9317.

95. Paul Y. Hammond, "NSC-68: Prologue to Rearmament," in Schilling, Hammond, and Snyder, op. cit., p. 281.

96. Samuel P. Huntington, *The Common Defense: Strategic Programs in National Politics* (New York: Columbia University Press, 1961), pp. 44-45.

97. "X" [George F. Kennan], "Sources of Soviet Conduct," *Foreign Affairs*, vol. 25 (July, 1947), pp. 566-82; Schilling, Hammond, and Snyder, op. cit., pp. 293-94.

98. Huntington, *The Common Defense*, p. 47.

99. This account of the background, origins, and production of NSC-68 is drawn from Hammond's in Schilling, Hammond, and Snyder, op. cit., pp. 279-330.

100. Huntington, *The Common Defense*, p. 51.

101. Schilling, Hammond, and Snyder, op. cit., pp. 318-19.

102. Ibid., p. 320.

103. Ibid., p. 341.

104. Ibid., pp. 300-304, 321-26, 336-40. The "climate of opinion" phrase and concept are Schilling's, in ibid., pp. 95-134.

105. Ibid., pp. 331-33; Huntington, *The Common Defense*, pp. 52-53.

106. H. Rept. No. 2018, 81C2, p. 5.

107. P.L. 351, 81st Cong., October 12, 1949.

108. *New York Times*, July 8, 1950, p. 1; July 11, 1950, p. 1; July 28, 1950, p. 1.

109. P.L. 624, 81st Cong., July 27, 1950.

110. P.L. 655, 81st Cong., August 3, 1950.

111. P.L. 771, 81st Cong., September 8, 1950.

112. P.L. 779, 81st Cong., September 9, 1950.

113. U.S. Congress, Senate, Committee on Armed Services, *Amending the Selective Service Act of 1948, as Amended, and for Other Purposes; Suspension of 1-Year Enlistments*, S. Rept. No. 2264, Report to accompany S. 4027, 81st Cong., 2d sess., 1950; *Congressional Record*, vol. 96, p. 12487.

CHAPTER THREE

1. For a summary of the relation between NSC-68 and the strategic assumptions behind our entry into the Korean War, see Cabell Phillips' report in *New York Times*, April 13, 1964, p. 1.

2. The phrase is from George A. Lincoln, et al., *Economics of National Security*, 2d ed. (Englewood Cliffs, New Jersey: Prentice-Hall, 1954), p. 20.

3. Stressed at length in Harry S. Truman, *Memoirs*, vol. 2, *Years of Trial and Hope* (Garden City, New York: Doubleday & Co., Inc., 1956).

4. Samuel P. Huntington, *The Common Defense: Strategic Programs in National Politics* (New York: Columbia University Press, 1961), pp. 53-64. The role of NSC-68 in the rearmament effort is examined in Paul Y. Hammond, "NSC-68: Prologue to Rearmament," in Warner R. Schilling, Paul Y. Hammond, and Glenn H. Snyder, *Strategy, Politics, and Defense Budgets* (New York: Columbia University Press, 1962), pp. 345-63.

5. U.S. Congress, Senate, Committee on Armed Services, Preparedness Subcom-

mittee, *Universal Military Training and Service Act of 1951*, Hearings, 82d Cong., 1st sess., 1951 (short reference: SCAS, Preparedness Subcom, *UMT&S*, Hearings, 82C1), pp. 37-73, passim.

6.   U.S. Selective Service System, *Outline of Historical Background of Selective Service and Chronology* (Washington: U.S. Government Printing Office, 1960), pp. 20-21.

7.   U.S. Selective Service System, *Annual Report of the Director of Selective Service for Fiscal Year 1952* (Washington: U.S. Government Printing Office, 1953), p. 90. (Short reference for reports in this series: SSS, *Annual Report*, FY 19__.)

8.   SSS, *Annual Report*, FY 1953, figure 1, p. 10.

9.   *New York Times*, August 30, 1950, p. 1.

10.   SCAS, Preparedness Subcom, *UMT&S*, Hearings, 82C1, p. 28.

11.   Ibid., pp. 494-505.

12.   For committee hearings and reports, see SCAS, Preparedness Subcom, *UMT&S*, Hearings, 82C1; U.S. Congress, Senate, Committee on Armed Services, *Universal Military Training and Service Act*, S. Rept. No. 117, Report to accompany S. 1, 82d Cong., 1st sess., 1951 (short reference: S. Rept. No. 117, 82C1); House, Committee on Armed Services, *Universal Military Training*, Hearings and papers No. 4, 82d Cong., 1st sess., 1951 (short reference: HCAS, *UMT&S*, Hearings, 82C1); House, Committee on Armed Services, *1951 Amendments to the Universal Military Training and Service Act*, H. Rept. No. 271, Report to accompany S. 1, 82d Cong., 1st sess., 1951. For compromises between House and Senate versions of the bill, see U.S. Congress, House, *Universal Military Training and Service Act*, H. Rept. No. 535, Conference report to accompany S. 1, 82d Cong., 1st Sess., 1951.

13.   SCAS, Preparedness Subcom, *UMT&S*, Hearings, 82C1, p. 533.

14.   *Congressional Record*, vol. 97, p. 1909.

15.   Ibid., pp. 3907, 3913.

16.   The full report of the Thomas Committee is printed in SCAS, Preparedness Subcom, *UMT&S*, Hearings, 82C1, pp. 817-24. The proposal of the Association of American Universities is printed in ibid., p. 454. For a brief summary of these and other student deferment plans, see The National Manpower Council, *Student Deferment and National Manpower Policy* (New York: Columbia University Press, 1952), pp. 27-29.

17.   The Trytten Committee's report is reproduced in SCAS, Preparedness Subcom, *UMT&S*, Hearings, 82C1, pp. 845-61. It is also included as an appendix to M. H. Trytten, *Student Deferment in Selective Service* (Minneapolis: Minnesota University Press, 1952).

18.   *New York Times*, August 10, 1950, p. 1.

19.   This declaration of general policy was approved by President Truman on January 17, 1951. It is reprinted in SCAS, Preparedness Subcom, *UMT&S*, Hearings, 82C1, pp. 553-55.

20.   Ibid., p. 56.

21.   National Manpower Council, op. cit., p. 26.

22.   S. Rept. No. 117, 82C1, pp. 42, 50-52.

23.   SCAS, Preparedness Subcom, *UMT&S*, Hearings, 82C1, p. 437.

24.   Ibid., p. 509.

25. HCAS, *UMT&S*, Hearings, 28C1, p. 461.

26. *New York Times*, December 19, 1950, p. 1.

27. Trytten, op. cit., pp. 91-93.

28. Ibid., pp. 56-57, 84-86, 90-91.

29. For the origins of this test, see Henry Chauncey, "The Use of the Selective Service College Qualification Test in the Deferment of College Students," *Science*, July 25, 1952, p. 73.

30. Trytten, op. cit., p. 35.

31. *New York Times*, April 9, 1951, p. 1.

32. Adopted without vote; *Congressional Record*, vol. 97, p. 3682.

33. For a succinct summary of Hershey's administrative philosophy, see his December, 1950, letter to all local board members, reprinted in SCAS, Preparedness subcom, *UMT&S*, Hearings, 82C1, pp. 538-40.

34. The strongest show of opposition came on a proposal simply to strike the program from the bill. This amendment was defeated 21-68; *Congressional Record*, vol. 97, pp. 2169-74.

35. Ibid., pp. 2186, 2205.

36. Ibid., pp. 3525, 3602.

37. Ibid., p. 3796; the teller vote was 140-232.

38. Ibid., pp. 2053, 2056, 3901.

39. Ibid., p. 2195.

40. *New York Times*, June 20, 1951, p. 1.

41. The commission's full report, dated October 29, 1951, is printed as U.S. Congress, House, *Universal Military Training*, H. Doc. No. 315, First report of the National Security Training Commission, 82d Cong., 2d sess., 1952 (short reference: H. Doc. No. 315, 82C2). For committee hearings and reports, see U.S. Congress, House, Committee on Armed Services, *Universal Military Training*, Hearings and papers No. 55, 82d Cong., 2d sess., 1952 (short reference: HCAS, *UMT*, Hearings, 82C2); *National Security Training Corps Act*, H. Rept. No. 1376, Report to accompany H.R. 5904, 82d Cong., 2d sess., 1952; Senate, Committee on Armed Services, *National Security Training Corps Act*, Hearings, 82d Cong., 2d sess., 1952; and same title, S. Rept. No. 1205, Report to accompany S. 2441, 82d Cong., 2d sess., 1952 (short reference: S. Rept. No. 1205, 82C2).

42. *New York Times*, September 26, 1951, p. 43.

43. Ibid., January 6, 1952, p. 31.

44. S. Rept. No. 1205, 82C2, p. 17.

45. HCAS, *UMT*, Hearings, 82C2, p. 2414.

46. *Congressional Record*, vol. 98, pp. 1830, 1840.

47. Ibid., pp. 1863-64. The vote for recommittal was 236 (D 81, R 155) to 162 (D 132, R 30); *New York Times*, March 5, 1952, p. 10.

48. *New York Times*, April 19, 1951, p. 1; July 31, 1951, p. 12.

49. For analysis of the motives and tactics of the reserve associations, especially the Reserve Officers Association, in regard to this legislation, see William F. Levantrosser, *Congress and the Citizen Soldier* (Columbus: Ohio State University Press, 1967), pp. 51-72.

50. U.S. Congress, House, Committee on Armed Services, *Reserve Components,* Hearings before special subcommittee, 82d Cong., 1st sess., 1951; *H.R. 5426,* Hearings and papers No. 49, 82d Cong., 1st sess., 1951; *The Armed Forces Reserve Act of 1951,* H. Rept. No. 1066, Report to accompany H.R. 5426, 82d Cong., 1st sess., 1951.

51. *Congressional Record,* vol. 97, pp. 13148-65; the bill passed under suspension of the rules.

52. U.S. Congress, Senate, Committee on Armed Services, *Armed Forces Reserve Act,* Hearings before subcommittee, 82d Cong., 2d sess., 1952.

53. For an account of the NGA's motives and the implications of this incident for assessing the NGA's lobbying tactics and power, see Martha Derthick, *The National Guard in Politics* (Cambridge: Harvard University Press, 1965), pp. 155-57; see also Levantrosser, op. cit., pp. 58-59.

54. U.S. Congress, Senate, Committee on Armed Services, *The Armed Forces Reserve Act of 1952,* S. Rept. No. 1795, Report to accompany H.R. 5426, 82d Cong., 2d sess., 1952; *Congressional Record,* vol. 98, pp. 8294-8306.

55. U.S. Congress, House, *Armed Forces Reserve Act of 1952,* H. Rept. No. 2445, Conference report to accompany H.R. 5426, 82d Cong., 2d sess., 1952; *Congressional Record,* vol. 98, pp. 8906, 9005-18, 9573.

56. U.S. Department of Defense, Office of the Secretary of Defense, Directorate for Statistical Services, *Selected Manpower Statistics* (Washington: Department of Defense, 11 April 1966), p. 19.

57. See Hershey's testimony in U.S. Congress, Senate, Committee on Armed Services, *Manpower Utilization,* Hearing before a task force of the Preparedness Subcommittee, 82d Cong., 2d sess., 1952 (short reference: SCAS, Preparedness Subcom, *Manpower Utilization,* Hearings, 82C2).

58. H. Doc. No. 315, 82C2, p. 8.

59. See Hanson W. Baldwin in *New York Times,* February 14, 1952, p. 15; February 15, 1952, p. 8; July 15, 1952, p. 2. Baldwin had presented similar arguments much earlier, in his book *The Price of Power* (New York: Harper & Brothers, 1948), pp. 272-73.

60. See, for example, Penn Kimball, "The Terribly 'Normal' Class of '52," *New York Times Magazine,* June 8, 1952, p. 14.

61. *Congressional Record,* vol. 98, p. 1423.

62. Trytten, op. cit., pp. 31-32.

63. National Manpower Council, op. cit., pp. 12, 32, 34, 67.

64. Brigadier General Louis W. Renfrow, quoted in *New York Times,* July 30, 1951, p. 31.

65. SSS, *Annual Report,* FY 1952, pp. 24-26; FY 1953, pp. 18-19.

66. SCAS, Preparedness Subcom, *Manpower Utilization,* Hearings, 82C2, p. 6.

67. SSS, *Annual Report,* FY 1952, p. 25.

68. National Manpower Council, op. cit., pp. 58-59.

69. Ibid., pp. 9, 25.

70. SSS, *Annual Report,* FY 1953, pp. 17-18.

71. SCAS, Preparedness Subcom, *Manpower Utilization,* Hearings 82C2, pp. 323-28; SSS, *Annual Report,* FY 1952, pp. 8-9, 72.

CHAPTER FOUR

1. Samuel P. Huntington, *The Common Defense: Strategic Programs in National Politics* (New York: Columbia University Press, 1961), p. 435.

2. See Glenn H. Snyder, "The 'New Look' of 1953," in Warner R. Schilling, Paul Y. Hammond, and Glenn H. Snyder, *Strategy, Politics, and Defense Budgets* (New York: Columbia University Press, 1962), pp. 379-524; and Huntington, op. cit., pp. 64-122.

3. *New York Times*, February 26, 1953, p. 14.

4. The president's letter to the commission, outlining the problems to be considered by each group, is reprinted in U.S. National Security Training Commission, *20th Century Minutemen*, Report to the president on a reserve forces training program, December 1, 1953 (Washington: U.S. Government Printing Office, 1953) (short reference: NSTC, *20th Century Minutemen*), p. iv.

5. *New York Times*, January 8, 1954, p. 10; January 10, 1954, p. 1; January 13, 1954, p. 12.

6. U.S. Congress, Senate, Committee on Appropriations, *Department of Defense Appropriations, 1955*, Hearings before subcommittee, 83d Cong., 2d sess., 1954, pp. 21 (Wilson), 56 (Stevens), 61 (Ridgway).

7. *New York Times*, December 10, 1954, p. 13; December 11, 1954, p. 6; December 15, 1954, p. 14.

8. See U.S. Congress, House, Committee on Armed Services, Subcommittee No. 1, *National Reserve Plan*, Hearings and papers No. 11, 84th Cong., 1st sess., 1955, pp. 1244-50. Unless otherwise noted, details in the following account of congressional action on the Armed Forces Reserve Act of 1955 are drawn from U.S. Congress, House, Committee on Armed Services, *Reserve Forces Legislation, A Legislative History of the Reserve Forces Act of 1955*, Hearings and papers No. 82, 84th Cong., 2d sess., 1956 (prepared by Eilene Galloway, National Defense Analyst, Legislative Reference Service, Library of Congress, May, 1956), pp. 7535-67.

9. The subcommittee's rewritten bill was approved and reported by the full committee in U.S. Congress, House, Committee on Armed Services, *National Reserve Plan*, H. Rept. No. 457, Report to accompany H.R. 5297, 84th Cong., 1st sess., 1955 (short reference: H. Rept. No. 457, 84C1).

10. U.S. Congress, House, Committee on Armed Services, *Full Committee Hearing on H.R. 2107, Reserve Facilities Bill, and H.R. 5297, National Reserve Plan*, Hearings and papers No. 17, 84th Cong., 1st sess., 1955, p. 2860.

11. H. Rept. No. 457, 84C1, p. 24.

12. Ibid.

13. *New York Times*, May 1, 1955, p. 39; *Congressional Record*, vol. 101, pp. 6112, 6495-97, D237.

14. *Congressional Record*, vol. 101, p. 6574; the vote was 126-87.

15. Ibid., p. 6657; the teller vote was 143-167.

16. *New York Times*, June 9, 1955, p. 1; June 11, 1955, p. 7; June 12, 1955, p. 2.

17. Ibid., June 18, 1955, p. 1; June 4, 1955, p. 5; June 20, 1955, p. 8; June 24, 1955, p. 10; June 25, 1955, p. 16.

18. U.S. Congress, House, Committee on Armed Services, Subcommittee No. 1, *H.R. 6900 and H.R. 7000*, Hearings and papers No. 26, 84th Cong., 1st sess., 1955.

19. *New York Times*, June 22, 1955, p. 1.

20. U.S. Congress, House, Committee on Armed Services, *Full Committee Hearings on H.R. 6277, H.R. 6600, Real Estate Projects, and H.R. 7000*, Hearings and papers No. 25, 84th Cong., 1st sess., 1955; the committee vote was 29-1, with even Representative Short supporting the new bill. *Congressional Record*, vol. 101, pp. 9801, 9811; the Powell amendment was defeated on a 105-156 teller vote.

21. H. Rept. No. 457, 84C1, p. 16.

22. U.S. National Security Training Commission, *Annual Report to the Congress* (Washington: U.S. Government Printing Office, 1956), p. 42.

23. U.S. Congress, House, Committee on Armed Services, *Military Posture Briefing*, Hearings and papers No. 9, 85th Cong., 1st sess., 1957, p. 128.

24. U.S. Congress, House, Committee on Armed Services, Subcommittee No. 1, *Review of the Reserve Program*, Hearings and papers No. 22, 85th Cong., 1st sess., 1957.

25. U.S. Congress, House, Committee on Armed Services, *Action of Committee on U.S. Army—Army National Guard Reserve Training Requirements*, Hearings and papers No. 16, 85th Cong., 1st sess., 1957.

26. Ibid.; Executive Order 10714, June 13, 1957; U.S. Selective Service System, *Annual Report of the Director of Selective Service for Fiscal Year 1957* (Washington: U.S. Government Printing Office, 1958), p. 10. (Short reference for reports in this series: SSS, *Annual Report*, FY 19__.)

27. U.S. Congress, House, Committee on Armed Services, Subcommittee No. 1, *Review of the Reserve Program*, Hearings and papers No. 35, 85th Cong., 1st sess., 1957, p. 1409.

28. Huntington, op. cit., pp. 98-99, 139-44; Martha Derthick, *The National Guard in Politics* (Cambridge: Harvard University Press, 1965), pp. 144-49; William F. Levantrosser, *Congress and the Citizen Soldier* (Columbus: Ohio State University Press, 1967), pp. 97-124.

29. U.S. Congress, House, Committee on Armed Services, Subcommittee No. 3, *Consideration of H.R. 3368, a Bill to Extend the Special Enlistment Programs Provided by Section 262 of the Armed Forces Reserve Act of 1952, as Amended*, Hearings and papers No. 7, 86th Cong., 1st sess., 1959, p. 419.

30. *Congressional Record*, vol. 105, pp. 4152-55, 12017.

31. SSS, *Annual Report*, FY 1960, pp. 46, 48.

32. *New York Times*, September 6, 1956, p. 1; September 7, 1956, p. 1; September 18, 1956, p. 1.

33. Ibid., October 19, 1956, p. 1.

34. Ibid., October 7, 1956, p. 1; October 20, 1956, p. 10; November 2, 1956, p. 1.

35. Ibid., October 24, 1956, p. 14; November 4, 1956, p. 84.

36. Ibid., November 25, 1956, p. VI-12.

37. Annual reenlistment rates are the percent of those eligible to reenlist dur-

ing the period who do sign up for another term of service. Reenlistment figures and rates cited hereafter are, unless otherwise noted, drawn from U.S. Department of Defense, Office of the Secretary of Defense, Directorate for Statistical Services, *Selected Manpower Statistics* (Washington: Department of Defense, April 11, 1966) (short reference: Department of Defense, *Selected Manpower Statistics*, 1966), pp. 51-53.

38.   P.L. 506, 83d Cong. For a review of the reenlistment problems and the old and new bonus scales, see U.S. Congress, Senate, Committee on Armed Services, *Providing for Computation of Reenlistment Bonuses for Members of the Uniformed Services*, S. Rept. No. 1640, Report to accompany S. 3539, 83d Cong., 2d sess., 1954.

39.   P.L. 20, 84th Cong. For an explanation and details of the act, see U.S. Congress, Senate, Committee on Armed Services, *Career Incentive Act of 1955*, S. Rept. No. 125, Report to accompany H.R. 4720, 84th Cong., 1st sess., 1955.

40.   The Cordiner report and the Administration's responses to it are discussed in U.S. Congress, House, Committee on Armed Services, Subcommittee No. 2, *Method of Computing Basic Pay*, Hearings and papers No. 76, 85th Cong., 2d sess., 1958.

41.   *New York Times*, January 15, 1958, p. 1; U.S. Congress, House, *Military Pay Bill*, H. Rept. No. 1701, Conference report to accompany H.R. 11470, 85th Cong., 2d sess., 1958; Committee on Armed Services, *Adjusting the Method of Computing Basic Pay for Officers and Enlisted Members of the Uniformed Services, to Provide Proficiency Pay for Enlisted Members thereof and for Other Purposes*, H. Rept. No. 1538, Report to accompany H.R. 11470, 85th Cong., 2d sess., 1958.

42.   SSS, *Annual Report*, FY 1953, pp. 16, 31; *New York Times*, January 9, 1953, p. 1. The standard set was a score of 10 (that is, tenth percentile) or better on the Armed Forces Qualification Test.

43.   *New York Times*, November 7, 1953, p. 33; March 7, 1954, p. 37; SSS, *Annual Report*, FY 1954, p. 31; FY 1955, pp. 35, 89.

44.   U.S. Department of the Army, Office of the Surgeon General, "Results of the Examination of Youths for Military Service, 1963," prepared by Bernard D. Karpinos, supplement to *Health of the Army*, vol. 19 (Washington: Department of the Army, May, 1964) (short reference: Department of the Army, "Examination for Military Service").

45.   U.S. Congress, House, Committee on Armed Services, *Amend the Universal Training and Service Act to Authorize Additional Deferments*, H. Rept. No. 879, Report to accompany H.R. 8850, 85th Cong., 1st sess., 1957, p. 2.

46.   U.S. Congress, House, Committee on Armed Services, *Full Committee Hearings on H.R. 8850, to Amend the Universal Military Training and Service Act to Authorize Additional Deferments in Certain Cases*, Hearings and papers No. 53, 85th Cong., 1st sess., 1957 (short reference: HCAS, *Raising Induction Qualifications*, Hearings, 85C1); *Congressional Record*, vol. 103, pp. 13662-64; the bill passed under suspension of the rules. Brief Senate hearings were held in August, 1957; see U.S. Congress, Senate, Committee on Armed Services, *Miscellaneous Bills, S. 2305, H.R. 7914, H.R. 8531, H.R. 8850*, Hearings, 85th Cong., 1st sess., 1957 (short reference: SCAS, *Raising Induction Qualifications*, Hearings, 85C1).

47.   U.S. Congress, Senate, Committee on Armed Services, *Authorizing the President to Raise Mental and Physical Qualifications for Induction into the Armed*

Forces, S. Rept. No. 1827, Report to accompany H.R. 8850, 85th Cong., 2d sess., 1958; *Congressional Record,* vol. 104, p. 13972.

48. SSS, *Annual Report,* FY 1958, pp. 27-28; FY 1961, pp. 18-19, 73; Department of the Army, "Examination for Military Service," p. 26.

49. U.S. Congress, House, Committee on Armed Services, *Full Committee Hearings on H.R. 3005, to Further Amend the Universal Military Training and Service Act by Extending Authority to Induct Certain Individuals, and to Extend Benefits under the Dependents Assistance Act to July 1, 1959,* Hearings and papers No. 2, 84th Cong., 1st sess., 1955 (short reference: HCAS, *UMT&S Act Extension, 1955,* Hearings, 84C1); Senate, Committee on Armed Services, *1955 Amendments to the Universal Military Training and Service Act,* Hearings, 84th Cong., 1st sess., 1955 (short reference: SCAS, *UMT&S Act Extension 1955,* Hearings, 84C1); House, *1955 Amendments to the Universal Military Training and Service Act,* H. Rept. No. 902, Conference report to accompany H.R. 3005, 84th Cong., 1st sess., 1955.

50. *Congressional Record,* vol. 101, p. 1326; the division was 15-106.

51. The two-year extension was defeated on a 62-153 division; ibid., pp. 1322, 1329, 8463, 9338, 9380.

52. SSS, *Annual Report,* FY 1955, pp. 46-47.

53. U.S. Congress, Senate, Committee on Armed Services, *Extending the Authority to Induct Certain Individuals and to Extend the Benefits of the Dependents Assistance Act,* S. Rept. No. 549, Report to accompany H.R. 3005, 84th Cong., 1st sess., 1955.

54. Most other provisions of the Doctor Draft were also incorporated into the Universal Military Training and Service Act at this time; see SSS, *Annual Report,* FY 1957, pp. 9-10. For views of the Defense Department and of medical groups, see U.S. Congress, House, Committee on Armed Services, *Full Committee Hearings on H.R. 6548, to Amend the Universal Military Training and Service Act as Regards Persons in Medical, Dental, and Allied Specialist Categories,* Hearings and papers No. 33, 85th Cong., 1st Sess., 1957. For passage, see *Congressional Record,* vol. 103, pp. 7568, 8941.

55. U.S. Congress, House, Committee on Armed Services, *Consideration of H.R. 2260, to Extend until July 1, 1963, the Induction Provisions of the Universal Military Training and Service Act; the Provisions of the Act of August 3, 1950, Suspending Personnel Strength of the Armed Forces; and the Dependents Assistance Act of 1950,* Hearings and papers No. 2, 86th Cong., 1st sess., 1959 (short reference: HCAS, *UMT&S Act Extension, 1959,* Hearings, 86C1), p. 13.

56. U.S. Congress, Senate, Committee on Armed Services, *Extension of the Draft and Related Authorities,* Hearings, 86th Cong., 1st sess., 1959.

57. *Congressional Record,* vol. 105, pp. 1941, 1951, 3827-28, 4003.

58. Data in this paragraph are from SSS, *Annual Report,* FY 1953-61.

59. Calls from the group of I-A's aged nineteen to twenty-five were filled in order of birth dates, oldest first; hence a decline in the numbers being inducted tended to raise the average age of those drafted. Selective Service practice allows qualified registrants to volunteer for induction; such volunteers are generally younger than the involuntary inductees, which reduces the median age of all inductees somewhat.

60. Executive Order 19714, June 13, 1957, put Selective Service into the busi-

ness of deferring reservists on a large scale by requiring assignment to Class I-D of all men participating satisfactorily in Ready Reserve training; SSS, *Annual Report*, FY 1959, p. 10.

61. SSS, *Annual Report*, FY 1954, pp. 51-52; FY 1955, p. 63; FY 1956, pp. 63, 65; FY 1961, p. 45.

62. U.S. Congress, House, Committee on Appropriations, *Independent Offices Appropriations for 1955*, Hearings before subcommittee, 83d Cong., 2d sess., 1954, p. 681.

63. For Hershey's concept of "functional standards," see his long discussion of recruiting and screening in U.S. Congress, House, Committee on Appropriations, *Independent Offices Appropriations for 1953*, Hearings before subcommittee, 82d Cong., 2d sess., 1952, pp. 307-8, 310-19.

64. SSS, *Annual Report*, FY 1956, p. 65.

65. HCAS, *Raising Induction Qualifications*, Hearings, 85C1, p. 3407.

66. Totals for Class IV-F for the three dates in the text were 1,737,000, 2,453,000, and 3,322,000, respectively. To these have been added a proportion of the unclassified pool (totaling 93,000, 796,000, and 1,653,000 on the dates used) who might be expected to be rejected upon examination; this portion of the totals shown in the text was calculated by applying the "overall" rejection rates of 27 percent for 1953 and 1957, and 32 percent for 1961, to this unclassified group. This somewhat underestimates the total rejectable, as the unclassified group includes some men already rejected, and excludes large numbers already accepted, on application for enlistment.

67. Executive Order No. 10496, July 11, 1953, amended Selective Service regulations to preclude granting deferment for fatherhood alone on evidence filed after August 25, 1953. See SSS, *Annual Report*, FY 1953, p. 66.

68. The extent of the proviso's effect is detailed in SSS, *Annual Report*, FY 1953, pp. 76-78.

69. The changes in regulations effected by Executive Order 19659, February 15, 1956, are outlined in SSS, *Annual Report*, FY 1956, pp. 10-11, 27-29.

70. See SSS, *Annual Report*, FY 1956, p. 28; FY 1957, pp. 25-26 (quotations), 29, 36.

71. SSS, *Annual Report*, FY 1955, p. 17; FY 1957, pp. 61-62; FY 1958, p. 51, emphasis added. The word "channeled" first appeared in the reports in 1957 (p. 61), describing the hopes for draining down the working pool of available men by expansion of the Ready Reserve. The 1958 report marked the first time that term was used in the general sense of deferment from military service.

72. SSS, *Annual Report*, FY 1961, p. 11.

73. SSS, *Annual Report*, FY 1960, p. 29.

74. Department of Defense, *Selected Manpower Statistics*, 1966, p. 36.

75. SSS, *Annual Report*, FY 1961, p. 11.

76. U.S. Congress, House, Committee on Armed Services, *Universal Military Training*, Hearings and papers No. 4, 82d Cong., 1st sess., 1951 (Vinson, 1951); HCAS, *UMT&S Act Extension, 1955*, Hearings, 84C1, p. 39 (Vinson, 1955); SCAS, *UMT&S Act Extension, 1955*, Hearings, 84C1, p. 197 (Russell, 1955).

77. HCAS, *UMT&S Act Extension, 1959*, Hearings, 86C1, p. 29; see also charts at pp. 32-33, and additional explanations at pp. 24-32.

78. SCAS, *Raising Induction Qualifications*, Hearings, 85C1, pp. 20-23.

79. John Graham, *The Universal Military Obligation* (New York: Fund for the Republic, 1958), pp. 8, 9.

80. U.S. Congress, House, Committee on Armed Services, *Utilization of Military Manpower*, Report of special subcommittee, Hearings and papers No. 69, 86th Cong., 2d sess., 1960.

81. Graham, op. cit., p. 13.

82. SSS, *Annual Report*, FY 1958, p. 50.

83. The 1940 lottery had been abandoned in 1942, at the time the registration age was lowered to eighteen, and the age-order of induction, by date of birth, was set in its place. The official history of the Selective Service System explains only that this seemed a more "deliberate," and equally impartial, means of integrating new registrants into the induction sequence established for earlier registrants by a series of three earlier lotteries. U.S. Selective Service System, *Problems of Selective Service*, Special Monograph No. 16, vol. 1 (Washington: U.S. Government Printing Office, 1952), pp. 26, 28.

84. Graham, op. cit., p. 9.

85. HCAS, *UMT&S Act Extension, 1959*, Hearings, 86C1, p. 86.

86. New York Times, January 17, 1960, p. 40; March 13, 1960, p. IV-7; November 3, 1960, p. 1; November 7, 1960, p. 31; December 21, 1960, p. 25; SSS, *Annual Report*, FY 1960, p. 27.

CHAPTER FIVE

1. *New York Times*, July 26, 1961, pp. 1, 10.

2. S. J. Res. 120, 87th Cong.; P.L. 87-117.

3. For a detailed review of the reserve call, see U.S. Congress, House, Committee on Armed Services, Subcommittee No. 3, *Military Reserve Posture Hearings*, Hearings and papers No. 66, 87th Cong., 2d sess., 1962.

4. See reports in *New York Times*, November 18, 23, 27, 29, and December 1, 2, 4, 5, 6, 7, 8, 9, 18, 1961; February 12, 15, and March 4, 6, 20, 21, 1962.

5. See, for example, his news conference reported in ibid., November 30, 1961, pp. 1, 14.

6. See Martha Derthick, *The National Guard in Politics* (Cambridge: Harvard University Press, 1965), pp. 129-32, 135, 148-53; William F. Levantrosser, *Congress and the Citizen Soldier* (Columbus: Ohio State Uiversity Press, 1967), pp. 155-82. Major documentary sources on the dispute, in addition to the reserve posture hearings cited in note 3, include: U.S. Congress, House, Committee on Armed Services, Subcommittee No. 3, *Report on Military Reserve Posture*, Hearings and papers No. 70, 87th Cong., 2d sess., 1962; Committee on Armed Services, Subcommittee No. 2, *Merger of the Army Reserve Components*, Hearings and papers No. 39, 89th Cong., 1st sess., 1965; Senate, Committee on Armed Services, Preparedness Investigating Subcommittee, *Proposal to Realine the Army National Guard and the Army Reserve Forces*, Hearings, parts 1 and 2, 89th Cong., 1st sess., 1965; Committee on Appropriations, *Defense Appropriations Bill, 1966*, S. Rept. No. 625, Report to accompany H.R. 9221, 89th Cong., 1st sess., 1965.

7. Annual and average rates for this period are detailed in U.S. Department of Defense, Office of the Secretary of Defense, Directorate for Statistical Services, *Selected Manpower Statistics* (Washington: Department of Defense, 11 April 1966), pp. 52-54. (Short reference to reports in this series: Department of Defense, *Selected Manpower Statistics, 19__.*)

8. U.S. Congress, House, Committee on Armed Services, Subcommittee No. 1, *To Amend Title 37, United States Code, to Increase the Rates of Basic Pay for Members of the Uniformed Services, and for Other Purposes,* Hearings and papers No. 6, 88th Cong., 1st sess., 1963; House, Committee on Armed Services, *Military Pay Increase,* H. Rept. No. 208, Report to accompany H.R. 5555, 88th Cong., 1st sess., 1963: House, *Military Pay Increase,* H. Rept. No. 773, Conference report to accompany H.R. 5555, 88th Cong., 1st sess., 1963.

9. Documentary sources on this dispute include: U.S. Congress, House, Committee on Armed Services, *Military Pay Bills,* Hearings and papers No. 13, 89th Cong., 1st sess., 1965; Committee on Armed Services, *Uniformed Services Pay Act of 1965,* H. Rept. No. 549, Report to accompany H.R. 9075, 89th Cong., 1st sess., 1965; Senate, Committee on Armed Services, *Military Pay Increase,* Hearings, 89th Cong., 1st sess., 1965; Committee on Armed Services, *Increase in Rates of Basic Pay for Members of the Uniformed Services,* S. Rept. No. 544, 89th Cong., 1st sess., 1965.

10. U.S. Congress, House, Committee on Armed Services, *Consideration of H.R. 2438, to Extend the Induction Provisions of the Universal Military Training and Service Act, and for Other Purposes,* Hearings and papers No. 3, 88th Cong., 1st sess., 1963; Senate, Committee on Armed Services, *Extension of the Draft and Related Authorities,* Hearings, 88th Cong., 1st sess., 1963 (Russell quotation, p. 10); *Congressional Record,* vol. 109, pp. 3930, 3935, 3937, 4327-28.

11. Harvard Law School Forum, November 19, 1965.

12. U.S. Selective Service System, *Annual Report of the Director of Selective Service for Fiscal Year 1962* (Washington: U.S. Government Printing Office, 1963), p. 54 (short reference for reports in this series: SSS, *Annual Report,* FY 19__); SSS, *Annual Report,* FY 1964, p. 36; FY 1965, p. 42; Department of Labor, *Manpower Report of the President and A Report on Manpower Requirements, Resources, and Utilization* (Washington: U.S. Government Printing Office, 1966), p. 109. See also *New York Times,* September 5, 1961, p. 37; November 24, 1961, p. 20; October 1, 1963, p. 31; January 5, 1964, p. 1; and Daniel Patrick Moynihan, "Draft Rejectees: Nipping Trouble in the Bud," *The Reporter,* February 13, 1964, pp. 22-24.

13. SSS, *Annual Report,* FY 1962, pp. 8, 19.

14. *New York Times,* February 18, 1964, p. 17; August 14, 1964, p. 2; August 17, 1964, p. 75; *Army Times,* August 26, 1964, p. 1; September 2, 1964, pp. 1, 13; March 17, 1965, p. 1; June 30, 1965, p. 8; U.S. Congress, House, *Department of Defense Appropriations Bill, 1966,* H. Rept. No. 1006, Conference report to accompany H.R. 9221, 89th Cong., 1st sess., 1965.

15. Department of Defense, *Selected Manpower Statistics,* 1966, pp. 97, 99.

16. P.L. 87-378, October 4, 1961; P.L. 88-110, September 3, 1963.

17. SSS, *Annual Report,* FY 1963, p. 9; FY 1964, p. 8; U.S. Congress, House, Committee on Appropriations, *Independent Offices Appropriations for 1965,* Hear-

ings before subcommittee, 88th Cong., 2d sess., 1964, p. 1013; Senate, Committee on Appropriations, *Independent Offices Appropriations, 1964*, Hearings before subcommittee, 88th Cong., 1st sess., 1963, p. 1340 (Hershey quotation).

18. SSS, *Annual Report*, FY 1962, pp. 8, 19; FY 1964, p. 13.

19. U.S. Department of Defense, Office of the Assistant Secretary of Defense (Manpower), *Project 61* (unpublished staff study, October, 1962).

20. For details of the early impact of expansion, and views of the joint chiefs of staff and the Army chief of staff, see U.S. Congress, Senate, Committee on Armed Services, Preparedness Investigating Subcommittee, *U.S. Army Combat Readiness,* Hearings, 89th Cong., 2d sess., 1966. For a critique of the impact of expansion, see Hanson W. Baldwin, "The Case for Mobilization," *The Reporter*, May 19, 1966, pp. 20-23; see also Baldwin's articles in *New York Times*, October 14, 1965, p. 24; February 21, 1966, p. 1; April 8, 1966, p. 4; May 8, 1966, pp. 4 and IV-3; and text of a rebuttal statement by Secretary McNamara, ibid., March 3, 1966, p. 16.

21. Lloyd Norman, "Anatomy of a Decision," *Army*, September, 1965, pp. 25-34.

22. P.L. 90-168.

23. Department of Defense, *Selected Manpower Statistics*, 1968, pp. 51-52.

24. P.L. 89-501, P.L. 90-207.

25. Robert T. Stafford, et al., *How to End the Draft* (Washington: The National Press, Inc., 1967), chart at pp. 132-33; John B. Spore, "The U.S. Army in Vietnam," *Army*, May, 1966, pp. 28 ff.; S. L. A. Marshall, *Battles in the Monsoon* (New York: William Morrow and Company, Inc., 1967).

26. P.L. 89-358; see also *Army Times*, March 10, 1968, p. 1; *New York Times*, February 11, 1966, p. 13.

27. P.L. 89-501, P.L. 90-207.

28. SSS, *Annual Report*, FY 1966, p. 19.

29. Ibid., p. 17; Stafford, op. cit., p. 133.

30. *New York Times*, August 24, 1966, pp. 1, 24; August 28, 1966, p. IV-11; September 4, 1966, p. 2; October 10, 1966, p. 6; October 16, 1966, p. 6; November 19, 1967, p. 1; *Army Times*, September 7, 1966, p. 5; March 1, 1967, p. 1.

31. *New York Times*, December 3, 1965, p. 1; March 31, 1966, p. 1; *Army Times*, February 23, 1966, p. 6; March 23, 1966, p. 5; June 29, 1966, p. 7; July 27, 1966, p. 8; SSS, *Annual Report*, FY 1967, p. 23; Department of Defense, *Selected Manpower Statistics*, 1968, p. 93; U.S. Congress, Senate, Preparedness Investigating Subcommittee, *Personnel, Training, Equipment, and Readiness Status of Army Reserve Components*, Hearings, 89th Cong., 2d sess., 1966, pp. 7-10; *Congressional Record*, vol. 112, pp. 18860-84, 19797-805, 22486-506, 25007, 25027-28, 25033-34.

32. *Washington Post*, October 13, 1966, p. A8; May 6, 1967, p. A6; *New York Times*, December 3, 1966, p. 3; Department of Defense, *Selected Manpower Statistics*, 1968, pp. 46, 93.

33. *New York Times*, October 27, 1965, p. 1; October 28, 1965, p. 5; November 15, 1965, p. 1; SSS, *Annual Report*, FY 1966, p. 17; FY 1967, pp. 22-23.

34. *New York Times*, March 12, 1959, p. 8.

35. The major bills were S. 2432 and S. 2960, 88th Cong. For Senator Gold-

water's comments, see *New York Times*, February 7, 1964, p. 16; and September 4, 1964, p. 12 (quotation).

36. *New York Times*, April 19, 1964, p. 1.

37. For a report of President Kennedy's instructions, see ibid., March 13, 1964. The Defense Manpower Study was a formal project in the Office of the Assistant Secretary of Defense (Manpower), under the direction of the deputy assistant secretary for special studies, William Gorham. Accounts of this study in this chapter are based in part on documents and other sources cited below, and in part on notes made during four visits with working members of the study group. Not all the documents produced by the study group have been published, so data and conclusions from these visits cannot all be considered part of the Defense Department's official findings and recommendations. Information on the study that is not otherwise documented is cited below as: Author's notes, September, 1964, January, 1965, April, 1965, and September, 1965. For announcement of the decision not to release the full study and recommendations, see *Army Times*, October 27, 1965, p. 3.

38. U.S. Congress, House, Committee on Armed Services, *Review of the Administration and Operation of the Selective Service System*, Hearings and papers No. 75, 89th Cong., 2d sess., 1966 (short reference: HCAS, *Review of Selective Service*, Hearings, 89C2). Additional data supporting the Defense Manpower Study's published conclusions are available in U.S. Department of Defense, Office of the Assistant Secretary of Defense (Manpower), *Reference Materials from the Department of Defense Study of the Draft* (unpublished document, July, 1966) (short reference: Department of Defense, *Draft Study Reference Materials*, 1966); much of this material appears in an appendix to the 1966 House committee hearings.

39. For details on the commission's appointment, work, and findings, see U.S. National Advisory Commission on Selective Service, *In Pursuit of Equity: Who Serves When Not All Serve?* Report of the commission, February, 1967 (Washington: U.S. Government Printing Office, 1967) (short reference: Marshall Commission Report, 1967).

40. For details on the panel's appointment, work, and findings, see U.S. Congress, House, Committee on Armed Services, Civilian Advisory Panel on Military Manpower Procurement, *Report*, 90th Cong., 1st sess., 1967 (short reference: Clark Panel Report, 1967).

41. For information on the New York conference, see Donald J. Eberly, ed., *A Profile of National Service* (New York: Overseas Educational Service, 1966); see also National Service Secretariat (Donald J. Eberly, ed.), "A Plan for National Service" (New York: Unpublished manuscript, November, 1966), for extended treatment of the new group's views. The approved statement of the Antioch conference is printed in U.S. Congress, House, Committee on Armed Services, *Extension of the Universal Military Training and Service Act*, Hearings and papers No. 12, 90th Cong., 1st sess., 1967 (short reference: HCAS, *Selective Service Extension 1967*, Hearings, 90C1), pp. 2481–84. The Chicago conference was sponsored by the university and financed by the Ford Foundation; background papers commissioned by the conference organizing committee, an edited transcript of the plenary sessions, and other related materials have been published in Sol Tax, ed., *The Draft: A Handbook of Facts and Alternatives* (Chicago: University of Chicago Press, 1967).

42. For Armed Services Committees' hearings, see HCAS, *Selective Service Extension 1967*, Hearings, 90C1; and U.S. Congress, Senate, Committee on Armed

Services, *Amending and Extending the Draft and Related Authorities*, Hearings, 90th Cong., 1st sess., 1967 (short reference: SCAS, *Selective Service Extension 1967*, Hearings, 90C1. For other hearings, see U.S. Congress, Joint Economic Committee, *Economic Effect of Vietnam Spending*, Hearings, vol. I, 90th Cong., 1st sess., 1967 (short reference: JEC, *Economic Effect of Vietnam Spending*, Hearings, 90C1); Senate, Committee on Labor and Public Welfare, Subcommittee on Employment, Manpower, and Poverty, *Manpower Implications of Selective Service*, Hearings, 90th Cong., 1st sess., 1967 (short reference: SCLPW, EMP Subcom. *Manpower Implications of Selective Service*, Hearings, 90C1).

43. Department of Defense, *Project 61*, Table B-2, following p. III-4.

44. Author's notes, April, 1965.

45. *Army Times*, September 22, 1965, p. 1; HCAS, *Review of Selective Service*, Hearings, 89C2, p. 9940; JEC, *Economic Effect of Vietnam Spending*, Hearings, 90C1, p. 350.

46. Results of three such surveys appeared in *Congressional Record*, vol. 110, p. 16122.

47. Author's notes, January, April, and September, 1965; HCAS, *Review of Selective Service*, Hearings, 89C2, pp. 9938-40; for details on calculation of these estimates, see Stuart H. Altman and Alan E. Fechter, "The Supply of Military Personnel in the Absence of a Draft," *American Economic Review*, vol. 57 (May, 1967), pp. 19-31.

48. See Walter Y. Oi, "The Economic Cost of the Draft," *American Economic Review*, vol. 57 (May, 1967), pp. 39-62; "The Costs and Implications of an All-Volunteer Force," in Tax, ed., *The Draft*, pp. 221-51; and Oi's testimony and submissions in JEC, *Economic Effects of Vietnam Spending*, Hearings, 90C1, pp. 292-309.

49. See testimony and prepared statement by Thomas C. Schelling in JEC, *Economic Effects of Vietnam Spending*, Hearings, 90C1, pp. 309-13 (quotation at p. 310).

50. See Milton Friedman, "Why Not a Volunteer Army?", in Tax, ed., *The Draft*, pp. 200-207; "An All-Volunteer Army," *New York Times Magazine*, May 14, 1967, pp. 23 ff.

51. For arguments on this point, see Samuel H. Hays, "A Military View of Selective Service," in Tax, ed., *The Draft*, pp. 7-22; Samuel P. Huntington, "Political and Social Aspects of Selective Service" (unpublished manuscript written for the Defense Manpower Study, 1965); and articles by Monte Bourjaily, Jr., in *Army Times*, January 20, 1965, p. 11; January 27, 1965, p. 11.

52. Harold Wool, in JEC, *Economic Effects of Vietnam Spending*, Hearings, 90C1, p. 339. Cf. Tables 15, 18, and 19.

53. See testimony of Representative Rumsfeld (R., Ill.) in HCAS *Selective Service Extension 1967*, Hearings, 90C1, pp. 2101-2; and statement of Walter Y. Oi, JEC, *Economic Effects of Vietnam Spending*, Hearings, 90C1, pp. 303,309.

54. From the statement of a Harvard University faculty study group, led by Professor Thomas Schelling, "On Meeting the Nation's Need for Young Men in Military Service," reprinted in JEC, *Economic Effects of Vietnam Spending*, Hearings, 90C1, pp. 357-60.

55. For examples of this suggestion, see Friedman's articles cited in note 50

above; and statement of Norman Thomas in HCAS, *Selective Service Extension 1967,* Hearings, 90C1, p. 2480.

56. *United States* v. *Seeger,* 380 U.S. 163 (1965).

57. The Marshall Commission produced majority and minority views on this issue. For a detailed review of the question, concluding in favor of broadening the concept, see James Finn, ed., *A Conflict of Loyalties: The Case for Selective Conscientious Objection* (New York: Pegasus, 1969).

58. HCAS, *Selective Service Extension 1967,* Hearings, 90C1, pp. 2506-7 (Hebert), 2509 (Vinson).

59. See contrasting views of Samuel H. Hays and Samuel P. Huntington, cited in note 51 above.

60. Dwight D. Eisenhower, "This Country *Needs* Universal Military Training," *The Reader's Digest* (September, 1966), pp. 49-55; Department of Defense, *Draft Study Reference Materials,* 1966, p. 21.

61. See Morris Janowitz, "The Logic of National Service," Terrence Cullinan, "National Service and the American Educational System," Margaret Mead, "A National Service System as a Solution to a Variety of Problems," Donald J. Eberly, "Guidelines for National Service," John Mitrisin, "Voluntary National Service," Richard W. Boone and Norman G. Kurland, "Freedom, National Security, and the Elimination of Poverty: Is Compulsory Service Necessary," all in Tax, ed., *The Draft,* pp. 73-113, 252-79; see also Morris Janowitz, "The Case for a National Service System," *The Public Interest,* No. 5 (Fall 1966), pp. 90-119; National Service Secretariat, op. cit.; and, for Secretary Wirtz's views, *Washington Post,* November 20, 1966, p. A7.

62. See Eli Ginzberg, with James K. Anderson and John L. Herma, *The Optimistic Tradition and American Youth* (New York: Columbia University Press, 1962), pp. 82-83; Bernard D. Karpinos, "Mental Test Failures," in Tax, ed., *The Draft,* pp. 48-49.

63. See articles by Morris Janowitz and Margaret Mead cited in note 61 above.

64. Author's notes, January, 1965; Department of Defense, *Draft Study Reference Materials,* 1966, p. 22.

65. *New York Times,* May 19, 1966, p. 11; Executive Order 11289, July 2, 1966.

66. For General Hershey's figures and the Defense Department's report on men age twenty-six in 1964, see HCAS, *Review of Selective Service,* Hearings, 89C2, pp. 9630, 9642, 9930, 10011. For Clark Panel's figures, see Clark Panel Report, 1967, p. 11. For reports on men age twenty-seven through thirty-four, see Marshall Commission Report, 1967, p. 23; and HCAS, *Selective Service Extension 1967,* Hearings, 90C1, pp. 1930, 2702.

67. HCAS, *Review of Selective Service,* Hearings, 89C2, pp. 9680, 9932; SCAS, *Selective Service Extension 1967,* Hearings, 90C1, p. 649.

68. Marshall Commission Report, 1967, p. 41.

69. SCAS, *Selective Service Extension 1967,* Hearings, 90C1, pp. 170-71.

70. For a detailed critique, see the statement of William R. Keast, president of Wayne State University, in HCAS, *Selective Service Extension 1967,* Hearings, 90C1, pp. 2716-18. For students' views, see *Boston Herald,* May 8, 1966, p. 1; *Harvard Crimson,* May 17, 1966, p. 2; and Michael Levitas, "2-S—Too Smart to Fight?" *New York Times Magazine,* April 24, 1966, pp. 27 ff.

71. HCAS, *Selective Service Extension 1967*, Hearings, 90C1, p. 2281.

72. Lewis B. Hershey, "A Fact Paper on Selective Service," in Tax, ed., *The Draft*, p. 5; for the Chapman-Ingold exchange, see ibid., p. 330.

73. Ginzberg, op. cit., pp. 79, 81.

74. Quoted by Henry A. Marmion in "A Critique of Selective Service with Emphasis on Student Deferment," in Tax, ed., *The Draft*, p. 55.

75. Author's notes, January, 1965.

76. HCAS, *Review of Selective Service*, Hearings, 89C2, p. 9638.

77. SCLPW, EMP Subcom, *Manpower Implications of Selective Service*, Hearings, 90C1, p. 13.

78. HCAS, *Selective Service Extension 1967*, Hearings, 90C1, p. 2616.

79. Quoted in *New York Times*, June 1, 1966, p. 4. For additional statements by this group, see ibid., March 2, 1966, p. 9; and *Congressional Record*, vol. 112, pp. 4543, 12178-84.

80. HCAS, *Review of Selective Service*, Hearings, 89C2, p. 9669.

81. SCAS, *Selective Service Extension 1967*, Hearings, 90C1, p. 619.

82. U.S. Congress, House, *Selective Service*, Message from the President of the United States, H. Doc. No. 75, 90th Cong., 1st sess., 1967.

83. Part of the information in the remainder of this subsection, and section IV following, is based on interviews with members of Executive departments, agencies, and an inter-agency committee, with members of Congress and their staffs, and with congressional committee staff members. Dates of interviews are cited, but in most instances anonymity has been preserved.

84. U.S. Congress, Senate, Committee on Armed Services, *Amending and Extending the Draft Law*, S. Rept. No. 209, Report to accompany S. 1432, 90th Cong., 1st sess., 1967; Congressional Record, vol. 113, pp. S6585, S6657-80.

85. U.S. Congress, House, Committee on Armed Services, *Military Selective Service Act of 1967*, H. Rept. No. 267, Report to accompany S. 1432, 90th Cong., 1st sess., 1967.

86. House debate appears in *Congressional Record*, vol. 113, pp. H6239-6300; the quotation is from a revision of remarks by Representative Joelson (D., N.J.), p. H6297.

87. U.S. Congress, House, *Amending and Extending the Draft Act and Related Laws*, H. Rept. No. 346, Conference report to accompany S. 1432, 90th Cong., 1st sess., 1967.

88. Interview, August 4, 1967.

89. Interviews, July 24 and August 16, 1967.

90. *Congressional Record*, vol. 113, pp. S8161, S8183, H7478; P.L. 90-40. Interviews, July 10, July 28, August 4, August 8, August 16, 1967.

91. U.S., *Budget of the United States Government for Fiscal Year 1971* (Washington: U.S. Government Printing Office, 1970), p. 265.

92. *Washington Post*, January 26, 1970, p. B9; February 12, 1970, p. E7; March 19, 1970, p. F9.

93. Ibid., January 27, 1970, p. A3; *Army Times*, April 8, 1970, p. 4.

94. *Washington Post*, December 18, 1969, p. F10; *Army Times*, July 16, 1969,

p. 4; January 7, 1970, p. 4; March 4, 1970, p. 1; April 8, 1970, p. 6; May 6, 1970, p. 6; U.S. Department of Defense, *Modernizing Military Pay: Report of the First Quadrennial Review of Military Compensation*, vol. I, *Active Duty Compensation* (Washington: U.S. Government Printing Office, 1968).

95.   U.S. President's Commission on an All-Volunteer Force, *Report* (Washington: U.S. Government Printing Office, 1970).

96.   Ibid., p. 10.

97.   *New York Times*, April 24, 1970, p. 1; *Washington Post*, April 25, 1970, p. F1. For additional arguments favoring all-volunteer forces see James C. Miller III, ed., *Why the Draft? The Case for a Volunteer Army* (Baltimore: Penguin Books, Inc., 1968); and Robert T. Stafford, et al., op. cit.

98.   Interview, August 2, 1967.

99.   *Washington Post*, April 29, 1968, p. A1; April 30, 1968, p. A9 (quotation).

100.   Harriet Douty, "Drawing the Line on Draft Evasion," *The Reporter*, April 4, 1968, pp. 20-26; *Washington Post*, April 2, 1969, p. A4; August 8, 1969, p. A3; January 20, 1970, p. A1; January 27, 1970, p. A1; April 23, 1970, p. A31; *New York Times*, March 8, 1970, p. E12.

101.   Executive Order No. 11360, June 30, 1967.

102.   *Washington Post*, February 17, 1968, p. A1; Scientific Manpower Commission and the Council of Graduate Schools in the United States, *The Impact of the Draft on the Graduate Schools in 1968-69* (Washington: Scientific Manpower Commission, 1968); Army Times, December 4, 1968, p. 3; *Science*, vol. 165 (July 11, 1969), p. 162.

103.   *Washington Post*, May 14, 1969, p. A1; September 20, 1969, p. A1; October 17, 1969, p. A1; October 30, 1969, p. A2; October 31, 1969, p. A2; November 6, 1969, p. A1; November 12, 1969, p. A6; November 20, 1969, p. A15; November 27, 1969, p. A1; *New York Times*, August 17, 1969, p. 9.

104.   *Washington Post*, December 2, 1969, p. A1; December 11, 1969, p. F1; *New York Times*, January 4, 1970, p. 66.

105.   *New York Times*, January 18, 1970, p. 1; January 25, 1970, p. E3; April 26, 1970, p. 32; *Washington Post*, January 24, 1970, p. A1.

106.   *Washington Post*, October 11, 1969, p. A1; October 12, 1969, p. A1; October 23, 1969, p. A1; February 12, 1970, p. A2; February 17, 1970, p. A1; March 13, 1970, p. A1. Hershey's observation on himself and Hebert was made in an interview on September 6, 1968.

107.   U.S. Congress, Senate, Committee on the Judiciary, Subcommittee on Administrative Practice and Procedures, *The Selective Service System: Its Operation, Practices, and Procedures*, Hearings, 91st Cong., 1st sess., 1969; *A Study of the Selective Service System: Its Operation, Practices and Procedures Together with Recommendations for Administrative Improvement*, Report of subcommittee, 91st Cong., 1st sess., 1970. See also James W. Davis, Jr., and Kenneth M. Dolbeare, *Little Groups of Neighbors: The Selective Service System* (Chicago: Markham Publishing Company, 1968); and Gary L. Wamsley, *Selective Service and a Changing America* (Columbus, Ohio: Charles E. Merrill Publishing Company, 1969).

108.   *Washington Post*, April 25, 1970, p. F1.

Index

Acheson, Dean G., 137

Active force strengths, 14, 30-33; actual, 7 table, 31-32, 63, 84 table, 85, 95 table, 123 table; 123-26, 177-78, 192 table, 253, 254 table, 256, 272, 273 table; and appropriations, xviii, 5, 10, 21-22; and balance among services, 63-64, 94, 95-96; and budgets, 85, 94, 98-104, 123-24, 135-36, 191, 253; ceilings on, 47, 50, 55-57, 103, 140, 149, 167-68, 178, 366; goals for, xviii, 12-13, 30-31, 36, 39-40, 44, 45, 47, 55-57, 84 table, 87-88, 94, 95 table, 96, 100-101, 102 table, 123 table, 123-26, 195, 238-39, 339, 351, 352, 374, 375

Agricultural deferments, 187, 222

Air Force. *See* Air power; Armed services; Army Air Forces (AAF)

Air Force Reserve. *See* Reserve force components

Air National Guard. *See* Reserve force components

Air Policy Committee, 388 n.17

Air power: vs. balanced forces, 91, 97-104, 120-21, 135, 137-38, 144-45; vs. universal military training, 18-19, 81, 91-92, 100-101, 104-5, 120, 126-27, 135, 181, 350, 352, 391 n.77

Air-sea power, 18-19, 69, 70-71, 107-8

Aliens, enlistment of, 111, 114, 165

Allen, Leo, 73, 111, 132, 201

All-volunteer forces. *See* Volunteer force

Alternative service, 226, 249, 306-7, 308. *See also* National service

Altman, Stuart H., 405 n.47

American Association of Colleges, 28

American Association of University Professors, 107

American Council on Education, 107, 184, 314

American Dental Association, 225, 226

American Farm Bureau Federation, 107

American Federation of Labor (AFL), 16, 27, 49, 107

American Legion, xix, 181, 212; plan of, for universal military training, 34, 37-38, 58, 68, 385 n.49; support of, for universal military training, 15, 59, 68, 72

American Medical Association (AMA), 164, 225, 226

American Veterinary Medical Association, 225

Anderson, James K., 406 n.62

Andrews, Walter G., 71, 73, 87, 109, 116

Antimilitarism, 49, 53-54

Antioch Conference, 287, 298, 404 n.41

Antiwar groups, 299. *See also* Peace groups; Political groups, left-wing; Religious groups

Armed Forces Reserve Act: amendment of (*see* Reserve Forces Act); enactment of, 1952, 173-77, 395 n.50, 395 n.52, 395 n.54, 395 n.55; and rejection of universal military training, 173-74, 175, 178

Armed services, xvii-xviii; and interservice relations, 91-93, 97-98, 124, 135, 136; segregation in, 72, 117, 125, 201-3. *See also* Air power; Army; Army Air Forces (AAF); Demobilization; Department of Defense; Marine Corps; Navy; Reserve force components

Army, 4-5, 6, 8, 14, 44, 73. *See also* Armed services

Army Air Forces (AAF), 12-13, 14, 81-82. *See also* Air power

Army National Guard. *See* Reserve force components

Army Reserve. *See* Reserve force components

Articles of War, 113, 114